SELL UP

AND SAIL

Sell Up and Sail

FOURTH EDITION

Bill and Laurel Cooper

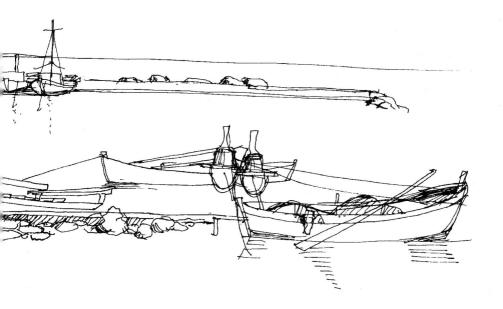

ADLARD COLES NAUTICAL

LONDON

Fourth edition published 2001
by Adlard Coles Nautical
an imprint of A & C Black (Publishers) Ltd
37 Soho Square, London W1D 3QZ

First edition published by Stanford Maritime 1986
Reprinted 1987
Second edition published by Nautical Books 1990
Paperback edition with amendments published by
Adlard Coles Nautical 1994
Reprinted 1995, 1996
Third edition 1998
Reprinted 2000

ISBN 0–7136–6086–4

A CIP catalogue record for this book is available from the British Library.

Design and typeset in 10.5/13pt Clearface by Tony and Penny Mills.
Printed and bound in Great Britain by
Cromwell Press, Trowbridge, Wilts

All quotations as chapter headings and elsewhere
are either by Laurel Cooper, or Captain John Smith *A Sea Grammar*,
published in 1627, unless otherwise attributed.

Contents

Dedicated
∼ to our parents and children ∼
who let us go

Other titles by the same authors:

Watersteps Through France: To the Camargue by Canal
ISBN 0-7136-4391-9
When Bill and Laurel Cooper decided to spend the winter in the south of
France, they took their seaworthy but half-finished Dutch barge *Hosanna*
by an 'overland' route through the canals and rivers of France. Climbing
the watersteps of the Massif Central, they passed through some out-of-
the-way places, made a wonderful variety of friends, and had a great
many adventures.

Watersteps round Europe: Greece to England by Barge
ISBN 0-7136-4399-4
After their journey through the French canals, the Coopers cruised their
converted Dutch barge around the Greek islands. Needing a replacement
engine, they hurried back to the UK to refit, meeting all kinds of
difficulties, delights and disasters on the way. This is the story of the
eventful 2300 mile voyage home via the Ionian Isles, Sicily, Sardinia,
Corsica and then through France and back to Great Yarmouth.

Back Door to Byzantium
ISBN 0-7136-4637-3
The spell-binding story of the Coopers' voyage by Dutch barge from the
North Sea, eastbound across flooded France, down the Rhine in full
spate, through the new Rhein-Main-Donau Kanal and down the Danube
to the Black Sea.

Sail into the Sunset
ISBN 0-7136-3951-2
Covering every kind of boating, from messing about in a dinghy on a
reservoir to boating on canals, chartering, racing and retiring to live
aboard, the Coopers have drawn on their own experiences to provide
a wealth of practical information and advice for people sailing in
their retirement.

Introduction

Not so many years ago, the number of people living aboard cruising yachts was small enough for them to be considered very eccentric. The situation is no longer the same.

In 1980, a survey for an Italian marina company produced a figure of 4000 boats which were lived in all the year round in the Mediterranean alone. Of this number, 25% were British and some 10% American. The number grows year by year, and to it must be added the substantial population doing the same thing in the West Indies, the Bahamas and the South Pacific, as well as the American community on the move up and down their East Coast Waterways.

The significant words are 'on the move'. We are not concerned with houseboat residents, or even those who live in a yacht in one place. This is about mobility, and we try to go into it quite deeply.

It is about escapism as well. Too many moralists infer the escape is from obligations, but this view begs a lot of questions. Many of us escape from regimentation, from interfering bureaucracy, from cradle-to-grave suffocation: we want to look after ourselves. We are rebels from the Welfare State. We discuss that.

But an urge to go is not enough. To a lifelong sailor the act of setting sail comes naturally and easily. Most people are not so experienced, and we are often asked how we have managed to enjoy fourteen years of early retirement in this way, when many others have set out but have not managed to keep going. A good deal of the answer lies in understanding what you are trying to achieve, in defining your aim, in ordering your affairs to further that aim, and then finally having the capacity to cast off the last mooring and go.

This is not a book on technique – seamanship, how to sail, how to maintain engines – though we do indulge ourselves from time to time. It is about attitudes, about ways of ordering existence on the move.

We are not concerned with obsessive achievers speeding round the world on curried split peas, without touching land except to have their GREAT SAILOR ticket punched at the more spectacular blue-water stopping places. Nor do we have time for bathtub sailors, navigators of barrels or floating bedsteads, or voyagers in re-cycled cornflakes packets and other unsuitable craft. Our advice to nautical loonies is to stay at home, buy a plastic duck and give the rescue services a break.

There are some who for various reasons can be only partially or temporarily committed to wandering. Those with a sabbatical and no time to waste and others

1

with a semi-annual approach, wishing to live aboard for perhaps six months at a time. Though not suffering from a terminal case of wanderlust as we are, they have a minor infection: perhaps we can help them too.

We are writing for people who are out to enjoy themselves in company with others in their new lifestyle. So we concentrate on those parts of the world to which the live-aboards tend to gravitate, and where our voyaging experiences are more recent.

We write also for dreamers, for most of us were dreamers to start with, and we hope we may encourage them to realise their dreams. There may be those unsure of their ability, of their endurance, or uncertain that the lust is real. Those too who have to cope with the wanderlust in a partner, and how it might affect them. We try to help these people analyse their attitudes in Chapter Two, 'Test your UQ'. The two of us have very different personalities and we see things different ways. To some extent, then, this is two books for the price of one, for we both express (as much between the lines as in them) what drives us on.

PREFACE TO THE THIRD EDITION (1997)

Since we first wrote *Sell Up and Sail* we have been delighted that, despite the lookalikes that followed, its popularity is undiminished. So why do we need a revised edition? As we predicted in a preface to the second edition, authority is now taking notice of the phenomenon, and wants to stick its oar in with regulation and certification. The psychology and the philosophy of sailing away remain the same, but the reasons change. If anything, the bureaucrats are getting worse, people of all lands are more and more fed up with the way they are governed, the speed and stress of cities, the noise and pollution. The incentive to get away from it all is stronger than ever.

The yachtie fraternity changes only slightly in emphasis. There are always the dedicated and starry eyed, always the adventurers, and the courageous pensioners who have waited so long for their reward. In the seventies there was a wave of Capital Gains sailors, afloat for one year to fulfil the letter of the law, and white escapees from African states, getting their capital out of the country in the only way they could, in one expensive package called a yacht. They were followed by Europeans laid off in the recession, using their redundancy pay to find a new life. Now, with the fall of Communism, a few brave hearts from Eastern Europe, with yachts stitched painfully together from leftovers, are joining the fleet. Prosperous Asians are appearing in boats, and we all continue to get on well together. The reasons for the Sell-up-and-Sail syndrome are so bound up with the economics of life that it is necessary to comment on the global economic situation as yachties are affected.

Traditionally the best cruising has been found in archipelagos. The Caribbean, the Greek islands, and the South Pacific are the three obvious ones. These places combined beautiful islands, less-developed economies where it was possible to live simply and cheaply, and generally hospitable inhabitants. It does seem that the last two of those advantages tend to go together. Many of the islands the yachties favoured were isolated, with small chance of profiting from conventional tourism.

The visiting yachtsmen, while not themselves rich in terms of their countries of origin, enjoyed a comparative wealth so that their modest expenditure was welcome to their hosts. Communications in many of these regions were elementary, and very often there were extremely strong traditions of hospitality that were still apparent, helped because the yachties imposed few changes: they used generally unaltered facilities (they preferred it that way), and made local friends, and learnt some of the language.

Along came commercialised tourism, and the investing vultures gathered round the idylls the yachtie had 'discovered', and once had to himself. Islands which at one time had a ferry once a week or less, one simple 'ethnic' café-bar/general store to serve the locals plus half a dozen or so yachties, now have an airstrip capable of landing Boeing 747s. Strings of restaurants and jewellers' shops are owned by people who do not live in the islands, but who visit only in high season when thousands of tourists are broiling on the beaches. The local people, instead of a life of a bit of fishing, a bit of gardening and a lot of sitting happily under trees, now find they are rushed off their feet as waiters, chambermaids or washers-up working a 12-hour day throughout the season for the benefit of foreign investors.

And the berths previously occupied by the yachties? The anchorage has now been developed, and in the expensive marina (with non-resident owners and operators of course) the berths are filled with charter yachts and glass-bottomed boats. To which are added the world-wide mass-cruising fleets, such as the ARC (Atlantic Rally for Cruisers) and the Round-the-World equivalents, who put up the prices wherever they go, never to come down again, as appalled individual yachties following in their wakes discover.

So we long-cruising folk move on as another once-delightful haven is off the list, except out of season.

It might have been thought that the European Union would have made things easier in Europe, and so it has from the point of view of bureaucratic procedures for citizens of its member states in other member states. But there have been two disadvantages.

One: though problems of entering and clearing countries and harbours may be simpler, other kinds of bureaucracy are galloping throughout the Union. Every country seems to have a pet area it wishes to regulate and by the time this has all filtered through Brussels we get not a distillation, not the lowest common denominator, but the Highest Common Factor, the sum of all the requirements. New rules for skippers' certification are in being, for inspection of boats, for hygiene, for insurance, for radio, life-saving equipment, fire-extinguishers. Many of these rules are not unreasonable in themselves, but boats and people are different one from another. We used to be able to use our own judgement in matters which were very personal and idiosyncratic to our own boats, which might vary from 66-year-old 60 tonne steel barges to new plastic dishes apparently weighing 60 kilograms.

The second disadvantage comes from the money that has poured from Northern Europe into the Mediterranean countries. Whether or not one approves of the massive corruption which accompanies these handouts, they have been on such a scale that the local people have been considerably enriched. We cannot cavil at the rising prosperity; they have come from a long way behind after all. From the point of view of our own narrow interests, however, the effects have been a dramatic rise in the cost of living in Greece (do voters in all the countries lining up to join the EEC realise this inevitability?), plus the filling with locally-owned boats of all those lovely small harbours that were improved with EEC money specifically to help visiting tourists. The world changes. Being fallible human beings, we grumble that others are bettered to our detriment. We should not. We move on.

We have noticed certain changes in the live-aboard fleet. In the traditional centres, the number of boats becoming quasi-immobile has risen, and these, too, take up berths that cruising boats might have used. A number have decided to call it a day and buy a cottage with roses. And the new recruits keep coming, and they keep being pleased, no matter that people shake their heads and say: 'It's not what it was'. It never is, was, nor will be.

To those on the brink of departure we say: it is still a grand way of life, even if one has to go a little further afield to find it these days.

FOURTH EDITION 2001

It's easier than ever, but not so simple. You buy a boat, and all the gadgets which steer and navigate, and tell you what the weather is going to be. There are hundreds of sea schools to teach you to sail. You can cross the Atlantic or sail round the world with one of the 'school bus trips'. And now the family is as close as the nearest cyber café.

As long as we can wrest ourselves from the baleful eye of Brussels and find an anchorage that hasn't been blocked by a fish farm or changed into a marina, as long as we can keep away from the fast lane, we think it's still worth doing, 26 years on.

But don't let's forget the days when it was all so simple, so fresh, and so adventurous.

UNITS OF MEASUREMENT

Well over 50% of yachts registered in English-speaking countries belong to people who use the old Imperial system. Of the remainder, most mature people will have used the Imperial earlier in their lives and be familiar with it.

Of the two major chart publishers, the largest prints in Imperial measure and, though the other is changing to metric, there are still older charts in use with the Imperial system.

It seems to us, therefore, that we should use the Imperial system as the principal one for this edition. But we hope this book will be useful for a long time, and because there is no doubt that the metric system is gaining ground, some of the more significant units have been converted. Now you know why.

1 • Why Do We Do It?

'What a greate matter it is to saile a shyppe or goe to sea.'

In 1976 we sold our house, waved goodbye to the family, and took to the sea in a boat we had built ourselves. We became long-distance, live-aboard cruisers, for whom no very accurate generic term has yet been established – 'Sell-up-and-Sailors' begins to be heard, though the nearest is perhaps 'Yachties'. Abandoning brick walls and gardens, property taxes, and interference from authorities who continually tried to order what we might or might not do, we took on the less comfortable but much more invigorating life of responsibility for our own actions, health, welfare and safety, and through this self-reliance achieved contentment.

Since then, the interest shown in our way of life has increased to a point where the number of people who wish to emulate us, and others like us, has become almost a social phenomenon. The idea of it seems to appeal to many. Although it is the antithesis to the collective responsibility of the Welfare State, that may be a perverse explanation for its attraction. It may also be why some people find they cannot handle the idea, since there is no doubt that great exchanges have to be made (we prefer not to call them sacrifices).

Sudden change is not good for the system. On a boat you can usually choose to change slowly, to stay a bit, or go on as the mood takes you. An Atlantic crossing is a very slow change, giving you time to get used to the climate, and hurling no insults at your biological clock.

Have we not, some people ask, merely exchanged one set of problems for another? Yes, in a sense. We have exchanged the insoluble problems of politics, the pace of life, the battles with bureaucracy, and the appalling proliferation of paper which push one to the edge of madness, for problems of wind and wave and how and where to go next, which we *can* solve. That alone does wonders for your well-being.

When the wanderbug bites you, the symptoms vary from person to person. The aching boredom and frustration of many of today's jobs – or worse, the lack of any job at all – produce understandable feelings of restlessness, and in some people a desire to travel. Many people in middle life feel that this is something they wish to do before they get too old. The young feel they would like to do it now, before family responsibilities and education become too great a burden.

Many feel that it would be a great way to retire. All have differing requirements and expectations. With some, the idea of travel comes at the head of the list; with others, the escape vehicle comes first and travelling in it second. There is a third category to whom the building of the boat is a sufficient release. They dream of going but remain at home, quite content.

There was no doubt in Bill's mind that he wanted to build his own boat, and travel in it. There was a great deal he wanted to get away from: a 9–6 job, very stressful, complications of property and officialdom, winters of ill health, the speed of life, and the trauma of too much change too quickly and for no good reason. I could see his point.

Why a yacht? Because it is a romantic dream that has a chance of coming true: you can build it yourself. And when you've built it, you can travel in it, which is another romantic dream. Building a boat, or acquiring one and refitting it to your own requirements, seems to appeal to something very ancient and necessary in man. Your life, and that of your family, depends on how well you build it and how carefully you plan the voyage. In a world where someone else is always to blame for any misfortune (and where with luck, you can sue), to take responsibility for your lives firmly on your own shoulders and find out that the burden is bearable brings feelings of worth and confidence.

A yacht has a freedom of travel that no other vehicle enjoys. The sea is, by and large, still free to all to cross from one side to the other, starting and finishing where you please, or to stitch your way round its shores. There are extremely few restrictions and regulations specifically affecting yachts, and what few there are would be complied with by a prudent mariner in any event. Close to land and in harbour, you will find the only restrictions you are likely to meet. In or near big commercial ports you will find one-way systems, parking regulations and choked traffic just as on the busy roads of any city. Away from the big ports, restrictions dwindle until they disappear altogether. A yacht marina is merely a specialised commercial port, and you can expect the same sort of restrictions, added to those of a caravan camp (no laundry lines, no barbecues). We avoid them if we can.

God help us if the day ever comes when we are all directed into marinas because commercial interests or overcrowding demand it, or indeed for any other reason. That will be the day when Bill and Laurel start building their kit-form space capsule. (Well, it's got to come, hasn't it?)

Until then, if your aim is carefree mobility, then a yacht is the ideal vehicle. Some people may find eventually that cruising is merely an interval between long stops in one place. Some find a place they love so much they never leave it. Would a caravan have been a better choice? It is certainly cheaper. To use a yacht to stay in one place means that you are not using to the full the expensive and specially designed equipment that was intended to give you mobility: like using the Rolls-Royce as a chicken shed.

If you find, after doing the UQ test which follows, that neither sailing nor travelling are really what you want, but that you would like to drop out of the Stress Layer for a while, or forever, and sink down to the quieter levels of the world, afloat or ashore, then it would make sense to search for your place in the sun by land cruising.

This involves driving at an average of 50 miles an hour instead of 5 knots. You need registration, insurance and a driving licence. In most places where you would feel like staying, caravans are strictly regulated into campsites. If you are not in a campsite, water and sanitation can be a problem. You cannot carry much fuel, and yet cannot move without it. You have to stick to roads, of more or less good quality. You are dependent on ferry services to get you across water, and filling stations for fuel, therefore you are at the mercy of strikes and industrial policy. But yes, it is cheaper. Still, find your small village or town or island, and you will in some ways be less isolated than in a bed-sit in outer London.

We find that in a stay of one month in a tiny port we can, even if not accepted as part of the village, at least lose our tourist status. It takes care and tact, however. Try to change nothing. Watch before you join in. Does Baba Iannis always sit in the same chair in the Taverna? Then don't sit in it yourself. Do the old men like to cluster in one corner and gaze out over the bay? Then don't block their view with a table full of strangers. If the village turns in at half past nine, don't keep them up with noisy chat and laughter, ordering strange drinks that the Taverna has not got. Try to talk a little in the language, to assuage natural curiosity as to your age, marital status, and number and age of children. Don't go on too long, though; they have the whole world to run in their deliberations, don't forget, and if they missed an evening who knows what could happen? Catastrophe.

If Selene brings out her distaff to spin a little in the evening, I go and sit near her with my knitting, and we can exchange wordless admiration without making many waves.

Sense the mood, so that you do not behave inappropriately. One day, when the ferry came in, everybody stopped smiling. We, too, put on grave expressions. The men ran down to the ship and came forth bearing a coffin. The women came down to meet it and fell in behind. It was taken up the little alley beside the Taverna to a courtyard where three old ladies had been wont to sit on the warm stones in the evening. Now only two remained: Eleni had been whisked off to hospital on the mainland the day before, and had died there. She was very old, so faces were grave, but not tearful. 'Poor lady,' said the baker, 'I gave her half a loaf of bread many times. She was too poor to pay me, so I forget always to ask for the money.' Everyone came to her funeral, as she had no relatives left. The village cared for her in death, as they had done in life. Can one ask more?

Some people can. They want to go and spend another month at a different place, learn to understand another kind of village and another sort of people, drinking rum punch on a coral beach or rough red wine in a bodega, or 'island tea' in a Turkish tea house, or cook their stew in fumeroles in the Azores and eat lobster-in-the-rough off paper plates in New England. I cannot think of a better way of doing this than to go with your house on your back like a sea snail, at a speed where your surroundings change slowly and without shock to the system.

What is this life, if on our cruise
  We have no time to sit and booze?
Conversely what, if full of booze
  We never get to sea and cruise?
What is this life, I'd like to know
  If I am always down below?
And if, upon the starboard tack,
  The loo is always out of whack?
And what if I am ill at ease
  With not a ripple on the seas?
What is this life? It suits us well.
  It's mostly heaven, rarely hell.

To have built your boat, or at least lovingly altered and equipped her for such a voyage, is a process which brings in itself many rewards. For us, the real reward was the travelling. We held on to this aim through many black days during the building period.

This is a book for dreamers, but especially for those who would like to achieve the dream. We would like to take the stars out of your eyes, and use them to illuminate practicalities.

While anyone contemplating long-term cruising would be foolhardy to embark without some nautical ability, the effort of acquiring it can be eased by planning and dreaming. Indeed, dreaming may be one of the most enjoyable aspects of the whole enterprise. If you never get beyond the stage of catalogues and cruising books by the Sunday fire, enjoy the book. Just before we sailed, the Lifeboat cox'n said to us, 'A lot of people want to do what you're doing. Difference is: you've done it.'

We were dreamers once. Dreams can become a reality. It is hard work, rather than magic, that gets it done.

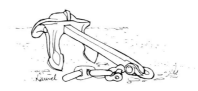

2 • Crucial Questions

'Make voyages! Attempt them! There's nothing else.'
TENNESSEE WILLIAMS – *Camino Real*

It was the insidiousness of it that got me.

From the day he retired from the Royal Navy, Bill began the 'one day we'll both go to sea' gambit. Over the years, punctuated by annual visits to the Boat Show (I always went with him – I almost always got migraine), the subliminal mention became less subliminal, and during his next two careers became friendly persuasion, then gentle insistence, and finally downright intransigence.

Not that I disliked either the sea or sailing; far from it, though my experience, while considerable, was largely on inland waters. I even liked the Boat Show. But I was entrenched in a comfortable little life and saw no reason to abandon it in order to get wet, cold and seasick away from my books, cats and children.

It became clear that if I was not to be shanghaied to sea willy-nilly, I should have to take certain steps. These were all backwards, and included countering every stated assumption that I would go by good-humoured negatives and careful references to '*your* boat' and '*your* voyage' and 'when *you* go, I'll have a cottage somewhere for you to come back to'.

After some years of this it dawned on my husband that I meant it, and that I did have good reasons for doubting my capacity at sea. With a sigh, he began to design singlehanded yachts. At this point I realised that he too meant what he said. My bluff called, negotiations began with frank and free discussions, and meaningful dialogues; and the next few designs were very different. If I was going, I wanted a say in the sort of boat I would live in.

• *The inevitable compromise* •

Bill says now that he built *Fare Well* round my books and my bath. For the next few years he worked on my sense of adventure and I worked on his sense of responsibility. We had two children whom we could not leave until it seemed they could do without us. We had cats (one horrid and one super) and a dog. How could Bill leave his tiresome, but very lucrative, job? We had a large house that I adored. My life was busy and interesting, and I loved the work I was doing. It was going to be very hard to sell up and go.

• *Departure* •

In the end, as so often happens, some decisions were made for us by events. Bill became very ill for a year or two, able only to potter about the half-completed boat; and there was no longer any problem about breaking away from the job – the firm had already filled the vacancy. The children grew up suddenly and moved out, leaving us in a house far too big and expensive on our own. The horrid cat died, and we decided to take the other with us – one of our more brilliant decisions, as was the idea of giving the dog to Bill's widowed father, leading to one of those man-dog relationships worthy of letters of flame.

It began to look as if the sooner we went, the sooner Bill would regain his health. There was the little matter of finishing a 55-foot ketch, and getting it to sea, but we had been working on that for some time anyway. (It took five years altogether and is quite another story.) Gradually the people who had been saying 'you'll never finish it' began to realise that we damn well would, and that we were damn well going.

Don't kid yourselves, it was hard. Morale was sometimes very low. It was as hard as I had thought it would be to sell the house, part with the dog, and say our goodbyes to family and friends. On the plus side, our son Ben decided to accompany us for a while. A sense of excitement began to grow as we worked, planned and stored ship; and found some pleasant people to share our maiden voyage to Gibraltar. This being, apart from trials, our first trip, and nearly my first ocean trip, Bill had decided to be prudent and take some extra muscle.

When we finally set sail from Lowestoft, six people and the cat Nelson, a burden rolled off my shoulders that I had never been aware of. I smelt the sea, saw the first of many ocean sunsets, and felt a freedom I'd never known before.

I wouldn't have changed places with anyone.

• *Looking back* •

I had always loved the sea in rather a romantic and sentimental way. I was born and brought up by the sea, and dipped my toes in it nearly every day of my childhood summers, or sat in the shallows and let the little waves bounce in my lap. You could pee in it without anyone knowing. You could watch the storms from the cliffs and be amazed by the crashing noise of the breakers, the cold hiss and rattle and roar of grating pebbles; even at that distance you must shout to be heard. In bed you could hear the waves above the fitful pelt and spatter of the winter rain. How blissful to be warm in bed, and not out in the dark on the wild sea.

As I grew up I learned to sail, on the Broads of course, as did the young Nelson, but I was 17 before I even crossed the Channel in a ferry, and the sea was still magic, and dangerous and attractive like an elder brother's motorbike.

That attitude was not very helpful when faced with a life at sea in one's mid forties. How would I cope with storms? How would I handle seasickness and exhaustion when we were short-handed? Could I stand my companions (let alone my husband) at close quarters and under stress? It seemed a good idea to find out about this sort of thing while the boat was still a-building. I do not advise anyone less dedicated to leave it as late as this. It is far better to do all this and more before you embark on a project that has a momentum as inevitable as the birth of a child, and to abort which is just as painful and a good deal more expensive.

• *Getting some sea-time in* •

My only real sea experience at that time (I discount dinghy racing where you are home and dry after a couple of hours) was a four-week cruise in 1954 with Bill, our six-month-old daughter and my brother. The yacht was a 5-tonner without motor or loo. I felt that there was some basis for confidence here, as although it was July in the Mediterranean we had had one of those unseasonable summer storms, and a thick fog in the Sicilian Channel shipping lanes to boot. I had by no means disgraced myself; I had cooked, washed nappies, kept watch, steered and been useful. The baby enjoyed every minute. I enjoyed most of it. So far, so good.

I had the great advantage of faith in my captain. Bill is an experienced deep-sea yachtsman, and an ex-professional navigator. He is also a seaman of the old-fashioned kind, which he describes as 'managing without what you haven't got'.

I felt I should have confidence in the boat, too; she was strongly built and looked seaworthy, and I was getting to know her by building her. I had had a lot to say about the design, and not just in the galley. The guardrails were to be very strong in case my congenitally dislocated hip failed me. (It didn't seem to worry Bill that his cruising companion was what had been successively known as crippled (1930s) handicapped (1940s and 1950s) disabled (1960s and 1970s) and differently-abled (1980s and 1990s) What will the millennium term be we wonder?) On the fore-deck we had strong netting to prevent a body slipping through the guardrails. Below, the furniture was built strongly enough to fall against in a seaway without damaging it, the corollary being that such solidity can cause a lot of mayhem to bodies bouncing off it. Despite the numerous handholds that we put everywhere, strong enough to Tarzan around the boat on, I still sometimes ping-ponged off the furniture. Gazing at my doleful bruises, I insisted on more cushions, in the cockpit as well. Bill hates them, but they do cut down injuries, not only mine.

We have mentioned the bath. For anyone with bone-aches like mine a hot bath is a solace greater than any medicine. Salt water can be used. Since it is now believed that more yachtsmen die of hypothermia than drowning, and a recommended remedy for the former is a warm bath, maybe it's less of a luxury than we thought.

I wanted a corner for drawing, and I refused to share the chart table, as I knew it would cause friction. I got it, a neat solution that was flexible enough to become a workbench when I started enamelling.

Double bunks were unusual in the late 1960s. You spend a lot of your life in bed, you might as well be happy there: we designed the first double bunk we'd

Laurel found a quiet corner on Fare Well *for her enamelling.*

seen that could be got at from three sides, instead of being shoved against the ship's side. I heard of someone who had an arm broken by a heavy bunkmate crawling over her in such a bunk, answering a night call. Twice.

• *Gaining experience* •

To get more confidence in myself, I went to the National Sailing Centre at Cowes (now alas no more) to learn some navigation (the coastal part of the Yachtmaster's qualification). Bill normally does all this, and to compete with him seemed foolish: if someone can play the Moonlight Sonata, should you join in on a penny whistle? But I felt a lot better for knowing something, and it might have become vital.

I gained more experience. When we could we helped friends who were new to sailing by doing short trips round the coast or across the Channel. I began to realise I was not the first in the crew to succumb to seasickness, that pills and sensible precautions to prevent overtiredness and chilling were better than being frightfully brave, and that I was so hungry I had to cook something. I found that a little yacht flying down-Channel before a stiff breeze was great. I discovered that I did not much like going to windward. We remained on speaking terms with our friends. It looked as if things were going to be all right.

The house was sold. I still writhe with pain when I recall this period. Although planning and forethought went into everything we did, it turned out there was still a lot to learn. Much of it, 26 years on, we are still learning by pleasurable stages, a little of it the hard way. Twenty-six happy years of cruising are witness to the fact that we did our homework, and that by the end of our maiden voyage a romantic dreamer had become something of a practical sea-person, and Nelson had enthusiastically embarked on the life of a one-eyed sea-cat.

Having described the process whereby I came to accept and enjoy living at sea, there are some relevant questions *you* should answer.

PART TWO: TEST YOUR UQ

Too little thought before you go,
And you'll be back before you know

We have devised a test to measure what we shall call your 'Ulysses Quotient' or UQ. While it should not be taken desperately seriously, it will nevertheless give you plenty to think about. You and your mate may even have your first disagreement over the first question. Ulysses, it will be remembered, roamed the seas for about ten years, looking for his homeland, the island of Ithaca. UQ can be described as a tendency to wander off for years in a small boat without actually getting anywhere much. (Though he was probably the worst navigator in history, he did, it is pointed out to us, suffer under the handicap of having an all-male crew!)

The desire, the will to go cruising, is paramount. We realise that nothing we say will stop you if you are determined; whether you are an unskilled, penniless tyro, incapacitated by alcohol and agues, embarking in an unseaworthy boat with a sack of lentils and aiming to be the first member of Depressives Anonymous to round Cape Horn; or a thrifty couple with a small but well-found boat, making well-planned voyages that are triumphs of ingenuity, courage and dedication.

However, we want you to enjoy your cruising; and time spent now on thinking and planning will save you money and misery later on. We cannot say this often enough.

You and your spouse, or mate, or lifelong companion, whatever (living at sea we have come across every combination of all four sexes) should do the test separately, in private, and without discussions or comparisons until all the scoring is finished. If you would like your children to do it, the same conditions apply: certainly they should join in the discussions which follow. Incidentally, I had better make it clear that I use the word 'Mate' throughout this book to cover: wife, husband, son, daughter, companion, friend, crew, lover, consenting adult – whoever is going with you to be your team mate.

You each (or all) have a lot of decisions to make, and you might as well know what your sticking points are now. They may prove to be immovable, they may need hard work and compromise to find a way round them, they may in time vanish like smoke, but at least you will know what you are up against. Name your enemy and the battle begins.

Note that your scores are nothing to do with winning or losing, or with being right or wrong. The test is an attempt to assess: (1) your present situation, which may of course change, (2) practical considerations which may have a bearing on your future, (3) your abilities and capabilities, and (4) your attitude to mobility and change. The scoring comes under three different headings: Alpha (A); Kappa (K); and Sigma (Σ). Their significance will become apparent later.

If you cheat – have fun, and carry on dreaming. If you are really keen on the idea, take a good look at yourself, answer honestly, and this could be the first step in your voyage.

THE ULYSSES QUOTIENT

SECTION ONE – BASIC QUESTIONS: DO YOU REALLY WANT TO GO?

1 Do you like sailing?
   (a) Yes, very much.
   (b) Keen to try.
   (c) Not sure, I think I shan't enjoy it.
   (d) Done it. Don't like it.
   If (a) score A4, if (b) score A2, if (c) score Σ5. If (d) score Σ15, and go to question Q3.

2 You are faced with a rough sea and a rising wind on a long beat into harbour. Do you:
   (a) Grin and bear it?
   (b) Say 'This is what it's all about' and call for eggs and bacon?
   (c) Get sick and miserable, and let the others get on with it?
   (d) Get sick and miserable, but try to produce the eggs and bacon?
   If (a) score A2, if (b) score A1, if (c) score Σ1. If (d) score A1.

3 Do you like travelling abroad? If Yes, continue. If No, score Σ4 and go to Q7.

4 If you have never been abroad score Σ4 and go to Q7.

5 When you are abroad, do you prefer to stay in:
   (a) A pension?
   (b) A campsite, or boat?
   (c) A hotel?
   If (a) score 0, if (b) score K1, if (c) score Σ2.

6 When you are abroad, do you:
   (a) Like eating local dishes?
   (b) Go for snake soup, raw goose-barnacles, and the honeybees coated in chocolate?
   (c) Prefer your normal diet?
   If (a) score K1, if (b) score K2, if (c) score Σ2.

7 Do you speak any language other than your own (enough to be polite and do some shopping)? Score A1 for each language more than two.

8 Can you afford this venture?
   (a) Yes.
   (b) In time, or maybe.
   (c) No.
   (d) I've just won the Lottery.
   If (a) score A2, if (b) score 0, if (c) score Σ3, if (d) score what you like!

• *Discussion on Section One* •

Q 1–2   These are germane questions. If you are unsure, you had better find out the answers for certain, for your own sake and the rest of the crew. Do this by sailing with friends, in as many different boats and situations as possible. If you ultimately intend to go singlehanded, skip the next paragraphs and go to Q3. If you are going to sail with a mate, and your answers to Q1 and 2 differ widely from your partner's, the battle lines could be already drawn. If you like ear'oling (sailing with the lee rail under) and spray in your face, and your mate prefers to go over on the ferry, you have a compatibility problem which needs to be resolved. How much can (and will) Salty Sam or Sue throttle back to accommodate the natural fears of less adventurous members of the crew? We have known voyages founder on the fact that the skipper was too harsh, hard-driving and self-punishing. This is fine for racing weekends but unbearable for a long cruise, which ought to be a pleasant experience; and feeble, weedy crews do not contribute to this either.

Be assured that if you go, and stick to it, you will both, or all, change, perhaps in unexpected ways. We have known people find strength and health and self-confidence. We have known tough looking characters fall apart. When push comes to shove, there are surprises in store.

Willingness is all, however, and much may be learned and achieved with determination. We have mentioned sailing with friends. Some might consider that a flotilla holiday would be the ideal way to do this. We do not. It makes a marvellous holiday and may tempt you into thinking you like cruising, but it is an artificial set-up. You will learn little that is of any use for your purpose, since flotilla sailing has less to do with long-distance cruising than the child licking the basin has to do with making the cake. It also suffers the curse of the ticking clock, that destroyer of relaxed cruises. ('We *must* get to the island of X before the taverna closes, we *must* get to Y to catch the bus to the airport.')

While many people get bitten by the cruising bug on a flotilla holiday, you will need a lot of practice in situations where you must get out of trouble on your own. That said, bareboating (ie chartering a boat to sail without professional assistance and as you wish) is probably a happy medium. You will learn a lot, and help should not be far away.

For Absolute Beginners there is a simple starter pack in Chapter Seven which will help you to be useful even on your first sail.

Q3–6 Do you really like 'abroad'?
We all love the thought of the palm trees, soft breezes, and swaying hula hula girls. But do you enjoy new tastes and smells, or would you rather have your joint and two veg and tea like Mother made (for Brits), or biscuits and red eye gravy (for Americans)? You can get McDonalds, french fries and Foster's almost anywhere.

Do you find it all interesting and exciting, or do you worry about the drinking water and the loos? Are you happy in a *pension*, eating with the family and making a stab at the language, or do you prefer a coach tour or hotel where a courier takes care of all the hassle? Are you, in other words, a self-reliant traveller?

Q7 If you are not good at languages, you can always go West, where most of the continent of North America and a good many of the West Indian islands, plus the Bahamas and Bermuda, are populated by people who speak English of a sort. You

AGHIOS EFSTRATIOS
EARTHQUAKE DAMAGE

can also go down to the Antipodes. If you go to the Mediterranean, and many other seas where the language is strange, you will have to cope with foreigners on entry to a new country; and you will have to store ship, get water and fuel, and deal with spares and repairs. This will be stressful if you are impatient with people who speak little or no English. The other side of the coin is the fun of it. When I was much younger and prettier, I left our boat *Phoenix* in Syracuse harbour and went looking for a fishhook with my Italian dictionary. 'Amo?' I said hopefully to the proprietor of the fishing tackle shop. His eyes lit up. 'I love you too!' he said. It was a while before I could get him back to the subject of fishhooks. When Nelson had a skin problem that I suspected to be a fungus, a young German came over to help. 'I hear your cat has the mushrooms,' he said.

Q8 Can you afford this venture? What is enough? Selling your house, or your business, if you own it, will provide enough money for a reasonable boat. But it has to be maintained, as you do; you will need to fit her out and store before you go, and you need reserves for contingencies – which may be drastic. Don't count on being able to find work on the way. The next chapter on Finance will give you some idea of probable costs, but a lot depends on whether you are in the champagne or local beer and wine bracket. Perhaps you need more time to work and save, in order to sail with debts paid, mortgages discharged, some reserves and a light heart.

If you scored all As or Ks in this section, you have crossed the first barrier with ease. If you scored all Σs someone probably gave you this book as a present. Tough. Enjoy reading it, however. If you came somewhere in the middle, you have some thinking to do. Now go to Section Two.

SECTION TWO – YOUR JOB: CAN YOU LEAVE IT?

1 Do you own your own business? If Yes, go to Q4. If No, continue.

2 Are you unemployed or retired? If unemployed score K2, If retired score K2. In either case, proceed to Q7, otherwise continue.

3 How do you feel about the job you are doing now? Choose any of the following:
   (a) I have a strong vocation.
   (b) I really like my job.
   (c) It's just a job.
   (d) I'm in line for promotion.
   (e) I'll be glad to leave.
   (f) I'm ready for a change.
   (g) I've embezzled the tea fund and I'd better go.

   If (a) score Σ3, if (b) score Σ2, if (c) score 0. If (d) score Σ1, if (e) score K1, if (f) score K2, if (g) score K10. Proceed to Q5.

4 Which of the following statements is nearest to how you feel? (Choose one.)
   (a) I can't let my work force down.
   (b) It's a family business: I have obligations.
   (c) I work all the hours God sends, and love every minute of it.
   (d) I used to enjoy it, but it's getting me down.
   (e) It's a good living and I'm content.
   (f) I'd sell if I could find a buyer.
   (g) I'd be glad to be shot of it.

   If (a) score Σ2, if (b) score Σ3, if (c) score Σ1, if (d) score 0, if (e) score Σ1, if (f) score K1, if (g) score K3.

5 Are you worried that you might lose skills and/or seniority while you are away?
   (a) No problem.
   (b) I'll catch up later.
   (c) Yes.

   If (a) score K2, if (b) score K1, if (c) score Σ4.

6 If you are a member of an occupational pension scheme, what happens if you give up your job now?
   (a) I get a reduced secure pension on retirement.
   (b) I get a return of contributions but no pension.
   (c) I have no protected rights.

   If (a) score K1, if (b) score 0, if (c) score Σ1.

7 Can you use your skills abroad? (A skilled craftsman is welcome almost anywhere, but the professions often erect barriers against foreign practitioners. See next chapter on Finance.)
   (a) Yes.
   (b) To a certain extent.
   (c) No.

   If (a) score K2 + A2, if (b) score K1 + A1, if (c) score Σ2

8 If in Section One (Basic Questions) you scored: As: more than 6, score a further K1. If you scored Ks: more than 5, score a further K1. Σs: more than 6, score a further Σ2

9 Are you any of these, or do you hold similar posts: Justice of the Peace, President of the Women's Institute or Townswomen's Guild, Provincial Grand Officer in the Buffs or Freemasons, chairperson or officer of any clubs or societies, mayor, councillor, alderman etc? Score Σ2 for each post you hold. If you hold more than three, score a bonus of Σ3. (NB: If you are dying to resign from them all, score K3.)

10 Do you spend more than two nights a week at meetings which are nothing to do with your job? (Here only, your job means what you are paid to do. In all other questions 'job' includes unpaid work such as housewifery, parenthood, voluntary work etc.) If Yes, score Σ4, but see NB above.

11 Do you spend more than two nights a week at meetings which *are* to do with your job? If Yes, score Σ3.

12 Can you give up the interests in Q9?

(a) Easily.
(b) With regret.
(c) No.
If (a) score K1, if (b) score Σ1, if (c) score Σ3.

• *Discussion on Section Two* •

Q1   Can you leave your job? These days, the concept of 'job mobility' is much in everyone's minds, 'serial professions', as envisaged by Alvin Toffler in his book *Future Shock*, are already with us: that is, a series of occupations where you will change jobs at around five-year intervals. Such flexibility will make leave of absence or sabbaticals between jobs a much more feasible proposition, and probably improve the mental and physical health of all concerned. On the other hand, there are signs (in 2000) that insecurity of tenure of jobs is causing increased tension; frequent changes are with us, but they are not always so beneficent as Toffler anticipated.

Q3–5   *If yours are technical skills in a fast-changing field, it will be hard to keep up while you are away. Technical journals are heavy: trusting them to foreign mails is expensive and chancy. Once we used to ask friends to bring them when they visit us, and were smitten with guilt when their heaviest piece of luggage turned out to be full of yachting magazines, a pilot book, the Sundays, 'and a few paperbacks' plus several Royal Institute of Navigation Journals.*

If you want to keep your options open, then leave of absence while you find out if you really enjoy the life, is the best answer. Otherwise you face a refresher course of some kind on your return, if there is one. This also applies if by leaving your job you lose status and seniority. It could be hard.

So we wrote in the mid-1980s. The above two paragraphs were still true for the last edition, but the internet has changed everything, and now keeping up with events, news and communication gets easier every day, if that is what you want. Some people manage to work via the internet and e-mail while still cruising.

If leave of absence is not possible and you cannot take your job with you on your laptop, you should look on your voyage as early retirement, with the possibility that you might have to return to work later. If your skills are really rare and valuable you should have no trouble finding a job when you come back, and your employer will not care where you have been, so long as it wasn't in gaol. If your skills are less useful, you could face re-training for a new career. In either case, we don't need to tell you that your curriculum vitae (resumé, to Americans) would need to be carefully worded. You will clearly be able to provide adequate, not to say impressive, reasons for your absence. The usual pack of lies, in fact. At least your health and vigour should have improved, and you might have acquired a whole new set of skills, but in the present climate you may face great difficulties getting back into the labour market, especially after a certain age.

Q6–8 If you are used to being a person of consequence, consider whether you will be satisfied with being 'just a yachtie'. We tend to come a bit lower on the social scale than some of you are accustomed to. You will be 'of no fixed abode', can't get a credit rating, and in some countries end up classed with travellers, beggars, tramps and chicken-stealers. There are many compensating and pleasurable feelings of achievement and satisfaction, but these do not scintillate outwardly in Ralph Lauren and Rolexes and a Rolls; rather in an air of contentment and relaxation.

And once having tasted real freedom, could you ever again settle to a 9–5 existence? We think we could if the devil drove – but he'd need a big whip.

SECTION THREE – YOUR HEALTH: ARE YOU FIT TO GO?

1 Do you feel unwell a lot of the time? If No, continue. If Yes, score Σ4.

2 Do you have a condition for which you regularly seek medical advice? If No, continue. If Yes, score Σ5.

3 Do you have a condition which worries you and for which you have not sought medical advice? If Yes, score Σ4. If the answers to the last three questions were all No, score K3 and go on to Section 4. Otherwise continue.

4 Do you remember your condition:
   (a) Hardly ever?
   (b) Some of the time?
   (c) All the time?
   If (a) score KI, if (b) score ΣI, if (c) score Σ3.

5 Would your doctor allow you long periods of self-medication?
   (a) Yes.
   (b) No.
   (c) He doesn't give a toss.
   If (a) score K1, if (b) score Σ4, if (c) score 0 and change your doctor.

6 Could your condition:
   (a) Prevent your standing a watch, night or day?
   (b) Endanger the boat or fellow crew members?
   (c) Necessitate expensive and/or time-consuming medical attention while on voyage?
   (d) Cause over-tiredness or require a rigid regime or schedule?
   If your answer to Q6 is No to all four, score K1. If your answer is Yes
   to (a), (b) or (c), score Σ2 for each Yes. If (d) score Σ1.

• *Discussion on Section Three* •

Q1–4　Are you fit to go? There is no doubt that we go to sea with the most amazing handicaps. We have met unbelievably courageous long-distance cruisers with diabetes, cancer, heart conditions and stroke, amputees, people with imperfect limbs and paralysis; not to mention those souls (perhaps more foolhardy than courageous) who were obese or alcoholic or addicted; to which list we should add several who were clearly bonkers. Nothing short of coma seems to stop us, as long as we are willing and able to 'manage' our disability with long-range advice.

A positive mental attitude will assist one's fellows to make a few (oh, very few) allowances, as will a determination to excel in the things one *can* do, while not shirking those tasks which will cause discomfort but not damage. Realism is of the utmost importance here, and the quality of enjoyment one can expect must be considered as carefully as physical well-being. A long talk with a doctor who understands exactly what long-distance cruising is all about will be necessary. If you have not already consulted on anything that worries you, ask yourself why.

Q5–6　At sea you will have to care for yourself. This requires more sense than bravado. A golfing doctor who doesn't understand what is involved will merely tell you not to go: professional people must be cautious about giving advice in unusual circumstances, as they could be held liable for the consequences. Find yourself a yachting doctor to consult. Where do you find him? Offshore at the Yacht Club, of course, where his patients can't get at him! If you are in luck you should get a realistic answer; pointing out dangers to avoid, how to monitor your condition, what drugs or medication to take with you, how to inject yourself safely, and what to exercise and how. (See later discussion on the Ship Captain's Medical Course in Chapter 15.)

Q6　Consider carefully whether you are a danger to the boat or crew. Red-green colour blindness, for instance, is a strong contra-indication since it is of vital significance on a night watch to be able to distinguish red and green lights on shore and on other vessels. Get round this by volunteering for extra day watches and/or making short voyages. A condition that causes you to tire easily, or requires a rigid regime or time schedule, should give you pause; since one of the great benefits of the life is being able to forget time and rigidity. Most of us long-term cruisers don't even know what day it is, and find that getting friends to airports on a particular day, let alone a particular time, is an unwelcome return to a scheduled world. That said, a little structuring of the day to accommodate your condition, whatever it is, ought not to upset your fellows if your presence brings compensating advantages.

A word on drinking. Most of us do this with great gusto, the rum or wine being cheap and the company enjoyable. But note that air pilots are forbidden to drink before and during flying. Naval navigating officers are not so forbidden, but nevertheless have a long-standing tradition of not drinking at sea. (Of course, when let off the hook you'll find them drinking ashore and sinking a gin; but

Laurel

GIGLIO, ITALY.

that's better than drinking at sea and sinking the ship.) Make up your own mind, but the sea is no place for alcoholics. We know of at least one yacht that was lost with all hands, where drink was a contributing cause, and a good many drownings from dinghies on the way back from the pub.

Don't forget that alcohol in the bloodstream increases seasickness. Not a few wild farewell parties have caused a sensible postponement of the sailing day. Nor is it unknown for a yacht, after the gongs, bells and cannons have wished them

Bon Voyage, to creep into a bay round the very first headland and drop anchor till their headaches improved.

Now the good news. On a well-organised voyage your general health will improve, as the outdoor life and the lack of stress seep into your body and mind. You will probably be cured of your migraine (as I was), your asthma (as Bill was), or your hay-fever, tummy cramps, eczema, PMT – anything with its true origins in tension and stress.

SECTION FOUR – YOUR FAMILY: HOW STRONG IS THE PULL?

1 Have you parents, children, or near relatives living? If No, score K1 and go to Q4. If Yes, score Σ1 and continue.

2 Are you worried about any of them? If No, score 0. If Yes, score Σ3 for each one.

3 Are you the only child? If No, score 0. If Yes, score Σ2.

4 Has your mate (if any) parents, children or near relatives living? If No, score K1 and END THIS SECTION. If Yes, score Σ1 and continue.

5 Is he/she worried about any of them? If No, score 0 and END THIS SECTION. If Yes, score Σ3 for each one and continue.

6 Is he/she an only child? If No, score 0. If Yes, score Σ2.

7 What age will your child (children), both yours and your mate's, be when you sail? Will you take them with you? Score as follows:

Age	Taking them	Leaving them
0–5 years	0	Σ5
6–12 years	Σ1	Σ4
12–18 years	Σ2	Σ4
over 18 and/or independent	Σ2	Σ1
over 18 and dependant	Σ2	Σ4

(The score is additive, thus if taking a baby and toddler with you, score 0; and if you are taking one four-year-old and leaving two of 13 and 15 years respectively, score Σ8.)

8 Is there someone reliable to care for children remaining at home? If Yes, score K2. If No, score Σ4.

9 Do you have children of school age? If No, END THIS SECTION. If Yes,
(a) Will you teach them yourself?
(b) Will you use a correspondence course?
(c) Will you send them to boarding school at home?
(d) Will you send them to local schools as you travel? And stay long enough to benefit?
If (a) score K2, if (b) score K2, if (c) score K1. If (d) score 0.

Note Q8 There is a wide range of possibilities here. Boarding schools fill the bill in term time, but usually other arrangements must be made in the holidays if children cannot join you. Compliant relatives may take your child on for a while; this was a common thing in wartime, and most of us did not seem to suffer from being parked on aunts and grandparents and changing schools at frequent intervals. The criterion has to be that the arrangement is satisfactory to all parties.

• Discussion on Section Four •

Q1–6 You will not enjoy your cruise if family responsibilities lie heavily upon you. It makes sense, therefore, to solve as many problems as you can before you leave, so that on sailing you know that the situation is as stable as can be expected. Good communications after your departure are important; apron strings pull in both directions, and your family will sometimes be as anxious about you as you may be about them. Several cruisers we know have a clued-up person back home, who may or may not be a member of the family, to act as a clearing house for news – so that one phone call only, and that a short one, need be made. A fortnightly (for instance) 'How's things?' 'Everyone's fine, where are you?' is worth a lot, being positive and up-to-the-minute reassurance. Messages to ring home often go astray, and we find we do better by telepathy, and so do others we've met. I'm not kidding: we always obey any feeling that we ought to go and telephone, as we are so often met with a relieved 'Ah! you got my message.' It wouldn't be quite truthful to say 'What message?' but one always does.

E-mail is now the answer, if you can. There are cyber-cafés in the most surprising places these days, under a roof of banana leaves or halfway up an icy mountain.

We discuss communications more fully in Chapter Thirteen.

Get the Social Services off your back and on the ball

If you have elderly relatives that you have been in the habit of visiting, it is well worth going along to the DSS and pointing out that you will not be available after such-and-such a date. The Social Services can often help a great deal, and will do more if prodded: a talk with them may produce home help, meals on wheels, and a regular health visit, for instance. Your absence will precipitate mild panic, and quite right too.

If you think more help is needed, Age Concern can tell you what might be available. A good neighbour can be your communication link in case of need. The more people who know the situation the better: doctor, lawyer, fellow club members, fellow church members, and reliable neighbours: anyone who could help to hold the fort if need be. Don't forget great-nephews and nieces, and grandchildren, all of whom should be concerned, and encouraged to visit and give what assistance they can. However, they will all expect you (if you are female) to reappear and wave a magic wand if anything goes wrong, and this can be tricky if you are one donkey, two ferryboats and a bus away from an air terminal, as I was on one occasion. Let alone the expense.

If you are male, then it is considered that you have an excellent reason for what you are doing, usually connected with the sacred word BUSINESS which excuses everything, and far less pressure is applied. So that's all right then. You may, however, be the only child and your relative may be isolated and friendless. The Social Services and Age Concern will be vital in this case, especially if the idea of moving to sheltered accommodation (for example with a warden) is met with resistance or is not possible for other reasons.

What if, after all your efforts, your obstinate 90-year-old tells the meals-on-wheels lady where to put her gammon and mashed, and slams the door on the Health Visitor as if she were the double glazing man? What if your old person, in fact, insists on self-sufficiency and independence, in a mountain shack or on the middle of Dartmoor? Presumably they do this from choice. You are a chip off the old block, aren't you? You'll be doing the same thing when you're their age. In the meantime you wish them good luck, and sail; also from choice. Only you can decide, but if things are unstable at home, it is particularly necessary for your peace of mind to have frequent communications, and a reserve of cash to travel home; and this will affect your choice of cruising ground.

Make sure your old ducks know how to use a computer for e-mail. The second best thing we two old ducks did when we reached 60 was to go on a computer course. This is now known as silver surfing. (The best thing we did, of course, was to continue sailing.)

Children

Take 'em or leave 'em? Many people have taken their children to sea, from birth to age 13 or 14, and few have regretted it. Books written by survivors of wrecks can frighten you off, but note that the children DO survive. Read the many articles written for cruising magazines by parents who find, in the main, that cruising with their children has been an enriching experience. Their tales of sailing to new lands, meeting new people, and how the children develop self-reliance and confidence and, better yet, a stronger family bond, will be an inspiration for you. We also have a feeling that crews with children on board take more care.

SECTION FIVE – BOAT SKILLS: HOW ABLE A SEAMAN ARE YOU?

1 Do you own, or part-own, a boat? Or have you in the past? If Yes, score A2. If No, score Σ1.

2 Do you maintain, or help to maintain, a boat? (Hands-on, not just paying for it.) If Yes, score A2. If No, score Σ2.

3 Are you a qualified Master with a lifetime of experience and over 30,000 miles under sail in your log? If Yes, score A30, and go to Q17.

4 Do you potter about in boats? If Yes, score A1. If No, score 0.

5 Are you a weekend dinghy or small-boat sailor? If Yes, score A1. If No, score 0.

6 Have you cruised locally at home or abroad in a yacht for more than 14 days? If Yes, score A2. If No, score 0.

7 Have you made a passage to a foreign country? If Yes, score A2. If No, score 0.

8 Have you kept a night watch by yourself at sea? If Yes, score A2. If No, score 0.

9 Can you take a compass bearing? If Yes, score A1. If No, score 0.

10 Can you make any of the following: bowline, clove hitch, rolling hitch, fisherman's bend, figure-of-eight knot, sheet bend? If you can do them all NOW, score A2. If you can do three of them, score A1.

11 If your car goes wrong do you:
  (a) Call in the garage?
  (b) Have a go at mending it?
  (c) Read the manual and then have a go at mending it?
  If (a) score Σ2, if (b) score A1, if (c) score A2.

12 Can you cook:
  (a) Under difficult circumstances?
  (b) With unfamiliar and limited ingredients?
  (c) Without getting seasick?
  If (a) score A1, if (b) score A1, if (c) score A1. If Yes to all three, score a bonus of A2.

13 Do you suffer from seasickness? If No, score A4 and go to Q17. If Yes, continue.

14 Is your seasickness controllable or reducible by drugs? If Yes, score A1 and go to Q16. If No, continue.

15 Do you recover after 24 hours or so at sea? If Yes, score A1. If No, continue.

16 Are you prepared to suffer the occasional day of misery? If Yes, score A1. If No, score Σ10.

17 Do you have a smattering of any of the following skills: carpentry, compass adjusting, diesel and petrol engineering, electrics (AC or DC), electronics, fire-fighting, fishing, food preservation, haircutting, how to move heavy loads, laundering (by hand), metalworking, meteorology, musical instrument (small), paramedical skills, painting, plumbing, radio, rigging, sail repair, scuba diving, sewing, soldering, swimming, upholstery? Do you really understand computers? Score A1 for each three skills you claim.

• *Discussion on Section Five* •

'If there be more learners than saylors all the worke to save ship, goodes and lives must be on them especially in foule weather.'

It seems to us that anyone who wishes to go in for the cruising life will have acquired some skills. Such is the availability of experience these days that failure to have done anything so far could indicate a lukewarmth: or maybe you are just dreaming.

Some definitions might be useful. In Q1–3 we clearly infer a sailing boat, though if for perfectly valid reasons you are thinking of going in a motor yacht, then adapt the question accordingly. Q4, on the other hand, could mean any type of boat, which is clearly better than none at all. Q5–9 involve many conditions which might be borderline: you must use your common sense. If you haven't any, subtract A20!

Q10 is a fundamental. At first we thought it should score very high; then we reasoned that we are not testing seamanship, but a kind of nautical wanderlust of which ability is only a part. Bill would not like anyone to go to sea without being able to do all these knots in the dark, or to drive even a motorboat away from its moorings without knowing the bowline at least.

If you are a novice and learn to tie these knots (or make these bends, or bend these hitches: what a rabbit warren old nautical jargon can get you into), then you will be already useful. We have come across many yachtmasters who make their yachts fast with snowball hitches that melt in the sun.

In Q11 we are after your willingness to get stuck into a dirty problem with some chance of solving it effectively. Too many of us dash at a problem without thinking first. Always start with the simplest explanation, because that is often the case. And emulate John Guzzwell who was crewing for the Smeetons when their yacht capsized and was badly damaged rounding Cape Horn. His first recon-structive action was to sit down and sharpen his saw. There are rites of passage in all crafts: preparation before deciding what form the work will take is good thinking time.

Cooking, Q12, is one of the basic skills of cruising. Skippers are not entitled to hide behind wifey's apron all the time. Poor food is as demoralising as bad weather and bad temper.

Seasickness, Q13–16 must be taken seriously, since it can affect the morale and capability of everyone who suffers. A determined effort should be made to discover whether you start to recover after about 18 hours at sea and then are immune for the rest of the voyage, as the majority are; whether pills help you; or whether yours is the truly resistant kind, in which case you will probably hate the sea for ever.

The list of skills in Q17 are those that we have needed (or lacked) in a quarter of a century at sea in a yacht. (It is not definitive: if we have missed out your special expertise, sorry.) We intend the level of competence to be that of a conscientious amateur. Being a pro does not score extra, but might improve your earning capacity. Moving heavy weights is an art worth studying if you don't want to get a hernia.

SECTION SIX – GOODS AND GARDENS: CAN YOU LEAVE THEM?

1 Have you lived in your present house/flat for:
   (a) Less than two years?
   (b) Two to five years?
   (c) Five to ten years?
   (d) More than ten years?
   If you love your house, score (a) Σ2, (b) Σ3, (c) Σ4, (d) Σ6. If you are ready for a change, score (a) 0, (b) 0, (c) Σ1, (d) Σ1.

2 Do you like gardening? If No, score K1. If Yes, score Σ4.

3 Do you like horses and riding? If No, score 0. If Yes, score Σ2.

4 Do you own antique furniture or fine pictures? If No, score K1. If Yes, are you prepared to sell it, or give it to parents/children? If Yes, score 0. If No, score Σ2.

5 Do you have a fine collection of anything too big or fragile to take with you: old cars, steam engines, carousels, mangles, Ming china, 13th century armour, books, bird's eggs or pornographic (excuse me, curious) literature? If No, score K1. If Yes, are you prepared to sell it, or give it to parents/children? If Yes, score 0. If No, score Σ2.

6 Do you have a sport or hobby that you cannot take with you, eg. billiards, model railways, pottery, hang-gliding, monumental sculpture or mink breeding? If Yes, score Σ2. If No, score 0.

7 Can you manage without the local library?
   (a) Yes.
   (b) With difficulty.
   (c) No.
   If (a) score K1, if (b) score 0, if (c) score Σ2.

8 Is there life without TV? Do you watch, per week,
   (a) 6 hours?
   (b) 6 to 12 hours?
   (c) more than 12?
   If (a) score Σ1, if (b) score Σ3, if (c) score Σ5.

• *Discussion on Section Six* •

To some people, possessions are status. It is important to them to have a quality car, a house in the right part of town, and the latest gadget. They get a lot of fun out of their things, and are not likely to be reading this unless escape by yacht becomes frightfully fashionable one year, when they will buy a frightfully fashionable yacht to do it in, and have a lot of fun doing it for a short time before wanting to get back to their other gadgets. In our world, some people travel as light as a soul to heaven: Dan was one of these, he crewed for us from Antigua to Bermuda on his way to Europe and seemed to possess what he stood up in, a tracksuit and some running shoes.

Between these two extremes lie most of us, with a heap of rubbish that we could gladly say goodbye to, some useful odds and ends whose passing we might regret, and a further pile of junk that we cling to fiercely and beyond all persuasion. The more of it you can get rid of, the less hassle you will have on your voyage.

Q5–6   Houses. If you are going on a long voyage, your house back home will be a nuisance. Besides, you are probably buying your boat from the proceeds of selling it. Renting it in case you want to return can cause a lot of headaches: the Hiscocks tried this at first but eventually sold the house as the tenants caused so many problems. We have this spring met a French couple whose summer cruise to Greece had already ended in Fiumicino near Rome: they had to return and sort out some legal difficulty with their house. We sold ours. It was a wrench at the time, but the wound heals.

Q5–6   Those possessions that we could not bear to part with we left with various members of the family to mind for us. Funny, I can't remember what some of them are now. A few we took with us. So, we find, did other people; and it is surprising what a variety of objects mean enough to someone for them to find room and make a safe stowage for. We saw a cello on the 26-foot *New Life*, lovingly cradled on the forward berth (the second best cello, to keep in practice) an icemaking machine which worked by burning camel dung or any other solid fuel on *Northern Light*, an electronic keyboard for writing songs on *Clarity*. We carry my enamelling kiln. Eight-year-old Ben Lucas on *Tientos* had a most impressive Lego set. *Snow Goose* was the first yacht we met with a PC aboard, the full early-eighties television-sized monty, before laptops existed. TVs, guitars, bicycles, laptops and mobile phones are run-of-the-mill; golf clubs and tennis rackets rather less so. A dentist we know keeps a neat case of the tools of his trade on board, so do most doctors; indeed anyone with skills might want the wherewithal to use them, with the possible exception of lion tamers and nuclear physicists. The *Sell up and Sail* Collection-Riddance Award goes at present to Mike and Carrie Hofman, who sold a collection of more than 20 British World War Two armoured vehicles and a field gun before setting off on their cruise. Beat that!

Beware of Grandsons, Goods and Gardens:
Here your wife's resistance hardens.

SECTION SEVEN – ATTITUDES: YOU'VE GOT TO BE CRAZY.

1 Is your dreamboat taking shape? Are you (or your mate) currently:
(a) Buying or building her?
(b) Planning or designing or choosing her?
(c) Still looking for the right one after ten years?
(d) Designing for the tenth time in ten years?
(e) Still building after 15 years?
If (a) score K4, if (b) score K1, if (c) score 0, if (d) score Σ1, and if (e) score Σ3.

2 All of us have fears and uncertainties about such a voyage. Let's look them in the eye. Which one of the following statements is most true for you, concerning:
Keeping a night watch alone
(a) I'll be OK.
(b) I'm a bit nervous.
(c) I'm rather nervous.
(d) I'm not keen on the dark.
If (a) score 0, if (b) Σ2, if (c) Σ4, and if (d) Σ7.

Becoming ill on the voyage (you or your mate:)
(a) We'll cope somehow.
(b) I don't know what I'd do.
(c) I'm going to first aid classes.
(d) We'll have a check up before we go.
(e) He/she would be helpless without me.
If (a) score K1, if (b) Σ1, if (c) 0, if (d) 0, if (e) score Σ2.

Bad weather
(a) I'm used to it.
(b) I think I'll be OK.
(c) I'm a bit nervous.
(d) I'm very nervous.
(e) I'm scared stiff.
If (a) score K2, if (b) K1, if (c) 0, if (d) Σ1, if (e) score Σ4.

3 Pick whichever of the following best expresses your situation:
(a) I'm determined to go.
(b) I'm looking forward to it.
(c) I can't wait, but I don't think he/she wants to come.
(d) If he/she won't come, that's the end of it.
(e) I love planning, but I'm nervous about going.
(f) If he/she really wants to go, I suppose I shall have to.
(g) If we go for a year, he/she might get it out of their system.
(h) The idea is great, but I can't leave my grandchildren/dogs/ cats/garden just now.
(i) I don't think he/she has enough experience yet.
(j) My friends seem dubious about my going.
For (a) score K4, if (b) K2, if (c) 0, if (d)Σ3, if (e)Σ1, if (f) 0, if (g) 0, if (h) Σ5, if (i)Σ4, and if (j) Σ2.

4 How long do you envisage doing this?
(a) For the rest of your life?
(b) For a year or two?
(c) For several years?
(d) Until you get too old?

(e) For the foreseeable future?
If (a) score K4, if (b) K1, if (c) K2, if (d) or (e) score K3.

5 If you are not yet committed to going, how long before you do commit yourself?
(a) This year?
(b) Next year?
(c) Sometime?
(d) Never?
If (a) score K3, if (b) K2, if (c) 0, and if (d) Σ5.

6 Why haven't you already gone?
(a) I'm really just dreaming.
(b) For reasons I don't wish to reveal, or am not sure about.
(c) I have.
If (a) score Σ5, if (b) Σ4, and if (c) you are fouling up the system! Behave yourself. If your score in this section is more than K15, you are somewhat imprudent: subtract A4.

• *Discussion on Section Seven* •

In terms of partnership, one person is usually the instigator and prime mover of the Ulysses plan and the other (or others) the more or less willing follower. Usually the man is the instigator, and is going to be Captain. Usually the women and children are followers, and are going to be mate and crew. To the discussion which follows, it does not really matter which way round it is, but in order to avoid saying he/she too often we will go with the majority.

Trouble is clearly going to arise if the views of the partners are too divergent. Now, before you go to great expense and disruption, is the time to find out: if you disagree fundamentally about whether to go at all; or less radically about the kind of boat, the amount of time and money to be spent, what areas you will travel to, and the standard of comfort required.

Women have been home-makers ever since the first cave-wife hung a skin on the wall of her cave, instead of wearing it or lying on it. The habit, after 5000 years, dies hard, and it is too much to expect your wife to live in a production boat, stark as a railway station gents (and probably smelling rather similar), without letting her cosify it, within reason. The happiest boats we meet seem to be the ones with the homely touches. I have seen the sideways look in a woman's eyes when her man boasts that 'We haven't altered or added a thing since we got her at the Boat Show: keeps up the resale value, you know.' I am far more inclined to Hal Roth's view: 'the layout and detailing of the little ship on which a man lives and travels ought to be as personal as his fingerprints.'

I cannot see that curtains, covers, cushions and decor ruin the resale price. Nor has any production boat designer thought of all the extra gear you need to live aboard: indeed in many production boats it is hard to find space for the oilskins and seaboots for every crew member. I shall say more about this later, when we talk about storage.

If you embark on this life with any hope at all, you have to trust and have faith in each other. It follows that there should be some basis for this trust, and that you should set out to acquire skills and experience that will justify it. It's no good sailing out into the sunset, Captain, with your manly hand on the tiller and your manly pipe clenched between your teeth, if your mate quickly concludes that you do not really know what you are doing or where you are. No good, Lady, posing like the yachting mag ads, in immaculate whites holding a rope that obviously goes nowhere, when your Captain needs knowledgeable help. You owe it to each other to learn as much as you can by sailing together and separately, with friends or by answering 'crew wanted' ads, for long or short journeys, in different kinds of boat with different kinds of skipper.

If you have both been living the 9–5 life, you will be used to speaking to each other about five to six hours a day: less if you are silent breakfasters, TV addicts or in the darts team. How will you cope with being in each other's company 24 hours a day, barring night watches? When in such close quarters, a seventh sense needs to be developed. You should know when another person's space and privacy should be respected, and words that can wait half an hour be left unsaid. Long companionable silences should be easily achieved, and just as easily broken at the right moment. When we have friends on board we find that siestas are a great idea. Everyone separates to their own patch of space, and quiet activities, rest or sleep prevail for a blissful couple of hours. On meeting again later the chat is all the livelier, and the wit keener, for having had a break.

Fears and fancies we all have (Q2), and they need dragging out into the light where they can be more carefully examined. It is no good saying 'Cheer up, it won't happen!' because it probably will; no cruise is without incident. If you are aware of danger you have already taken the first step to prevent it; but be sure that you are guarding against realities, and not bogies under the bunk. You will reduce unnecessary worry to a minimum if you develop confidence in your boat, your Captain or crew, and yourself. Fear is allayed by encountering, and coping successfully, with trouble; this is what experience means. From the statistics, one ought to be far more terrified of crossing the High Street than keeping a night watch, but the first is a known and familiar danger and the second an unknown one. Eventually it becomes as ordinary as crossing the road, and rather less dangerous, though never to be taken lightly.

Illness on the voyage (either oneself or one's partner) is one of the thoughts that perturb us. Why do we not worry as much over becoming ill in our ordinary life at home? Because help would be available, in the form of doctors, hospitals, and friends. We have only to seek advice, and the burden is straight away on other shoulders: all we have to do then is follow instructions. If you wish to have the freedom that the cruising life brings, you have also to accept that you are going back to the pioneer days of being self-reliant.

Having said that; you will certainly be a lot healthier than if you'd stayed at home; and it's surprising how often there is a doctor in the next boat just when you need one. We have come to no serious harm in 26 years of cruising, some of it in very remote places. (See Chapter Fifteen and appendix for prevention of illness and accidents, and Website surgery.)

I suppose most of us are afraid of bad weather, though some of us are reluctant to admit it. It's no fun at all to have your house bucketing about at all angles, and the corners of your galley attacking you when you cook; and when the cat burrowing on to your lap under your oilskin while you steer is the only bit of companionable warmth you'll get till the weather improves. But if your boat is strong and your Captain capable and prudent, and perhaps above all you have got your sea legs, then it's possibly a little better than two hours in a packed commuter train.

No blame attaches to people who are afraid to go to sea, any more than those who would fear mountain climbing or motor racing, or (in my case) pot-holing (I'm already not too happy on the Underground.) Some people do these things precisely because they are afraid, and singlehanded too. To such brave hearts we give our admiration, but this book is not for them. Cruising is a game that two or more should play: no sane person goes mountain climbing or deep diving alone, and people who go off on journeys which they mentally label 'One Man against the Elements' or 'Alone in the Southern Ocean' are taking greater risks than we would care to. There is no need to be that crazy.

Nevertheless, if you want to undertake the life, you must develop a self-reliance that is unusual these days. We yachties are felt to be eccentric, a curious cross between hermits, voluntary exiles and adventurers. We feel very normal, of course; and only at gatherings of landpeople do we realise that we are perhaps a bit peculiar – when our answer to the inevitable question 'And where do you live?' is followed by an odd little silence, or a rush of enthusiastic clichés covering extreme social embarrassment. If you can't be classified, you are too alien to converse with. If they don't know where to put you in the social order you naturally go to the bottom. It's quite comfortable down there, there's no competition!

So, you do have to be a bit crazy. But at least do it with planning, forethought and prudence.

SUMMARY			
Now, write down your scores:	A	K	Σ
Section One	. .	. .	. .
Section Two	. .	. .	. .
Section Three	. .	. .	. .
Section Four	. .	. .	. .
Section Five	. .	. .	. .
Section Six	. .	. .	. .
Section Seven	. .	. .	. .
Totals for each type of score:			

Now add up the totals for A and K, and multiply by 100. Divide this figure by your total Σ score: this gives your Ulysses Quotient, ie

$$UQ = 100 \times (A + K) \text{ divided by } \Sigma$$

where A represents your Aptitude and Ability for cruising, and K represents Kinesis which is the mobility force in your personality, while Σ: (Sigma) represents Stasis which is the inertia in your personality.

If your UQ is below 100, you are a static person from a cruising point of view.

If your UQ is between 100 and 200, you are moderately kinetic: go with someone who has a higher one.

If your UQ is between 200 and 300, you are kinetic: you'll get by.

If your UQ is over 300, you have marked kinesis.

If your UQ is over 1000, you are a bit weird; why haven't you already gone?

There is a possibility of obtaining a total Σ score of zero, which would lead to a UQ of infinity. This is only possible if you are already following the life of a Ulysses, and are thoroughly content. Go on and enjoy it in good health.

PS: If you can't do the arithmetic, you probably wouldn't be able to work out the tidetables, or understand the GPS manual. Stay at home.

3 • Finance

*'The Purser doth keepe an Account of all that
is received and delivered'*

When we were giving talks following the publication of the first edition, we were frequently asked about finance and it is clear that this is a preoccupation with many prospective voyagers. However, now that this book has achieved international status we have to face the fact that it is impossible to cover the subject taking into account world-wide currencies and different taxation systems. We will confine ourselves to some outline views and opinions based on our own 26-year experience. There will inevitably be a British emphasis, but we believe that, mostly, the same principles apply elsewhere.

TAXATION

In the first edition we wrote that the important thing on the income side, assuming you have any, is to be able to stop most of it falling into the hands of governments or assorted middlemen. Since that time, taxation in Britain has changed dramatically, the main change being the big reduction in personal taxation level, now standing at 23% basic, and a mere 40% maximum rate for the rich. Some may recall that in the 1970s the marginal rate in Britain was 91.25%, which was one of the reasons we sold up and sailed. It made working not worth the mental struggle.

The present UK level (23%) is actually less than the Value Added Tax in some countries, and because VAT is much more difficult to evade it is likely the process of lowering income tax will continue, or at least not be reversed. There comes a point when the costs of setting up schemes to minimise income tax are too high for the benefits. We do not think it is any longer necessary to devote energy to this when there are more enjoyable things to do.

• *Non-residence* •

There thus remains only one important (UK) tax advantage to obtaining the status of non-residence, and that is exemption from Capital Gains Tax. If you have a business to sell, it is worthwhile starting the process of emigration and obtaining provisional non-resident status. This will need professional advice. Remember that an important factor is to emigrate: you need not immigrate anywhere; that is a completely different thing. The two verbs are quite opposite in meaning, and one does not necessarily involve the other. Tax men, not being noted for verbal skills, can get quite confused about this, but they give way if you persist. 'But what is the address of your villa?' they asked repeatedly. One was tempted to give them a lat and long. In mid-Atlantic.

Apart from Capital Gains Tax, I do not feel that non-residence is worth the bother unless you are very rich, in which case you will get better advice than we can give. One of the reasons is that when non-resident, susceptible income is taxed from the very first pound: one does not get any personal allowances. There is a complex formula which the Inspector should work out to decide whether you would be better off being taxed as non-resident or as resident (it is too difficult to go into the formula here), and you pay the lower figure.

On what, you may ask? Can one not invest entirely in those magical gilts which are tax-free to non-residents, and thus pay no tax at all? Yes, you can, but with the yield on long gilts (government bonds to the cousins) below 5%, you are not exactly doing very well. It is better to get 77% of something, rather than 100% of damn all.

Incomes of husbands and wives are now taxed separately. It is likely there will be several changes in the rules because the Treasury never gets anything right first time, but it seems at the moment possible for a husband to be a non-resident and to have all the non-taxable income while the wife remains resident and has all the inflation-resistant but taxable income in her name. If the husband has a good pension, then the position would be reversed. At the moment, contrived double taxation arrangements for those with no fixed abode do not seem to be worth the candle. Under the new self-assessment system in the UK there is an added disincentive to becoming non-resident. If resident, it is possible to arrange with your tax inspector to render returns every five years if you have stable income sources (ie pensions). If non-resident, the return has to be rendered annually, another example of the meaningless bureaucracy we are all trying to escape from.

Being non-resident exempts you from jury service but does not necessarily deprive you of a vote. However, the regulations governing this type of voting make it very difficult for yachties to qualify. Consult your MP before going if this interests you. Non-residence also enables you to do some very interesting things with the taxation of motor vehicles which we cannot go into here because its legality is dubious. Some people who settle in the Med do return to the same wintering port year after year, and they sometimes find it worth having a car. We refer to other aspects of this later.

Do not forget that the British old-age pension (or whatever the mealy-mouthed, politically correct politicians call it this year) is very good value. Keep up the voluntary contributions if you can: the DSS has leaflets on this.

• *VAT* •

The exemption from VAT that can be claimed by non-residents when buying goods in Britain for personal export is no longer the advantage it once was because it is no longer available to EU countries. You have to give a bona fide residence in a non-EU country to which the reimbursement cheque will be sent. Of course, we do not suggest that you need to organise a squad of trusted friends in faraway places.

The rules for VAT on boats in the EU changed in 1993. Consult the RYA's publication. If the yacht has had VAT paid on it in any EU country, it may travel and change hands anywhere throughout the EU without incurring further liability. Any boats built or imported into the EU before 1985 are assumed to have paid VAT even if documentary evidence is unavailable. One small example of common sense in an area not noted for it.

The snags arise because each EU country is unable to interpret the new rules with any certitude. Greece has had occasional fits of hyper-activity and fined some tax-evaders very large sums. It seems that they get help in identifying evading yachts from the authorities in other countries. You must also face the fact that in certain countries informers get a proportion of the fine as a reward.

In various Mediterranean countries, it is virtually impossible to get an authoritative ruling on anything. France is apparently interpreting the rules liberally, not wishing to drive away the vast fleets of foreign boats resident in their marinas, while in Italy it seems to depend on who you know.

We have not heard of anyone being harshly or unfairly treated. The only awkward cases concern boats that were exported from the UK without payment of VAT and have since been passing their winters in Cyprus or Malta. Technically these vessels are liable for the tax on their first entry into any EU port. EU citizens buying a boat should ensure that European VAT has been paid if they plan to stay in Europe or wish to sell the boat on to a European. Citizens of other countries thinking of selling on their boat in Europe must allow for this tax, which would have to be paid by the buyer. The amount of VAT varies from country to country. Currently it is 17½% in Britain, but much higher elsewhere. If you have to pay VAT, study the rates, which vary from year to year, and choose the cheapest country to pay it as it can be a substantial sum.

• *Organising your Finances* •

For those looking forward not to settling at sea for life but to having a limited break, finances become different. When the break is for a comparatively short period (say two years), one must be careful to define the aim. Many try to greyhound round the world and get their 'Great Sailor' ticket punched. Because we do not go for this approach does not invalidate it, but the finances will be much the same.

If you are going to be away for a period such as two years, do not dismantle your personal finances, because every major change involves fees and costs. You will not be able to become non-resident of the UK, so your strategy will remain that of a resident. Try to minimise the property (in its widest sense) that could cause problems while you are away. Many will want to keep their residence, but it will need protection, and delegated authority to deal with problems is essential.

• *In the USA* •

For citizens of the USA, the main problem in avoidance of US taxation is the possibility of losing citizenship. Having seen examples of correspondence shown to me by American friends, I can affirm that the relentless po-faced tone of the USIRS makes the UK Inland Revenue seem like knock-about comedians.

Our American friends still fill in their tax returns and send them off each March, whereas most English do not unless they have a pension.

EARNING YOUR KEEP

Earning one's living locally is theoretically possible but in many cases not wholly practicable. Even if unemployment is not a problem, elaborate precautions are taken to protect locals from foreign competition. The question needs looking at in three ways: first, how can one earn in a way that does not upset the locals, wherever one is? Second, what jobs, trades, or professions are generally welcome anywhere? And last, what about the EU?

• *Not Upsetting the Locals* •

- Be discreet
- Bring skills that are not available locally
- Don't be too successful

• *Welcome Jobs* •

There are various occupations that can be carried out aboard, the income there-from not being obtained locally. Artists come under this heading, provided they are not seen to sell in direct competition with the locals, though even here there is often a degree of tolerance not evident in most fields. The keynote is discretion; it does not seem to matter how much you make, it is the degree of ostentation involved which is important. We have personal knowledge of this field. Artists in general are very tolerant of one another, respecting genuine talent in any form. The chief source of possible objection comes from the local art gallery or souvenir shop, but sales direct to other foreigners excite little attention. Bermuda has really restrictive laws – be careful there. Places where the artist can make a little something are the West Indies and the Bahamas, where the locals do not do much towards providing a souvenir industry, and where the majority of tourists are comparatively wealthy Americans dying to spend on something local. Greece is interesting, for it can be chauvinistic or even xenophobic at times, but it is genuinely liberal towards artists and musicians. However, I suspect there exist several ways in which they could cope with unfair exploitation of this liberality.

Writing is not an easy way to earn. It wins a little respect in some countries, and bestseller writers live like kings, but a couple of well-known novelists living afloat in the West Indies do so modestly. Writing for yachting magazines is hard work, and a very poor return for the time spent. One would need to produce a very large volume of words to make much of a living. Magazine writing has to be seen as a way of making an occasional bonus, especially as there has been a growing tendency for the magazines to become more glossily professional. Which means that they tend to prefer articles written by full-time journalists who do not know much about sailing and have little time to sail, rather than by experienced yachtsmen or women with little time to write and meet deadlines.

Away from writing, there is one lady sailor who makes very high-quality bikinis for the boutique trade. She is now well known, and hers is a good example of a well-planned, suitable home industry, carried on in winter in order to sail in the summer. We know people who bake, or make preserves. We know woodcarvers, craft jewellers and scrimshankers. Any craft worker should be able to make a bit where there are tourists to buy their work.

I would also put under the first heading (Be discreet) the carrying out of services associated with boats for other foreign yachtsmen. I have made some pocket money adjusting compasses, no problem in the USA, but in Greece I had to get the approval of the local Coast Guard Captain (I swung the Coast Guard cutter for him). Persons capable of doing electronic repairs are very hard to find. A good working knowledge of technique, and ability to read a circuit diagram, are required, while electronic parts are often easier to buy retail in less well-developed countries. Competent refrigeration engineers should get enough work anywhere to prevent them enjoying life. So should sailmakers and upholsterers.

Those skills which are universally welcome are not so numerous. Trained nurses are in demand world-wide, but doctors definitely are not; the latter seem to have devised some very nasty restrictive practices against their fellows in other lands. Mechanics can do well in some parts, though often it is a question of a direct job for another yottie, but really skilled men are almost always needed, especially in some West Indian islands. Shipwrighting jobs can be found, though these are usually in the busy season which is when the dedicated cruiser wants to be doing his own boat. This applies also to casual labour; even if found it is likely to be when one would rather be sailing. Qualified teachers can sometimes get work, especially those with a certificate to teach English as a foreign language.

• *The European Union* •

Persons from one member country are supposedly allowed to work in the others. I am only aware of the situation round the Mediterranean coasts, where the French seem to be honouring the treaty. Not unreasonably, they demand that any

Stonington, Conn.

foreigner working there should pay French taxes and social service dues; however, the bureaucracy is a wilderness for the foreigner to get lost in, and it is necessary to take care. In general, I have found French authorities are sympathetic, and fair about unintentional breaches of regulations, but they do not take kindly to attempts to pull a fast one. Keep in the open; they suspect anything of a clandestine nature.

If French bureaucracy is difficult, the Italians' is a complete enigma that even the natives do not try to solve. I get the impression that everyone lives illegally, and pays up when, or if, caught! It is a completely undisciplined society, and the illegal work going on is widespread. Italians, however, are the most tolerant and least chauvinist people in Europe.

Greece is settling into the EU slowly and complainingly, after having spent the cash which accrued. They were quick to exploit the handouts, which they called Delors's Drachmas (they have now the highest BMW count in the EU) – not much has actually been spent on the works for which various subsidies were intended, however). Conformity to EU rules is taking much longer, and is disagreeably painful. The rules for working, starting businesses etc now seem to be being honoured in law, even if in practice the process is not so easy. Greece is a Levantine country and West European methods and business ethics are foreign to the Greek culture. But we do believe that they are trying to adapt. In the meantime be very wary of doing anything that could be wrongly construed: the Greeks are among the most

hospitable people in the world provided they do not think their hospitality is being abused. Then they can become quite annoyed. A Greek who is quite annoyed is about equivalent to an Englishman who has gone ballistic.

GETTING MONEY TO WHERE IT IS NEEDED

It isn't funny to run out of money.
Having some for contingencies, avoids stringencies

We now come to the problem of transferring funds and drawing money. It is best to have a bank account in any country where you have income originating. Transfer from bank to bank is hopeless. Transfer from an office of a bank in one capital city to an office of the same bank in another capital city is not much better. For example, a sum of $7000 dollars sent by the London office of the Bank of New York took 32 days to become available in New York, and that was fast going. Another sum took 53 days to get from the London office of Credito Italiano to one of their offices near Rome. Even Barclays took three weeks to get money from their head office in the City of London to their associate company in Antibes. All of these were telegraphic transfers.

As if to confuse matters, those old-fashioned bankers to royalty, Coutts & Co, have transferred a sum to Holland for me in two days, which is astonishing. It seems it can be done, perhaps only by bank clerks wearing frock coats. And we must remember that Anglo-Dutch banking has always been good, ever since the burghers of Amsterdam saved the Bank of England from default in 1697, in return for which we took William of Orange off their hands. They drive a hard bargain, the Dutch.

I see no sign that internet banking, or any other form of electronic activity, has improved financial services in any way. Rather, the reverse. One used to get next-day delivery when dealing in UK government bonds. Computer science has enabled us to 'catch up with the Americans'; we now have four-day delivery as they do – if you are lucky.

• *Drawing funds for everyday living* •

This can be done in several ways:

Eurocheque services are being withdrawn this year. I am told that this is because they are no longer much used. Holes in walls are better for drawing cash, though the eurocheque used to be useful for larger amounts.

Travellers' cheques are acceptable generally, but beware of cheques drawn on little-known banks, and that means little known at the back of beyond. ('Who is this Barclay that he has a bank?' I was once asked.) These also have a ridiculous charge payable when you buy them, though in view of the fact that you are lending money to the bank, unsecured and interest-free, you ought to be paid a fee. A big snag with travellers' cheques is that they are difficult to get once one has left one's native banking scene. They can be bought abroad, but if you already have the money, why buy the cheques? Not unreasonably, banks will not send them through the post.

Postcheques are available to those with a National Girobank account. They come in chequebook form and enable withdrawal of up to £100 daily in local currency at post offices in Europe and the Middle East (with a few exceptions). There should be no commission on each cheque, but about 50p is charged per transaction. This is possibly the cheapest way of getting funds at the modest level. Apart from Italy, I have found post office queues rather shorter than those in England. They are much the same length in Italy, but service is even slower.

Credit cards can be used for a variety of purposes, but are not universally convenient for ordinary shopping except in cities. Elsewhere, most shops in the scheme are the high mark-up, luxury type of shop which we do not patronise. Cards can rarely be used for buying diesel oil except at up-market marinas, though they can be used to buy petrol at garages. This seems an anomaly, as this would be the most convenient use for such a card. On the whole, for retail use alone cards are barely worth the bother, though most European supermarkets accept them these days. With the growth of the hole-in-the-wall cash dispensers, they do represent in many places the only convenient way of drawing cash. At a price sometimes, but you have to bear in mind that tourists (and one becomes one sometimes, like it or not) exist to be ripped off. I started out with a full set of cards, and here are my views on four of them based on experience:

- American Express: This card has a high service charge, but its administration is completely unsuited to the needs of the long-distance sea-going traveller, being more geared to the business tripper. Like most cards, it can be used for airlines and luxury hotels – so what? I thought it would be useful in the USA, but shops refused it or asked for an extra payment if I wished to charge the purchase. An exception to this was car hire: it is virtually impossible to hire a car without a card, but it does not have to be American Express. When I did charge something, there were so many billing errors that the whole procedure became a nightmare. One advantage of this card is that there exist AmEx travel offices in certain places where one can draw both travellers' cheques or cash in quite large amounts. Unfortunately these centres are mostly in capital cities or major tourist venues which, apart from Antibes, are unlikely to be of much use to yachtsmen.

- Diner's Club: Much of the above about American Express also applies, except that it is not nearly so widely accepted, and has no travel offices. I gave it up very early. The annual charge is too high.

- Visa/Barclaycard: This has been the most useful. I have used it for drawing cash in both USA and Europe with good results, having once established that one needs a credit limit of several times one's normal monthly drawings, owing to delays in payments clearing and getting into the authorising computer abroad. It is widely used in Europe without much difficulty.

- Access/Mastercard: Almost as good as Visa, but it is difficult to find co-operative outlets in France, while the Italian outlets seem to limit very severely the amount drawable.

Bank cards with the cirrus device on them are now giving good service more cheaply than other means of drawing cash.

The only card I need now is plain and simple Visa. We have not found it necessary to presume superiority by presenting Gold or Platinum cards or whatever else they tempt you into paying more for. We have an arrangement with our bank in Britain to pay the accounts on presentation, which keeps our credit limits up and avoids unnecessary interest charges on otherwise inevitable late payments. American Express refused this eminently sensible arrangement, expecting travellers to pay within a few days from a position in the middle of the Black Sea.

• *Carry cash* •

There is a lot to be said for regarding the dollar bill as the perfect travellers' cheque. There is no charge for issuing it, and it is acceptable everywhere, often at a premium. A few years ago in Turkey, the up-market newspaper *Çum Huriyet* published the black market rates every day. But there is no safeguard in the event of loss. Nowadays, inflation has become so rampant in Turkey that practically all transactions take place in Dollars or Deutschmarks, and in Eastern European ex-Iron Curtain countries a one-dollar bill will buy almost anything you need.

• *Getting a large amount in an emergency* •

This is a big problem; fortunately it is not likely to occur often. Possible causes might be a fine by local Customs (however undeserved, it has to be paid before being appealed) or the purchase of a major piece of equipment. Generally, major repairs take long enough for money to be remitted by routine means, but it is possible for estimates to be exceeded giving rise to an urgent need. In some countries medical expenses may have to be paid up front before reclaiming them on Form E111 or your insurance.

As a precaution, negotiate the maximum possible credit limits on credit cards, which should be good for £10,000 each at the very least (and preferably much more), in order to give quite a good sum available at very short notice. Both Visa/ Barclaycard and Access/Mastercard will make personal loans above the credit limit and are very prompt, so it might pay to carry appropriate application forms. We believe there are some institutions who will consider e-mail applications for loans, but have never pushed one of them to the ultimate step of parting with money. As with all advertisements and claims by financial institutions, there is always a hidden condition that means you are not eligible. Everybody else is, it seems, especially those who have no need of the service. Only you are not. We have explained, haven't we, that people with no fixed abode and therefore no postcode have no credit rating? A latitude and longitude position just doesn't seem to appeal to computers.

In theory it ought to be possible to draw a certified cheque on the London (or New York) branch of a foreign bank and present it to the local branch of that bank for immediate payment. In practice, it just doesn't work out.

Obtaining really large amounts (in this context) is an intractable problem; there is no certain solution that can be applied in all countries. I do recommend keeping a personal relationship with your home bank manager so that, if there is a crisis, an understanding at a personal level can oil a lot of wheels. The trouble is that retail banking is getting less and less personal and one cannot be on friendly terms with a computer, even if it does address you with inappropriate familiarity by the forename that you do not actually use. If you are going to be in one country for a fair time, consider opening a local account and make yourself known to the manager. Less trendily advanced countries still tend to have managers. Local advice at a friendly professional level is usually worth it.

All in all, the best way of getting a large amount in a hurry seems to be to get a lot of small amounts by various means and add them together. A nuisance, but effective. We once had to pay a stingingly large engine repair bill (well, it was in Sicily) and went to nine banks to collect the money together. All Sicilian banks are fortresses, seemingly held by one set of Mafiosi against another. They all have a security interlock entrance lobby, one person at a time, X-rayed for weapons. In every one, Bill set off the alarm with his aluminium spectacle case, and was set upon by grim men with guns who would not allow him to have the case back till we left. One even took away his spectacles as well, making it difficult to fill in the forms. Perhaps that was the idea. If you think it might be necessary to get a large sum, organise methods in advance.

BANKING OVERSEAS

In the first edition I wrote 'Considering the problem of getting cash country by country, I think it is fair to say the British will generally be astonished at the lack of customer convenience at retail banks in many parts of the world.' Nowadays the boot is largely on the other foot. People in other parts of the world would be astonished at the way mainstream British banks treat their customers. French banks, for example are much more friendly.

• *The USA* •

Here, banking is still fragmented and localised; there is no cheque card system, and cheques from local banks (and there are no others) are not cashable in the next town, let alone the next state, so Visa or Mastercard are essential for drawing cash. Foreign money is very unwelcome anywhere; even the Canadian dollar is alien and suspicious. Financially, the country is parochial; it is easier to make transactions between countries in Europe than between states in the USA.

• *The West Indies* •

Here one finds Barclays to be efficient and they will accept UK cheque cards. It is not generally realised that Canada does a lot to help the more backward islands and Canadian banks are common, well organised and helpful. In a world league of bank helpfulness, Canada is near the top. Apart from the French islands where French banks and currency are used, and there are no significant problems, most islands either use the US dollar as legal tender (the British Virgins, for example) or tie their dollar to the US dollar, and both currencies circulate side by side. Even on those islands with British sovereignty or strong connections, the pound sterling is not welcome, and this applies to the Bahamas and Bermuda too. Before leaving places with dual currencies, make sure to change local currency into US dollars, as it can be difficult to do so afterwards.

• *Europe* •

French banking is reasonable. The most appallingly inefficient is in Italy, where banking is supposed to have been invented and the system does not appear to have changed since the prototype. Commissions charged are higher, chaos and error abound, and it is one of the few environments in Italy where they are habitually rude to the customer. The best banking services for the tourist are to be found in the more backward countries that are heavily dependent, economically, on tourism. Greece is an example where the service is very good. In Turkey, everything is very polite and correct but takes a long time with much cross-checking. Spain and Yugoslavia are tolerable, but it is useless to try anything out of the routine in the ex-communist countries.

EXPENDITURE

Now let us have a look at expenditure. I would like to quote a cost of living figure, but tastes differ so much that it would be meaningless. We met a couple in 1986 who claimed to live (exist?) in a small yacht in the Med on about £40 per week (at present price equivalence) for everything. I would treat this with a little caution because I cannot see how their craft could continue to be maintained properly, though at the time it appeared to be well enough. Such a life-support existence would be feasible if the cruise were short and no maintenance were done; no replacements, no emergencies to be met, no sickness or injury, and few, if any, excursions into the interior, which are certainly part of our life.

In the later chapter on victualling and marketing, Laurel will discuss the relative costs of food and stores from country to country. With a fair-sized boat one can take advantage of differentials or bargains and buy some things in bulk. By moving from place to place, many costs do average out, except between continents.

The Med used to be undoubtedly the cheapest area to live in but is so no longer, largely because of the EU which has raised prices everywhere in the northern shore countries. Turkey is very reasonable and so is Tunisia. In the year 2000, everywhere was cheaper than Britain. One of the reasons why some countries are cheap to live in is that many imported or luxury goods are not available outside the big cities, which is conducive to economy.

At present we budget £50 ($75) per person per week for food in the Med, but often do not spend this much. This will cover all housekeeping, food, wine, refreshments and an occasional meal ashore – except in Italy, where although food costs are much the same, restaurant prices are high for value received. (In the new millennium, there are signs that this may be improving.) The figure does not include fuel. It is, however, catering on a reasonably liberal scale: we could do it a lot cheaper and still enjoy life.

In the West Indies and the Bahamas, where the economy is dollar based and much is imported from the USA, the cost of living reflects this.

INSURANCE

The costs of insurance are substantial in the type of boat suitable for living in. In some countries, notably Italy, France and Greece, *third party cover* is obligatory, and we have heard it is also so in Spain. I think anyone not so covered is an antisocial menace, anyway. However, there are a number of yachtsmen who do not carry *full* cover. If going to those countries where it is compulsory, get your insurers to provide a certificate of cover *in the local language*. This is important.

We have had good value for over 45 years from the gentlemen of Lloyd's, who behaved splendidly when we were struck by lightning. However, it became clear to them that they were not writing the right sort of policies, and instead of changing their policies our syndicates decided to write none at all. We now insure via GJW Direct (which is still underwritten at Lloyd's), and have had one claim in 12 years which was treated very civilly and settled promptly and fairly. One can ask for little more. One word of advice: if you want your claim settled promptly, do not try to put one over the claims officer of your insurer. He has been in the business a long time, has seen it all, and can sniff out the preposterous with uncanny ease. His suspicions can delay the overall settlement considerably. Do not suppose, though, that good companies seek to delay payment unfairly. Most insurers are aware that if there were no claims there would be no insurance industry.

There is no doubt that it is difficult to get good cover at reasonable prices for an ocean-cruising boat, and virtually impossible if there are only two persons on board. I cannot convince underwriters that they are wrong here; they maintain that a small crew can get tired keeping watch-and-watch in poor conditions. They seem to forget that the Battle of the Atlantic was won by men, many of them yachtsmen by inclination, keeping watch-and-watch for weeks on end in truly appalling conditions. If the boat is your home, you are not going to take risks deliberately. Number and kind of crew is perhaps not as the underwriters see it. We were dismasted one stormy night off the Kentish Knock, not so long ago. We sorted the mess out ourselves, the two of us; it was difficult and exhausting, but we managed it, and decided to make for Ramsgate instead of heading down-channel to the Solent as we'd intended. After eight pretty exciting hours, we made harbour. We discovered that close by in the same storm another vessel had also been dismasted, a well-found yacht belonging to a bank, with eight husky young men on board. The lifeboat towed them in.

If you do get good cover, then keep in touch with your underwriters. Become known. Send them postcards, tell them where you are and what you're doing.

It seems to me unlikely that anyone will get good cover in the Med for much less than 1.7%, and that rates will be a lot higher elsewhere.

If you are going to do much canal cruising, it might pay to get cover from one of the specialist French insurers. They know the risks,so their rates are generally lower. Consult the pages of the French magazine *Fluvial*.

The ocean-going yachtsman badly needs a policy that will insure him against any third party claims, fire, lightning strike, and any structural damage, collision and grounding, but excludes cosmetic finishing. It is often the latter that runs away with costs, and it is something most of us are prepared to do ourselves. Note that marine policies do not cover piracy and various forms of civil unrest. With the increase in piracy in certain places, it seems to me that some cover for these risks should be available. At extra cost, of course.

One odd feature of the insurance scene is that US underwriters charge more for cover in European waters than for cover in the Western Hemisphere, while European underwriters rate the risks the other way round. This strongly suggests that rates are based entirely on personal hunch rather than on statistics.

SYNDICATES

The majority of craft we come across are manned by a married couple (the word 'married' being interpreted a little loosely), but there are a number of boats being sailed by syndicates, and as these are essentially financial arrangements this is perhaps the place for some comment. There are two broad kinds of syndicate:

In the *running syndicate* the expenses of running the boat and living aboard are shared, but the boat herself belongs to only a part of the syndicate, perhaps to one person only. In a *property syndicate* all the members have shares in the boat, though not necessarily equal shares. It is evident that it is possible to have a combination of the two sorts.

• *The running syndicate* •

In this, there is no question of ownership of assets, thus the syndicate is comparatively easy to start, break up, or alter as it goes along. Many running syndicates have no formal agreement; they run happily on a shared interest and good fellowship. Given goodwill all round, a break can be just as easy: the person who wishes to leave just packs up and goes. Cautious people might like to have a more positive agreement; I would, but few actually do.

It has to be recognised that the boatowner(s) have the right to withdraw their vessel. But they cannot reasonably exercise this right suddenly in a completely isolated port and thus leave the rest of the syndicate stranded. Likewise, members must not leave the owners stranded, supposing the boat needs a crew to sail. A period of notice needs to be agreed, and it should be expressed in two ways, both in time and in geography; ie there should be a minimum notice of say, two weeks, but that the break shall only take place in a reasonably accessible port, to which the vessel should be taken as soon as possible. New members can be added at any time, but I know of problems, where, for example, one member wishes to bring in a marvellous girl he met last night, and the others just do not see eye to eye with him about her value to the syndicate as a whole.

The loose agreement might at least define what types of expenditure are cover-ed, eg housekeeping, ship's stores, fuel, repairs, replacements and so on. It should

The owner presumably gave up a good job and went from riches to rags.

certainly appoint a book-keeper. It should ideally set up a contingency fund to help meet accidents or disaster; the decision to use the fund has to be a majority one, and it should be used only for an item too large to be met out of two (say) months' total contributions. Most people would accept simple provisions like that, otherwise there is no point in starting. If disagreement becomes serious, expulsion or dissolution has to follow, even if a somewhat different syndicate re-forms.

In these circumstances the major problem is often the distribution of the contingency fund, especially if it is long standing and/or substantial. In theory it is possible to work out the refunds arithmetically, but a lot of syndicates have fairly frequent changes, and the mathematics might be daunting. One terminating syndicate I knew (a German one) threw a fantastic party, inviting all yachtsmen in the port to drink the fund, which was eventually done. The real problem is that goodwill is often thinned on a dissolution.

A running syndicate problem occurred when an aggrieved party considered that a major repair that became necessary arose from neglect by the owner before the formation of the syndicate, and that the repair could enhance the value of the vessel after the syndicate broke up. He felt this was a capital matter, not maintenance; the owner thought otherwise. Such arguments cannot be pre-defined, or pre-determined. They are questions that have to be answered as and when they occur. All parties to a running syndicate must accept the vessel 'as is, where is', and they have to use their judgement as to future liabilities. Of course, an arbitration agreement would help.

• *The property syndicate* •

This second type of syndicate is concerned not only with running a boat from day to day, but also with the ownership of, and responsibility for, a very valuable piece of property. In these circumstances an agreement *must* be made in proper legal form, for though there will be no problems if goodwill prevails, the scope for bitterness, anger and nastiness when tempers become frayed after some real, or imagined, injustice or slight is so immense that the exercise can turn into a lawyers' benefit. Better a small fee for legal advice at the start.

The syndicate agreement must, therefore, lay down clearly:

- Who is the skipper for purposes of running the ship (there can be only one).
- How decisions, other than navigational ones, are reached.
- Procedure for changes in the syndicate.
- How unforeseen liabilities will be paid, eg reconstruction due to previous neglect or hidden defects.
- Procedure for final dissolution.
- Arrangements for arbitration.

No syndication agreement should ever give any one person a right of general veto. When all goes well, such a right is exercised with tolerance. But if one person gets disaffected, or has a breakdown perhaps, then such a bloody-minded partner can ruin everyone's life. For similar reasons, agreements should contain a clause that in the event of a death the remaining syndicate members have the right to buy out the deceased partner's equity at a valuation arrived at by a stated method. Though all the partners might be the best of friends, this happy relationship may not extend to an executor, or to a legatee of one of these friends. If the capital values are substantial, and exercising the right is liable to cause embarrassment to one or more of the partners, then it is possible to obtain a temporary, contingency insurance on a number of lives payable to the survivors on the death of one of them, though full-scale tontines are illegal.

I do not think the concept of time-sharing has any relevance to the type of cruising we are considering. Come to think of it, I do not think it is much good for anyone except the organising entrepreneur.

MARINE MORTGAGES

Though vessels can be bought with marine mortgages, it would need a lot of careful weighing up before sailing off with such a burden. The finance companies would not be overjoyed to see their security, mobile as it is, disappearing to parts of the world where they could well have great difficulty and expense exercising any rights in the event of a default. Even if they granted a loan, it would have to be considered less secure than a loan on a boat owned by a man in a steady job, and who never left the country in her, and this would probably lead to a higher rate of interest.

And how would you pay the regular, very large, instalments? Out of a substantial pension, perhaps, if you are lucky enough to have one – but otherwise one is very unlikely to earn that sort of income while actually cruising. It has been done by investing a large sum in property and using the net rental of the property to meet the mortgage payments on the yacht, but this presupposes that the former is greater than the latter.

Remember that the finance company is in the investment business too, and in my experience it would be a very special investment opportunity that would make that sort of deal profitable after taking into account all the on-costs of the various arrangements.

To try to earn enough as one goes along to meet mortgage payments is crazy, other than for best-selling novelists, artists who can regularly sell a load of rubbish to the Tate Gallery, or hard-drug smugglers. The latter will assuredly have their yacht confiscated when they are inevitably caught, so the less equity they have in her the better. They should mortgage to the hilt.

WHAT WILL IT COST TO SELL UP AND SAIL?

It must be possible to get some idea.

I have been persuaded, against my better judgement, to be a little more specific about the costs of wandering abroad. This is, of course, to be on a hiding to nothing, for I will be trying to say how long your piece of string is. On the other hand, I do have some data, thanks mainly to Laurel's elementary but effective accounting methods, and I do have a certain amount of both personal and borrowed experience of several boats, so here goes. The jargon may be mathematical, but I will give some examples at the end. We are forecasting, remember. **Currency is immaterial** for this exercise, provided you do not mix them; reckon using the same one throughout.

Let the price or current value of the craft be **P**.
Let the building material factor be **B** (see Table 1, below).
Let the rig factor be **R** (see Table 2).
Let the age (boat, not crew) factor be **A** (see Table 3).
Let the physical capability of each of the crew be **E** (see Table 4).
Let the displacement of the boat in tons be **T** (to the nearest whole number).
Let the cost of the sea-going inventory be **F**.

Table 1 Building material factor B

Fibreglass (GRP)	1.0	Steel	1.35
Aluminium alloy	1.1	Teak	1.35
Ferrocement	1.2	Other timbers	1.4

Table 2 Rig factor R

Sloop	1.0	Wishbone or staysail schooner	1.15
Cutter	1.05	Other schooners	1.2
Yawl or Ketch	1.1		

If craft is gaff or sprit rigged multiply each of above by 1.1.
For example, a gaff schooner would be 1.2 x 1.1 = 1.32.

Table 3 Age factor A

Less than one year	1.0	10 years but less than 20	1.4
1 year, but less than 5	1.05	20 years but less than 50	1.8
5 years but less than 10	1.2	50 years or over	2.6

Table 4 How about the crew E?

A really fit person well used to manual labour	3.0
Average person 16–40 years, according to fitness	2.0–2.6
Average person 12–15, or 41–60 according to fitness	1.8–2.3
Average person over 60, according to fitness	1.1–1.9
Someone willing and capable, but completely out of condition	0.9–1.1
A partially disabled person but willing and able to keep a lookout, pass tools, brew tea, and give first aid.	0.5–0.8

• *Maintenance cost* •

The total annual maintenance cost is divided into two parts, of which one is dependent completely on the ship and her gear, while the other takes into account the capacity of the crew to do things themselves. Obviously they cannot do everything, or it is very rare that this is the case, and it would require unusual combinations and levels of skills. Our assumption is for an amateur and willing, but not especially skilled, crew. The formula works only for sailing craft because I have no data for motor yachts. The costs of engine maintenance in a sailing yacht are included with the broad assumption that the boat and her engine are proportional to each other in size and condition. Well, I do have to make some assumptions, don't I?

The first part, m_1, is:

$$m_1 = 0.02 \ (P \times B \times R \times A + F)$$

which represents maintaining engine, structure, rigging, and replacing them from time to time. It is a long-term annual average.

The second part, m_2, is:

$$m_2 = \frac{B \times R \times A \times T \times 40}{\text{sum of E}}$$

The total expected annual maintenance cost for the ship, M, is given by adding these two, thus:

$$M = m_1 + m_2$$

If you are still with me, you must be keen, so let us look at some examples; we will take three to show a fair cross-section of types.

A A 50-year-old gaff schooner, built of pine on oak, displacing 36 tons, costing in good sea-going order £50,000 and with an inventory of about £8,000.

So $P = 50,000$; $B = 1.4$; $R = 1.32$; $A = 2.6$; and $F = 8,000$.

$$
\begin{aligned}
m_1 &= 0.02\,(50,000 \times 1.4 \times 1.32 \times 2.6 + 8000) \\
&= 0.02 \times (240,240 + 8000) \\
&= 0.02 \times 248,240 = £4965 \text{ per annum.}
\end{aligned}
$$

She will have four young crew: a sporty accountant, and his wife who is something of an athlete, a bricklayer, and his wife who is not too fit. These might rate, in order: 2.6, 2.3, 3.0, and 1.4, giving a total crew worth, from this point of view, 9.3 as **E**.

Thus $m_2 = (1.4 \times 1.32 \times 2.6 \times 36 \times 40) \div 9.3 = £744.$

One might expect to budget for maintenance, then $M = 4965 + 744 = £5709$ per annum. (Always round up.)

B A bermudan steel ketch, 10 years old, displacing 20 tons, worth £70,000 with a £10,000 inventory. She is crewed by a 54-year-old fit man, his out-of-condition wife, and a 15-year-old fit daughter. In this case;

$$
\begin{aligned}
P &= 70,000; B = 1.35; R = 1.1 \times 1.1 = 1.21; A = 1.4; F = 10,000. \\
m_1 &= 0.02\,(70,000 \times 1.35 \times 1.21 \times 1.4 + 10,000) \\
&= 0.02\,(160,083 + 10,000) = £3402 \\
m_2 &= (1.35 \times 1.21 \times 1.4 \times 20 \times 40) \div (2.2 + 1.0 + 2.0) = £352
\end{aligned}
$$

So her total expected maintenance **M** would be $3402 + 352 = £3754$ per annum.

C A new fibreglass sloop, costing £75,000 with inventory costing £9,000, displacement 9 tons. Her crew is an elderly couple; he is 64 and fairly fit, but his wife has arthritis and has difficulty with ladders.

$$
\begin{aligned}
m_1 &= 0.02\,(75,000 \times 1.0 \times 1.0 \times 1.0 + 9,000) = £1680 \\
m_2 &= (1.0 \times 1.0 \times 1.0 \times 9 \times 40) \div (1.2 + 0.7) = £189
\end{aligned}
$$

So her maintenance, $M = m_{1} + m_{2,}$ might well cost an estimated £1869 per annum.

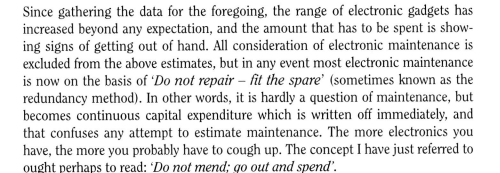

Since gathering the data for the foregoing, the range of electronic gadgets has increased beyond any expectation, and the amount that has to be spent is showing signs of getting out of hand. All consideration of electronic maintenance is excluded from the above estimates, but in any event most electronic maintenance is now on the basis of '*Do not repair – fit the spare*' (sometimes known as the redundancy method). In other words, it is hardly a question of maintenance, but becomes continuous capital expenditure which is written off immediately, and that confuses any attempt to estimate maintenance. The more electronics you have, the more you probably have to cough up. The concept I have just referred to ought perhaps to read: '*Do not mend; go out and spend*'.

• *Insurance again* •

If the boat is insured there will be another annual expense equal to the value of the boat with her inventory multiplied by the insurance rate, that is $i(P + F)$, where i is the insurance rate which, as discussed earlier, usually lies between 1.0 and 2.5% depending on cruising areas.

If the boat is uninsured, the crew should keep a contingency fund. Start this off at the beginning with 1% at least of the boat's value; but add to it regularly. I think it ought to be a budget item of about 0.25% of the boat's value. If the boat is insured, then a sum equal to the excess (the 'deductible' in the USA) should be kept on one side in a realisable investment, or in a deposit account on short call, especially in syndicated boats, unless it is a small enough amount to be coped with from current income.

• *Personal costs, Food, etc* •

Food, etc   We cover this in Chapter Ten.

Pleasures   What your pleasures are, and how expensive, I have no way of knowing, nor do I think I ought to tell you what ours are. You'll just have to sort this one out for yourself.

Miscellaneous   There are other costs that have to be budgeted for, and these are particular to the person too. There will be the occasional trip back home to see the folks, which is coupled with buying spare parts, thus mixing sentiment with hard-headedness. You will have expenditure on any property or chattels you keep in the old country. You will perhaps have medical insurance, which is no cheap item. World-wide cover is expensive and we discuss health in the Chapter Fifteen.

Obviously, I cannot comment on what allowances you make to cover your personal leanings, but we would say that, if you do it all in a thinking way, you should not be more than 50% out. That is not a bad approximation in these circumstances.

4 • A Yacht to Live In

'Were I to chuse a shippe for myselfe I would have her sail well yet stronglye built, her decks flush and flat, and so roomy that men might pass with ease'

The yacht is to be more than just a nautical vehicle: she is to be a home. This puts a very important requirement into the considerations, because many boats that are a joy to sail would make abominable homes, and vice versa. From reading accounts written by mile-hungry ocean voyagers, it is apparent that few, if any, spend more than 40% of their time at sea. In our case, over 26 years of full-time, year-round cruising, our average number of days when we were at sea was 91 days per year, about one day in four. In our busiest year with three ocean passages, it was only 118 days at sea.

Many others spend less time at sea, especially those who stay in the Mediterranean where sea-going in winter is, to say the least, not obviously congenial and sometimes downright dangerous.

It must also be borne in mind that even at sea one is living aboard the yacht, and that is a different thing from doing a fortnight's cruise. A degree of discomfort or inconvenience that is acceptable for a week or two rapidly becomes intolerable over a long period.

SIZE AND TYPE

The reader has to balance the amount of boat to the amount of money and to the size of the available crew, and the answer has much to do with personal preference.

It is a mistake to try to live in too small a boat. Small size admittedly requires less energy to handle and to maintain, but the extra difficulty of moving about, the unavoidable close intimacy, and the obtrusiveness of all those stores for which there is no locker, make a breeding ground for irritation. We know a couple still living aboard a 25-footer after crossing the Atlantic in her, but they are young and very much in love, as well as being short of personal possessions. A German couple lived in a 24-foot boat with an Alsatian dog. The following year we met them in a 68-foot converted Baltic trader, having gone from one extreme to another.

A yacht that is too big can be a liability, of course. A physically fit couple cruising carefully and prudently could expect to cope fairly easily with 75 feet or even more, as we have done ourselves for the past 14 years, but one has also to think of mooring fees and maintenance. Surprisingly, gear does not always cost more in the bigger sizes; often chandlery for yachts is fancy, of materials chosen for their looks rather than their strength, and the ability to use fittings made for small tugs or barges can save money in some cases. And do remember that, to your astonishment, you will get older.

Fare Well is a 55-foot ketch of about 30 tons displacement. We sailed her long distances over 11 years, and Laurel, my wife and mate, and usually sole crew, is a lightweight 5-footer with a congenitally dislocated hip. Since then we have motor-sailed our 60-tonne sailing barge, and though we have been less adventurous, we are beginning to find her a bit more tiring than we used to. Our boats are fine, but we age faster than they do.

Probably the ideal monohull for any age would have a waterline length of 33 to 37 feet, a beam of just over a third of that, and not too V-shaped in cross-section. That would provide a home that can be comfortable, have enough storage space, be easy enough to manage even when years advance, and be reasonably economical to moor and slip. If you decide on a little ship that is outside this range, be very sure your decision is soundly based on reason and experience, rather than emotion.

• *Multihulls* •

This is the time to mention multihulls. They certainly give more boat for the money, but they have disadvantages. When heavily loaded, and in our life they *always* would be, they seem to lose proportionately more performance than a monohull. Some even become dangerous. It is also necessary to go up in size to get enough headroom in the living accommodation. One can get by with a shorter overall length than a monohull, and whereas the latter might run to some 40 or 50 feet, a multihull might provide as good accommodation on 33 or 40 feet. But again there is a disadvantage in the multihull's beam: berthing becomes more difficult, and when it has to be paid for, much more expensive, the loading being 50–100%. This is a big factor in the crowded ports of the Mediterranean; it is less significant in the West Indies where one spends a lot more time swinging to a single anchor. It is even less significant in the Bahamas where many of the best harbours are closed to the deeper-draughted monohulls. It's horses for courses.

• *Motor yachts* •

It is not easy to be a long-term deep-water cruiser in a pure motor yacht, partly because long passages are virtually impossible, and also because one must be much more cautious about the weather. We do know of several, split between the Mediterranean and the USA Intra-Coastal Waterway. In the former they have access to the attractive European canal system, and in the latter there is much scope for short sheltered passages. The Intra-Coastal Waterway is rather a special case as, apart from a few Canadians, most yachts there are in their home waters. The European inland waters are ideal for those who get seasick.

Fare Well, *a 55 foot ketch of about 30 tons displacement, at Marineland Marina , Florida.*

As Laurel and I seem to be unwilling to give up this life, maybe motoring will be our eventual mode. Certainly in *Hosanna,* we have been motoring more as we get older.

A motor yacht provides considerably more comfort than a sailing yacht of the same length. I see no reason to adopt a superior attitude to the dedicated cruising motor yachtsman. Typically he runs his boat well and safely, and conforms to cruising etiquette much better than the bare-boat charter people, even those in sailing yachts. Long-term cruising is an attitude of mind.

• *The motor-sailer* •

There is much to be said for the motor-sailer in the Mediterranean. The powerful engine capable of hull speed into a force 6 wind and short sea is most reassuring in the unsettled weather at the beginning and end of season, while the ability to set a fair spread of canvas on a long passage saves fuel and gives her a much easier motion. The option of two adequate power systems impresses me. I wish now that we had installed a bigger engine in *Fare Well* than 62hp. It's nice to be able to move about the engine room, but a bit more potential thrust would have been a good use for the space.

Modern engines, having much improved power/weight ratios, have more or less turned most present-day sailing yachts into quasi motor-sailers. Perhaps the term is beginning to mean less than it did.

I hope it is unnecessary to advise against the petrol (gasoline) engine. I have swept up after too many nasty accidents involving petrol in boats, and I maintain that even in the hands of the experienced user the system is dangerous. In the USA where the low price of gasoline has favoured the petrol engine, there are draconian rules about the installation, and they are enforced. Nevertheless, I detect at last a trend away from them. In the Mediterranean it is often difficult to get petrol except in cans.

NEW BOAT OR OLD? ONE-OFF OR PRODUCTION?

This is the time for sweeping generalisations and, oh boy, are we going to have plenty. It is a highly opinionated part of the book because choosing a boat to live in is as subjective as choosing a wife. Objectivity is impossible. I suspect that these days it is becoming easier to correct an unfortunate choice of spouse than to change boats. Anyway, because I, Bill, am writing this it is bound to reflect my opinions:

- Production boats make less good homes than one-off vessels
- Professional yacht-designers seem to have no idea how to design a boat for long term cruising

Looking at these two generalisations, first go back a few years to the days when a

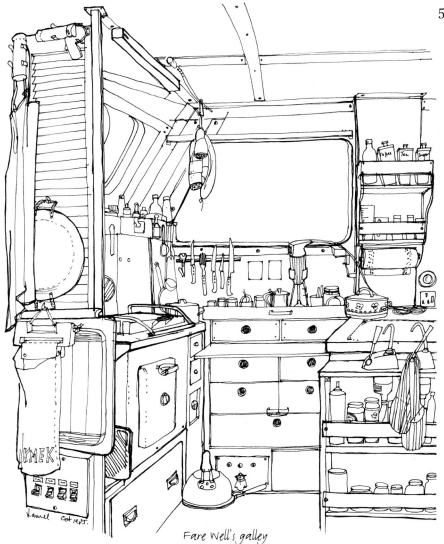

Fare Well's galley

designer would be commissioned by a gentleman to produce a yacht for a specific purpose. The designer would try hard to satisfy his client, and would go to some lengths to find out exactly what was needed. Now and then he must have succeeded, or we presume so, because in those days owners tended to keep the same boat for a longish time.

Nowadays people keep boats for a short time, except among the live-aboard fleet where typically the boat lasts until the family comes ashore again. We have had two boats in 25 years, and may well finish up with a third, but that is partly because we have erred on the side of having large and unusual boats.

There is not so much profit for the designer in the modest one-off for a private owner. By designing a prototype for a production run the naval architect hopes for extending royalties and a wider dissemination of his name, for the designer is in the rat-race too. Because this is the market he is aiming at, his general arrangement plan will have more to do with production engineering and marketing than with real suitability for the sea. Though the word 'cruising' will appear in the advertising, fashion will dictate the boat's shape and rig, she will have more than a nodding acquaintance with the glamour of the IOR rating rules, and the marketing men will demand as many bunks as it is possible to get in. Probably, when sold, she will spend most of her life at moorings, and that is about the right place for her.

Since we first wrote the above we have been interested to read a paper by Hugo de Plessis, an experienced naval architect and ocean cruiser, pointing out the dangers of lightweight boats for long-distance cruising. To sum up his contentions, with which we heartily agree, he says that lightweight boats cannot carry the loads necessary to support a crew over long distances, and that when they are, inevitably, overloaded they become dangerous. When loading a boat for a four-week (say) passage, the increase in weight for a lightweight boat is proportionately much more, and her sailing characteristics would be much more seriously affected. His arguments are convincing. We know that the food and drink for four people on an Atlantic crossing weighs more than 1 tonne. His article should be reprinted by a yachting magazine for wider circulation.

The vast majority of so-called cruising yachts being marketed these days, particularly by Continental builders, could reasonably be said to exemplify the description 'lightweight'.

If one needs a ready-made boat I believe in going to the second-hand market, and even then picking a vessel that is capable of some alteration without losing her charm. There are good boats about, and they often have the advantage of a good inventory that saves a lot of money. In general, boats from the boards of American designers tend to be more suitable for long cruising than those of other nationalities, though the Dutch are not far behind.

The chief differentiating factors are that less attention is paid to rating rules, leading to more attention being paid to load carrying and stowage, ease of handling under both sail and power, crew comfort and a nice appearance.

If you are building from new, or carrying out any major task and feel you need professional advice, then try to find a naval architect who has actually lived in a cruising yacht. They are understandably rare, because one would not make much of a living swanning about the oceans, but it is quite an important point, like choosing a land architect who lives in a house of his own design. Have you noticed how most of them seem to live in Georgian houses?

Has anyone ever heard of a live-aboard marketing consultant?

WHERE TO BUY SECOND-HAND

If you are trying to buy second-hand, do not expect much help from yacht brokers. Even if you itemise exactly what you are looking for, you will be sent, for a time, details of craft that are manifestly unsuitable for your purpose, and then shortly you will be sent nothing further. This is because brokers generally do not understand what living aboard is all about, but then it is difficult to do so unless you have actually done it.

Britain is not the only place to look for a boat. There are many starters in this life, who for one reason or another, do not get very far. Perhaps they have not done their homework. In any event there are often bargains to be picked up in Gibraltar, the Canary Islands, southern Spain or Portugal where they have been abandoned by a disillusioned crew.

Many yachts winter on the Côte d'Azur, and although most of these are likely to be holiday or luxury craft there is a substantial turnover, so there are often suitable boats on offer. Brokers are used less in France because of the silly commission rate, and marinas often have many boats with '*a vendre*' (for sale) signs.

Larnaca (Cyprus) is a busy wintering hole. Various Turkish marinas are popular too, but Turban, who run several marinas there, have increased their prices considerably now that chartering has become big business. The Balearics and Alicante are further winter haunts. As the number of Mediterranean live-aboards has increased dramatically over the past five or ten years, so wintering places crop up in ever more diverse ports.

In the Western Hemisphere, Fort Lauderdale and vicinity seems to moor as many craft as the whole of Europe put together, and the Chesapeake cannot be far behind. Given the high standard of some US cruising yacht design, one should find something there, but beware: even there you will find builders who cynically build rubbish for the ignorant mass market.

English language magazines where suitable boats may be advertised are *Cruising World* (Newport, RI), *Sailing Today* (England) and *Yachting Monthly* (England). *Yachting World* (England) for the larger boats, and *Practical Boat Owner* (England) is useful for the smaller sizes. *Boats and Planes for Sale* is a good source. *Fluvial* (France) has many advertisements for barges and rivercraft on the Continental waterways.

BUYING A BARE HULL

If the extent of alterations required is large, or one's requirements are very esoteric, one should consider buying a hull and then finishing it. This is basically what we have twice done, though I did have some say in the design of *Fare Well*'s hull too.

Completing a hull is not so difficult as may be imagined. Generally, the cost of the bare shell itself is a surprisingly small fraction of the total cost of a professionally built boat, often about one-sixth. This means that there is a lot of work in finishing it, and it is a long, time-consuming project. *Fare Well* took 4000 logged man-hours of amateur work, and *Hosanna* took even longer. A few jobs have to be done by professionals, but be careful: good freelance professionals are hard to find, and you may end up as we sometimes did, having to re-do work. An intelligent and manually competent person with access to a good reference library can out-perform some of the ham-fisted cowboys who menace today's British yacht industry.

> I will arise and go now, and go where the wind is free,
>   And a fine keelboat build there,
> Of wood and metal made.
>   Nine summers will I sail her,
> With a cat for the company;
>   And live content in the awning's shade.

WEATHERLINESS

'A well bowed shippe so swiftly presseth the water as that it foameth, and in the dark night sparkleth like fire. If the Bow bee too narrow . . . she pitcheth her head into the sea; so that the meane is the best, if her after way be answerable'

I have already referred to the yacht that is a joy to sail but hell to live in. Understandably, most dreamers and planners contemplate a boat with good performance; yachting editors and cruising correspondents write endlessly about it, recalling with enthusiasm the drenching they got batting to windward for a few hours last weekend. A glorious sail! Yes, but they went home afterwards for a hot bath and change of clothes.

It's a bit different doing it for days on end, trying meanwhile to prepare and cook good meals, to do the maintenance and repairs, and to keep dry clothing. Many dedicated cruisers never beat to windward at all. Our own motto is 'if you have to beat, you're going to the wrong place'. 'Gentlemen do not tack' is another, though most live-aboards are not used to being treated like gentlemen. On a long passage it is occasionally necessary to compromise, but we have been known to heave-to in mid-ocean when confronted by a heading force 6 and wait for it to change. Do not trust ocean sailors who bang on about windward ability: suspect them of masochism.

It is a question of enjoying life and having all the time in the world to do it. Generally, in *Fare Well*, we did not approach closer to the wind than 55°. If we did it was usually for a short leg or to keep a better offing, and even then we tended to run the engine at half revs, which contributes some ever-welcome amps as well as thrust and gets the unfortunate episode over sooner. In *Hosanna*, we motor much more. She has eight sails in all. In the Med the two of us are often too lazy to set them all for a comparatively short voyage, and setting only a few is not enough to maintain a fair speed. You will often see us with the upside down triangle in the rigging forward, indicating that we are motorsailing. Another reason is that she is a heavy boat to steer, and with an engine ticking over we get power-assisted steering.

• *High performance* •

One sometimes finds the opinion that high sailing performance is a potential safety factor. Let us examine this hypothesis. In 40,000 miles of cruising in *Fare Well*, and over 20,000 in *Hosanna*, extending over 25 years, the following were our 'dangerous situations':

- A fire at sea.
- A hurricane.
- Damage from a heavy squall, or it could have been a waterspout, in the Gulf Stream.
- A lightning strike.
- A shaft coupling disintegrated, leaving a big leak.
- I fell and injured myself in a gale off Cap Corse.
- The forehatch was left improperly secured and the forepeak filled with water.
- The genoa furling gear failed, and at the same time I allowed the trailing sheet to foul the screw while approaching a crowded anchorage. (Classic!)
- We were dismasted in a near gale in the southern North Sea, with a lee shore not far away.

In addition we have endured 11 other gales of force 8 or over, with no worries other than understandable apprehension.

At no other time in over 60,000 miles over 25 years were we in danger, and at *no time at all* would high performance on the wind have been of any benefit whatsoever. Nor any other high performance for that matter.

Let us contrast that with the racing fleet, which we suppose to be the exemplars of high performance. In the Fastnet Race of 1979 the fleet met a short summer gale of admittedly above average severity, but managed to score a world record for the number of distress signals per square mile of sea. The RYA enquiry served to encourage the already enormous complacency of the ocean racing industry. It concluded that there was no firm evidence that any particular design feature was common to all the sinkings or damage, but failed to bring home the point that the lightness of construction was a common feature together with the flimsiness of spars and rigging, and even more so the unseamanlike nature of the sail plan encouraged by a rating rule that is dangerous. However, the enquiry failed to take evidence from cruising yachts that were in the area at the time, who didn't make a fuss, and came through without assistance.

We know that a small American cruising yacht sailed through the worst of that storm with the owner, his wife, and two children aged under four on board, and wrote home merely that they had 'had a rough passage'. So far as I know the RYA did not seek their evidence, which was that of very experienced cruising sailors.

Since then the Sydney to Hobart race has experienced similar tragedies among the generously crewed, expensively equipped and supervised racing fleet while cruising yachts survived unharmed.

In the 1996/7 Vendée Globe Round the World Race, the yachts were heavily sponsored and designed by leaders of their profession. They were built and fitted out at enormous expense using state-of-the-art materials. Their keels fell off, their rudders broke, their masts fell down, and several of them capsized and sank. Worse,

*This is a modern fibreglass version of a traditional Greek boat,
ideal for the Eastern Mediterranean.*

there was loss of life. The boats, sailed by competent, experienced sailors, were built to win races, not to survive bad conditions. Do ocean-racing yachtsman feel no shame at the way the world's rescue services are being exploited to the tune of millions of pounds to help satisfy someone's lust for personal glory? Yes, it's rough down there in the Southern Ocean, but the designers know that, don't they?

For reliably safe cruising one should seek well-tried and proven dispositions of sail, with everything much stronger than mere theory suggests. Use of new materials should include a generous safety factor to take care of the unknown. So arrange matters that any sail can be furled or trimmed by one person without recourse to power assistance.

In Mediterranean conditions, where winds are often light and the seas unexpectedly and uncomfortably short and steep, we find we use the engine much more than we expected to. The number of engine hours per year remained fairly constant for a time, but has started to increase a little as we age. In any case, with fridge, running lights and other domestic conveniences, some battery charging is needed. In the Med, many passages are of 30 to 50 miles, and if the wind changes or drops, as it often does in the evening, there is a strong incentive to set the iron topsail for an hour or so to ensure timely arrival in a good berth before the whole port is full of noisy Italian motor yachts or the ubiquitous flotillas.

In the Bahamas and West Indies things are somewhat different. Winds are more reliable, it is easier to sail to an anchorage and/or weigh under sail, and the line of the Windward Islands runs, as their name tells you, conveniently across the wind, generally giving a comfortable reach in both directions.

EASE OF HANDLING AND THE RIG

A constant assumption throughout this book is a short-handed crew. The yacht must handle easily, whether sailing, motoring, berthing or unberthing. It is no good having a beautifully balanced sailing boat if your attempts to back her into an awkward slot in a strong cross-wind leave you tired, cross, and feeling foolish under the eyes of the whole town out for their evening stroll.

These things are not incompatible; it is just that some designers, particularly those who have made their name in racing, have never learned how to relate them one to another. Screw propellers do not behave entirely as they should in theory.

To be able to handle sail quickly, and without too much effort, is vital to both comfort and safety. No matter how much you tell yourself that by keeping alert you will never have to do anything in a hurry, sooner or later you will slip up, as we have, several times.

We once rounded Cape Malea in southern Greece, leaving it close aboard, ghosting under every stitch of canvas we could set, including the poop awning. The cape is a steep cliff some 2000 feet high, and as we rounded we could see hissing white water ahead. As the Admiralty Pilot warned, on the other side there was a katabatic wind of great force. The log was reading 10 knots before I got the mizzen staysail down, and I never did furl the big genoa. It would not let me. As we sped south towards Africa at right angles to our intended course, the wind gradually eased and we re-established tenuous control.

On another occasion I fought the genoa for more than an hour at the end of the bowsprit which was dunking me every half minute. With each dunk the sea surged up my trouser legs leaving by the neckhole in my oilskins, and doing unmentionable mischief en route. Real cruising men are pledged to avoid such heroics, so shortly after these incidents we bought roller reefing/furling gear for the headsail.

Good roller gear, which can reef as well as furl a sail, solves a lot of problems, but in the large sizes it still requires a lot of physical effort, though reasonably reliable electrical or hydraulic winding gear is now available. Roller headsails are sometimes held to be less aerodynamically efficient than hoisted headsails. I do not think the difference when the whole sail is set is significant to the cruising yachtsman, while the ability to reef a headsail a little, a lot, or a little bit more or less compensates for marginal losses. The whole system of roller reefing/furling is completely appropriate for short-handed sailing. Jams, snarl-ups and breakdowns are not more frequent than conventional foredeck foul-ups, and the cost of the gear is offset by the fewer headsails required.

It would, I think, be advisable not to follow our example of fitting the headsail roller with a big, 175% overlap genoa. *Fare Well*'s was 67 square metres and a lovely puller, but it was also a bit of a menace on occasions when the wind got up, being difficult for one person to tack it round the inner forestay.

For a cutter foretriangle I think the roller headsail should be a slightly oversize yankee, a sort of yankoa or genkee, called a tow-foresail by old smack fishermen. This means that arrangements must be made to set an occasional light-weather

The long-distance cruiser's status symbol, especially in France. In my opinion, such domes are little use. They soon become scratched and crazed, then more and more opaque. It is better to have a proper wheelhouse.

genoa, probably involving a second forestay. If you have two forestays there will be occasions when the unused forestay gets wrapped into the furling sail, usually while rolling up before a strong wind, but one soon gets a technique for avoiding this. Luff extrusions with two parallel slots exist.

It is impossible to recommend any particular roller gear because new ones come and go frequently. It is not advisable to seek sailmakers' advice, as most sailmakers either have their own gear or are agents for one or two, and objective advice is difficult to get. Few people, and I am not among them, have experience of more than one or two different makes – deep-sea experience, I mean. You just have to use whatever advice you can get and apply your own judgement. Fortunately the technique of rolling has advanced considerably in recent years.

Roller mainsails are not as good as headsails. The long luff of bermudan mainsails means that the sort set externally to the mast tend to sag away from it, and to add very considerably to the compression strain on the spar without the vibration-deadening effect of the continuous contact via the slides or luff rope. Mainsails that roll inside the mast are available. I have no intimate knowledge of them, but I would be much concerned about possible chafe of the sailcloth at the mast slot on the sort of voyages many long cruisers habitually make. Foul-up problems are probably not significant and unlikely to be much worse than with a headsail. Some gears have a social problem in harbour, when with strong winds, the mast slot turns itself into a gigantic organ pipe, and the whole place is disturbed with hooting like a demented owl. Makers once notorious for this defect now claim to have solved the problem. Watch out when buying second-hand!

We have mixed reports of in-boom rolling. It involves having a rather over-size boom and a rigid kicking strap or martingale. Personally I would prefer it to in-mast gear because it is more accessible. I do not like climbing masts at sea.

Whatever rig you have, make sure there is no sail you cannot furl singlehand-ed, and quickly. In these circumstances the divided rig makes a lot of sense, but remember that one cannot furl or reef all the sails simultaneously. Standing rig-ging should not be the flimsy affair of the racing fleet: it must be able to support full canvas in gale-strength squalls, then as sail is reduced things will get better. There is one case to watch which I have found little appreciated nowadays: in gaff-rigged craft when the main is furled before reducing the headsails, there is still great compression in the mast and without the pull of the mainsail hoops to dampen vibration, it is possible to lose the mast. In spite of knowing all about this we still managed to lose *Hosanna*'s solid wooden foremast off the Kentish Knock, but it had been weakened by a soft spot round a small knot. We had known about that and were on our way to look for a suitable tree.

REEFING SYSTEMS

In general a well-balanced ketch rig virtually eliminates the need for reefing. We almost never reefed in *Fare Well* because the possibilities were such that one could always find a comfortable way of setting whole sails, even if you used fewer and smaller of them. An exception was a very deep reef on the main which was meant to avoid the need for a trysail. We used it once in ten years. The mizzen had no reefing system.

If you have a mainsail that requires reefing, then the system depends on person-al preference influenced by size of sail. For short-handed crews, *slab reefing* is dubious above an area of 400 sq ft (40 square metres), but sails that big are getting dubious in our context anyway. It is in sloops and cutters that reefing becomes very important, and the frequent necessity of getting up on the high bit of boat in bad weather is a strong argument against the single-master. *Reef points* should be avoided: you have to be up there even longer. Recently (2000), I have noticed that

An extendable gallows allows the boom end to be held out over the water.

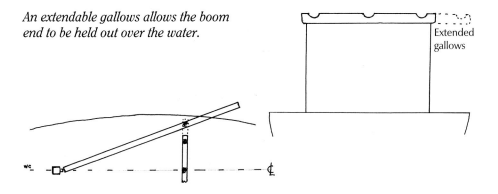

Extended gallows

fewer ketches feature among production boats. Most boats are bought to sit on moorings all year round, so the dearth of ketches may be due to cost cutting by the manufacturers. I do not think anyone sensible has made out a case for sloops or cutters as being better than ketches or schooners for short-handed deep-sea cruising, except perhaps for small yachts under 33 feet (10 metres) LOA.

All booms, but especially main booms, should have a stout gallows, not only for stowing in harbour but also with slots in the outboard ends so that the boom can be easily bowsed down to leeward to be worked on. It is far easier and safer to hold onto a rigidly fixed boom than to cling to one that is allowed even a little movement. If the gallows is fitted about two-thirds of the length of the boom from the mast it is possible to arrange a slot on the extreme end of the gallows, so that the end of the boom when stowed is a foot or so outboard of the ship's side. This provides a good lifting point for bringing heavy weights on board, or recovering people from the sea.

What applies to furling, applies to sheeting too. When one is short-handed, all sheets and controlling cordage of all types should, if possible, be led to a sheltered place, preferably a cockpit. It will not do to have one or more sails flog while you sheet the others. Even a few seconds' hard flogging in a severe squall can demolish a clew.

With roller furling, if heavy weather is expected then over-roll a furled sail by a few turns. I once left our 8oz genoa loosely rolled, with perhaps a square foot or so still off the roll. When a Gulf Stream squall hit us in the middle of the night the force was enough to pull all taut and effectively unroll a few feet of sail, which disintegrated into ribbons in seconds. An 11oz sail that was set survived in usable state but a conventionally, though hastily, furled 12oz mainsail was ripped out of its gaskets and was lost too. One cannot go about continually taking precautions against squalls of this extreme violence, but where their occurrence is possible or likely, then one should.

Roller reefing/furling does partially solve a problem of stowage, for sails so set remain above deck and one needs fewer separate sails. Space below in a long-cruising boat is so valuable that many stow their sails on deck. It is possible to have a sailbag such that a headsail can be put in it while it is still hanked on its stay. It does not look very elegant, making the average yacht look as if she has a nosebag on. It is quite important that all sails should be covered when not in use. Simple light covers will do: all that is necessary is to stop ultraviolet light damaging the synthetic cloth. I have seen no evidence that this ultraviolet problem has so far been solved (2000).

HULL SHAPE

While for most passage-making a deep keel is desirable, except perhaps over the Bahamas Banks, there are innumerable little ports and bays where the deeper boats cannot go but where a shallow draught can find wonderful peace (provided the wet-bikes stay away!). There are also opportunities for exploring canals and rivers, especially those of France, or the lovely Intra-Coastal Waterway of the US east coast. These factors point the need for a compromise, so consider a monohull draught of 5 feet 4 in (1.6 metres) or less. *Fare Well* was designed for 6 feet (1.85 metres) and for her size that is quite modest, but she did not end up that way, and cruising yachts never do, because no one can ever believe the incredible weight of things that they need to carry on long voyages.

- **Golden Rule:** *in every case, draught when cruising with full living load will be at least 6 inches(15cm) more than expected.*
- *There are no exceptions.*

Centreboards are not an ideal answer. When the Bollay family took their Rhodes-designed centreboard sloop *Snowgoose* into the French canals they eventually exported a good part of the mineral wealth of the country, which had got itself jammed up the trunking, and it took a lot of getting out. Centreboards can be awkward to manage in larger boats because they have to be heavy to be strong enough to take the big lateral cantilever strains. In smaller boats the draught need not be so very deep anyway, so that centreboards are perhaps an unnecessary complication.

It is worth mentioning that *Fare Well*, while drawing 6 feet 7 in (say 2 metres), cruised the Bahamas and the full length of the Intra-Coastal Waterway without any serious problems. We found the bottom a few times; once we stuck on a coral head in the Bahamas for a tide, but got off unaided by laying out two bower anchors.

Long overhangs have a sporty look, but are expensive in mooring and construction; they add to the maintenance and contribute little to usable boat. I do not think they are an advantage for our purpose.

The sugar-scoop or retroussé stern and spade rudder hung right aft pose problems for a cruising yacht. Not only does one lose a commodious locker and some valuable deck space without any corresponding saving on mooring fees, but if one berths stern-to, as in most Mediterranean ports, this configuration can be a positive hazard. Lying bows-to is an alternative that has its own disadvantages, which I will refer to under anchoring. The problem with a deep rudder right aft is that quays in the Med (and elsewhere) seldom have vertical faces to their full apparent depth. Often they are ballasted to just below water level, and odd rocks, together with the assorted detritus of centuries, extend some distance from the quay.

The sloping transom makes landing to and from the quay more difficult, but

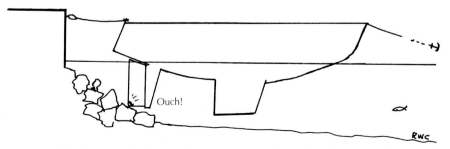

A deep rudder hung well aft near the transom is vulnerable when mooring stern-to.

on the other hand it is a good site for a permanent bathing or boarding ladder, and a little platform there forms a safe(ish) place to stow a can of petrol (gasoline) for the outboard motor.

Twin screws are an unnecessary luxury for sailing yachts in the sizes we are contemplating, but for the pure motor yacht they would make a lot of sense. Although undoubtedly vulnerable in canals, there will be occasions in less frequented parts where the ability to limp home might be a blessing. Away from the British or US coasts help is not so readily available, or even not at all. In some parts we have visited, VHF Channel 16 may be of more use for ordering a taxi.

HULL CONSTRUCTION

It is in craft over 33 feet (10 metres) waterline that steel becomes an economical material. Then it becomes possible to have a hull of plate thickness sufficient to stand a variety of abuses, including abrasion and impact. In fact, the only short-term danger to a steel hull is the tin-opener effect typified by striking a sharp rocky pinnacle. It is the most effectively resistant material to ice, though that rarely concerns us.

Once the plate thickness rises above $^3/_{16}$in (4mm), this danger recedes for the speeds we are likely to reach. The bottom of *Fare Well's* keel is $1^1/_2$in plate, rounded up at the forefoot, and when we sledded up 2ft (60cm) out of the water after striking a coral head at 7 knots, the scratches on the steel were less than a millimetre deep.

• *Paint* •

Maintenance is heavier with steel, but it is unskilled labour for the most part, and the dedicated cruiser is there all the time to do it. If the hull is initially shot-blasted to an even grey (S3), then instantly coated with epoxy-based cover to a thickness of half a millimetre, you have a good basis, but it is important to touch up damage to this film as soon as possible.

Fare Well's initial paint job lasted eight years, and even then only needed redoing near the waterline. Some people like zinc or aluminium spraying, but I believe this actually weakens the bond of the epoxy to the steel, though there may be some merit in epoxy-zinc as a paint. I think one can get too clever over this problem. The vital thing is to get the strongest possible skin to adhere in the strongest possible way, and any minor damage to the coating below the waterline ought to be taken care of by fitting good sacrificial zinc anodes, whose life and effectiveness can be periodically checked.

The banning of TBT antifouling has undoubtedly worsened the case for the steel boat. I personally think, given the comparatively small proportion of steel and aluminium yachts compared with wood or fibreglass, that an exception could have been made for existing vessels, many of which were built with the expectation of having non-reactive antifouling available to them. But the Greens are like the Roman Church in the Middle Ages: any criticism of them is a heresy.

OTHER HULL MATERIALS

Steel hulls do not leak, except through contrived openings. Similarly, *fibreglass* hulls ought not to leak, but strength and reliability depends on the quality of the materials and also on the conscientiousness of the laminators – factors that are difficult to assess in a second-hand boat later on in her life.

Fibreglass hulls have been known to crack, particularly where skegs or keels adjoin the hull, and this seems to happen irrespective of the reputation of the yard, and particularly with light-construction boats from weight-conscious designers. The material abrades easily, which is very important if one visits non-yachty harbours where there are fishing boats with sharp steel projections, like metallic porcupines. GRP burns and is a poor conductor of electricity, which can cause it to disintegrate in lightning strikes, which are much more common in tropical climes. Like steel, it is not habitually eaten by any known animal (except Greek goats), but it does have its equivalent to corrosion, osmosis, which can be difficult to deal with. It is expensive on a one-off basis but this can be ameliorated by using the sandwich method, which has the great advantage of insulating the skin and is therefore an appreciated method of building for the hotter climates.

Ferro-cement boats have a bad reputation, which is not fully deserved. The well-built hull is very good indeed, but poor technique gives rise to nautical disasters. (Buried in the Medway marshes is a hull constructed by a professor of building technology, which fell to pieces.) I would consider a hull made by the Wroxham firm of Windboats to be worth a second look, as I have seen some good work of theirs, and good boats have come from New Zealand builders. New Zealand seems to be the skill centre for this technique. As for the material, abrasion resistance is poor compared to metal, though better than GRP. Impact resistance is good for boats with a heavy steel reinforcement, but chicken wire, often used by amateurs because it is cheaper, lighter and easier to shape, is vulnerable. Maintenance is less of a problem than with steel. Ferro is thought of as being the cheapest material for a one-off amateur-built hull, but so much depends on standards. In any case the cost of the hull is likely to be between one-sixth and one-fifth of the total cost of building. Resale of these boats is supposed to be difficult, but those with experience tell me they are much like any one-off: it depends on the quality.

A *wooden* hull has a lovely feel about it, but it presents many problems. All sorts of things eat it, and it rots and grows fungi, problems which are all worse in warm climates. Hulls built traditionally are subject to leaks. Wood can be easily repaired in backward communities, though often good hardwoods are hard to come by, and this is a worsening situation as the Greens gain ground. Abrasion resistance is moderate, and whereas impact is unlikely to penetrate because of wood's elasticity, it can lead to planks springing, or to distortion with multiple small leaks that can be hell to stem.

I now have some knowledge (though not expertise) of the more recent wood techniques. Boats built in the West System (a sort of epoxy-saturated wood method, which seems to combine the advantages of GRP with the advantages of wood) have impressed me and their owners all seem satisfied. I have recently watched at Bure

Marine Ltd, Great Yarmouth, a boat built in this system being expertly repaired after being damaged and sunk (she had impaled herself on a pile on a falling tide; an interesting salvage job). She was double-diagonally planked and seemed to have much to commend her. Her heavy epoxy coating would proof her against insect attack.

An *aluminium* hull has some of the properties of steel, but is lighter and not nearly so resistant to damage, a fact that is apparent in many a large repair yard. One of its principal problems is that it is softer than steel and dents easily. It is vulnerable to electrolytic problems if great care is not taken over the selection of alloys and fittings, and it is by no means unknown for the wrong alloy to creep in because the right one is temporarily unavailable at the yard. It is expensive to build and extremely difficult, not to say impossible, to get repaired neatly outside the major sophisticated yachting venues.

It is now possible to have hulls built of steel with superstructure of marine-grade aluminium, without all the bother of bolting, insulating (to prevent electrolysis), and worrying if it is all going to hold together. Aero-Spatiale of Toulouse has invented a way of welding aluminium to steel. It cannot be done on site, but they sell strips in the form of a sandwich of aluminium and steel with a filler of thin titanium, the three 'welded' together by the pressure of detonating explosives. This strip can be conventionally welded to steel on the one side and to aluminium on the other, and seems not to suffer from electrolytic action. It is easy to use, but expensive.

Decks should be made of sheet material and should never rely on caulking for their watertightness. If they do, they will leak, which is a catalyst for rot and marital discord.

LONG-TERM VALUE

Whether a particular yacht will retain or lose pecuniary value depends on many factors. Investment analysts have a lot of trouble accurately forecasting future prices of quite simple things; it seems to me very dangerous to base decisions on projected future assumptions about prices of one second-hand yacht against another. Some points are worth bearing in mind:

- A long-cruising yacht will get much more wear and tear than a similar yacht seldom out of its shed, or off moorings. On the other hand, it will be better looked after.
- A strongly built boat which is unfashionable today may well be a 'character' boat when today's fashionable trade-in models are in the scrapyard, provided hull, engine and gear are in good condition and she's not too massive.
- Resale prices are heavily dependent on fashion.
- Are you buying a boat for life? If not, how long do you envisage cruising? If over seven years, it seems to me that resale worries should not be allowed to cause sleepless nights. Almost everything I worried about seven years ago seems to have solved itself in the meantime.

The most important thing is to buy a boat that suits you well. You would not buy a car that was a bastard to drive just because someone suggested it had a good resale value. We once knew a couple who had started out to live aboard, and thinking that they might not like it they had chosen a Finnish production boat with a good reputation for being easy to sell. A moment's thought would have shown its complete unsuitability for long-term living aboard. Of course they did not enjoy the life; they had ruined their prospects by forgetting what was the principal purpose of the boat and instead choosing on other criteria. Still, they got a good price for it.

If you are not going long-cruising as a completely new way of life, but as a short break of perhaps two years in a working career, your attitude to resale prices will be somewhat different. You will still need to consider your aims carefully in order to live reasonably well, but you would be a hostage to financial fortune to ignore the likely proceeds from the sale of the yacht, which you are unlikely to want to keep for ever. It is quite reasonable to forecast two years ahead, and a good broker's advice will be valuable in this respect. Do not, however, pay much attention to his advice on what sort of yacht to cruise in unless you are sure he knows what living aboard is about; I have never met one who does. Your aim may be different from the aim of a long-term cruiser, but you will still have an aim that is not entirely centred on resale. You make the compromise.

A YACHT TO GROW OLD IN

*'The saylers are the antient men ... and nothing
but experience can poffibly teach it'*

This is a difficult subject to find a name for, mostly because we have all got into the habit of using euphemisms for 'old age'. My preference for calling spades spades has not changed much since becoming a pensioner, but I discarded the word 'geriatric' because my elementary knowledge of Greek suggests to me that the word really means an old doctor.

When we originated the first-ever cruising symposium on the 'Sell Up and Sail' concept, we were very impressed by the strong interest in the subject shown by people who had retired. We were in process of changing to a boat more suitable to our own increasing years, and were somewhat shamed by the ambitions of some of our fellow symposers. It became evident to us that there is a positive demand for boats suitable for retired people to do a lot of sailing in, even if not to live aboard fulltime.

This is the time of life when living aboard becomes especially attractive. No more worries about careers, children growing up, and income, because you should have seen to all that by now. The only problems are to do with one's physical capability, and the fact that it can be expected to decline as the years go by. (You can also go bonkers, but many of us are quite a long way down that road already.)

If you are buying a boat to retire into, it is important to project ahead what you can cope with. Certainly your skills will improve to offset failing strength, but there will come a time when skills reach a plateau and strength goes on declining.

It would be unwise to contemplate frequent changes of boat. God knows, it is hard enough to find one superboat in a lifetime without giving yourself the task of finding several, and every change is expensive. Nevertheless it requires quite a lot of self-discipline to buy a boat that will not perform to the full extent of your present capabilities. If you are not ready to face this prospect yet, come back to the subject in a few years' time.

We wrote in a past edition that we thought production boats not very suitable for the live-aboard. In this we found ourselves at odds with some yachting journalists, who are no fools and not inexperienced. It just goes to show that opinions can differ. But note that when a former editor of *Yachting World* retired, he wrote that he found the production boat not exactly ideal for old age, and he had his retirement yacht specially designed to suit him. I didn't like this boat either, but that is beside the point. We note with amusement that one editor who disagreed with us has now sold his production boat and taken delivery of a one-off. Anticipating retirement, perhaps.

We faced the problem of changing boats 12 years ago. We do not pretend that our personal solution would be the best for other people, but we feel it might help some folk if we described the arguments that led to our decision.

Firstly, prospective old salts should consider their personal qualities. For example, Laurel is small, and somewhat lame. Her disability will not improve; rather the opposite. Bill is big and very strong in the short-term sense, but shortness of breath prevents him exerting himself for long periods without resting. None of our problems will improve.

If we were each at 90% of our best-ever capacity when we first set sail as live-aboards in 1976, we were probably at about 65% at change-over time in 1987, which represents a decline of about 2% per annum. This had to be projected forward. We had owned *Fare Well* for about 15 years, this meant that our new ship *Hosanna* might be our ultimate if she would last us another 15. What will be our physical capacity then? Probably not good.

We have known and met a fair number of yachtsmen who have gone on cruising far and wide into old age, and we have become aware of some of their difficulties. We have helped some with their problems, for example, diabetes, which is only one of the possible scourges of the elderly. Many of these problems can be coped with, at least until they become debilitating. Some old salts we can think of clearly went on far too long. It is one thing to rely on other people's help in an occasional crisis, but when one can no longer cope without frequent and almost regular assistance, it becomes time to think about swallowing the anchor, however much it sticks in your throat.

The obvious solution to the problem is to settle for a smaller boat than would the younger person. I say obvious because it seems to be everyone's instinctive answer. I don't think it is necessarily the right one. A lot depends on what you think you will be able to handle. Surprisingly, size is not as important as, for example, whether the boat itself acts like a gentleman or a hooligan. Some boats are intractable yobs.

The process of adapting to decreasing faculties can be approached in two ways. One is to have a boat that will be easily coped with until death us do part, come hell or high water. The other is to have a boat that is comfortable and reasonably seaworthy, but which will both require and allow one to modify one's cruising range when that becomes necessary. We chose the latter course, but let us consider the other option first.

Maintenance is not so much of a problem because it can be undertaken in slow time. It is unwise to take on an impossible burden, but apart from that, maintenance should not figure too largely in the argument.

Assuming one is going to come down in size, what is the right size? We have to have good living conditions, so the boat cannot get too small. Small sporty boats need quick physical reactions, something we tend to lose as we get older. Space is needed for the things one likes to have about one, souvenirs, photographs, small treasures and so on.

On the other hand, it is desirable that the boat should be of a size that can be pushed or pulled short distances in harbour by old-man power without gut-busting effort, and that her gear should be light enough to be handled without causing hernias.

These two opposing factors indicate a boat of up to 15 gross registered tons, and sails that do not exceed 350sq ft (35sq m) each. To get good living comfort in this range one is going to have to sacrifice some speed and sportiness. Good fat lockers lead to good fat boats, and contented old skippers.

Inside, the accommodation should be arranged so that tired people do not have to step over things, so that a person falling does not fall far, so that edges and corners are padded, and there are innumerable handholds. It should not be necessary to demount the table in order to have a restorative nap.

Unless there is a deckhouse configuration, which has its points, the accommodation should be on a level, thus avoiding those irritating little 3-inch steps that naval architects seem to think essential, and which even able crews are always falling over. Much better to have two or three standard-sized steps, which keep you in practice, than a host of trip-you-ups.

There should be a good seat at the galley, and bunks that are not too difficult to make. A lot of the problems down below become the woman's problems; she may stay fit longer than her old man (she may well be younger into the bargain), but how many yacht designers have been deeply into the ergonomics of an old lady at sea? Going to the loo in a small yacht arguably produces more broken bones than any other nautical accident, strong handholds in the head and a sit-down shower are essential. Even such a simple thing as bed-making can be difficult with awkward enclosed bunks; fitted bottom sheets and a duvet can help here.

On deck we come to the real difficulties. Admiral Goldsmith, one of the earliest dedicated live-aboards, died in his eighties while hauling up his anchor. I had tried to talk him into having electrics in his boat, but he was adamant. 'Ampères are the curse of mankind' he bellowed at me from a distance of about 3 feet. Admirals tend to do that.

I am torn while writing this bit because if I had the chance to choose a way of dying, this would be it, except for the awful problems it would leave my devoted crew. But isn't it better for many reasons to have an electric windlass and a self-stowing anchor? Heart attacks apart, there are times when, caught perhaps by a squall in an anchorage, one is obliged to work cables and anchors under trying conditions. Getting exhausted doesn't help.

Nowadays there are some excellent little windlasses on the market. They use a lot of amps, but not for long; most of them pull in at over 20 feet (6 metres) a minute, so weighing would not normally take more than three minutes. Forty amps for three minutes is two ampere/hours; not very much, is it? Especially as one would almost certainly have the engine running at the time.

Sheet winches do come with electric motors, but the prices are prohibitive, as one needs a fair number of them. It is better to have geared winches with plenty of power. When getting on it is easier to give six gentle turns than three hard ones; it takes longer, but so little extra in cruising terms. Winches should be just above waist height if worked standing up, which is the best position for the effort. If you have to work them sitting down, then even more power is required. Don't risk straining the back.

The steering position should be in a wheelhouse. There is positive evidence that old people can be distressingly unaware of the onset of hypothermia. I know that the evidence applies strictly to very old persons, but I do not suppose that the condition jumps suddenly to danger level overnight: its development is almost certainly spread over quite a period; its onset probably arrives with your bus pass. Do not suppose that hypothermia is unknown in the tropics. Of course on a starlit night with a gentle force 3 blowing from the quarter there is no problem, but during Hurricane Alberto I was wearing a thick sweater down below. (I didn't go on deck; I was too scared.) And remember you don't always stay in the hot climates. In the Med in April or October it can get quite chilly. We lit our wood-burning stove on 15 May close to the Mediterranean coast.

The wheelhouse should have opening windows for fine weather, and a good chair to rest in. In *Hosanna* we have seats from which both of us can see around at the same time, and why not? It is still essential to have somewhere to sit outside, and even to entertain on a small scale, but do not place too much emphasis on sunbathing; one gets tanned quite well enough without ever going into the direct sun, though the process takes a little longer. Many people who have spent long periods in the tropics now have skin problems.

Sail plans must be arranged for ease of handling rather than sailing efficiency. All sheets should come to a cockpit. All halyards or roller furling lines too. It should be possible to douse a sail without having to put on an act like a chimpanzee in a circus. In my view this makes roller sails virtually essential, and means either leaving the spinnaker behind or saving it for when junior pays a visit.

Have really big cleats. Hands and fingers get less agile, and fumbling with irritatingly miniature fittings is bad for one's frame of mind.

Give a lot of attention to lifelines. The aged do not pick their feet up so easily as

Hosanna *under all plain sail.*

the young, and we have seen older people tripping over deck fittings; the average deck-level lifeline is a perfect tripwire. It needs some experimenting, but a lifeline at waist height may be the best. One tends to crouch a bit in bad conditions, and it might be easier to duck under than clamber over.

Mooring is a pastime which can tax old bones. Though Old Tom will undoubtedly be more experienced than Young Fred, his reaction time will be slower. Ensure you have a boat that is responsive under power and steers well at slow speed. Even if the boat is less than 15 tons, a miniature bow-thruster is probably a better buy than a lot of electronic navigating equipment (though I do not discount the value of anything which takes some of the physical burden off a small crew).

A motorsailer is probably the best type of craft, for one will need a good engine. Consider how you could manage if one of you had to cope on their own. I could have sailed *Fare Well* back to harbour by myself, Laurel would not have had the strength. If the event had arisen then she would have had to motor back, and it is essential that the boat has engine power to make headway in a rough sea.

As one gets older one tends to use the engine a little more, whatever one's original intentions. I see nothing wrong in this: in my view the prudent mariner is the one who uses all or any of his resources to the best advantage.

We have written about this subject at greater length in *Sail Into the Sunset* (Adlard Coles Nautical).

So how have we solved the problem of a boat for the elderly?

First of all Bill, designed a steel boat in accordance with all that we have said above. We never built it. We approached the basic problem by considering the cruising grounds we enjoyed the most, and those we had not yet cruised but wished to. Some would require more nautical effort than others; quite clearly some are getting too much to contemplate unless done soon.

Having graded these by degree of ambitiousness we found we had more than a lifetime's cruising ahead of us, and we decided to cut down by removing those such as the China Sea, which are unlikely to become congenial to the casual yachtie for some time.

It was about this time that Laurel indicated that she wanted to bring all her library, so we threw away our lists and Bill proposed putting in a bid for the *Queen Elizabeth II*. When the argument settled down again we both went to look over the market in sea-going Dutch barges in their raw, unconverted state. Bill had seen several conversions in the West Indies and in the USA which had sailed there on their own bottoms, and it seemed to him that one of modest size might suit us well. When sea sailing got too difficult we would have all those European canals and rivers to potter about in. In the meantime we would be limited to the fine weather zones in their more reliable periods, but our list was mostly that anyway. We tend towards a quieter life.

When we found a beautiful little barge available for what was virtually the price of her engine, we dealt. It was our intention to cut out 4 metres of length and make a full motorsailer of her. After the two of us had driven her in ballast across the North Sea in February in rough conditions we became impressed with what we had bought. Bill looked again at Laurel's pile of books. He decided we could cope with the Little Dutch Barge under power under all but survival sea states, once one or two things were improved. The cost of cutting out 4 metres, if invested, would produce enough income to maintain 4 metres.

So *Hosanna* has ended up entire and whole and perfect, a token of our love, with three fixed keels and a sail plan divided into three low masts, and all sails rolling. She has three engines, three screws and a bow-thruster. And probably 3 tonnes of books.

Since writing the above we have circumnavigated Europe, cruised *Hosanna* all over the North Sea, the Med, the Aegean, and the Black Sea, as well as various canals and major European rivers, including the Rhine and Danube. Navigationally speaking, her size has caused us little anxiety. Occasionally in bad weather the two of us have found her a bit exhausting: the worst case was being dismasted at 0400 in a rough North Sea, though the most tiring experiences generally have been in the great rivers. Now 14 years on we will have to contemplate another change because the maintenance shows signs of becoming too much for us. We do not want to allow Hosanna to deteriorate as we have sometimes observed in old people's boats. One has to be sensible. A couple ten years younger than us could cope well enough. We now need time to think, though we expect you will be able to see the likely direction of our thoughts. Pity about Laurel's books.

5 • Above Decks

'For a man of warre a well ordered taunt-mast is best, but for a long voyage a short mast will bear more canvasse and is less subject to beare by the boord'

NAUTICAL TERMS

Neither Laurel nor I are sticklers for using a lot of nautical jargon. We are both inclined to talk of our bedroom, windows or ceilings, to give three examples. But there are items or doings which are peculiar to the sea, which are well described by sea terms, and for which no other words are adequate. Sometimes these terms have been debased by yachtsmen using them wrongly, so to clear up doubts over what we are going to discuss, I want to define a few terms:

Guardrails are a 'safety fence' running round the vessel; they can be solid rails, or they can consist of wires supported by stanchions.
Lifelines are wires rigged between various rigid parts of the vessel so that crew can hold on or clip harness onto them when moving about.

The remaining words concern anchors. Apart from names indicating the design, such as Danforth or Bruce, anchors may be described either by their function or by the part of the vessel from which they are used. *Bower anchors* are normally stowed on either bow, and are the normally used anchors by which a ship comes to anchor. A *sheet anchor* is a spare anchor usually kept forward, for use only in very bad conditions. Though 'sheet anchor' is an expression much misused by politicians, it is not necessarily noted for its size or unusual holding power; generally it was a last resort because it was a bit of a pest to manage (like politicians). A *stream anchor* is one stowed at the stern; let go from there, usually in conjunction with a bower, so that the two anchors and the ship lie parallel to the stream and do not swing with its changes. A *kedge anchor* is an anchor used to point the ship or to move her about. The rope used between ship and kedge anchor is called a *warp*, which is also used to describe ropes used between ship and shore or between ship and a buoy, also for moving the ship. The kedge, which in these days of tugs and bow-thrusters has largely died out, was usually lighter than other anchors because it was typically carried away from the ship to be laid by boat. The word does not mean a light anchor, but defines the use to which it was put.

The big racing yachts did not want to anchor during a race unless the wind was light and they might have to stem the tide. As their lightest anchor was enough for this purpose they would save weight by landing their bower anchors, and thus the racing fraternity debased the word 'kedge' because that was the way the professional crews referred to their light anchor. In the same way, yachtsmen came to refer to the rope on the anchor as a warp, when the correct word is *cable* whether it is cordage or chain. In the USA it is often called a *rode,* an older word, so also correct. I will refer to the length of cable in use as the *scope*, which should not be dependent on the size of the ship but on the depth of water, though the relationship is not a linear one.

With chain cable a scope of five or six times the depth of shallow water is prudent, but for deep water, over 20 metres say, this can fall to three times the depth. Double this for nylon unless a heavy angel is used. An angel is a heavy weight lowered down an anchor cable to provide an extra 'spring' to prevent the cable coming up bar-taut and snatching (see p. 94). I have been told some yachtsmen call this a 'chum', and discover this is because some enterprising manufacturer used this as a trademark.

For Med mooring with an anchor, use as much scope as possible, but also try always to use an angel with nylon. (This use is a prime example that cable does you no good when in the locker. Use the lot if you can, the more the better.)

When two anchors (or more) are used we usually say the vessel is moored, which strictly means made fast to the bottom. The angle at which an anchor cable leaves the ship is referred to as its *stay*. If it is almost horizontal and enters the water a long way ahead of the ship, it is called a *long stay*. A *short stay* is when the cable hangs down almost vertically.

RIGS AND RIGGING

If one discounts the requirement of high windward ability, one brings into question the suitability of the bermudan rig. Why do so many long-term cruising yachts sport this rig? *Fare Well* was so rigged, and as I designed it, I suppose I should have an answer. I don't. It must have seemed the right thing at that time.

For tradewind cruising it certainly is not the best rig. For short-sea sailing when short-handed, the modern type of bermudan rig with a small mainsail and a very large foretriangle may be very efficient when on the wind on a long tack, but it is far from convenient when putting about. A period of short-tacking in a largish boat can exhaust a crew of two: the rig can become a monster.

The perfect answer does not exist, but I think it pays to look at the question from viewpoints other than maximising tractive effort per square foot of canvas.

One of these is ease of maintenance and repair, and I will touch on this in Chapter Eight. Another, already mentioned, is ease of management, especially when short-handed or tired, in setting, furling and trimming the sails. On longer voyages there is the important matter of chafe. There is initial cost, as well as cost of maintenance of masts and rigging as well as the sails themselves.

With roller reefing/furling gear, some older rigs that did not prove altogether suitable for yachts, or which never caught on, bear some re-examination. Some years ago, Blue Bradfield circumnavigated the lovely little ketch *D'Vara,* just over 30 feet,

I designed Fare Well *with a bermudan rig which made it inconvenient to manage when short-sea sailing short-handed.*

which had an American-designed *wishbone rig,* well subdivided. He swore by this rig, saying that it gave him any combination or balance he required in any weather conditions. It seems to me that the wishbone mainsail with a downmast roller system would be effective and easy to manage with the wishbone set aloft permanently.

The *spritsail* also needs a revival. Being essentially quadrilateral, it could be set on a shorter mast with a vertical roller, and with vangs on the sprit. We tried it on *Hosanna,* and it set well, though we sometimes had trouble with the down-mast rolling gear. I had to throw money at it to get it exactly right, but it is better now. Shorter masts make a lot of sense when cruising, especially when off to distant parts, but one does need to keep a fair area of sail up aloft where the wind is stronger. I could like Mr Hoyt's *cat-rigged* Freedom boats but for the necessity of stepping heavy masts through the deck, which has never appealed to me. I favour the tabernacle; perhaps it is my East Anglian breeding.

A *square-sail* is a great asset on a tradewind passage, but it must be easily handled. The Dutch sailor Harm set a big one on his old Colin Archer using the 'drawing curtain' method of brailing the sail in from either side to the mast. I am told he did not keep it long, and others have said this way can be a nightmare in a squall. Has anyone yet set a square-sail from a horizontal roller gear inside a hollow aluminium yard? Such a sail, easy to reef and set, would appeal to me.

If one does have a shorter mast, then standing rigging is simplified. It is possible to save money from this simplicity, and some of this will come with the sailmaker's bill, for example. Sails made very simply for a rig that is not state-of-the-art generally last twice as long and cost half as much as those from fashionable sailmakers with gimmicks and big advertising accounts.

Mast steps are seen on many long-distance cruisers; along with windvanes and astro-domes, they became, for a time, a status symbol of sorts, but are less seen nowadays. *Fare Well* had steps, but I would not waste money on them again. One does not want to go up a mast that often; a 60-foot climb at my age is no light undertaking; and at sea, when rolling, my moment of inertia at that radius is more than I can cope with and still do a job. Instead I use a cloth bag type of boatswain's chair. Nonetheless, a pair of steps conveniently placed about 3 feet (a metre) or so below the cap or wherever work is likely to be needed would enable one to steady oneself, frap oneself down, and thus leave both hands free to work.

• *Collecting rainwater* •

With a boomed conventional mainsail it is possible to have a hollow aluminium boom made with a simple 'fairing' riveted on either side of the track to collect rainwater that falls down the sail and to allow it to pass into the boom. A 1-inch BSP hole tapped underneath, close to the gooseneck, allows a hose to be connected and the water fed straight into a tank. One can collect a lot of waterduring a squall. This could also be a feature of in-boom furling (see opposite).

• *Running rigging: cord or wire?* •

This is a great expense, and I prefer cordage. Wires are tolerable if turned on to a reel winch, but they have disadvantages. First, they have a tendency to spring into kinks which, if inadvertently pulled taut (in the dark, say) will seriously weaken the wire and also stop it passing easily through blocks or eyes. Second, when minor damage occurs, some of the small wires break and the ends project. The discovery of one of these can be painful and even disabling. Third, it is apparently impossible to find sheaves properly designed for wire rope. I once took part in elaborate Admiralty tests to discover the best size and section of sheave for modern wire. It turned out to be a question not of finding the best, but of finding the least worse, but the trials did show a requirement for very large diameter sheaves, about 20 times the wire diameter, and a deep narrow groove of roughly semi-circular section.

Cordage, on the other hand, chafes. It also stretches, but in lengths up to 20 metres or so I have never found this much of a problem with polyester. It cannot be conveniently wound on self-stowing reel winches, and thus it can leave one with lengthy snakes about the deck. These can have their ends washed overboard where they will surely find the propeller, even if it is only trailing. (Someone defined a screw propeller as the perfect self-tailing winch.)

This leads on to winches. I believe in the self-tailing type, and have found those little blue rubber gadgets that can be added to existing winches to be less than perfect. This is a department where the money should be found for the proper job. It is not necessary to go for the metallurgically perfect, every part turned by a master-craftsman, models that cost more than the boat. For cruising, a sturdy well-made job with simple bearings that can be kept clear of salt and well lubricated without having to dismantle them into a kit of parts every few days is what is needed. But do fit big enough ones. Under-sized winches cause accidents in squalls or emergencies.

See also Chapter Four.

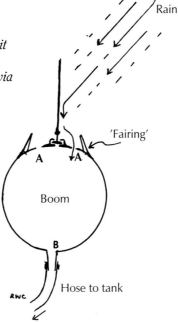

Catching rain water with the mainsail. The fairing strips trap water next to the sail track where it runs into the boom through holes (A) and drains away to the tanks via an outlet (B) near the gooseneck.

STEERING AND SAFETY ARRANGEMENTS

The chore of steering a boat for long periods is usually eased by self-steering vane gear or autopilots, which I will discuss later. One finds that they are in use for 99% of the time, but the occasion will arise when hand steering becomes unavoidable and a comfortable position is essential.

I am all for a wheelhouse. The open sports car syndrome becomes less relevant as one matures. The Royal Navy were the last professionals to grow up, and it needed the atom bomb with its fallout problems to convert them from open bridges. For my part, I do not like a wet shirt and a flowing sea. A first-class permanent awning is necessary over the conning position if there is no wheelhouse. Without an awning, the tropical sun will boil your brains or else the rain will drown you. As the rain can also come at you horizontally, we are back to wheelhouses again. The windows should open, and one of them should have a substantial watershedding device. The Kent Clearview Screen is good, though in the smaller sizes the clear area is not big enough. There are some very powerful windscreen wipers on the market which work well.

• *Guardrails* •

Whether or not a wheelhouse is possible, make sure the cockpit is well fenced in. Some modern designers, obsessed with getting more berths and walk-through headroom everywhere, have put cockpits high up on top of the accommodation. It may surprise you to know that I do not object to this from the point of view of height (it raises one above a lot of the spray), but only because, to keep a racy profile, such yachts are usually given too little cockpit fence, either to keep a sea out or to keep stumbling, tired crew in. If you find a ready-made yacht with a high cockpit but which otherwise suits you, contemplate fitting a strong rail round it. The upper edge of the cockpit coaming should be at least a metre high where one can stand up close to it, but where a seat or bench is in front of it then a little extra is desirable.

Guardrails become even more important when short-handed or family cruising. In the early days of offshore racing we did not have them, and I went overboard and missing one night, so I have intimate knowledge of this; not many of us survive to be able to discuss it.

There are some very expensive 70-footers (20m) on the market with guardrails suitable only for laundry lines. From 33ft (10m) LOA upwards, the *minimum* height of the top rail should be 30in (75cm) and the maximum vertical gap 12in (30cm). Anything else is a perfect trip-wire. They need to be strong enough to arrest the progress of a heavy body falling across the beam of the boat, assisted by flowing water, and that exerts a very large force indeed. This is not an area to take chances with: one has to consider the extreme case and then add a safety margin, and remember that disasters are rarely caused by something being too strong, only by being not strong enough.

Another aspect of guardrails is their vulnerability when mooring. Novices have

Fare Well's *laterally pivoted side davits, an adaptation of the merchant ship type and much more practical than swinging davits. Note the strong guardrails. The fitting at top right takes the awning.*

an irresistible urge to push boats about by heaving on their stanchions, and given the apparent numbers of novices about it is desirable that the rails withstand this deplorable but widespread practice. Modern motor yachts are designed with high freeboard and considerable flare at the deck edge: for the comparatively low-free-board sailing yacht, these features make mutual fendering very difficult. The ability to fender against one's guardrails is an asset. *Fare Well's* guardrails were 80cm high, that is 55cm above the gunwale. The stanchions were 40mm x 40mm x 4mm RHS steel welded on at 120mm intervals, the intermediate rail was welded and the top rail was all teak. They were sufficiently strong to allow the unbraced top of a stanchion to take the sheet lead block of the 67-square metre genoa, and I felt happy about them. Up forward there was a different arrangement with netting, as the foredeck had fewer impedimenta to interrupt a fall, and netting is nicer to fall into than steel bars. Laurel has only one good leg and needs protection from falls. Don't we all.

Harness is very important on deck in rough weather. My opinion is that, given good strong guardrails as a back-up, one can move about better without clipping on to lifelines, but instead use two clips and move from one ringbolt to another. In small yachts with light guardrails, narrow side decks, and the necessity to do a lot of work on the coachroof, some forms of stout wire lifeline are required. One should extend from cockpit to mast on each side, and another from mast to headsail tack. Wire of 8mm diameter is about right, but must be made fast to strong fittings. I fear that a falling body could pull the mooring cleats out of some of the production boats I have seen, let alone the lifeline seating.

There is something to be said for a fair-sized yacht having a folding davit by her midship gangway rail-break. It would not only be of great help recovering heavy weights from the sea, but would be good in harbour for doing ditto from the dinghy.

When we commissioned *Fare Well* there was no windvane steering gear strong enough, so we had a Sharp Mate autopilot which was the simplest I could find. In consequence I know little about pure windvanes, except that the Mediterranean's variable winds cause problems for them. The Sharp was a good companion; it only let us down once (on the first day out on an Atlantic crossing!) when a diode failed. (No dedicated cruiser should be without a stock of diodes, and a basic understanding of what they do: they are everywhere.) One little peculiarity of autopilots is that they occasionally go barmy and go round in a 360° circle before resuming the previous course. They give trouble running before a big quartering sea; and I believe vanes, too, are not so good at this difficult point of sailing.

In *Hosanna*, because Sharp had gone out of business, we fitted a Cetrek model 272 (now discontinued), which is a much more complicated, all-singing-all-dancing affair with an 'intelligence' that measures weather helm and trim and automatically allows for them. After a measuring time, of course. For a sailing boat this is a big snag for the T.O.M. cannot be made to anticipate a gybe, so that one has to steer by hand for a time, just when one should be tweaking sheets and things. Try to find an autopilot that permits you to pre-adjust it with knobs, so that as you set the alteration of course on it you can also change the side of the trim. Proper knobs, not dainty little fairy buttons that gloved fingers cannot feel, and preferably dials with light-emitting diodes, which can actually be seen in tropical sunlight.

How we regret the passing of knobs! Buttons were all right when you could feel the things with cold wet fingers, but now they are designed as faint elevations behind a sheet of smooth plastic – often the best one can manage with a large finger is to press about four at once.

LIFERAFTS AND TENDERS

I suppose most people contemplating long cruises have read with interest, if not alarm, the accounts of yachts lost and the experiences of survivors. One feature that is worth stressing is that an inflatable liferaft is not designed for long-term survival, while there are several cases where persons have been recovered from rigid dinghies after long periods adrift. I have moved back to the view that the best

Fare Well's *tender, a small Norfolk lugsail dinghy, was useful for pottering up creeks as well as ferrying us to and from harbour. I made side davits for it which meant that it could be stowed on deck in rough weather.*

liferaft for an ocean or well-offshore cruising yacht is a good rigid dinghy, even in the severest storm where survival needs an element of luck anyway. The dinghy must have first-class inherent buoyancy, and a stout cover or at least a partial one, and rope-loop handholds below the gunwales. The Panic Bag should be kept in it at sea (it is the best place for the vegetable locker in any case). It requires no annual service, which is not only very expensive in some countries (it bears VAT in France and Italy for a start), but also difficult to arrange and check. It is also virtually impossible to verify that the work

(TOP) *A mini-motorbike takes up little space and, if under 50cc does not require licensing in many countries.*
(BELOW) Hosanna *was big enough to allow us to take a small car, in this instance a Fiat 600 – the smallest car that Bill was able to climb into.*

charged for has actually been done, and in too many cases it has not, or not properly at any rate. A dinghy has many other uses.

Which leads us to tenders. Once we had a rigid dinghy and an Avon, but we found that we used the rigid one for choice; it was so much easier to row. When we met a fellow traveller whose inflatable Avon had perished in the sun, we contemplated the inevitable deterioration of this asset and sold it to him. We have rarely missed it. Our dinghy is a small Norfolk lugsail dinghy, now 27 years old, still good for pottering up creeks and by-waters, but it is not a heavy load carrier. In *Fare Well* we hoisted it on side davits which I made myself. We had stern davits too, but a stern-hung dinghy is a nuisance in the Med, though a stern-hung inflatable makes a good emergency fender when lying stern-to a quay. The advantage of the side davits is that the dinghy can be turned in and stowed on deck in rough weather or when manoeuvring, where it is much safer and makes an extra locker. With *Hosanna*, being a bigger boat, we hoist the dinghy in and out with either a derrick, or side davits.

We got rid of our 2hp Evinrude outboard. We used it very seldom, it was noisy, troublesome, and in our view had more potential as an anchor than as a propulsion unit. Our dinghy sails and rows well, and for when we were tired we had a very cheap Sears Roebuck electric outboard that ghosted us about at slow speed, needing no maintenance and not waking the neighbours. In the end we disposed of that too, because we find it fun to sail, and the exercise of rowing ashore is good for us, helping to remove the results of too much Greek food and wine at the tavernas.

On the other hand, our American friends have a large Zodiac with a powerful outboard, and they tend to zip into some harbours for a little shopping without berthing the yacht. Unless the harbour is very encumbered I feel berthing is rather less trouble than fiddling about with dinghies. Once we returned to Gouvia very late at night, formally dressed, Laurel in long skirt and so on. The chap who was taking his dog for a walk and took our lines for us as we berthed asked where we had been in formal dress. 'To the theatre', we said. 'What?' he said, 'In a 50-foot yacht?'

Another form of tender is a vehicle. Many dedicated cruisers are advertised by a bicycle on deck; larger boats sometimes have a mini-motorbike, which, if under 50cc, does not require licensing in most countries though it may require insurance. The obligation of a crash helmet is spreading; France and Tunisia insist and there may be others. Motorbikes should have a painted sign 'Tender to . . .' instead of a number plate. Perhaps the trendy scooters would suit some.

Hosanna, being a barge, is able to carry a small car, a Mini or a Fiat 600, on deck (there we go, very one up on the Jones's that is!). In the canals it is worth it on occasions, but on the whole it was more trouble than asset, and the practice has been discontinued. It rusted before our eyes in the salt spray. For anyone living aboard a barge that is committed to the canals, it should be considered, but it must have its own loading crane. Second-hand hydraulic cranes can be obtained cheaply from truck-breakers.

ANCHORS AGAIN

The long-term cruiser will have to take more thought to his anchors than the marina-based animal who probably never anchors at all. During 1982 we spent 134 nights riding to single anchor, and a further nine moored with two. In 1995/6 we spent 410 consecutive nights riding to anchors in one way or another. We dragged once or twice. *Fare Well* was fitted with two 75lb (34kg) CQR bower anchors which self-stow over rollers close either side of the stem. To port we had 45 fathoms (82m) of ⁷/₁₆ inch (14mm) chain, and to starboard 40 fathoms (72m) of ¹/₂ in (12?mm), both handled by a Simpson-Lawrence 521 electric windlass. This layout owes a lot to big-ship experience, and it meant that Laurel, the vertically and orthopaedically challenged cable officer, could manage anchors and cables in all normal circumstances without any help. Foul anchors are another thing altogether.

The size of bower anchors is very important. Most published tables of recommended anchor sizes seem to have in mind the marina denizen or the ocean racer, and not the sea-going cruising yacht. For example, I followed the advice of Simpson-Lawrence (now taken over by South-Western Marine Factors – choice is disappearing fast), but wish I had fitted larger anchors. Their table:

Waterline length	Displacement in tons	CQR anchor weigh
40ft (12m)	25	60lb (27kg)
45ft (13.5m)	30	75lb (34kg)

In my view, to enjoy peace of mind, one should have bower anchors larger than this. My table, in just metric this time:

Waterline length	Displacement in tons	CQR or Bruce anchor	Chain cable links
10m	17	25kg	10mm
12m	25	30kg	11mm
13m	30	40kg	12mm
15m	35	50kg	15mm

When moored bow- or stern-to a quay with an anchor out, the wind on the beam has a sweating-up effect on the anchor cable, and a strong wind can multiply the tension in it several times. Add to this the fact that a wind on the beam acts on a larger area of boat than a wind from ahead, and it is not surprising that anchors of apparently adequate size come home. If you expect to spend much time in the Mediterranean an increase in size of both anchor and cable is desirable. The alternative, which we follow, is to have two bower anchors and use both if a strong wind is expected. The practice of waiting until the wind gets up and then laying out a second anchor by dinghy, upwind, may solve the layer's problem (if he succeeds, it's not always easy). It inconveniences those across whose cables he lays his second anchor, who may justifiably call him names. Indeed, we have seen this gambit not only fail to secure the yacht in question, but trip the anchors of several others, leading to drag acts quite as dramatic as anything on stage.

If I had thought further ahead I would have fitted *Fare Well* with a self-stowing stream (stern) anchor with its own capstan or windlass. It would have been useful on several occasions, especially in restricted tideways such as the Intra-Coastal Waterway. *Fare Well* had no kedge, and I saw no need for one as there is little point using a lighter, less secure anchor when the heavier, safer bowers could be managed more easily. She had a spare 75lb (34kg) Danforth which we never used. If the need arises to send away an anchor in a boat (after a grounding, say) I have always used a bower with enough chain cable; one does not need a lot if it is shallow enough to run aground.

On those rare occasions when the wind blows across the swell and rolling becomes a nuisance (it happened in Mustique in the West Indies, and also at Pargos in Greece), it is possible to spring the cable to point ship across a moderate wind (see diagram).

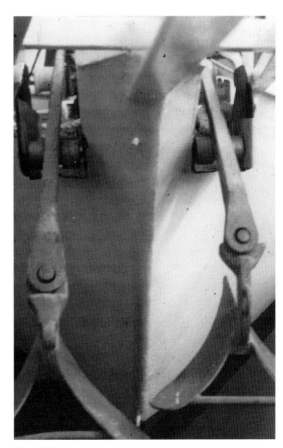

For *Hosanna* we have adopted a different approach to berthing end-on. We use a stern anchor that is twice the weight of the bower. We go ahead into the berth with a stem fender over the bows, and nudge the quay with our stem. No matter what the wind, we can leave the boat pressing end-on against the quay, leaning on Greece say, with the centreline engine going slow ahead and the rudder adjusted to allow for any cross-wind. In this condition we have all the time in the world to put out head ropes, set taut the stern anchor cable, and get out gangways. This is only possible in straight-stemmed steel boats, but it enables us to berth a very big boat with just two people. However, nothing comes free, and leaving the quay and

Fare Well *was fitted with two CQR bower anchors which self-stow over rollers close either side of the stem.*

The contrast between long and short stay anchoring. The cable in the foreground is going to be many yards out before it is deep enough to be safe from being snagged by a passing boat.

weighing the big stern anchor while the bows quest in all directions can be a bit nerve-wracking in strong winds.

Choice of anchor type is a personal matter. They are mostly difficult to stow other than as described above. But the criterion of choice should not be a tabulated holding strength in one or two particular conditions, but a good all-round security in most conditions where sea sense indicates anchoring is worth considering. No anchor holds on smooth marble as one discovers at Xania in Crete.

Taken overall I have found the CQR satisfactory, but respect that some friends prefer Danforth, Bruce or Fortress, though I would approve the latter very cautiously and only as a back-up. It's their choice. All these anchors were very carefully designed. Avoid imitations. The CQR and Bruce anchors will stow over rollers. I have an idea that the Bruce is not so good in the smaller sizes as it is in the larger; perhaps this is another case where one should read the next line in the table. It is worth noting that the Bruce was designed for positioning oil rigs in deep water. Here, security is paramount, but absolute holding power is achieved with the help of very long cables. The Danforth will hang conveniently upside down over the guardrails in a smallish yacht. Admiralty Pattern and Fisherman's anchors are really not worth it, except as rock picks, while ship anchors, such as the Hall's pattern, only come into their own over 100 kilos.

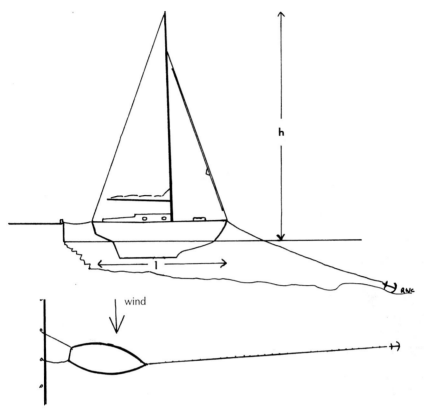

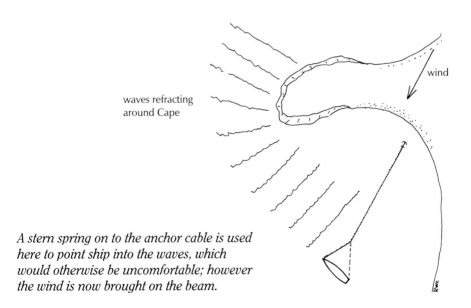

A yacht moored to a quay with an anchor out is not free to swing and a wind from the side has more windage to act upon and causes far more strain on the cable and upwind mooring lines.

A stern spring on to the anchor cable is used here to point ship into the waves, which would otherwise be uncomfortable; however the wind is now brought on the beam.

CABLE

I favour chain cable, though with frequent use the galvanizing does wear off and begins to look dreadful. Re-galvanizing is expensive outside the UK, and often badly done too. As a palliative, turn the cable end for end, wire-brush it, and keep it soaked in boiled linseed oil, which is the only suitable oil without a nasty smell (it smells of old cricket bats). If you do need anything re-galvanizing, it can be done at Pireaus, near Athens, and at Marseille.

Nylon has advantages, and for the lightweight yacht which is normally in a marina and does not often anchor, it is a good choice. There is on the market a coil of flat-braid polyester which I consider dangerous. Though the principle of rolling up a flat braid is excellent and practical, the material should be of nylon, which is highly elastic, and not of polyester, which is meant to be inelastic. The importance of elasticity in an anchor cable cannot be over-estimated. In doing anchor trials for the Admiralty, I found that anchors were started to drag very easily by a series of jerks, whereas they would not move for a much greater tension in the cable if the pull was steady. It is the catenary weight of chain cable that acts as a good spring, and if you do want to use the polyester braid I would recommend lowering a weight (the angel, mentioned above), which should be about half the weight of the anchor, down the cable to about one-third of the scope from the bows.

One sees reference to nylon being subject to chafe or cut over coral, but I have no personal   knowledge of this happening, probably because my friends are

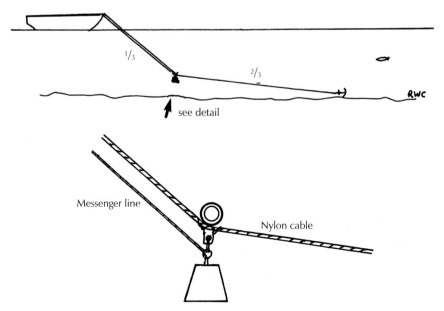

An 'angel' designed to hang on the anchor cable at about a third of the scope out from the bows, with its own light messenger line to lower and retrieve it. The weight should ideally be half that of the anchor.

sensible enough not to lay out a nylon cable over sharp coral heads, which in any event are not good holding ground. More important is the fact that nylon will abrade over sand and in fairleads, especially when strong winds have the ship yawing and sheering. Nylon is more awkward to stow coming in than chain, especially as one needs double the scope, and another consideration, in the Med especially, is the question of security in crowded harbours when other boats are manoeuvring. Nylon cables lead at longer stay than chain, and thus enter the water much farther away from the bows, and are easily cut by another vessel manoeuvring with difficulty. The question of legal liability is not the half of it: the case might well have to be argued in foreign tongues in foreign countries, and that still is not all. The reason why the cutter was in trouble in the first place was probably a strong wind. The ensuing dance of yachts cut adrift and/or disabled with a rope round the screw soon develops the characteristics of a gang-rape among elephants, with comparable dangers to life, limb and property. Though

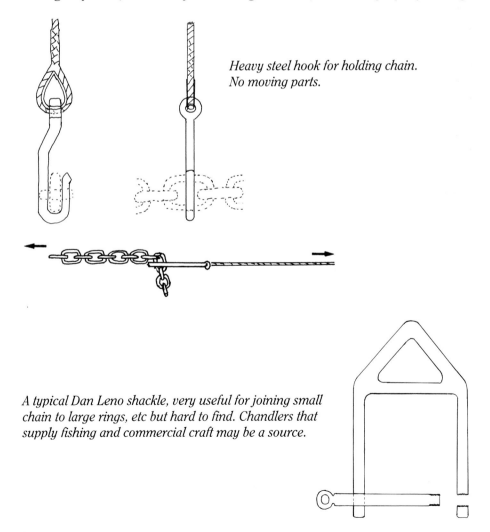

Heavy steel hook for holding chain. No moving parts.

A typical Dan Leno shackle, very useful for joining small chain to large rings, etc but hard to find. Chandlers that supply fishing and commercial craft may be a source.

legal opinion has it as the cutter's responsibility, that is based on big-ship cases heard before the days of nylon cables, and it could be argued that these, at long stay in crowded harbours, are unseamanlike and a contributory factor to trouble.

Perceptive readers will have noticed that the advice given in this paragraph has not been followed by the yacht on the cover of this book. We have no control over this yacht, or her Skipper and, thank God, yachties may still do as they please. She is there as a bad example. You can amuse yourself noticing the other things that make her undesirable as a live-aboard yacht, but there are no prizes on offer.

It is the ease of handling self-stowing bower anchors with a good windlass that makes berthing stern-to a quay the best proposition for craft needing an anchor of about 20 kilos or more, even though skippers will find it simpler to manoeuvre ahead, rather than astern. If one had a self-stowing stream anchor the case might be altered, but a bowsprit does make boarding difficult and larger boats with normal sheer find the stemhead a little high.

There will be more on anchoring in the chapter on navigation, because it is such an important feature of live-aboard cruising.

OTHER MATTERS

Backing into a berth (making a sternboard) is not as difficult as it appears and is soon mastered by most. Exceptions are yachts with an outward turning, off-centre screw. The secret is to get enough way on, for she will not steer until this is achieved. The speed required depends on the amount of cross-wind, and in very strong cross-winds it may not be possible at all. Most ship-handling textbooks counsel a softly-softly approach until one has mastered the feel of her, but in this case it is not the best approach. The prudent mariner will go off somewhere secluded and do a bit of practice.

A recent development has been the introduction of moderately priced (comparatively!) bow-thrusters, and I have seen several fitted. For short-handed single-screw yachts above, say, 40 feet (12 metres) such a device might be a better investment than electronics if you are planning to moor in popular harbours.

For serious cruising it is essential to have very strong bitts or cleats, because one is occasionally obliged to berth in harbours where the shelter is not perfect, and a swell or scend will have boats constantly dancing in their berths. Most deck fittings seen on production boats are criminally inadequate; this seems to be the area where the builder goes barmy to save a pound or two. The main centreline bitts forward should be strong enough to take the weight of the boat, and one needs two shoulder cleats or bitts fit to spring on. Two midship cleats ditto and two substantial bitts aft, strong enough for towing. Spring bitts or cleats should be on the gunwale, thus avoiding the need for fairleads which are seldom as good as their name. For fairleads read chocks in the Western Hemisphere.

In many primitive harbours chafe of ropes on quay copings is a nuisance. A common Med practice is to have a loop of chain at the end of the rope, sometimes with a carbine hook. Unfortunately the size of chain equivalent to the strength of the nylon would be impossible to heave. In any event, stand clear of people throwing chain about. A nylon rope of 16mm diameter has a breakload of 4000kg, which is much more than that of a 13mm chain and more than twice that of the biggest carbine hook. One suggested solution to this problem is to use a soft wire eye at the end of the nylon, or if you wish to use chain, first use a picking-up rope of lighter nylon and afterwards substitute the main berthing chain and/or rope which can be quite short.

It would be wise to insert here a word of caution about vandals who cast boats adrift while the crew is ashore. It has happened to us in Savannah, Georgia (courtesy of drunken US Marines), in Schweinfurt (where our home almost disappeared into a hydro-electric station – equal that as a conversation stopper!), and also at Cambrai, France. Vandals favour the easy way of doing things and though they are quite prepared to cut ropes, they tend to dwell a pause before releasing chain. Even so, we now padlock heavy chain round the steel bitts with a super padlock after making sure there are several tight turns round the shoreside bollard. Of course, it is better if the quay has rings. No, we are not paranoid. We only do it if we are unsure of security, and if the wind and/or tide is strong.

Most people use airfilled plastic fenders, and for lightness and convenience a few of these are more or less essential. But they are not ideal. Hot sun decomposes the plastic material of which they are made and they turn into sticky, grit-covered, abrasive puddings. Secondly, they are expensive; and thirdly, they do not stand up to hard wear alongside rough concrete or chipped stone quays. A couple of small motor tyres are advisable for bad conditions, though it is not nice to use them against someone else's topsides. We know that the marks are easy to remove, but some of the fancy yacht brigade can get upset and there is no point in causing offence. (We paint our tyres with white chlorinated rubber to avoid this.) Your neighbour may yet be happier about the grit-encrusted plastic ones.

• *Awnings* •

'An awning . . . spread over their heads . . . especially in hot countreys to keep men from the extremity of heat or wet, which is very oft infectious.'

I have mentioned already the need for good permanent shade over cockpit or conning position. In harbour, where one spends most of one's time, temperatures are higher, breezes are attenuated, and some form of living in the open air is desirable in hot or sticky seasons. I designed *Fare Well*'s poop as a verandah: it was 4 metres by 4 metres at its widest point, planked in teak with very few impediments. It became a delightful living room under a big awning, with folding table and chairs. *Hosanna* is big enough to have a permanent covered verandah, which is where we live in the hot weather.

It is possible to have a simple awning, for example, a sheet with a batten sewn

A strong, simple awning is a cool solution to hot-weather conditions and makes an inexpensive extra living room.

into the hem at either end. When spread over the boom, and with the ends of the battens bowsed down, it is a very cost-effective solution. I prefer a long-term investment of a good heavy cotton awning, roped all round and strong enough to be set over the mizzen boom in all but very strong winds. *Fare Well*'s mizzen boom had a sliding gooseneck so that it could be raised up well above head height in harbour, and the awning had hose connections sewn in: in the West Indies, where fresh water is quite hard to come by, there are frequent showers and we could get 15 gallons from a half-hour's rain.

The Americans have long had the Bimini awning, which is excellent, and it can be fitted so that it can be spread under the boom and therefore valuable while sailing. British sailmakers are getting good at making these; for smaller boats they are the best.

Remember that all boats are a compromise, and that you will never find the perfect boat. All you can do is to find one that is good enough to love, then you can ignore her faults.

6 • Below Decks

'On each side of the Stearage roome are divers Cabins . . . with many convenient seates or lockers to put any thing in, as in little Cupberts.'

KEEPING WATER OUT

Though there is a natural emphasis on comfort in a long-term cruising boat, we mustn't lose sight of the importance of comfort at sea, otherwise we will end up with something like a Chelsea houseboat. So important is the ability to maintain efficiency and safety at sea, that the question of comfort, whether in harbour or offshore, has to be fitted round the requirement to survive such rare testing moments that the yacht might encounter. Important factors in keeping going at sea are minimising both physical and mental strain, and the possibility of water entering the accommodation, which in effect will comprise most of the hull.

In our view, watertightness is a vital part of living in a boat. Inevitably one has more possessions on board than the holidaymaker, some of which are perhaps precious even if only for sentimental reasons. Sea water is the great destroyer, and it has allies with which it works. Dampness breeds mildew, mould and rot. And bad temper. Avoid it. It may not always be possible to stop every whit of water entering the bottom, but do get a watertight deck and windows. (It surprises us that in this day and age this still needs saying.) The aim is to be able to clean one's bilges with a feather duster, and it is perfectly achievable.

But water *will* get in. Spray flies, waves do wash over the deck; a moment's inattention when tired and there goes the sea water, slopping down the hatch or skylight. Only a paragon can maintain eternal vigilance and what a bore he'd be to live with.

We once had a terrible night beating down the Ionian Sea towards Kephalonia into a rising force 6 to 7, the spray flying the length of the ship as her head ploughed into each short sea, making us duck rhythmically behind the sprayshield to avoid the worst of it. Then, worried because she seemed to be diving a little more deeply than usual, Bill misjudged a duck and was able to see the forehatch lift, only an inch or so but enough to swallow a gallon or two from the water swilling about the deck. We bore away instantly, foregoing the pleasure of mutual recriminations, and investigated the forepeak which is fortunately separated from the accommodation by a watertight bulkhead. Bill later calculated that there must have been 4 tons of water in it, and all because we each thought the other had screwed down the bad-weather fastenings. And that was not all: it was a night when Professor Murphy drove home several points. Detritus and mud from the anchor cables had blocked the pump intake, but then, they say, there has never been a pump as fast as a frightened man with a bucket.

You could not enjoy living in a yacht with the watertight integrity of a submarine. There is a mean, and how far one goes in either direction depends on the chosen voyages, the chosen times, the chosen crew.

One way water can get below, even in harbour, is on the crew's clothing. A surprising dampness can build up this way over a period of prolonged rain or spray. Bill makes fun of Laurel's bath, but at sea it is an invaluable temporary drop for wet oilskins. Another source of damp is condensation, something that yacht designers have yet to appreciate fully. One modern quality English-built yacht in which a young couple was wintering in Corfu was dreadful: they were unable to use two of the bunks because of condensation dripping from the aluminium window frames. Now this is bad design and it is something to look out for when buying a boat. Older ships used to have 'save-alls' under scuttles and portholes to gather the overnight condensation or the odd leaky drops. With plastics, why are not save-alls moulded into the scuttles of the production boats that are often the worst offenders? A palliative is to cover the aluminium with some layers of masking tape, when the top layers will prevent the under ones from hardening out, but it doesn't look all that nice. If you are building from scratch, ensure that no bunk has a hatch over it, then it can't leak over your bedding

INSULATION

Wooden boats are composed of material with its own insulating properties, but all other constructions need insulation, and as steel or aluminium are the worst from this aspect, let us consider these.

The best steel hull insulation is to cover the interior above the waterline with about an inch (at least) of sprayed-on, closed-cell polyurethane foam, which is also an excellent protective coating for steel.

Some years ago, this foam used to be flammable and gave off toxic smoke if it ignited. In *Fare Well* we sprayed it with fire-retardant paint, which coped with a small fire caused when an anti-mosquito candle melted its plastic case in the saloon. (A word on this: we had a blind girl staying with us, and of all the terrors, fire is one of the very worst for the blind. We were all so shocked by this experience that now we never use insect repellents with naked flames.) The foam scorched but did not ignite.

While insulating *Hosanna*, we discovered that this foam is now available in a highly fire-resistant form. We used this and found it good, so much so that it was possible to make small welds on the opposite side of the steel plate without igniting the foam. We even cut a hole with oxy-propane, and the foam melted and blackened, but did not burst into flame. Of course, we drenched the area with water immediately. In these circumstances, and with care, this foam is ideal for boats that are going to be lived in.

Other insulation methods are to line with glassfibre wool (Rockwool), which does nothing to protect the steel. I have seen an old steel ship with hardpacked natural straw and another (Dutch built) with scrumpled-up newspapers packed behind the linings (and she was 100A1+ at Lloyd's, which gives one pause for thought). In my opinion, the sprayed foam is best.

How to protect the steel behind the insulation? The foam will adhere well to an epoxy-based holding primer which should be sprayed on immediately after sand-blasting. New steel, which it is inconvenient to sand-blast, is best treated with a 20% solution of ortho-phosphoric acid, the surplus acid neutralised with industrial alcohol (>75% is best), and then painted with a good quality primer, but the foam will then adhere only to the paint skin. Foam is really effective only on sand-blasted steel. *Hosanna* is an old ship and the after accommodation (the *roef* in Dutch) was in excellent condition after 55 years untouched (we could tell by the dates of the newspapers). She had been coated there, behind the panelling, with a mixture of old engine oil and paraffin wax. We tried to sand-blast, but over the years the mixture had penetrated into the steel itself, and as there was no sign of rust, we slapped on another coat of the same gungy mush. The Dutch know a few things about steel boats, and they do not like wasting money.

Ventilation alone will not cure condensation when dewpoint conditions are really ripe. In fact, ventilation can import dampness when the air outside becomes saturated, so some means of closing off ventilators is desirable.

Designers might reply to my criticisms of them that they do not attempt to design boats for living aboard in winter. This is probably true, but why not? A yacht should be capable of use whenever its owner wants, unless its unsuitability for a particular use is openly stated.

SEAGOING CITADEL VERSUS OPEN-PLAN

Our own solution of the comfort/seaworthiness dilemma was eased by *Fare Well's* size, but I believe the principle is adaptable further down the scale. It is important to recognise those bits of boat that are vital to the navigation, those that are desirable for harbour comfort in winter or summer, and then those that are common to both, such as galley and heads. Then design a layout with a sea-going 'citadel' separated from the rest of the boat, not completely, but so that in bad weather there is no need to go beyond it. In our citadel, mostly in the deckhouse which was at half-deck level, we had the galley, chart table, radio, refrigerator, switchboards, a sea bunk, a small table, tool chests, oilskin locker (big – 21 x 24 inches x full height), and close by, but down a ladder, the bathroom. (This actually contained a bath, essential in our case for therapeutic purposes and, as we said above, it also makes a first-class place to dump soaking-wet clothes.) The deckhouse was also the access to the engineroom, which was beneath it.

A touch of luxury afloat: Hosanna*'s saloon; this spacious barge had room for Laurel's extensive library.*

In the ends of the yacht (excepting the forepeak and the lazaret) were the saloon forward, and a small guest cabin and our own double bedroom aft. This latter was not a cabin; we use the word 'bedroom' deliberately to emphasise the comfort and peace of the place, which is the biggest single space in the whole ship. I do not say that our conception of the best (there is no perfect) layout is the only one, or even the right one for another couple. It worked very well for us, for a long time, for deep-sea and short-sea cruising and winter living. The only substantial improvement we would have made would be to have had a real wheelhouse instead of the then shelter, which we subsequently did when we converted *Hosanna*.

Others we know have an open-plan layout, one enormous airy space. It's nice for a party, and it suits the smaller yacht. It does suffer from 'one place wet – all places wet', and there is a lack of privacy when one has guests. Some have a small, separate after cabin as guest accommodation. These are very good for children, but having once been a guest in a Seadog ketch where I needed a shoehorn to get myself into bed, I suspect their long-term use for the grown man is a question of hope rather than reality.

A more conventional use for the half-deck deckhouse is to make it the saloon. This certainly looks better on demonstration models at the Boat Show. It does feel nice to have a light and airy saloon, but in Laurel's view it is also nice to have a light and airy galley. The catering tends to improve if the cook is not condemned to working in an ill-lit, ill-ventilated dungeon, conducive to seasickness. In the climate we aspire to, most of the living is on deck, which is the ultimate in light and airy. In a Mediterranean winter our saloon does have its disadvantages because our side ports are often blocked by neighbouring craft, but it is mostly in the evenings that it is used and it gets dark early in winter.

We are not really able to talk about *Hosanna* in these terms. Even a small barge like ours is almost big enough to hold a village dance. We have in fact as much space as a small flat and are in danger of becoming spoilt. But we are getting on now, and will have to move to a smaller boat soon, so the subject is very much in our minds.

THE INTERIOR IN MORE DETAIL

• *Fuel* •

There are many good arguments for having only one fuel aboard, one that is easily and universally available, and easy to load. The commonest is one that most of us are obliged to have in any event for propulsion. So let us first consider diesel oil as a sole fuel. (See also Chapter Nine.)

First, it not only drives the main engine but it can also drive an auxiliary generator if you should want one. It will drive an outboard; unfortunately these are heavy though powerful, and not very convenient. In the low power range one can have a battery-run electric outboard, thus using diesel oil at one remove.

There are very good diesel heaters on the market. At the simple end I like the Danish-made Refleks heater, which requires no fan and is therefore silent, but of course it heats only the compartment in which it is mounted. English-manufactured Taylor's are similar, and actually look a little neater. There are American and Dutch heaters too, all having gravity feed and dependent on a sort of carburettor made in the USA.

I am not so happy with blown-air oil heaters, having seen a serious fire in Antibes which happened when the crew were ashore for a very short time. It is possible in a bigger boat to have proper central heating with a normal oil-fired boiler. There are very good boilers working on the same gravity feed system we mentioned above. The basic boiler is quite small, but it can be installed in multiples. One can also get water heating coils in the Refleks and most similar heaters, but they are limited in output, though they would provide hot water and one small radiator.

Diesel This can also be used as fuel for cooking. There is a Canadian stove, the Dickenson, which not only cooks but provides hot water and central heating too. There is no other single-fuel arrangement.

Bottled gas Used for cooking, gas will save considerable initial cost and weight, some of which will be lost because of the price, size and weight of the necessary number of cylinders required for reasonable independence from the shore. It will bring problems apart from its propensity to explode, which can be controlled: practically every major country has its own size and design of gas bottles, very often with differently threaded connections. To change bottles at a retail supplier, it is necessary to hand in a local bottle. Odd bottles can sometimes be refilled at depots, but then there is the problem of transport, for the depots are seldom conveniently placed for yachts. I remember helping another boat take their bottles to a depot in Greece, and beating a hasty retreat as I observed the workman pouring liquid gas into an open cylinder through a funnel while he was smoking a cigarette. Possibly the mixture was too rich to explode, and the fumes did not rise.

I would think very carefully before opting for gas as the sole method of cooking, except in a small boat when I would agree that it is the only solution. If the boat is big enough to have a powerful separate 240 volt generator, then one can maintain the one-fuel principle by cooking with electricity. We do this in *Hosanna*. It can mean a lot of generating, even in the evening, when it can cause bad feeling among neighbours in a quiet harbour, but it is becoming more and more common especially among charter yachts. We have a four-plate hob, two of which are electric and two gas, and using the gas below and the barbecue on deck is a good way of solving the noise problem if too close to neighbours, the amount of gas required for this occasional use being very small. *Hosanna* has on deck a little sheltered summer kitchen with a single miniature gas ring for brewing up late at night. We do tend to swing at anchor rather than moor cramped up in harbours, and it's more peaceful for us too.

Paraffin (kerosene)   This is not suitable for the ordinarily hedonistic live-aboard. We have small oil lamps in gimbals which we keep lit at night at sea, turned very low, when they provide a faint glimmer which allows us to move about without switching on electric lights and spoiling night vision. Coarse, cheap paraffin is hard to find because rural or isolated communities are changing to liquid gas, while the refined, treated anti-pong variety is available in tiny bottles at very high prices.

Alcohol cooking   It is a menace. It surprises me that the Americans have tolerated it for so long, and I am happy to note a trend away from it at last. In some popular Caribbean anchorages one can sit enjoying a Planter's Punch after sunset while watching neighbouring Americans tossing overboard their flaming alcohol cookers. Some keep them on the end of a wire so they can easily haul them back inboard.

Solid fuel   The lovely old sloop *Diotima*, in which the late Admiral Goldsmith lived the life of a dedicated singlehander (and on the foredeck of which he died, weighing anchor at Monemvasia) had a solid fuel stove which was lovely in winter but noticeably warm in summer. Fuel was never a problem for him; he just gathered it from the beach. What a lovely little yacht! We last saw her in Hydra, now owned by a Greek sculptor who cares for her. *Hosanna* has two wood-burning stoves for winter evenings; we can sometimes find enough driftwood to feed them for free. We have a derrick, and finding a full-sized eucalyptus tree floating off shore in the Ionian, we hoisted it aboard, acquiring fuel and at the same time removing a danger to navigation. We then landed it to cut it up with a chain saw. We were told off by the Port Captain for making too much mess, but we swept up the sawdust which made good firelighters when soaked in old engine oil. The cruising life teaches you to use any resource you come across, usually this is better than the latest gadgets.

• *Refrigeration* •

This is the biggest energy user in the boat, apart from propulsion. Nowadays there are only a few families living without refrigeration, usually in a small boat. When you get acclimatised, it is not too bad, as I remember from days of yore. But now I do like a cold beer, and both white wine and rum punch are better chilled. Some say that the only way to take retsina is so cold you cannot taste it.

In *Fare Well* we had a top-opening refrigerator of about 3 cubic feet, and beneath and accessible through it a storage freezer of 2 cubic feet. This was a good installation, driven by a Grunert compressor unit, with a large holdover tank. The control was manual with an externally reading thermometer. The compressor was driven by 24 volts DC from the battery. It was mainly switched on during the daily battery charge. It was a robust system, as strong as a brick privy.

For *Hosanna* we could not get an American installation and had to fit one made in Italy. This works from time to time, but needs a lot of expensive attention, and the service agents (apart, we must say, from the one in England) have not proved noticeably co-operative or effective.

For smaller boats the 12-volt units working on the Peltier system are very simple though not highly efficient, technically. They are unlikely to make ice, but they will keep a small amount of food cool using two miniature fans; take spare fan units as these do not last for ever.

There is now on the market a range of normal-looking refrigerators, some of which have limited freezer space, which can work on 230 volts AC, or 12 or 24 volts (110 volts 60~ is also available for the cousins) according to the current available. Two larger ones, made by Engel and sold by AquaMarine Ltd, and a smaller one marketed by Penguin Engineering Ltd (addresses in Appendix), are known to us. This is a great advance in boat refrigeration. They use a powerful lot of DC current and need to be run either when the generator is going, or by a good solar or wind-driven generator. These fridges are not so cheap as ordinary domestic models (the smaller one above currently retails at £444.00 + VAT, for example), which latter can occasionally fit the bill, and probably represent the best solution for a boat too small to have a custom-built job.

That sums up the custom-built refrigerator, which has as many variations as you care to give it. The alternative is to buy a conventional household fridge at low initial cost and run it via the AC converter referred to above. The custom-built is probably more energy-economical as its insulation is usually better, and cooling the refrigerant is usually by sea water. The domestic system cools by air, which can heat up the accommodation if not ducted out. In the event of major breakdown, the domestic system is much easier to replace.

If you have a boat with an existing fridge using Freon gas, note that this gas is

SIMI

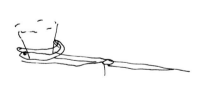

now virtually unobtainable outside primitive countries. It can be replaced by R49 gas which will keep the Greens happy until they find something wrong with that too.

If considering the alternative of an ordinary domestic fridge with power from a converter of some sort, be careful. The starting loads of most domestic fridges are about ten times their running loads. This means that a fridge with an advertised power drain of 100 watts will need about 1000 watts for a second or two while starting up. This would be enough to blow an electronic power inverter, but the rotary type will take it in its stride. I favour buying American refrigerating machinery; the country is so obsessed by ice that they seem to have solved more of the problems than most.

There are refrigerators working on the absorption method, getting energy from a gas or paraffin flame. I once tried the latter, and though I was quite pleased at the time, there is no doubt that the present system is much better. The absorption system can be troublesome at sea because tilting and movement inhibits its operation. I am told that the use of naked flames in absorption-type refrigerators is now forbidden in boats in the UK. I am not sure who in our Constitution has the power to forbid this, but it does make sense anyway. For use of the freezer, see Chapter Ten.

• *Water systems* •

In small yachts these are usually manually pumped; the larger boats normally have a pressure system. The best I know of is made by Godwin, but alas they have ceased to make them. As in most things, the Rolls-Royce job is getting hard to find and we have to make do with Mickey Mouse gear. Power consumption is negligible, and in *Fare Well* we had running hot and cold via the Perkins cooker. In *Hosanna*, the generator heats the water when neither the engines nor the central heating are running.

I know of some boats which use a header tank. One has a tall, narrow 5-gallon cylinder inside the mainmast with a visual sight glass. The skipper pumps water up each morning and has a very exact check on consumption. Knowing him, I bet he has a lock on the pump! Usually live-aboards use more water than holidaymakers; again it is a question of wanting a higher standard of living for long stays.

I would make sure that the yacht has capacious fresh-water tanks; most production boats, being dedicated to weekend use, are poorly fitted. *Fare Well* had 400 imperial gallons, and without any drastic economy measures we used about 10 per day. With two guests extra, this rose to about 13. For an ocean voyage we exercised a little economy and used 5 gallons on average, laundry day always being an upset to the calculations. Probably tankage of 200 gallons, or 1000 litres, is the minimum for comfortable living and water security. (NB: American gallons are smaller than British, the rogues!)

Water-makers are becoming a practical proposition at last. We once wrote that they converted a gallon of diesel into a gallon of barely usable water, but the ratio has improved. It is still an expensive way to make fresh water and it needs maintenance. Having a good awning with a hose connection is an effective rainwater catcher. The canvas must be strong – water is heavy.

• *Stowage* •

One of the major factors in the accommodation aboard a long-term cruiser is the relationship between bunks and stowage. Ocean racers can get by on half a cubic foot per man, but such an allowance would make for marital discord, and in time a pretty smelly crew. (It is hard to think of a cubic foot in metric terms, the units are just not amenable to such matters. I suppose a cubic foot is about 28 litres, though I think of litres more in connection with drink.)

In tropic conditions, when humidity can be high (and the same applies during a scirocco in the Med), the best way of stowing clothes is the hanging cupboard or wardrobe. Though women's clothes are smaller and lighter, the female needs (and demands, and uses) rather more space than a man. If we were to decide on a requirement of 4 feet (1.2m) of wardrobe bar for a couple (and this is a bit on the mean side) it would indicate 70cm for her, and 50cm for him. Generally guests need only about 15cm each.

The problem is that while living afloat one has to carry on board full outfits of hot weather decent, hot weather indecent or casual; the same for temperate climes; and finally bulky winter garments for both sea and shore. Whereas a man is moderately content to put on a shapeless old sweater to do the winter shopping, most ladies prefer to look a little less like an itinerant scarecrow.

Each person living on board ought to have about 12 cubic feet (say 350 litres) of good dry locker or drawers for clothing, quite apart from the wardrobe and any oilskin stowage. I like to provide a guest with 2 cubic feet, enough for a two-to three-week stay.

Food stowage is not such a problem in most EU countries where one is seldom far from a good market, but in the oceans, remote Greek islands, the West Indies or Bahamas, one does need a fair bit of tin space. The bilges are traditionally used for this. With dry bilges, tins keep for long periods, years even. We did once have a labelling problem by stowing tins in the bilge just above the prop. The vibration made the tins rotate slowly and wore off the labels, leaving the tins brightly polished. It took some time to trace the cause for we didn't go down there while motoring.

Stowage for tools and spare parts

Tools are very important, and by keeping the boat dry, I have had few bad rust problems without taking any elaborate precautions. One has to keep some tools handy. *Fare Well* had five large drawers, each one subdivided, in the deckhouse close to the main hatch. There is seldom a hardware store round the corner at sea.

By the same token, spare parts are a problem. Most of the spares we started with are still intact in their wrappers: it has always been something else that has gone wrong. So the quantity carried has grown and grown, and the ship has settled deeper and deeper into the water. It is necessary to make a list of the spares to carry:

- Class A spares: the lack of which would cause severe problems.
- Class B spares: from those suppliers who are so bad, slow or unreliable that one is obliged to carry them on board.
- Class C spares: from those companies who can be relied on to help you out of a hole if their product goes wrong, by sending a spare by a fast and convenient carrier.

One should make a policy of buying the products of companies in class C: they deserve every encouragement. Unfortunately there are occasions where one has to patronise a mediocre outfit, and the more you do, the more spares you have to carry.

Chart stowage

Designers seldom give sensible thought to this. I have seen a claim for a boat to be well endowed with space under the chart table for 25 charts, a height of about ½ in (12mm). A yacht's outfit (a full one would be much larger) of charts for the UK to the Med, the Med itself, Black and Red Seas, the Middle Atlantic, the West Indies, Bahamas and the USA comes to a stack 2ft (60cm) high, and is probably the heaviest movable item on board. And quite possibly one of the most expensive, too.

Navigational publications for the same areas, ie pilot books, tables, almanacs etc, occupy 10ft (3m) of bookshelf; and while it is true that I have one or two old chums among these which are not a great deal of practical use any more, the figure is not far out. We have 16 Admiralty Pilots alone. Then there are catalogues, a few books giving advice on problems, multi-language nautical dictionaries, and instruction books for equipment. To the suggestion that one does not need all these charts or books at once, the answer is that they have to be on board because the ship is one's home. There is no other place: no shed at the bottom of the garden, no convenient storage at Grandma's that one can easily get to.

Other books can be a problem too. People who have been brought up to read seem to need books to keep in practice, and books abhor damp. The worst are those printed on glossy paper, whose pages tend to stick together. (Yachting magazines are bad offenders.) Thank heaven Penguin and others publish a good list of paperback reference books.

• Ventilation •

The frequent mention of dampness leads naturally to ventilation and light. We have already referred to the possibility of moisture coming in the ventilator, but unfortunately other things can get in too. A good wire mesh (which should be of bronze because rats eat plastic) is desirable to exclude mosquitoes, rats and mice. (See Chapter Seven for more on pests.)

In really hot weather it is nice to have windows that open, though our steel boat is often cooler down below than on deck, largely because she is well insulated. The problem with opening windows is that they are seldom completely watertight, nor are windows and openings of whatever type. Our fixed windows have aluminium frames, as do the skylights. They all give a little trouble from time to time because after eight years the sun has perished the rubber-like compound in which the glass or acrylic is bedded, and one comes to the conclusion that the aluminium-framed opening or window is not really good enough for the long term. Replacing seals is a tedious job, and I cannot recommend an alternative system, though we all badly need a better one.

It is not necessary to have windows of the miniature mousehole size so often counselled by the old salts in the magazines. I have heard tell of Messrs Camper & Nicholson selling a large yacht to an American who, to demonstrate that their windows were not strong enough, hit them and broke them with a hammer, telling the builders that that was the type of force that they would need to withstand. While having every sympathy with an owner in quest of confidence in his vessel, I feel also for the builders, who had already fitted extra strong glass, which was almost certainly adequate. Don't forget that the windows have to be very well fastened into the surrounding hull.

We have had a couple of very severe storms in *Fare Well* and been knocked down until the deckhouse was submerged, but our hull and deckhouse windows (considered too large by some) have done well. (A few squirts got through, but they were not particularly noticeable in the ensuing disorder.) The 10mm toughened glass in the deckhouse windows measured 94 x 48cm, while that in the biggest hull window was 43 x 30cm. It is possible to build the boat like an armoured submarine: the best thing for the nervous is to have removable deadlights of ¼ in (6mm) aluminium plate, and enjoy the pleasure of good windows for 99% of the time.

As beforementioned, though it may be very nice to contemplate a cooling breeze coming down a skylight or ventilator just over your bunk, do not do it. Sooner or later the breeze will come with water. It takes just one second to get your bedding wet; it takes ages at sea to get it even tolerably dry. One can tell the boats with this design fault as they arrive in Barbados or the Azores: their drying mattresses are slung across the main boom, and the telltale banners of their shame are drying in the rigging. Surprising how often these boats have been well reviewed in the magazines.

One sees many boats with miniature fans. We have an exhaust fan above the galley stove, but no other, and I am not inclined to add one, though visitors fresh from the cool of an English summer sometimes mention the heat. In big ships, I have had to sleep under a hot steel deckhead with two fans directed onto my unclothed body, but this should be unnecessary in a well-ventilated and insulated yacht.

BOUZOUKI SHOP, CHIOS

• Heads •

'The Beak-head is . . . of great use as well for the grace and countenance of the ship, as a place for men to ease themselves in' [This is the derivation of the sailor's term head.]

Two heads are better than one, for sooner or later one will become a blocked head, usually while guests are on board. This is not always due to items being put down the heads without being eaten first (watch out for people who swallow their cherry stones), though that is often the trigger. The underlying cause is usually scale owing to the salinity of the water. It is necessary to dismantle the flexible tubing every six months or so and beat it against the quay, preferably when there are few people about, and when wearing a hat. An alternative method is to flush the loo a few times with a 10% solution of hydrochloric acid, which can be bought over the counter in most Med countries for just this purpose. It is not a way endorsed by the manufacturers, but it works. The Mediterranean Sea has high salinity.

We changed the heads on board to Lavac because this loo has a separate pump above the basin. We carry a spare pump so if a loo pump becomes blocked it is a comparatively simple task to fit the spare, leaving the unpleasant servicing job to a more convenient time. We originally fitted a holding tank head because it looked as if everywhere was going ecology mad, but well-meaning attempts to control yacht heads generally ended in an administrative shambles, as in the USA where, except for waterways with locks, the legislation was discreetly ignored.

Since then, the ecology war has hotted up. Turkey has become most aggressive. It seems that both the informer and the magistrate get a proportion of the fine levied for infractions; there must be some inducement for the local peasantry to be so eager to shop foreign offenders even for emptying the washing up basin, and the fines are disproportionate. We accept that in certain marinas, such as Marmaris, where the enclosed harbour is anyway in a bay with little water movement, and the Arsenal Basin in the centre of Paris, some control is necessary at the height of the busy tourist season. Even so, we have found the regulation being rigidly enforced in a quasi-open port where the town's sewage system already drains untreated into the sea.

We anchored in a bay in Grenada where it was forbidden to use the ship's heads. There were five other boats there, in a water plane of about 5000 square metres. With a tidal range of a metre, that bay was flushed twice daily by 5000 tonnes of water. Just how sensible or necessary are some of the restrictions that the more barmy ecologists so enthusiastically impose?

Now, in *Hosanna,* we have two 140-litre galvanised soil tanks which will cope with a fairly long stay in port, especially with only two of us on board. And *no,* we have never yet been accused of pollution: we are not by nature polluters, we just exercise common sense.

• *Washing* •

If the electrical situation will stand it, it is worth having some sort of washing machine. In the larger boats, where the machine is usually plumbed in, take care that the whole system has some sort of drip tray under it, for almost all machines spill a little water, and even if your hull will not rust, the gungy soapy mush will soon expand like hair-setting mousse and fight you for possession of your ship.

Most authorities recommend that sullage tanks, to take drainage from sinks, showers and washbasins below the waterline, should be enclosed. Our experience is the opposite. *Fare Well* had an open sump in the keel, in which was a submersible pump and an automatic switch operated by air pressure as the water level in the sump rose. (Float switches are unreliable.) Received opinion is that this is supposed to be smelly and nasty. It was situated in the engine room, which was well ventilated, and it did not seem to smell at all, or at least not as much as the engine, and it had the big advantage that any gunge could be easily observed and readily dealt with.

• *Guest cabins* •

Some yachts equip themselves with guest cabins in the hope that they can do the occasional charter to help pay their way. I am in two minds about this. It seems to me that chartering is getting ever more professional and customers are demanding more and more facilities. In these conditions, agencies are not too keen on the casual charter, which in any event is never so lucrative as the professional. Charterers can also be hard to find just when the owner wants them. The alternative is to devote that space to more comfortable living. Of course, when friends come to visit they have no super-cabin, but our friends are the sort who would holiday with us in a 5-tonner, and we can accommodate them better than that. However, it does not solve any financial problems for the owner. Double bunks are now accepted but it is as well to have a method of dividing them, even for non-marital reasons. Part of our padded headboard can be lifted out and slotted fore and aft to make two very comfortable sea berths.

All in all, do not over-concentrate on the boat as a boat. Think of her as living room for a good deal of the time. If you can do so before buying or finishing her, sit aboard and use your imagination. Surprising what you might come up with.

HOW TO COMPARE CRUISING BOATS

'Considerations for a Sea Captain in the choise of his ship'

It is comparatively easy to contemplate a yacht which one is going to use for a purpose that is already thoroughly familiar. However, not many people will be familiar with the complete dedication to the way of life required of a confirmed live-aboard long-distance cruiser. If they are, then they are unlikely to need any help choosing a boat, but for those who would like to consider another person's outlook, I have devised the following rough assessment system. I do not expect it to stand rigorously when applied to any and every boat, but it can be used to give an idea of whether a yacht is a suitable design for long-term cruising. One can then eliminate a lot of the rubbish and end up by choosing on one's personal tastes and that feeling of attraction to a craft that is the foundation of a true boat marriage.

For my part, I like to say something is lousy if I have good reason for saying so. You could probably say it about this evaluation scheme: I know it's not perfect, it is just something of a contribution to the debate.

• *Cooper's Yacht Evaluator* •

Take a piece of paper and a pen. Draw two columns, head one *Sea* and the other *Comfort*. The questions are arranged so that an affirmative answer will score as indicated in one column or the other (sometimes in both), while a negative answer will not score. Where a question is complicated there will probably be a few words of clarification immediately following. Part One is divided into two parts, for monohulls and multihulls; obviously each yacht can be considered under only one of these headings.

QUESTIONNAIRE

MONOHULL SECTION

		Sea	Comfort
1	Length overall of ship: is it under 30ft?	0	−2
	30–35ft?	1	1
	35–40ft?	2	3
	40–50ft?	2	4
	over 50ft?	1	4
2	Draught: is it under 6ft?	0	4
	6–6$^1/_2$ft?	2	2
	6$^1/_2$–7ft?	2	0
	over 7ft?	2	−4
3	Is the length of the keel bottom more than half the waterline length?	2	0
4	Is the after lower tip of the rudder less than $^1/_5$ of the length overall from the stern?	−3	−1
5	Is there a retroussé transom?	−2	−1
6	Is the keel bottom horizontal, or nearly so?	1	0

MULTIHULL SECTION

		Sea	Comfort
7	Length overall: under 26ft?	−1	0
	26–33ft?	0	1
	33–40ft?	1	3
	over 40ft?	1	4
8	Is there an automatic sheet-release gear?	2	0

COMBINED, ALL TYPES

9	Is there clear standing headroom throughout at least 50% of the accommodation?	0	5
10	Is there a wheelhouse?	1	3
	Or, if not, is the conning position well protected?	2	1
11	Deck integrity. Is the area of cockpit (including seats) below the level of the main watertight deck:		
	nil?	5	0
	less than 24sqft?	3	0
	between 24 and 40sqft?	0	0
	over 40sqft?	−4	1
12	For each hatch or skylight score	−1	1
13	For each Dorade-type ventilator over 4in dia. score	0	1
14	For each hatch or skylight over a bunk	0	−4
15	Is the mast(s) in tabernacle(s)?	0	1
16	Is there a triatic stay?	−1	0
17	Is there room for a bicycle on deck?	−1	1
18	Can a rigid tender be carried aboard?	1	2
19	Is it easy to get aboard from the water?	1	1
20	Easy access from shore by either bow or stern?	0	2
21	Are there more than four openings below the waterline?	−2	0
22	Add together the breaking strain of all standing rigging that reaches the deck (see table at end). If the total is greater than:		
	7 x displacement in tons	10	0
	6 x	7	0
	5 x	4	0
	less than 5 x	0	0
	less than 4 x	−6	0
23	Mast compression: if greater than:		
	2 x displacement in tons	10	0
	if greater than: 1.5 x	5	0
	if less than: 1.5 x	−10	0

Calculation of compression strain is somewhat complex; there are yacht designers who have never heard of Euler's formula. If you can find out from a mast maker, well and good; or you could try the approximation given in Skene's *Elements of Yacht Design*; or omit this question.

24	We define the foretriangle as the distance from the foot of the forestay to the foreside of the mast at deck, times half the height of the mast as far as the highest foresail halyard sheave.		
	If this is greater than 40% of area of all plain sail	−4	−2
	If greater than 50%	−6	−3
25	Are there running backstays?	−2	0
26	Is there a permanent gallows for the main boom?	1	1
27	Are there internal halyards?	−2	0
28	Is there roller reefing/furling on headsail?	4	3
29	Is there roller gear on main and mizzen?	3 1	1 0
30	For each sail over 400sq ft?	−3	0
31	For a yacht over 10 tons displacement are there two or more geared sheet winches?	2	0

ANCHORS ETC

32	Is the bower (main) anchor self-stowing?	2	1
33	If the bower is over 40lbs (25kg), is there a power windlass?	1	3
34	Bower anchor cable. Is it chain, more than		
	150ft (40m)?	4	0
	less than 150ft (40m)?	1	0
	all nylon?	−2	−1

Bower anchor size. Calculate frontal area of craft: multiply mast height from waterline by beam of hull, both in feet. (I know the boat is not that wide at the top of the mast, but the wind is a lot stronger up there and this is a good approximation.) Divide this area by 8. This gives desirable anchor weight in pounds, and applies to Danforth, CQR and Bruce anchors. Anchors of other types score nothing, and that includes imitations of above.

35	If no anchor of above size	−5	0
	If one anchor of above size	4	0
	If two	6	0
	If three	7	0

(One might reasonably have one or two additional anchors at about three-quarters this size for use as a kedge or lunch-hook.) Q35 applies only to conventional sailing yachts.

36	Chain cable size. Take one quarter of anchor weight in kilos, add 2, and this gives cable diameter in mm.		
	If chain diameter over or equal to above size	4	0
	If chain smaller	−4	0
	(Minimum acceptable 1/4 in (6mm).)		
37	Is the engine petrol (gasoline)?	−4	−2

No.	Question		
38	Does fuel tankage in litres exceed 12 x engine hp?	1	4
39	Is there a second means of generating electricity?	0	3
40	Are deck and hull skin well insulated?	0	4
41	Are there two separate batteries?	1	2
42	Fresh-water tanks. At least two, with total capacity in litres more than 40 x displacement in tonnes?	0	4
	Two tanks but more than 6 x	0	0
	One tank only (ignore rubber tanks)	−1	−6
43	Can you sit down on all four sides of the engine?	0	2
44	Do you have access to the engine without dismantling half the accommodation?	0	1
45	Is the heating system independent of electricity?	0	2
46	Is cooking by either diesel, paraffin or bottled gas?	0	1
47	Is the cooker either gimballed or fully fiddled?	0	1
48	Is there a fiddled draining board or putting-down space?	0	1
49	Is there a refrigerator?	0	1
50	Does total dry locker space for clothes exceed 6 cu ft (160 litres) per permanent bunk?	0	2
51	Number of permanent berths. Divide displacement in tons by number of berths:		
	if over 5	0	6
	under 5 but over 4	0	3
	under 4 but over 3	0	1
	under 2	0	−5
52	Is there separate saloon and sleeping accommodation?	0	3
53	Is there a WC compartment with shower (heads)?	0	2
54	Non-clothing stowage, above the cabin sole: is there more than 1.5cu ft (40 litres) per ton displacement?	0	2
55	Is there a good clear area of deck for lounging?	0	1
56	Is there an autopilot?	2	4
57	If no autopilot, is there a windvane?	2	2
58	Is an echosounder fitted?	1	0
59	Are there at least two deck cleats, eyes or bitts, each capable of taking a lateral pull of half the weight of the boat without pulling out?	4	0

(How to tell? Well, it's a bit difficult to provide a complete answer: such a fitting will probably look too big, but won't be. If in any doubt, it's not big enough.)

TABLE OF APPROXIMATE BREAKLOADS

for 1 x 19 stainless steel wire, for use with the above Questionnaire:

Circumference (in)	Approx diameter (mm)	Breakload (lb)
5/8	4	4700
3/4	6	8000
1	8	12000
1¼	10	17500
1½	12	30000
1¾	14	46000

To evaluate the boat add the scores of each column separately. The *Sea* column is meant to give some estimate of whether the yacht is fit to go to sea at all as a cruising boat. Do not expect the score to be conclusive; I am quite sure that there could well be exceptions, but most really worthwhile cruising boats should score well over 50 points.

The *Comfort* column has a broad coverage of those factors which affect one's standard of living; the idea is not to provide sybarism to a grand standard but to try to achieve a living above the 'grotty squalor' level, the sort of compromise between comfortable existence at sea and relaxed life in port. A good score in the Comfort column would be 60, but 50 might be treated as a minimum.

We have inevitably leaned heavily on our own preferences and opinions but have tried to allow for other points of view. If you have a strong opinion on some factor that differs from ours, then give it your own weighting; the important thing is to use common criteria for all vessels surveyed.

For interest, we reckon *Fare Well* scores 58 + 65. Bear in mind that all boats are something of a compromise between sea-keeping and comfort.

A problem with this 'evaluator' is that it takes time to assess each yacht; it is a detailed examination giving a weighting of some sort to most things worthwhile in a live-aboard yacht. To save time one should have a means of quickly discarding unsuitable craft by drawing up a shortlist. Keep the two broad criteria, seaworthiness and comfort. l suggest the following are seriously on the debit side in assessing seaworthiness in the context of this book:

- Deep, short, fin keel which tends to directional instability.
- Rudder hung right aft, which is vulnerable to damage, and also becomes inefficient when pitching in a following sea.
- Large foretriangle with bermudan rig is tough on small crews.
- Main shroud chainplates well inside deck edge (leads to higher tension in shrouds and greater compression in mast).
- Anchors not self-stowing, hard on weaklings like us.

- Running backstays are a pain in the transom.
- Bendy masts often bend too far, right over perhaps.
- Two or more sails over 400 sq ft (40 m²). Tough on small crews.
- Steeply cambered decks are a poor foothold. In theory OK on one side when heeled. In practice, at sea one is never at a constant angle.
- Guardrails less than 30in (75 cm) high are tripwires.
- Cockpit that is not self-drained, and adequately so.

All things are a compromise, but I think I would not like to trust my life in a yacht with more than five of the above debit points.

Items that detract seriously from the joy of living in a yacht are more idiosyncratic. Make your own list, but consider:

- Lack of good shelter at the steering position.
- Lack of separate sleeping/daytime accommodation.
- Cockpit that is uncomfortable to lounge about in.
- Lack of a simple heating system.
- Insufficient fresh water (less than 250 gallon (1000 litres)).
- Poor hanging lockers.
- Poor ventilation.
- Engine access in living space.
- Pokey little galley, ill-lit or ill-ventilated.
- Less than 20ft (6 m) of bookshelves.

I would not be very comfortable in a yacht with many of these points. Set your own limit: five perhaps.

In the end, whether you are looking at the short assessment or the more detailed, you have to face the fact that logic often plays second fiddle to love in the choice of both spouses and boats. Did you really go through all this sort of thing before choosing your wife? Minus three for a long nose, plus two for good puddings? Of course you didn't (I hope). And you probably won't choose your yacht this way either, but you might have fun looking at a few.

NAMING YOUR BOAT

When we came to registering our new home (*Hosanna*) we had to face up to the problem of naming her. We would have liked to keep her existing Dutch name, *De Tijd zal 'tLeren IV,* which means 'Time will teach you', but we do not like names which have numbers after them, and we had found it impossible to cope with the Dutch name outside Holland. Almost unpronounceable to the English, it would be completely so to the French, Italians and Greeks; it promised us a lifetime

The boarding ladder made a useful platform when Laurel repainted our name at Porto Sto Stefano.

devoted to spelling it out in full and having radio messages garbled out of recognition. *Hosanna* she became. It is a word that is reasonably common to all languages, it is cheerful, and it doesn't tread on anyone's toes. Things which have to be thought of, or should be, if one is off to foreign cruising grounds. Also it is one of the traditional Lowestoft fishing boat names; names with a ring to them like Kipling's trawler-minesweepers;

'Call up *Unity, Clarabell, Assyrian,*
Stormcock and *Golden Gain*'

If you intend long-distance cruising it is as well not to give your boat names like *Ploughboy of Loughborough*, or *Pwllhelly Phyllis*. Make up your own little list of impossibles. We once came across an Italian yacht called *Titty*. And off the coast of the USA we overheard a distress call from a boat called *Sexy Lady*. It was very difficult to take it seriously, and who wants ribaldry if in trouble.

In the West Indies, where all the local traders keep watch on VHF, we heard a very aristocratic English voice calling 'Scuba Shop, this is *Darling Two*'. Eventually a deep bass Paul Robeson voice answered, 'Halloo, Darling!'

Even our beloved old *Fare Well*, which you might have thought was straightforward enough, was written down sometimes as *Fairly Well*, or *Fairy Well*, and on one never to be forgotten document in Turkey as *Fart Well*. Take care.

7 • People, Pets and Pests

*'There are so many young Captaines and those that desire to be
Captaines, who know very little, or nothing at all to any purpose'*

A great many preconceived notions can be left on the quay on departure with the cardboard boxes, empty beer crates, broken gadgets bought at the Boat Show, and other cruising detritus. Among these could be stereotypes long overdue for discard, such as: old ladies cannot be expected to climb on board boats, girls can't row, children are not useful, and pets are a nuisance at sea.

You now enter a world where many a nippy granny leaps lightly into a dinghy and trims it without being asked as others follow. She has probably steered a yacht in a gale on an Atlantic crossing. Yon lovely girl, so slim and ethereal, can probably get the starboard jibsheet to the winch and hove in while you are still thinking about it, let alone row you a mile ashore. The rope you have just thrown to a likely-looking native, who is standing there looking perplexed while the wind carries you rapidly away from the quay, is apt to be seized by a tow-headed eight-year-old, who makes a bowline in the wink of an eye, drops it over the upwind bollard, and disappears down the companionway of that little Dutch sloop. As for pets, my crew would never be complete without a cat.

Without too much prejudice, then, let us look at who can do what on board, and how to avoid unnecessary conflict.

It is no longer true that 'Captain' equals 'male'. Many girls and women are Skippers these days, so when I speak of Captains please believe that they are not exclusively masculine. I am more familiar with a male Skipper, and being told what to do as regards navigation and ship handling. Other areas are my concern: the feeding, health and welfare of the crew are in my charge. In case of bodily accidents, I take over; not because I know more than Bill, but because in that situation I have a cool head and don't mind the blood. Much. Also, Bill still has to sail the boat. (Ah! you say: but what if the Skipper has the accident? We'll come to these things in Chapter Eleven.) I am also in charge of victualling and storing for long voyages, which is as it should be since I am usually also the shopper and cook.

HOW TO BE CAPTAIN

'The Captaine's charge is to command all.'

Our good Captain Smith once again says it all in a nutshell. The one person who need not worry about his status is the Captain: it is never in doubt. No company president, managing director, or even eminent surgeon on his rounds tailed by milling underlings, can know the power of being Master Under God (as the Lloyd's policy puts it) of a ship, however small. The rest of us, according to another well-known source, are a little lower than the angels, which presumably puts the Captain slightly above them. This gives him a natural authority instantly recognised by landsmen, which is not surprising. What *is* perhaps surprising is that the quiet authority of a good Captain is recognised by all, including his/her spouse even when he/she is in bare feet and ragged shorts.

No ship can ever run satisfactorily as a commune: the job of a Captain is to be Captain. I have never been Captain (except for a few hours entering the Turkish port of Datça, when Bill had a bad attack of Saladin's Revenge), so of course I have every right to comment on the subject, especially from the point of view of the crew. I use the word 'Capting' to signify bossiness without leadership, so if I answer my spouse, 'Yes, Capting', he knows I consider he is merely throwing his weight about and not giving sensible orders. He does not do it often.

- A good Captain explains a manoeuvre in advance, and thus does not need to shout complicated instructions at a bewildered crew at the last minute.
- His orders are clear and unambiguous, thus he does not need to repeat them with rising hysteria and ever-increasing decibels.
- If his crew make a mess of it, he wastes no time cursing. He says, 'All right, folks: we go round and do it again.' (He is allowed to grit his teeth, however.) Always start from *now*!
- If he makes an error of judgement he accepts it without fuss and does not blame his crew for it.
- He does not get too excited if the anchor cable comes in slowly, when it always does come in slowly.
- He shouts when ambient noise at the crew's end makes it necessary.

Having said that:

- Captains are the ultimate authority on everything connected with the ship and crew. Wise mates and knowledgeable crew may help him to make the decisions, but he is the arbiter.
- He should make sure all on board know his policy on certain important mishaps and events, such as fire, shipwreck and man overboard.
- He should be able to delegate many tasks, but it must be clear whose responsibility they are, and he should be prepared to back up his delegate with authority. It is important that he should be loyal to his crew, as they are to him.

The Captain: ultimate authority over everything connected with ship and crew.

A good Captain is recognisable not by his autocracy and didacticism, but by the respect in which he is held by his crew. It is not necessary for him to be the best qualified one on board, since it is possible for highly qualified people to be bad Captains. This is not to say that experience and knowledge are not to be acquired wherever possible; but courses of instruction should be carefully selected by recommendation rather than picked with a pin from alluring ads in the yachting press. Thus you will avoid those courses run by old and bold military men who are nutty about semaphore, and condescend to your wife. 'This the little woman?' they roar, 'Soon make a good cabin boy out of you, eh? Can she cook?'

The Yachtmaster's Certificate, for example, is all useful knowledge and updated at intervals; but to have gained it is not the be-all and end-all, nor is the Coast Guard Captain's Licence in the USA. There is a danger, in fact, that such certificates entrain dubious feelings of an all-powerful super-knowledge of the sea. Bill has occasionally had to be very tactful (which doesn't come easily), when given shouted and peremptory advice by Yachtmasters off their home patch, advice which would have been inappropriate at best, and dangerous at worst.

Both these admirable qualifications tend to be oriented towards local waters and conditions, and should be regarded as forming merely a basis for a great deal of further experience: there will be much to learn about sailing in distant parts, and much nautical wisdom yet to be acquired. After over 50 years at sea, one thing we have learned is to give advice only when asked for it, or when a real and unnoticed danger threatens. We, too, are still learning.

A good Captain conducts an orchestra in which he may not play the bassoon too well, but he knows its function as part of the whole and all the players look to him for direction. Or to *her*, of course, since conductors and Captains may well be women these days. This causes no bother to most people, as she is usually in this position because her crew feels comfortable about her being there. It is again a question of respect. If certain bigoted and reactionary people find it intolerable to take orders from a woman, they must go and find a bigoted and reactionary Captain who will suit them better.

Every Captain will make mistakes, and sometimes they will be serious. Apportioning blame may be balm to the wounded spirit, but it is unproductive. After disasters, start from *now*. He may find himself in dire straits through no fault of his own, or indeed anyone's, and he will still blame himself. We left Bermuda with an excellent weather forecast, heading north with the expectation of leaving the West Indies well before the hurricane season: June, the rhyme goes, is too soon (for the hurricanes to come). On 18 June, two days out, we got warning of a tropical storm, which had rapidly deepened into Hurricane Alberto. After the vortex had passed us, with no great damage, we were struck by a violent squall and a flash of lightning, early in the morning.

Bill's only crime was being on watch when it happened, but the shock of it, and the despair at seeing our sails in ribbons, laid him very low for a while. We were three on board. The watch below, Nora and I, were precipitated up on deck by the noise and the knockdown. Even if richly deserved, recriminations are unaffordable luxuries at such times, and this squall had been far too sudden for any action to be effective. Nora and I made comforting and reassuring noises to our stricken Captain, and as soon as I could get the stove going we fed him on quantities of scrambled egg, since we were in no immediate danger and all had headaches from the lightning strike. Then we took a deep breath, and under his direction began to restore the ship to order. We were still 400 miles from land and it was going to be a slow and uncomfortable voyage, but it had to be faced. We arrived in Newport Rhode Island 11 days overdue, with considerable material damage, but no bodily harm. Neither Master nor crew can say in the middle of a difficult passage, 'I don't want to play any more.'

What if the Captain and crew really don't get on at all? Suppose your Skipper, at the yacht club bar so smooth and full of salty tales of successful voyages and dangers overcome, turns out to be sufficiently bogus to be a menace to both his ship and crew? Suppose he retires to his bunk at times of stress, abdicating to his crew decisions which he should make, and for which he will later blame them? (This is a true story, and happened to a friend of ours who is a very experienced crew, on passage from the Bahamas to Gibraltar. She continued to the end of the voyage, and although the ship reached Europe some 600 miles north of the position the cataleptic skipper thought he was in, no physical hurt or damage occurred, probably due to a good crew on the watch for trouble.)

Suppose the apparently athletic girl taken on for crossing the Atlantic screams when the boat heels, or is afraid of the dark and won't keep night watches? Or the strong lad turns out to be impossible to live with? Most incompatibilities of this kind can be avoided by a shakedown cruise, with no commitment on either side. Living aboard is about long-term tolerance, so a series of weekends or holidays afloat are not really the answer, though they may reveal intolerably irritating habits or personality aspects. You need to fight your way through a few situations to find out how you are going to get on under stress. To be able to duck out of trouble too easily, as you mostly can on weekend and holiday cruising, negates the point of the exercise. Most of all, you need time to work together and evolve an everyday smoothness of running, so that routine tasks become second nature, and there is more time and energy to cope with unexpected surprises. Thus, while no one is perfect, you will not set off on a long cruise with someone who rubs you up the wrong way. I have said elsewhere that marriages may not survive the strains imposed on them by the cruising life (this goes for friendships and Captain/crew relationships too), but marital breakdown, mutiny, mid-Atlantic mayhem and murder are outside the scope of this book. Not far outside, though.

As you will have noticed, many observations that can be made about Captains are inextricably entangled with those about crew, since they are two sides of the same coin.

• *The Pierhead Jump* •

Should a short-handed Captain take on a 'pierhead jump' (an unknown crew who joins at the last moment)? It is a desperate measure, fraught with risk and uncertainty. Only the Captain can weigh need against risk. In the West Indies, such a crew must possess an air ticket outward before being allowed to sign off the crew list of any vessel. It is the Captain's responsibility to ensure that such a ticket exists, or he risks being landed with the person indefinitely. We have sometimes taken on someone at short notice: all but one were a great success, all but one came with recommendations from people we knew and trusted. Many couples we know have had a very different experience, however, even resulting in vowing never to take crew again however short-handed they were. The sins of the said crew varied from drug abuse, smuggling, theft and laziness, to actually taking command of the yacht in mid-Atlantic from an elderly couple who were powerless to stop them.

Only once we took a crew whose recommendation did not come from someone who knew them well and had sailed with them. We relied on the endorsement of someone for whom they had done a painting job. We regretted it all the way from Gibraltar to the Azores. (Our insurers had sprung on us, at the last minute, a requirement to have more than two persons on board for ocean sailing, a requirement they have since modified at our suggestion.)

Be aware that if drugs are found on your boat, the boat is liable to confiscation, even if you were unaware of the existence of the drugs. It is not necessarily the hippier-looking people who take or deal in drugs. Which takes us back to reliable references, living with prospective crew for a little while to discover their attitudes and habits, with, these days alas, a certain amount of healthy suspicion of anything that does not quite add up. At close quarters, one has a better chance of finding out before it is too late. We come, inevitably, to:

HOW TO BE CREW

'The saylors are the elder men, for hoising the sailes, haling the bowlings, and stearing the shippe'

There is no task in a boat that is sexually exclusive. Some jobs require brawn, and there are women who can do them and have enough breath left to whistle at the same time. Others of us are rather less muscular, but perhaps good at fiddly jobs requiring great patience. Apart from being helpful, tolerant, humorous at the right moment and tactful, it helps to have a little knowledge.

For *absolute beginners* and a few others we could name, we include a 'starter pack' on one or two essentials. While unlikely to prove the definitive work on the subject (indeed, this book is not about seamanship), *no one who has taken in the full import of this section is useless.* Anyone who can make a bowline, and has learnt the intelligent use of fenders without bumping into the rest of the crew, is already of considerable help; I particularly address myself to those windblown lovelies who are so disrespectfully called 'crew's comforts' by their companions.

• *Laurel and Bill's Starter Pack for Would-be Cruisers* •

'Here mayst thou learn the names of all ship's gear'

No one should embark on a long voyage or a life afloat without having acquired a minimum competence, which should be got not only by study but also partly by doing some boatwork. It is all very well to plan that the skipper will sail the boat to all intents and purposes as if singlehanded, and that his chosen crew will be entitled to consider themselves solely for catering and/or decorative purposes. It never turns out that way.

Circumstances will arise when it is a case of 'all hands to the something-or-other' and a certain basic knowledge of somethings-or-other would be no bad idea. Likely areas of difficulty are when berthing, or when others are berthing on you. There are occasions when sails will not do as they should, and no skipper, however brilliant, can see to both ends of a rope at once. People do fall overboard, they also fall in in harbour, especially from dinghies, and things do break or part.

Let us look at a checklist for the absolute novice so that he or she has, at the least, a basis on which experience can build.

WHAT A CREW MEMBER SHOULD KNOW

• Learn the names of important bits of boat or gear, so that you know what the skipper is talking about, especially if he is excited or overwrought. Examples: bows, stern, jib, genoa, mainsail, mizzen, sheets, halyards, topping lift, forward, aft, port and starboard. Know what he means when he says take a turn (or whatever term your own skipper uses to indicate bringing a rope to a cleat or winch), turn up, make fast, fend off, check or ease sheets, luff or bear away, haul, veer, cast off. Concentrate on the phraseology of your own skipper: it is more important to have certain and accurate communication than the precisely correct nautical jargon.

- Learn to tie a few nautical knots. We suggest the bowline is very important. Then comes the rolling hitch, the round turn with two half-hitches, the clove hitch, the sheet bend and the figure of eight. The reef (square) knot may be better than a granny, but it is a bad knot except for tying reef points, and perhaps also for tying two Boy Scouts together.
- Learn well that in boats over 10 tons, on no account try to stop them moving with hands or feet unless you have an amputation impulse. A fender is built for the job and does it very well if you play your part.
- Learn that when boats move towards a quay or each other there will be little or no damage if someone (why not you?) interposes a fat soft object (no, not you) so that the impact is absorbed.
- Learn that these fenders can be pre-positioned as a precaution and to save time, but that does not remove the need to see that in the event they are in the right position (where the impact takes place) and not too high or low.
- Learn to heave a line. Most yachts in the sizes we are writing about can be controlled by rope light enough to be thrown quite a long distance. (Remember to hold on to one end of it.) If berthing, when you have thrown your rope to the quay and some kind soul has made it fast there, adjust your end so that the rope has no slack and take one full turn round the cleat and back it up. There is more to it than this, but that is a basically useful thing to do: if the skipper wants the rope hauled or veered (tightened or let out), or made fast, he will say so. If you should be so unlucky as to make a riding turn (one that binds and cannot be undone while the strain is on it, and sometimes welds the rope inextricably even when the strain is off), your Captain will ensure that you learn rather quickly what it is, how to avoid it, and never to do it again.
- Learn to steer a compass course. It is not difficult and it gets easier with practice. It is a lovely feeling when you master the art.

When you are able to cope with the above you will be very useful on board if you keep alert and use your loaf. Your typical Able Seaman is no great genius. He has a few basic skills, some basic knowledge, but most comes as he sails. A lot of the mystique is pure bullshit.

With even this small amount of knowledge, you would be welcome in most yachts. Such happy beginners are more use than the theoretical know-all we once had on board, who while on watch and unbeknownst to the skipper, devised a splendid new lead for the jib sheet, which carried away the starboard rail when he tested it. He'd been to evening classes.

Next step: to be of real use as a trusted watchkeeper a crewmember should know:

WHAT A WATCHKEEPER SHOULD KNOW

- Where everything is kept, and what it is called.
- How to switch on the engine and use it for simple manoeuvres.
- What the normal reading should be for all dials and meters.
- How to lower and row the dinghy.
- The Rule of the Road at Sea (part B first, then C and D).
- Enough to plot a GPS fix on the chart.
- Basic sail and shiphandling.
- How to steer a compass course.
- The first steps to take in several various emergencies (MOB (man overboard), fire, taking in water, collision, grounding etc).
- How to use the VHF or other radio.
- How to use the GPS to steer a course, and key in the Man Overboard Position. (MOB)
- How to identify echoes on the radar and read off their ranges on the right scale.

(The RYA publish brochures which list recognised sailing schools, with details and prices of the courses run. Go on one, or go to evening classes; there's nothing wrong with them as long as you regard them as the beginning, and not the end, of your nautical education. You will learn some basics that will help you to understand a very rich craft and words of the vocabulary you will need to learn the language.)

We now have to recall that the crew and Captain are likely to be members of one family, or friends (long may they be so), and there is a lot to be said for everyone learning everything. In *Freya*, whom we met in the Chesapeake and the Bahamas, the family, with two young daughters, changed tasks daily so they all had their turn at engine bleeding, navigating, cooking and so on. This system might suit you very well. Diffident crew members also appreciate being given an area of personal concern, and time to research and study it. Such areas could be meteorology, cooking and victualling, radio, engines or first aid. The Captain does not have to do the navigation.

Bill and I use the 'specialist and backup' system. He is such a good navigator that it is hard for me to compete; but it would be obviously stupid for me not to know my coastal navigation. In the old days I could take a sun sight and work it out, however slowly and painfully, but satellite navigation has changed all that. Our GPS (Global Positioning System) has taught me so much about navigation that I am probably almost as dangerous as someone who has been to two evening classes. I can feed in waypoints, but get Bill to check that I've fed in the right points, with their correct latitude and longitude. It never does any harm for a second person to check these things. As with all computer-based programs (but with potentially lethal results if you are driving at sea in earnest and not from 4 Dagmar Terrace), if error goes in, error comes out. Errors at sea can mean rock, wreck and ruin.

I am a far better cook than the Skipper is so I do most of it, but when he has to

Laurel.

do it for a while we do not starve. When Bill is upside down in the engine room on a rough day at sea I am guiltily aware that I would far rather be steering, cooking, sail trimming and piloting (all at once) plus handing him his tools, tissues and tea, and receiving in exchange bad temper, blasphemy and blame. The 'dirty bits' of the boat are not for me, unless I am required to wriggle into some small corner that Bill is too big to get into. This gets me the job of packing grease into the shaft tunnel greasebox, and painting inaccessible holes and corners. In fact, I do most of the painting, after Bill has done the preparation. The miserable

Calvi,
Corsica

job of antifouling, so called because it *is* foul and most people are anti (the work, not the paint scheme), must be shared.

We are well aware that most cruising crews consist of one man and one woman, most of the time. It behoves both of you to be capable. Running a yacht properly requires teamwork of operating theatre calibre.

Whether your crew is large or small, we will suppose that they have been chosen after a shakedown cruise, and you have weeded out (or selected, according to pref-erence) smokers, vegetarians, flat-earthers and bridge fiends. Even when the crew has been tailored, as it were, to fit, irritating habits should be curbed. In a small space the utmost tact and tolerance is essential. Snoring, nail clippings, washing (either too much or too little), black hole filing systems and food fads are all annoying; make your own nasty little list. If the crew is the basic man/woman one, there should be room for you to sulk (as we do) at opposite ends of the boat till tempers are recovered. At sea, this is hardly necessary, since the days are busy, and we hardly meet at night except to hand over the watch and are usually pleased to see each other by breakfast time.

We have a little rhyme that describes the sort of crew we do not want to take with us. It goes:

> *No no-hopers, no topers,*
> *No one round the bend,*
> *No no-soapers, no gropers,*
> *No windbags (either end).*

CHILDREN AND BABIES

The children we meet who live aboard yachts are almost invariably courteous, at home in any company, pleasant to talk to, willing and reliable. They are integrated with their family in a way that is fast being forgotten when children no longer work alongside their parents at any demanding task, especially against time and the elements. Children in general now do not help with the harvest, mend the nets, help launch the lifeboat, or dig for victory as used to be the case; and so do not share with their parents the satisfaction of a difficult job well done. A sea voyage, however, is something that is achieved by the whole family; and the pride in it shines out of the children's eyes.

A single child often misses the company of other children, and plenty of opportunity should be found for mixing, since it is too easy in an adult environment, where responsibility is the watchword, for the child to forget how to be a child, and to find difficulty in relating to his own age group when the time comes.

If the child or children accompanying you are of school age, you have to face their education. Whether you do this alone, or with help from their teachers, or by correspondence course, you are in for a tough time. In Australia, France and the USA, correspondence courses are quite usual. Ten-year-old Ben Lucas on *Tientos* was working on an Australian course, which needed assistance from his mother Pat. The parents of Grant Dawson on *Iolanthe* had tried both the Calvert system (USA) (see Appendix C) and the British PNEU course. They preferred the latter as being more of a challenge. The Calvert system needed no assistance from parents since everything was provided down to the last pencil and eraser, and the child could be left to tackle it alone. Most parents prefer to be more actively involved, however, though it costs many hours of work.

One British couple we met had had remarkable co-operation from the state school that their child had attended: a stack of about 20 books was provided and a syllabus of work covering the next two years – which must have taken some dedicated teacher a lot of time and trouble to prepare. We doubt that such help would be available in the new millennium, given the present education budget problems.

However you go about it, it is no joke having to cope with lessons when you would rather be swimming; and this is as hard for the supervising parent as it is for the child. If you are temporarily in a yachtie community it can help to run 'the school' on one boat, in rotation: the children benefit from interaction and competition even if they are doing different courses, and only one parent need supervise the gang. Mornings are best for the heavy work, while the minds are fresh (you will notice that a good school timetable puts the maths and Latin before the first break if they can), leaving the more pleasurable side of things till later.

Thank goodness, there *is* the other side of the coin. Great delight and interest can be found in visits ashore, studying people and places, the local museums, the customs and culture of many lands; and some of the language does not come amiss either. There is also a wealth of sea and shore life: fish, birds, plants, dwellers in rock pools and in sand holes, shells, trees and flowers. Recognition books for all these things should be part of the 'school library'. A scrapbook will find a place for exotic bus tickets, postcards, programmes, labels and so on.

A well-kept log by each child combines many disciplines: writing, drawing, recording things seen, self-expression and observation are only a few of them. A rough book would help the preliminary layout of an attractive page. Since such a log will one day be a treasured reminder of the voyage, it would be worth presenting the child with a really important-looking hardcover book, such as are now available with unlined pages and attractive leather-type bindings, to encourage best efforts and the production of something to be immensely proud of.

With a laptop, encyclopaedias and other educational material in CD-Rom form take up little space, though in our experience they do not tell you a lot about, say, the island of Samos. Think of the effect on children to discover things from what they see and hear ashore, or from brochures at the tourist office, which they can write in their log: *things that the encyclopœdia does not know*! It goes without saying that computer skills will stand any child in good stead on their return to formal schooling. Computer games that all the family will enjoy might be good in bad weather, but on the whole shipboard life is too full and busy to need them, or indeed the telly, and it's such a relief to leave them behind.

Small babies pose few problems at sea. In a basic small yacht with a lack of gear that would raise eyebrows today my six-month-old required only feeding, a change of nappies (no disposables then) and a safe place to sleep; nothing else. She did not seem to be at all worried by even quite violent motion, and was certainly not seasick: this seems to come with the toddler stage. At times of stress (ours, not hers) we put her in a carry-cot wedged between the two forward bunks where, to our amazement, she learnt to stand up – briefly, before sitting down suddenly when we hit a wave.

As for feeding: battling with baby bottles and a Primus on a stormy night is a very good way to get scalded, as I discovered. Bottled milk is not nearly so convenient as draught, especially at sea: I have yet to hear of anyone coming to any grief through breastfeeding. You certainly don't get scalded. Nowadays I should probably use a cold-water method such as Milton for sterilisation of the bottles, and think of a foolproof way of warming the milk.

Baby food, in jars or tins, is widely available in the western Mediterranean, the USA and the bigger West Indian islands, but stock up if you are venturing farther, or to Eastern Europe (especially the old Communist Bloc). Take with you a small Moulinex, or some easy gadget to purée food for babies or invalids.

When my mother took me sailing at six weeks old (a daring thing to do in those days) she put me in a box of bran with a muslin square under me, and tossed out the damp bran as necessary. I have heard of sawdust, sand and seaweed being used in the same way. Kitty litter is feasible, but a little lumpy; it is great in a bucket for adults when the head gets blocked, but it is not available in the wilds. Nowadays we have disposable nappies (diapers to the cousins) and you would think that washing nappies was a thing of the past. So it is, in many parts of Europe and the USA where disposables are readily available. If you are going to remote places, however, they will be expensive and hard to find. They are too bulky to store many on board. Remember that disposal is getting more difficult as marinas and non-tidal basins get more and more fussy about what you throw, drain, drop, discharge, put, pee or spit into the water. You may have to revert to the terrycloth or muslin squares of Grandma's day, at least some of the time.

Mark and Felicity on *Scout* used a mixture of disposables and terry nappies for young Teresa. The terry ones were given a preliminary cleaning by towing astern, a watch being kept for dolphins who enjoy stealing them to play with. The nappies needed a thorough final rinse in fresh water, or terrible chafing and soreness would result. At 18 months, Teresa loved the shipboard life. She was used to being dunked in the water (many yachtie babies can swim at six months) so she had no fear of going underwater, but she could not quite swim yet without her inflatable armbands.

Yachts with small children on board usually reinforce the guardrails with netting, to fill in the gap down to the toerail that a small child might slip through. We had netting on the foredeck of *Fare Well* as we felt it was just as well to stop adults and sails falling through.

It has to be remembered that toddlers are all little Paganinis: great fiddlers. I watched recently, fascinated but unable to intervene, as three-year-old Suzanne on the neighbouring boat unpegged her mother's bikini from the guardrail and, chuckling, dropped it over the far side. We lent them our shrimping net, always handy for such events. Teresa loses tools and other objects by posting them into the rubbish bin. Sea mothers need even sharper eyes than their shore counterparts, since there are so many knobs, switches, buttons and hand pumps on a yacht; and they cannot all be put out of the reach of an active and curious toddler. I have seen a variety of ingenious devices to protect vital switches: shockcord, wedges, Perspex lids over a whole bank of them – necessity is the mother of invention.

In times of activity or crisis, babies are plonked in a safe place. This is essential for parents to get any peace at all. It takes the form of a playpen, or a well-wedged carrycot or 'padded cell'. The best idea, which I have seen many variations of, is

A very good safety idea for toddlers onboard – a car seat securely fixed to the cockpit with the baby safely strapped in.

the pilot berth transformed into a miniature nursery, well cushioned, with a strong net that snaps in place over the front. The baby comes to consider this as 'his', it is comfortable, full of his soft toys and comfort blankets or pillows, and he seldom objects to being put there for a spell. And even if he wimps a bit, you know he's safe and can be ignored till the rush is over or you have had your siesta. We have recently seen a toddler's car seat firmly fixed in the cockpit with the toddler happily strapped in, part of the family but safe in times of crisis or activity.

Children are people too, and while their skills are yet few they can be aided to feel valuable. They should join in all the activities they are capable of, and be taught the right way to do them. They should be given definite jobs to do, such as care of the fishing gear: teach them how to stick the hooks into a cork for safety. On long passages, they can be asked to read the speedlog at intervals and record the result. It can be their job to identify and record birds, fish and sea creatures seen. The tasks must be seen to be genuinely useful or rewarding, and take them to the limit of their capabilities, so that they are not shrugged off when they are not in the mood: responsibility starts early at sea. It all helps to prevent boredom. (Yes, long passages can be boring.)

HOW TO BE NAVIGATOR

'The Master is to see to the conning of the shippe'

Traditionally a man's task, this is changing fast. There is no foundation for believing that women are less numerate than men: many were badly taught. Women can, however, learn. A female navigator is a threat only to very old-fashioned

Captains who have forgotten that centuries ago no Captain, usually a moneyed aristocrat, would have been able to 'see to the conning of the shippe' since that was a well-protected mystery known only to the Master, a mere professional. The wealth of published pilot books, tables and charts that we had when we were young did not exist 200 years ago. Only much later did the job of the Shippe man and the Captain merge, when it was realised that a practical seaman made a better Captain than the aristocrat who knew nothing.

Navigation is a practical skill. The theoretical side can be learned on courses (see the yachting press for ads) and there are also evening classes, usually associated with various certificates.

To acquire the practical knowledge, there is no substitute for doing it. Like driving, it is a skill that is probably *not* best imparted by one's spouse if peace is to reign. The practical courses at the National Sailing School at Cowes were excellent – what a pity they no longer exist. Similar courses are widely available and ensure that you do not remain an eternal student, without confidence in your convictions, but return with a self-assurance born of knowledge, coupled with a respectful wariness for those who have done it for longer and further.

A GOOD NAVIGATOR . . .

- Tries to be always aware of his ship's position in space.
- Is always checking the instruments that tell him where he is.
- Checks his compass daily: in coastal waters against known transits; at sea against the rising or setting of the sun or moon.
- Will not rest until he has solved the problem when something puzzles him or does not add up. He pays regard to a strong feeling that something is wrong.
- Is rigid about keeping his DR (DEDuced reckoning, DED not DEAD reckoning) going, and expects you to do the same when it is your watch. He will be very unhappy if you fib about the course and speed, either because you nodded off and did not pay attention, or because you would prefer your helming performance to seem rather better than it was.
- Checks his sextant for index error in case someone has fiddled with it.
- Notices and jots down what time the electronic log failed, and remembers to allow for the half-hour you spent going round in circles when the jib furling gear jammed.
- Never leaves anything to chance. You do not hear him say, 'Yes, I think that's Cape Krio, we can alter course now.' He checks till he *knows* that it is Cape Krio.

Otherwise, you end up like the honeymoon couple we met in the West Indies, who mistook the radio mast on Union Island for that on Mayreau Island, and instead of (as they thought) entering harbour ran their boat on the reef off Carriacou.

The advent of GPS changes little of this: you still have to spot when it's lying, only you now have to be really creative in explaining to the Captain why the boat is in the wrong place after you've been steering for an hour. ('Well there's a current, isn't there? We've been set down' doesn't work these days, your cross track error should have told you that.)

Harmony can be maintained at the chart table by not getting ink, cocoa rings, gravy, chewing gum, setting lotion etc on the charts. Pencils should not be allowed to drop, otherwise the lead breaks at half-inch intervals all the way through, causing terrible anguish as pencils are always sharpened when the Master doesn't know where he is, and the irritation effect is cumulative. Practise with a cheap plastic sextant, and you won't be worrying about damaging that gorgeous brass and varnish antique that your spouse is so dotty about (and see Chapter Twelve for electronic marvels).

Avoid using the navigating notebook for shopping lists, and the dividers for opening tins, and perhaps the cook's wooden spoon might not be used for stirring bilge paint.

HOW TO BE THE WEATHER-MAN

'It overcasts. We shall have winde, foule weather'

I don't think it is discriminatory to say that women are (by my observation) much better at languages than men. It may be that we are more willing to try. Perhaps it is to do with having to make sense of what the very young and the very old are saying to us: we seem to have a greatly enhanced aural perception. That is to say, we can listen to a toothless old biddy in the marketplace speaking a thick dialect in a language we don't understand, then turn to our astonished menfolk and say, 'It's four and a half Filas for a Katlo, and please will we bring the container back.'

This leads to the women getting the job of listening to foreign language weather forecasts, which at times of bad reception sound far worse than the market lady and there are no nods, gestures and mime to assist comprehension. Thus, we get to be the meteorologist, too.

If you have previously studied nothing more weighty, weatherwise, than aching joints portending rain, it is time to find out why you can't break Buys Ballot's Law, why weather systems have fronts but no backs, and why:

> When in port you choose to stay
> The Goddam gale will go away,
> But when to sea you choose to go,
> The Goddam wind comes on to blow.

Courses in Meteorology for yachtsmen in the UK are run mostly in conjunction with the yachtmaster's certificate. They are a subject that can be taken as evening classes (see your Local Education Authority list, usually out in August for classes beginning in September.), and also as practical weeks or weekends as part of a cruising school course, which can be of various lengths, with emphasis on meteorological and practical forecasting according to students' needs, as well as the usual navigation, seamanship etc.

You can learn by CD-Rom if you have a computer; an excellent one is the Meteorology CD in the *Tomorrow's Yachtmaster* series by PC Maritime, address and website in Appendix C.

Since most weather forecasts are read at normal speed, you need shorthand of some kind. While there are international symbols for weather phenomena, they are not adequate even if you know them by heart, and you will need to supplement them with your own. Do not believe the RYA booklet *Weather Forecasts* when it blithely tells you that the international symbols 'will enable you to appreciate at a glance the information which is contained on any weather map which you may see displayed in Clubs or Ports of call'. This applies (as do most RYA statements) only to Great Britain. Elsewhere in Europe, the Mediterranean, the West Indies and America (except for some huge and expensive marinas, which rarely concern the cruising yachtie,) the weather reports are in words, on teleprinter or standard form in the local language and often the local handwriting. A few years or so ago a very few Port Captains were beginning to post grey-on-grey Weatherfax reproductions, which were so appallingly smudgy and hard to read that they always put the plain word teleprint form up as well. Even in a foreign language, it was easier to read. Now you get Navtex printouts (in English) almost everywhere. Both the RYA handbook and *The Macmillan Reeds Nautical Almanac* have a weather vocabulary in several languages, which are very useful. Most weather handbooks explain weather symbols, and tell you how to take down broadcast information, link it to your own observations, and construct and understand weather maps.

Nowadays radios with an inbuilt recording facility save a lot of trouble, since you can replay the forecast for words you might have missed at first hearing, and worry it out at leisure. Best of all, you don't have to stay up till 0100 or rise yawning in the grey dawn to 'Get the Weather'. You will get used to the orderly progression of the forecast, and the sound of the words in a foreign language, and soon be able to take it down direct.

Italy used to get the Gold Sou'wester for the best TV weather report in the Med, on RAI Uno (Radiotelevisione Italiana Channel 1), but the senior Air Force chap who did it with proper synoptic charts has been supplanted by attractive but vacuous people with pictograms. France (TF1) has a good forecast, after the eight-o-clock news, though the presenter's gimmick is to talk as fast as he can. Most of the European radio reports are good, and Greek Radio translates them into English after their early morning bulletin.

Nowadays almost every yacht has Navtex for weather and shipping notices, either the one that prints out and fills the boat with paper, or the one with a miniature screen. We find it invaluable, and not only because I no longer have to get up at an unearthly hour to 'Get the Weather'.

The only weather services which reach right across the Atlantic in either direction used to be in Morse, which has now been phased out. Satellite radio will bring you weather information, in mid-Atlantic, or Southern Ocean, or wherever, but is too expensive for most of us. *The Admiralty List of Radio Signals*, Vol 3, is certainly the most comprehensive book of weather broadcasts in the world, but it is usually out of date by the time it is published and is laid out like a Chinese puzzle. A new book, *The ALRS for Yachts*, is to be published by the Hydrographer.

Officers in big ships get bored on long passages and will pass on a weather forecast. However, do not expect to see more than two or three ships, big or small, on your entire Atlantic crossing (unless you stumble across the ARC), and do not try calling up US warships, as we did in mid-Atlantic. At first, they would not even admit that they were there at all, reminding us of a large Newfoundland puppy trying to hide in a daisy patch. Then they seemed to think that the weather forecast was a classified piece of information. After much delay and seeking of permission they gave us a cautious description of the weather we were actually experiencing at the time. The Russian 'trawler' shadowing them was much more helpful. That said, the long-distance cruising yacht is very much on its own and must be self-sufficient. We act at all times as if there were no such thing as rescue services, which indeed is the case in mid-ocean, unless you are a racing yacht or a media celebrity. We are proud of 25 years of deep-sea cruising with no calls for assistance: if we were in trouble, we coped with our own resources. Judging what the weather was going to do next if you could get no forecast was (and is) an important and normal part of that resource.

Finally, if you ever need detailed weather forecasting in home waters, if you are looking for a weather 'window' to start a particular voyage for example, you can, for a price, get expert forecasts tailor-made for your boat, your crew and your voyage, over the period of a month, from the British Meteorological Office. If you speak French well, you can phone Météo Consult in France to get in touch with professional forecasters, who will advise you directly.

There is good weather information available from amateur radio sources. Do not worry if you have no amateur radio licence; you are free to listen in. (See our list of ham radio nets in Chapter Thirteen on Communications.)

• *Weather on the internet* •

If you carry a laptop, there is a great deal of weather information on the internet, but this will only be available offshore if you have satellite or HF radio facilities, which are expensive. Websites will be found in Appendix 3. If you have access to a PC ashore, Météo France's shipping forecast is all bells and whistles, with a four-day satellite animation, besides which the BBC's shipping forecast, words only and no outlook, looks very tame.

HOW TO BE COOK

'The cooke is to dresse and deliver out the victual'

It is a poor cook who is not also a psychologist. This comes fairly easily to most women who, knowing how to cook on shore, have a head start at sea, and therefore get landed (not the most apt word here) with the job. Notwithstanding centuries of professional contempt thrown at the historical sea cook, and the extensive list of rude names for his dishes and his person, his contribution was vital and his lack of it often lethal. It is a job of immeasurable importance. Preserving morale in bad weather or other adverse conditions may rest heavily on the cook. 'Fate cannot harm me, I have dined today' said Sidney Smith. There is something unbelievably heartening about hot food and drink, and anyone who can rustle up an appetising one-pan dish in hell-and-high-water conditions is more to be prized than a Cordon Bleu. I've not noticed that men are any better at this than women: I have a strong feeling that it depends sometimes on who is hungriest. But the young male still tends to give cooking a low priority, and will stuff himself with anything that costs him no trouble rather than remembering the welfare of others, as a true cook should. I remember with gritted teeth the wally who was only 'vegetarian' when I was doing the cooking. Left to himself, vegetables were too much trouble. He opened tins of corned beef.

Practical help on cooking and victualling will be found in Chapter Ten, but before you embark be sure to take a few books to help you cope with the odder products of nature. You may not actually have to eviscerate a duck-billed platypus, or lightly kill an armour-plated turtle that is looking you straight in the eye, but you can see the way my mind is working. You may be leaving the fish fingers and pre-packed drumsticks far behind, and encountering unfamiliar fruits and vegetables as well. Asking the market women advice on how to prepare and cook their produce is very rewarding, if you can understand the replies.

Be sure you learn to make bread, in all its varieties. Fresh hot bread is as good for the spirits as the sight of land after a long voyage.

HOW TO STEER AND KEEP A NIGHT WATCH

'Steer steady and keep your course so you go well'

Steering looks so easy. To some people, it is: they fall into the way of it immediately. Others find it hard. They wrestle and wrench the wheel; they oversteer and the ship hunts this way and that like a dog after truffles. The compass confuses them and the watch below groan as the ship's motion deteriorates. These hapless helmsmen chase the spinning compass card till they are dizzy, and seem to have no tenderness or coaxing in them to sense the ship's needs. Naval Officers of the Watch of Bill's day had an order to deal with this phenomenon. They bellowed wrathfully down the speaking tube: 'Steer Small, Blast you!' (use less rudder). Less rudder lets the boat go faster.

Fortunately, most of us learn to be at least adequate helmsmen. In bad weather, half an hour may be quite enough at the wheel or tiller. It is hard work; you are likely to be steering because it has become more than the autopilot can cope with, however excellently (better than most of us, rot it) it can perform in calmer seas, and your concentration quickly tires. A certain mad exhilaration can set in with a force 7 behind you; you think you are doing very well indeed, like a drunken driver. It took quite a bit of persuasion to pry me loose from the wheel on one such occasion when it could be seen that I was tired, losing control of the ship, and likely to gybe all

The crew have to be versatile – here Laurel is practising her hairdressing skills on Fare Well's *deck.*

standing. I was soaking wet, singing loudly, drunk on the weather and indignant when firmly removed. They led me, babbling, below and quelled me with porridge.

Steering is more than just fooling about with the wheel. Unless told otherwise, the helmsman 'has the con'. This means that he is currently in charge. As well as steering the correct course, he should have an eye to the following:

- Are the sails flapping, or setting correctly? Has the wind or weather changed?
- If the engine is in use, are the revs, the fuel gauge, the oil pressure and temperature all reading normal?
- Other ships in the vicinity, the lights they carry, their probable course, speed and distance away. (Both by eye through open windows if you are in a wheelhouse, as well as by checking the radar.)
- The sea: is it getting rougher, or a swell developing? Is the visibility getting worse?
- Can you see any shore lights or lighthouses?
- Odd noises or smells repay investigation: we have often prevented something dire by due attention to these.
- If the log fails, the time and reading should be logged at once, and thereafter you must estimate the speed as best you can. You will also have to be honest about the course you actually succeeded in steering, however reluctant you might be to admit less than perfection, since the DR (deduced reckoning) depends upon it. Check, similarly, if you have one, that your GPS is really working properly, and if it has lost power, or its satellites, note the time. Nowadays, the GPS will read off the course and speed made good.
- Finally, the ideal watchkeeper will know when to call the Captain for something he really needs to deal with, and when he can be left to sleep.

All this probably seems a lot to pay attention to. It is just as well that it seldom happens all at once, and that a night watch can be a period of great peace or even paralysing boredom. The autopilot takes some of the strain, but conversely if nothing much is happening it can be a good idea to switch it off and steer by hand for half an hour, to keep you on your toes. If there is a moon and stars, and enough wind to carry you gently along: that is dreamstuff, and happens often enough. If you are in a nasty sea left by the last storm and slatting about with no wind, it can be exasperating. To pass the time some mentally write books, some listen to the personal stereo (what a boon this is: no more do the loud-music freaks, whether adherents of Bach or Blur, Shostakovich or the Spice Girls, disturb the sleep of the watch below). Bill invents things, plans *coups d'etat* and generally puts the world to rights. I have imaginary conversations with the Great, and write poems and songs, which I sing (quietly).

It can be a long night.

HOW TO BE A DECKHAND

'The younkers, or common saylors, for furling the sayles, bousing or trising, and taking their turn at the helm'

If you are a team of two, it pays to do nothing in a hurry. Whether changing sails, or berthing, or any other bit of seamanship, take a little time to think. If you are entering a new harbour, the crew should check through the binoculars where any other yachts are, whether the mooring is likely to be stern-to or alongside, and whether the quay is provided with bollards or rings; or (as sometimes happens in remote Greek islands) a park bench and a lamp post.

It is also important to note where the ferry berths, and whether there is an irate little harbour official blowing a whistle and waving you off your chosen spot because that big freighter that you have only just noticed is coming in there and you are badly in the way. Having avoided these things, and the shallow end where all the little fishing boats are, you now get out what mooring ropes you need and place your fenders where they will do some good. If there are bollards, it is often a good idea to put a good-sized bowline in your line before you even throw it, especially if there are no obvious sailors on the quay. Wait till everything is ready, and untangled. There is usually *time*.

This avoids the panicky hurling of tangled ropes at the last minute, which inevitably fall short; we see this happen countless times every summer. Since there is so often a rapt audience, it is nice to do these things well. It is sad to see a headrope thrown towards the shore too soon, so that it stops short and falls in the water. Skippers should not expect a 40-foot line to reach across a 50-foot gap just because they say '*Now!*', and deckhands would do well to practise (on a quiet quay out of sight of mockers) coiling and throwing a line that is at least 30 feet long. A good able seaman can throw an unweighted line 60 feet on the level.

A few good practice heaves will kill two birds with one stone (perhaps literally if you use that nasty ferryboat trick of having a weighted monkey's fist at the rope's end). One, you learn to heave the line with your whole arm; and two, you learn to judge the distance. Thus you avoid throwing too soon, and having the line snake out beautifully to its end, only to fall short into the sea. Or that movement akin to closing a chest-high filing cabinet which gives the same result: the rope slithers into the (inevitably) oily water and heads like a homing pigeon for the screw. There should be no need, given the necessary forethought, to go through that rib-tickling performance that has all the other yachts in stitches: the last-minute disinterment of what seems to be a doormat knitted in 12mm nylon, heaved despairingly ashore for the dock committee to wipe its feet on, before the entire mat is dragged back into the water by the rapidly receding yacht attached to its other end. To bring the house down, the line has only to catch in the prop as the yacht circles.

Anchoring also stands a bit of secret practice before your public debut. You will still occasionally drop your anchor neatly into the dinghy (thoughtfully brought to the bow as you knew you were going stern-to, and subsequently forgotten) or get the chain caught in the hawse pipe, or fetch up a snarl which jams in the fairlead. You will get it right nine times out of ten, and avoid the really calamitous things like failing to make fast the end or, as I did once, pulling an extra metre of chain cable up through the navel pipe, absentmindedly allowing it to slip off the gypsy that controls the links and onto the smooth warping drum. Since there was no longer anything to stop it, I watched aghast as with a thunderous roar the entire 45 fathoms of chain cable ran out into deep water. Right to the bitter end. Which was properly made fast and fetched *Fare Well* up with the sort of jerk you give the lead when your puppy is about to eat something disgusting. Bill achieved new heights, both in jumping up and down and creative language, while we slowly got it all back in again.

PETS AND PESTS

'Hale the Cat!' – Captain John Smith

Of course he does not mean cat like our Nelson. Our egregious Captain, from whom we quote so much, lists the following on a man-o'-war in 1627: the Cat, the Hounds, the Falcon (a kind of cannon) the Crab (a launching device), the Crow's nest, the Crow's feet, the Fish block, a Goosewing, Hogsheads, Marlin, Ratlines, Monkey, Sheeps' feet, Sheepshanks and Whelps.

Apart from these, many and various are the birds and animals we have met at sea. Their company is comforting, not only to singlehanders (who can otherwise end a three-week voyage talking non-stop for hours to the first person they meet), but to any crew who are not averse to animals. People will put up with a lot to have their pets with them; we have known a tiny yacht weighed nose-down with two enormous and beloved dogs, stowed forward like a couple of bower anchors. They had to be rowed ashore every few hours. Their owners got a bigger boat the next year. We met a Dane in Spain who swore he had rowed his dog ashore twice a day all the way from Denmark.

We have met parrots, large and small. Nelson is very fond of birds. So are we, but not to eat. The first parrot we met was a huge scarlet macaw on the island of Minorca which came up our gangway on its owner's shoulder. On confronting Nelson – black, alert, chops a-slaver – it squawked and committed an indignity on its owner's shirt, and had to be shut in his car in hysterics. That was the start of a great friendship. Moored next to us in Aegina, near Athens, a young circumnavigating family in *Active Light* had a tiny green parrot. Nelson was not hungry, but even a sleepy cat was enough to frighten poor Birdie across the street and onto the awning of the taverna opposite, where she had to be coaxed and climbed for. We met them again in Grenada in the West Indies, where we were all at anchor, and were able to exchange pleasant visits with bird and cat safely apart.

While birds are easy to look after, dogs are a horse of another colour, to mix metaphors. If you are doggy-minded you will take your dog with you and care for it like an extra child: which it will be, not being as self-sufficient as a cat or with the simple needs of a bird. A dog produces large turds, which (unlike the cat) it does not know what to do with. It is theoretically possible to get your dog to use the scuppers, or to home in on a short length of tree attached to a stanchion, or a square of artificial grass. We have heard of all these being tried, with or without tempting bottles of 'Do it here, Doggy' perfume. In the cold real world, however, we observe that all dog owners have to use a shovel and hose the deck down pretty frequently; or row the culprit ashore at intervals which interfere with one's beer-time.

Dogs do not like being left. It takes only one of them, howling because its dad and mum have gone ashore, to turn a quiet anchorage into Banshee night in Wolf Forest. On the other hand, they are a good deterrent for thieves (though our Nelson could be a bit frightening, with the eldritch shriek she used to fend off unwanted toms, and the moonlight glancing off her one eye, an emerald as large as a saucer). At least dogs are Faithful Pals. Cats are anybody's: if you upset them (by hoovering or varnishing, for instance) they go and live with someone else for a few hours, whereas a dog will grin miserably and put up with it. Cats are better in rough weather, it seems to me. They seem to be like humans as regards seasickness: some are and some are not. We know of one kitten that had to be found a shore home because it was very seasick, but we also know a very large number of contented ship's cats. Till recently, we had one of each, one insouciant up to force 5; the other hibernated in the lifeboat the minute the motor went on. As a matter of record, Nelson was with us at sea for ten years and upwards of 40 000 miles, and the recent cats clocked up seven years and 14 000 miles.

I have heard that keeshonds (Dutch barge dogs) were trained to leap ashore with a headrope in their teeth and drop a bight over a bollard. We never managed to get our keeshond to do this in the days when we took children, dog and all, out for the Sunday cruiser race. Ours was a good dog in a boat, so breeding helps a bit; he kept out of the way and did not moan, and when we were tacking up the narrow rivers of the Broads he would leap ashore on one tack, use a tree, wait until we tacked back again, usually having made only a few yards in two tacks, and jump back on board. He was so much a part of our racing crew that if we

Our one-eyed ship's cat, Nelson, was with us on Fare Well *for 10 years.*

crossed the finishing line without him we were threatened with disqualification.

For long-term cruising, however, cats take a lot of beating. They are neat in their habits, and when you run out of kitty litter, they tolerate sand or pebbles. (This once led to a misunderstanding when a young pebble-trained cat, who was my guest while his people went home for a week or two, decided that my Christmas bowl of walnuts was The Right Place.) They are philosophical about bad weather; an example to humans, in fact. They find the warmest, driest spot on board (on your lap under your oilskin for example, or the airing cupboard, or the lifeboat) and hole up for as long as possible. When it's all over they emerge, all smiles and hungry. Nelson could suspend all bodily functions for about 36 hours when necessary: if only we humans could too. If she had to go and her tray was awash, she would come and tell you so, complaining indignantly until you put it right. Braced, intent and swaying with the ship's motion while producing her own, she then did her housework rather more rapidly than usual, skipping with relief back into her chosen hideout. Sometimes this was her box behind the compass (cats are not magnetic) but sometimes she liked to wriggle well down into some folded canvas; a bundled-up staysail became such a haven for her when on a transatlantic passage that we let it be, unused until we reached the Azores.

• *Pet vaccination* •

It used to be a difficult task to get your cat or dog vaccinated against rabies in England. In 1976, at first I was told that it was impossible, but with a little persistence I got a bit higher up the chain of command and asked how, as we were going to sea, to get Nelson vaccinated. 'Oh, a Ship's cat' said the man. 'That's all right.' So Nelson became a ship's cat and was duly vaccinated. The vaccine was not normally used in Britain because the country, being rabies-free, insisted on sixth months' quarantine for incoming animals, and tests at once revealed if such animals were infected. These tests are much more equivocal on vaccinated ones and uncertainty would have set in. When the inevitable happens and someone smuggles in a rabid cat or dog, or quite likely brings in a horse (yes, horse: they are allowed to enter and leave the country freely to go to race meetings, with no rabies quarantine restrictions) and rabies comes to Britain, the rules will change and vaccination will become normal. So I wrote in 1985, and by the 1998 edition it seemed we were on the brink of change.

• *February 2000: pet passports at last* •

Vaccination against rabies has improved to the state of being trustworthy, as long as the animal is clearly identified by tattooing or microchip, and pet passports are now available, thanks to the Pet Travel Scheme run by MAFF (Ministry of Agriculture Fisheries and Food.) Before you get too excited, however, understand that it is as yet a pilot scheme, and there is no question of fetching up in Falmouth after a round-the-world trip with dog or mog and expecting to get away without quarantine. Not for some years, anyway. A restricted trial is in progress, and could suit you if you go no farther than Europe, and bring the animal back (with required documents) *not in your yacht,* but by train, air or ferry, and then only to certain designated ports. Installing the microchip and getting ancillary certificates will cost £150 to £200 on the British side. On the French side, the appropriate flea and tick certificates are obtainable at the Channel ports, the process costing between £5 and £50.

In a nutshell to qualify for the pet passport scheme (pets means cats or dogs, nothing else at present) note the following points:

- Countries from which your pet may arrive are limited. (In January 2001 MAFF extended the list of countries from 22 – 50, but check this out.)
- Services on which you may travel are limited.
- Ports of entry that operate the Pet Travel Scheme are limited.
- Your pet must be fitted with a microchip.
- Your pet must be vaccinated against rabies, and six months later have blood test to ensure that the vaccination has succeeded.
- 24 to 48 hours before you enter the UK with your pet, it must have treatment against ticks and tapeworm, with an appropriate certificate.

So you have to think about it in plenty of time, and the first stages should be completed before you start your cruise.

There are circumstances in which your pet, if complying mainly with the rules, could get quarantine time reduced. If you require more detailed information, see Appendix C for MAFF address and website.

In the meantime, the veterinary headquarters of your county should be able to assist you with rabies vaccination if you are leaving Britain for good. Make sure you tell them it's a ship's cat, as this cuts through a lot of red tape.

Up till now, I have for 20 years or more carried documents attesting to vaccination against rabies for any ship's cat or cats on board. No authority in *any* country has ever asked to look at them. In Gibraltar, Nelson was vaccinated willy-nilly; British rules then prevailed about bringing in animals, a bit odd considering that any squirrel or fox can trot over the border to or from Spain when it feels like it. Cats and dogs were confined to the yacht. Gibraltar has recently relaxed this rule: now if you are a resident of Europe visiting Gibraltar and your pet has a valid certificate of rabies vaccination dated not less than 28 days before your arrival, and providing you do not arrive from North Africa, it will be allowed ashore.

Malta, a country from which you may not enter Britain with your pet, still has the British regulations. Being an island, it makes some sense. However, they have no quarantine facilities and do not allow your animal even to be confined to the yacht. They used to employ the draconian solution of shooting them. This led to a high rate of pet smuggling in Malta, which defeats the aim of the regulations. I recall a lady who gave both her small dogs sleeping pills to get them into Malta in her yacht. One woke up too soon and was duly destroyed, but she succeeded in smuggling in the other. She was not British, but Brits are not all blameless in this matter either.

• *Rats and mice* •

Cats eat mice and kill rats. Until you have had one of these pests on board you have no idea what a good thing cats are. We met a yacht in Corfu in a state of siege after one month of Spanish Rat: they could buy only enough food for one day, which had to be kept in the oven, which was the only rat-proof place they had, as it had eaten through clothes, flags, Tupperware, and even teak lockers. They had already tried traps and poison and they were ready to sell their lovely little yacht for a song, rat and all, but they acquired a small cat and had no further trouble.

In some parts of the world, you are still required to sign a document concerning the health of any shipboard rats, in case you are carrying the plague. We found one of these in St Thomas's in the Virgin Islands, but rather piquantly rephrased: they wished to know 'if there was any unusual morality among the rates on board' (sic). We were also required to state the health of our rats as we entered Turkish waters in the Bosphorus.

Mice are almost as destructive as rats; it just takes them a little longer to chew through your Tupperware. They are also fond of other varieties of plastics. We once had the saloon lights fused by a mouse that bit through the electric cable.

This was one of Nelson's failures: she went through a phase of posting lizards and beetles down the forward ventilator into the roof space. Once, when she wasn't hungry, she posted a live mouse. It couldn't get out again and the roof space was only an inch or so high: too small to feed the cat into it.

Calling Nelson many dreadful and unpopular names, we removed a panel and tried some Italian Mouse Glue, a fearful substance that you spread on a piece of card which you then lay in the mouse's path. You then sit back and wait, hoping that the mouse is stupid enough to walk across it and stick, like Brer Fox to the Tar Baby.

I must confess that I was not anxious to deal with the pathetic results that seemed bound to ensue. I need not have worried; the mouse was not that stupid. After some days the stuff slumped off the card and began to drip down the cabin wall. The regular scrotch, scrotch, of chewing mouse went on. We took the panel off again and threw the card, now dusty and ineffective, away. The drips down the wall remained sticky for weeks and appeared to have no solvent known to man. I was relieved when the mouse, tiring of polyfoam, decided to try a change of diet, bit through the electric cable and fried itself.

This one shameful incident apart, however, Nelson was all that one could hope for: she never allowed a wharf rat on board unless she personally accompanied it. In Mahon, in Minorca, she ratted diligently. After snoozing all the warm day, come Cat-time, that darker-than-twilight time when cats and shadows blend, she would yawn, stretch, test her claws on the rope doormat and slink down the gangway to vanish instantly. Other cats would appear from the waste land and derelict warehouses, a whisker here, a flash of white sock there, but Nelson, black as ebony, invisible, was marked only by an occasional sharp rustle, followed by twitters and squeaks as she pounced and bit swiftly through the neckbone. Rats were serious business, and she did not play with them as she did with lizards and mice.

Some people, especially in the States, have neat-looking metal rat-guards on all their mooring lines, usually an aluminium disc about 30 centimetres across. Sorry, but to circumvent a determined rat, and there is no other kind, they should be at least a metre in diameter. It is hard to find stowage for four or five of those. I prefer a rat-guard that purrs. The purr of a cat is also a great tranquilliser, and has no side effects.

• *Insects* •

Sooner or later you will have insect trouble; flies in the galley or midges round the barbecue.

Mosquitoes In a few places, the mosquitoes are large enough to make life a misery. You will know where, because you will notice on shore the screened verandas, and the eerie blue light and sudden sputter of the electric bug frier. A very promising party of ours in Calabria broke up in disorder when, at dusk, swarms of mosquitoes drove us below decks. An hour later they were all gone, and we were able to reassemble.

On entering the Intra-Coastal Waterway in America, we asked the advice of a weathered waterman about mosquito screens. 'Well,' he drawled, 'ya might put one on yo door there; but our mosquitoes are too big for yo windas.' As we did the trip in winter and spring, mosquitoes were absent and we had no trouble.

Where mosquitoes abound we have tried anti-mosquito candles, and nearly burnt the boat. We have tried Off and Autan and Oil of Lemongrass; Boots' Jungle Formula has been highly recommended. The bugs don't come near you but nor do your friends. A vicious little breed of mosquito is found in the Eastern Mediterranean. We went ashore to have a barbecue and noticed what appeared to be a shepherd's bed in the branches of a tree, about 2 metres off the ground. While our supper cooked we made many jokes about savage beasts that couldn't climb trees (we couldn't think of many), and became more and more uneasy as the sun set. Then, in the space of about one minute, we learnt the reason for the tree bed: we were set upon by millions of tiny but savage little beasts, kinky about ankles, none attacking above the knee. After the quickest clean-up and evacuation ever, we rowed back out to *Fare Well,* our tingling ankles peppered with bites as close together as the dots on a smocking transfer.

One gadget that seems to work in a small space is the mini hotplate on which venomous pastilles are warmed till they give off fumes noxious to insects. These are widely available. The warmer did not suit our electrical system, so Bill contrived one in a Kit-e-Kat tin which worked well. Then *White Whisper* told us of their simple and effective solution: put the pastille on some copper gauze above the oil lamp. Turned down to the absolute minimum, it makes the pastille fume nicely.

There is a pocket battery device which is said to scare bugs away with ultra-sound. I know what I'd think about people who carry vibrating objects in their pockets.

If you are in an area where malaria is rife, then take no chances and sleep under a mosquito net. This at least does not smell, cause fires, or make your friends look at you oddly.

Cockroaches   Inevitably, we come to cockroaches. When we built the boat, we wrote to Shell asking them to recommend a long-term insecticide. We sprayed two coats of it on the foam that covered the interior of the steel hull, on top of the fire retardant paint and inside the linings where no one was likely to touch it. It was obviously lethal, as it kept *Fare Well* insect-free for six years. Not until we were coming back from the West Indies did we finally 'catch' cockroaches: not (luckily) the 'Mahogany Mice' of the Caribbean but a smaller breed. However, like the illegitimate baby of the 1930s, even little ones count. It seems few now recall the famous reply of the housemaid taxed by her prospective employer with having had an illegitimate baby. 'That's true ma-am' she said 'But it was only a very little one – and surely doesn't count?'

We took steps. Nelson ate some (they were crunchy). I took out the loose Formica linings from the galley drawers and sprayed them with Baygon (the Greek anti-*katsarida* kind which bears very little relation to the lily-livered stuff of the same name which is all they will allow you to have in the Western Med).

As a precaution, I had bought in the USA a trap called a Roach Motel, and I dug it out for use. It was well named: it seemed to invite them in for a hamburger and a night's sleep, and then let them go with me picking up the bill for their entertainment, which was not cheap as I had bought two of them. I found only one cockroach in it, and that was slightly bent as if Nelson had chewed it a bit first and it had gone in there for a dry Martini and counselling. When we came to the conversion of *Hosanna* ten years later, we found that the attitude to insecticides had 'Greened' and hardened; it was very difficult to get a long-term insecticide. Some of them have been completely banned, and the use of the remainder is restricted to industry, who are supposed to be more responsible about the use of such dangerous substances than we poor mortals with only our cats and our children to think about. (Since 'industry' has given us the blessings of BSE and antibiotic-resistant bacteria, it makes you wonder.) We, the public, are no longer trusted with anything that really works: laudanum, antifoulings, insecticides, weedkiller. (Where will it end? These measures restrict the detective novelists' poison arsenal considerably.) For a long time it has required great persistence to track down a killer insecticide, and now, in the twenty-first century, it will soon be impossible. It will be necessary to use physical prevention (traps, cats, netting, smoke-candles, pastilles and creams) and the watered-down sprays with biokindly propellant that are all you can get now. Perhaps we need to consider keeping insect-eating pets, chameleons perhaps, or a cuddly little toad? Encourage spiders.

We tried a secret anti-cockroach mixture imparted to us by the German skipper of a charter yacht, alongside whom we had berthed in St Lucia.

'Haf you cockroaches?' he asked us. 'No,' we said proudly.

'Now you vil haf,' he said, and gave us his recipe, Jorge's revenge: sweetened condensed milk and powdered boric acid. (Now wash your hands please.) The cockroaches yaffle the mixture, and the boric acid concretes up their insides till it's like treading on plum stones. (No, don't try it as a remedy for the runs. It is cumulative and dangerous, so prevent the puss from eating doctored cockroaches.) I found that Jorge's mixture dried solid and was ineffective after a few days, so I mixed icing sugar with it instead. Hal Roth, in *After 50,000 Miles*, quotes entomologists at the University of California as saying that any additives to the boric acid are unnecessary and counter effective. Well, my mixture, put in a flat tin and wedged where children and cats couldn't get at it, must have got up the cockroaches' noses and choked them. Something worked, we have no cockroaches at present.

It must be the size and obviousness of cockroaches which upset people and cause a disproportionate amount of hysteria, since in fact they are not known to be the carriers of any disease.

Flies   These are infinitely more dangerous than cockroaches, but do not cause the same reaction. A fly alighting on the table to lick up a beer spill elicits a half-hearted wave of the hand, instead of the panic and recourse to major artillery in the shape of slippers, pilot books, and even winch handles, that characterise the appearance of a cockroach. And yet, friends:

The fly that on your bread has wiped its feet,
Has also been and wiped them on the meat.
But worse than that, this morning (for a treat)
It trod in something nasty in the street.

Whether buzzing round the galley, or groggily dive-bombing your nose in the bunk, they have got to go. I keep the galley noticeably cleaner in warm weather to discourage them, covering any exposed food or fruit and leaving no water in the sink (flies too have to drink). We have a fly swat, disgusting but non-pollutant. We also have a flyshooter, which gives visitors endless harmless amusement and even kills a few flies. If desperate, we use an aerosol spray. No need to gun down individual flies: this is total war. Shut the windows, spray the area, and go up on deck for a while. Then come back when it's all over, like the politicians. Of course, you empty the rubbish as often as you can.

In Greece, every household keeps a pot of basil to keep the flies away. This is the little-leafed basil, not the one with large leaves grown in Italy to go with tomatoes. The Greeks tuck a sprig behind one ear or carry some in their hands; you will see the pots on their caiques and yachts as well. I have tried many times to grow my own pot of basil. It used to succumb to salt-blast, or else go overboard in a choppy sea. (Onboard gardening in *Fare Well* always ended like this. In *Hosanna*, we have a flourishing herb garden in a square metre 'frame' that flowerpots cannot fall out of, protected from wind, and covered at sea to keep the salt out.) Since Greece is one of the few places where you can still buy old-fashioned flypapers, the pot of basil may be a triumph of hope over experience.

Wasps   In September, the wasps arrive, unless you are well out to sea and stay there. This leads to breaks in the conversation while you or your guests perform Kung Fu, ending with a wham on the table that makes the glasses rattle. Eating on the poop becomes a little less than perfect, and bare feet are inadvisable as wasps are dying all over the deck.

You can rig up a diversion in the shape of a tin containing enough soda pop, Sprite, or 7-Up for them to drown in: they seem very fond of it, but there will still be a few left to zzzz round the salad. After one especially efficient attack with the fly swat we watched the stretcher-bearers arrive in the shape of hornets, come to carry away the dead. One tried to carry two corpses at once and ditched slowly into the sea, like a crippled Lancaster with two bombs slung under it. It made nearly as much noise, too. The less ambitious hornets cleared our decks of dead and dying wasps in no time at all.

Ticks   We knew a yacht that took on board a pathetic little Greek kitten, only to find that it was infested with pathetic little Greek ticks. Their bedding burst forth from below like spinnakers on the downwind run, and clothing bloomed in the rigging, scented with pyrethrum. I've seldom seen a gayer sight, even at Carnival. Frying ticks with a cigarette end is nauseating but effective. You can also use ether on cotton wool, but mind you don't anaesthetise the pet, or yourself. I found a tick on my neck once in the French canals; it took a lot of ether on cotton wool before I could persuade it to drop off, by which time I was as tight as the tick.

Slugs and caterpillars   Pests that come into the boat on fruit and vegetables, apart from those already dealt with above, can be reduced by discarding cardboard boxes on the quay. Salt in the washing water deals with slugs and caterpillars (always make the fussiest person on board responsible for the chore of washing fruit and salads, and see that they wear their glasses). Use clean seawater with a little permanganate of potash to pinken it.

Weevils   These are rarely come across in well-packaged goods these days, but they will occur in the West Indies and the Eastern Mediterranean, when buying pulses, cereals or rice from the sack or in paper bags. If you can put the stuff in some-body's deep freeze for 24 hours, in a plastic bag, this will kill any eggs, and you can then transfer it to beetle-proof containers. Watch things like instant mashed potato and dry dog and cat food, which are very prone to attack. If you find a few beetles in something, you need not throw it out as they are not in themselves harmful; but never add coarsely ground black pepper to your risotto until you are sure there are no weevils in the rice: they look too similar. If there are more than a few it becomes psychologically unappetising and is better thrown away.

• *Other pests* •

Worms   In the early days of 'abroad', when we were in our 'teens, both Bill and I caught roundworms, Bill from a Spanish paella, and I in Morocco from heaven knows what. This caused a lot of excitement; passing a creature about 9 inches long and quite firm in texture is a startling event. My doctor reverted to alchemy and prescribed extract of male fernseed. It was not surprising, therefore, that I tried to find some remedies to take with me before we left on the Great Cruise.

When the chemist came out of his little white stillroom to find out what hophead was buying 12 packets each of Stugeron and Kwells, and decided that maybe this little sailing lady was not hooked on seasickness pills, I began to ask him about worms. He backed off and disclaimed all knowledge. Fortunately, in 25 years of cruising, not all of it in civilised places, we have not had occasion to use any remedy (but see Chapter Fifteen).

All the baby books mention threadworms, but not the round or tape variety, which in Britain seem to attack only dogs and cats. It is easy to get multi-worm tablets for your pets, and you should take some, as infestations are often picked up on shore. Roundworm eggs are carried on fruit and vegetables, and tapeworm eggs in undercooked meat. The eggs are not visible to the eye, but heat kills both types. Since we do not like to forego our salads and raw fruit, we wash them well, in a little potassium permanganate (a few crystals, enough to pinken the water), just before eating them. I'm even more thorough about washing raw food now since one does not know what chemicals it has been sprayed with.

There is no great cause for panic if you do acquire one of the above internal guests, as those mentioned are more upsetting than harmful, unlike hookworm and other tropical murderers.

Wet-bikes A new pest has appeared since we first wrote. It is dangerous to swimmers and wildlife, aggressive and extremely noisy, shattering the peace of anchorages wherever it appears. It goes under the generic name of a wet-bike, and can be ridden uninsured and unrestricted by anyone of any age and at 60mph. At present there is no remedy that will not land you in gaol, but *The Sunday Times* ran a campaign for safe waters which includes a ban on wet-bikes. If you are a wet-bike fan, roar about where there is already high ambient noise, so you will be seen but not heard.

> Anchored in a quiet bay,
>   Watching birds and fish at play,
> Hush of evening rent asunder
>   Wet-bike whines, a chainsaw thunder,
> Decibels near ultra sonic
>   Overturn our gin and tonic;
> Yell aloud and shake your fist – I'll
>   Go below and fetch the pistol.

Monkeys A word about monkeys. We were berthed close to a rather theatrical family in a small yacht in Sicily. They had two young children, and two monkeys. They were bad-tempered, noisy and ill disciplined. (The children, however, were charming.) The parents ego-tripped up and down the quay with the monkeys on a lead, getting lots of attention. Nelson watched from her top-of-the-gangway sentry post, with distaste. Next day the parents were bored with their pets and sent the children to walk the monkeys. They got a little too far from their boat and were cut off by a large friendly dog, who barked at them playfully. The monkeys' reaction was instantaneous: with shrieks they shot up to the children's heads, where they loosed their bowels ready for further flight. For the next hour the dock committee watched with suppressed glee as the parents, tight-lipped and grim of mien, scrubbed their hapless children under the dockside hose with magnums of shampoo.

Other people's unwanted pets, whether roaming toms after your maiden moggie's virtue or those rangy pooches who seem to be able to pee for half an hour on your freshly washed mooring ropes, are discouraged by the handgun in the form of a water pistol, or (the heavier artillery) a squeezy bottle of water, if possible iced, directed at the active member.

I'm told that goldfish get seasick.

8 • Maintenance and Repairs

'. . . Decayed by weeds or Barnacles . . . which will eat thorow all
the planks if she be not sheathed'

There is a class of yachtsman who says 'Get it fixed', and Lo! it is fixed, and he signs a cheque. He is usually one of the racing fleet, or he keeps his boat in luxury style. He is unlikely to be a dedicated live-aboard for we are fairly firmly in the do-it-yourself class. Nevertheless, at either end of the economic scale there are those who occasionally employ a little casual help, or who actually provide that help. In any case we are all watching pennies, and tend to spend winters or refit periods where moorings and living are cheap.

Sadly, it is in just those areas that spare parts are hard to find, that local labour, while cheaper, is not up to the latest techniques, and that communications with the industrialised world are a bit tenuous. Which is why those places are so attractive. It is important, therefore, that all maintenance and minor repair work be able to be performed using onboard resources, or at worst using comparatively primitive facilities.

It is not a function of this book to instruct in elementary nautical maintenance, so we will refrain from travelling too far down that path, though we will wander a bit now and then. Rather, we want to consider how the live-aboard can minimise his inevitable problems by appropriate action before starting out.

SPARS, SAIL AND RIGGING

First, a story. We met a modern yacht that had been dismasted off the Canary Islands. They were still there ten months after their mishap, waiting for a replacement aluminium spar. By contrast, an old schooner discovered rot in the heel of the foremast while cruising Turkish waters. A new heel was scarphed in in ten days, the labour cost then being around one pound per hour.

Now, new masts are not needed that often and one may well cruise a lifetime without the necessity, but those stories illustrate a general rather than a particular point. Sooner or later repairs will be necessary to something, and if those repairs can be effected from local resources then one gets sailing again cheaper and sooner. The lesson applies, though with less force, even when cruising to sophisticated countries where certain basic standards differ. For example, electrical replacements

Greek hospitality at its best out of season. We are invited to an Easter lamb roast in Meganisi.

The opposite extreme to 'Keep it Simple'. ▶
Hosanna's *saloon in its winter clothes.*

One gains by the ability to haul out by traditional means. Hosanna *in Levkas.*
▼

One of  *the oldest cruising traditions: leaving your mark on the old breakwater at Horta. Not nearly as easy as the new one.*

◀ Help your neighbour: using Hosanna's derrick to re-step the mast in the little Canadian schooner Peer's Fancy.

In island
harbours
there's
always
something
going on
next door. ▶

◀ *Fair*
exchange:
the loan of
a sewing
machine
for an
injection
for tennis
elbow!

▶
This is
an effective
way of
coping with
the very
young while
continuing
to do things.

◀ *The Intra-coastal Waterway in the USA.* Farewell *passing a big barge.*

Farewell *in Navpaktos.* ▶

◀ *If you go to popular ports in high season, things can get hectic. Here, at Hydra, much tolerance is necessary, but it's fun.*

following our lightning strike in the USA were more difficult and expensive to obtain because our equipment is 24 volt, which is not common over there.

A good solid spar can be got almost anywhere trees grow, except in the sophisticated countries. I had immense trouble getting a new wooden mast for *Hosanna* in 1996 in England. Eventually I gave up and she had a galvanised steel foremast. In 2000, we replaced the other wooden masts with steel as well. They are much the same weight and twice as strong. I have heard of an impecunious French owner who stole a telegraph pole for the purpose; though this displays initiative, it is not likely to enhance the reputation of yachtsmen. Nevertheless, it makes a point.

Going with a wooden mast will probably be a lower sail plan, cheaper galvanised wire rigging, and cheaper sails. Some people chop and change their sailmaker, looking for an advantage here, or a bargain there. My family have used Jeckells for several generations, and though we might get a sail that is less than perfect on rare occasions, I do get excellent service, and I think anyone else would. This would probably apply to a regular customer of any other old firm such as Cranfields. As an example, following loss of an old mainsail in high summer we had a replacement arrive in the USA within nine days, at a cost of approximately half the lowest quotation there, and that was when there were over $2 to the pound. The old sail, blown out in Hurricane Alberto, had lasted eight years; it was still serviceable as a spare. A good cruising sail, if protected from the sun when not in use, should last ten years.

That does not apply so surely to roller jibs, which somehow seem to get unfair wear. Sacrificial strips along leech and foot are a nuisance. I designed our replacement genoa to be mitre cut with the cloths parallel to leech and foot, and with the outer cloths of stronger material. I have always found cloth to be stronger lengthwise, and old smacksmen knew this too, for it is the way they cut their 'tow foresails', which were the forerunners of the modern genoas. If the leech or foot deteriorates in the sun, it is comparatively easy to replace the affected parts.

Do not leave jibs rolled up when out of use for a long time or over winter. This is a common practice to be observed in marinas and a temptation with roller

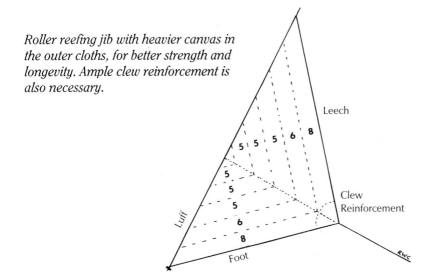

Roller reefing jib with heavier canvas in the outer cloths, for better strength and longevity. Ample clew reinforcement is also necessary.

headsail gear. There are many lazy yachtsmen about, and the live-aboard cannot afford to be lazy.

Generally, sail and rigging maintenance is a continual process, mainly because it is one of the more pleasant chores. But once a year at least all sail seams should be checked, because they are the weak points. We have a modern Singer sewing machine capable of zigzag stitching, but we cannot sew several layers of heavy cloth very well. Neither can our friends on their Reads, sold as a sailmaking machine. I have a feeling that an old-style hand-driven Singer would be best. Sew one's homeward-bounders in straight stitches. We have tried gluing on patches with contact adhesive when hard pushed; it looks terrible but works for a while.

PAINT AND PROTECTION

If one is living aboard and cruising continuously, it is sometimes easy to overlook passing time and the need for annual checks. In the Med these are done in winter, but even then one has to allow for bad weather when work is impossible or inconvenient. In Corfu it rains a lot. At Bodrum, we had gales and even snow. One winter in Rome we had snow on several occasions and even ice on the deck. Painting in these conditions is not really a good idea.

Painting is important in a yacht. I have a feeling that fibreglass boats could do with it from time to time, but for wood or steel it becomes essential. We try to keep a little paint in a small glass jar to touch up instantly any damage, and some is bound to happen. This way the annual chore, for that is what it is, is eased. GRP boats should keep on board two-part filler and gelcoat. The big paint job is so purgatorial that it has to be carefully planned. Part of it will be on the slip or hard, but upperworks can be done afloat, though we were dismayed in Porto Xeli in Greece to be arrested by the Port Police for painting our guardrails. As a Greek boat nearby was doing the same thing, it was clearly a bit of Greek xenophobia, and some vigorous argument solved the problem.

Stop Press (June 2001) We have just discovered that a new Dutch law forbids painting yachts except in special locations, so we find Dutch yachts re-fitting all over Flanders. There is pressure on the EU to make the ban Europe-wide, which would mean the end of DIY boat-owning. Our comments are not fit to print.

The chief purgatory is the preparation: whether sanding, wire-brushing, descaling or whatever, bits fly and a door left open soon leads to marital disharmony. With sand-blasting it is even worse, and it is evident that one should respect one's neighbours.

I am going to interject a word on behalf of the mate here. It is necessary to work hard and long at this chore to get it over sooner, and if 'sir' expects 'madam' also to do a full ten-hour day with sander or brush, then it is unfair to expect her to cook the evening meal afterwards. We see as essential to the cost of the exercise having baths and a dinner, however simple, at a local hostelry each evening.

Talking of sand-blasting, it is possible to buy portable equipment from a firm in

Reading. In a large steel boat this might well be worthwhile, though a big compressor is needed too. The same requirement limits the use of a needle gun for cleaning steel. Electric needle guns exist, but the on-board variety come under the description of toys – not man enough for the job.

Preparation, somehow or other, is the key. I have been concerned with painting steel ships for a lot of my life and have become disenchanted with paint companies. Apart from doing the job under laboratory conditions, the paint industry has made no real advance in protecting steel at sea since the First World War. The chipping hammer, red lead and oil paint routine I knew when I first went to sea lasted just as well as the latest advice and products of the industry. Here, for amusement, is a parody of a paint company's specification:

> *Steel should be sand-blasted to North Korean standard X24. This must be done with relative humidity below 10%, and in total darkness. All loose dust must be removed, and the steel should be coated with 5 microns of our No 7 priming solution within ten minutes of sand-blasting and with relative humidity above 70%. The primer should be covered by alternating coats of our 303 super-effective barrier, and our 404 semi-permeable undercoat until a thickness of 25 microns is built up. Overcoating time of the 303 and the 404 is between 12 and 13 hours, but the 404 should only be applied in bright sunlight and rising humidity. Failure to meet these conditions invalidates any warranty.*

What I really want to emphasise is that paint companies make paint for use only in ideal conditions, and write their specifications sitting in an office. All too often conditions at the sharp end of life involve a worsening weather forecast and an obligation to be off the slip by tomorrow, inevitably leading to the decision to slap it on and hope for the best.

With *Hosanna*, a steel boat, chlorinated rubber paints have been successful. Their remarkably short overcoating time, 15 minutes in a Mediterranean summer, means the job can be done quickly, largely overcoming weather changing problems. You would not call it a 'super yacht finish', though it is effective enough. I have heard that the Green loonies have campaigned to get this paint banned and that they may be successful. As Laurel swears by it, we are stocking up; to paint guardrails and have them dry before anyone touches them makes so much sense. It seems to me we will soon be back to Neolithic times, when the animal-lovers will stop us clothing ourselves in furs and skins and we will all freeze to death.

Varnish is not compatible with our existence, at least not on the upper deck. Beautiful Italian yachts gleam from the attentions of vast crews of nautical charwomen (this is how they solve their unemployment problem; they are all cleaning the rich men's yachts). Sometimes one has pangs of envy and this leads to a token bit of varnish in the cockpit, but it is not really a practical affair in hot sun.

Antifouling becomes a problem as one moves from one area to another. International Paints are available world-wide and while I think their paints sold in Britain are among the best available, they are not made to the same specification in every country. In the USA they print a full analysis of the paint on the tin, and this is very helpful. One wonders why there is no obligation to state the same valuable information in other countries.

Since there is now virtually a world-wide ban on Tri-butyl-tin (TBT) antifoulings for pleasure craft, owners of steel boats are in a fix. Paint companies are now advising us to use products they previously said were unsuitable! We do not have an answer, except that a boat over 25 metres is exempt from the ban. Considering how few small steel and aluminium boats there are, they could have sought exemption if the RYA had been better organised. In 1997 in various Greek ports there was a flourishing black market in merchant ship antifouling, to be delivered after dark. Presumably it had fallen off the back of a container ship. We have heard that some countries, notably the Netherlands, have banned all forms of antifouling on pleasure boats. Of course we do not want to poison the water, but this is lunacy.

HAULING OUT OR SLIPPING

The place where you haul out needs selecting with some care. In general, the more primitive the equipment the more it costs, an example where sophistication seems to have its benefits for the yachtie. The Western Med, which is littered with more marinas than it seems there are boats to fill them, each with its own boatyard, is in need of business so competition keeps the price down; while the equipment, generally a Travelift or similar, is fairly new and reasonably well operated. It is in these places that a yacht of whatever type can be dealt with.

Further east in the Med the number of marinas decreases, and with it the number of Travelifts and their standard of maintenance. And the prices rise; it has never been properly explained why it should cost six times as much in Greece to haul a yacht as it does in Spain.

Yachts with a long straight keel can be hauled out on the old-fashioned ways, or on a proper marine railway. We have been out on the municipal slip at Barcelona, and at the de Gasperi yard at Porto Santo Stefano (surely one of the best yards in the world). At both of these the care and competence were of the very highest. We came out on an old cradle over a shingle beach at Erol Ayan's yard near Bodrum, one of the high experiences of our lives; a wonderful place, but the whole thing was hair-raising and not at all cheap.

In the Western Hemisphere, we hauled out at Hazzard's slipway in Georgetown, South Carolina, a lovely family boatyard and cheaper than Greece or Turkey. We had planned to haul again, but found that the high cost of antifouling paint made it pay to wait until we got to Spain. I found the lift operators at the Club Nautico in Palma and also at Trehard's in Antibes to be good, and at both places the charges were reasonable. Facilities are not good in the West Indies. There is a slip at Grenada and another at English Harbour; there may well be others. There is, however, a 3-foot tide in some parts of the Caribbean, and it is possible to do something of a job between tides. The big problem there is the long grass-like weed that grows close to the waterline, but it is no great chore to drop over the side and remove it every few weeks. I found a home-made scraper like a butter pat made out of $1/4$ inch ply very effective.

In the USA Travelifts are frequent, though as most Americans own boats of a similar size to those in northern Europe, most lifts have a maximum load of 20 tons (bigger ones do exist). Some American yards tolerate do-it-yourself, though most of them demand that you buy paint through them. In most of the Mediterranean DIY is considered the normal course of events. In Turkey, labour was so cheap that I employed jobbing painters who worked very hard but used about 30% more paint than I did. Conditions are changing in Turkey; the marina at Kuş Adası has a Travelift, and one is planned for Bodrum now that harbour works have made the place safer.

Keep a few photographs of the yacht's underwater profile and section. This is helpful to lift and slipway operators. They cannot always read lines drawings, though in a good yard these are a help when slipping. Clearly mark the strength bulkheads on the hull. If you do not like a permanent mark, identify them with chalk or sticky tape when necessary, so that props and shores are wedged into the right places. It is a good thing to mark the gunwale permanently with the positions of the log impeller and any other sensitive device or projection. There is no reason why a steel boat cannot have lifting eyes welded to the gunwales, so dispensing with slings which often scrape off quite a lot of the paint that you have laboured so hard to put on.

REPAIRS AND FAILURES

Quality of repairs varies enormously from place to place. The more primitive the place the more ready are the local craftsmen to undertake anything, usually with tolerable results. You do not buy spare parts, you have them made at half the price. It is only when one rediscovers the village blacksmith that one sees what Western sophistication has lost: the Mr Fixit, par excellence. In the West Indies, however, the development and education of the local people is such that there are very few local craftsmen. Exceptions occur: there are competent wooden boatbuilders at Bequia, and they get some good wood up from South America.

Let us stop to consider the skills that are likely to be found in all but the most primitive places. I suggest:

- Diesel mechanics of some sort. Most places now have diesel engines in trucks, tractors and fishing boats. It is rare to find somewhere without some diesel ability, though it might be a bit haphazard.
- Simple welding and brazing.
- Elementary woodwork, carpentry rather than joinery. Often there is shipwright ability, particularly in planking and caulking, the latter being competent owing to the roughness of the former.
- Metal turning, and casting of small parts, but seldom enough to turn up a new shaft for instance.

- A sewing machine, usually old enough to be strong enough to stitch anything bendable.
- Hydraulic knowledge. This may surprise you, but it is becoming a common feature in agriculture and trucking.

What is rarely to be found outside yachting centres?

- Aluminium welding.
- Stainless steel welding (sometimes at basic level, but almost never with the right rods which is important).
- Electronic capability and spares.
- Electric capability above household or car level.
- Swaging or Talurit wire fittings.
- Sand-blasting, except unintentionally in strong winds.
- Facilities for hauling out fin-keel boats.
- Spare parts for nautical equipment.

Unless one is going to confine one's cruising to the coasts of Britain, the Riviera, or the USA, it is worth pondering these two lists. To take to the out-islands a boat built of exotic materials, with state-of-the-art rig and electronics and the current racing-yacht hull form, is to run a big risk of having pleasure spoiled by non-functioning, non-repairable, sophisticated gear. There is a lesser but definite risk of disaster due to the inability of both local craftsmen and yourself to service or repair even quite minor damage.

Insurance underwriters might well take more note of the repairability of the craft they insure, bearing in mind that the majority of claims are for damage rather than total loss.

If one tried, one could have a very pleasant boat that would reduce or cut out a lot of the payments the owner has to make to others. She would have shoal draught, a reinforced cutaway stem and a powerful stream anchor. She would avoid marinas; just drop anchor and put her bows to the beach. Rig the passarella over the bows. Have four 5-ton screw jacks vertically in tubes through the hull next to the bulkheads and at refit time just jack her up clear of the water. I would not think they would cost more than a couple of haulouts, and from then it's paying for itself.

Simple strong masts, simple strong rigging. Basic electronics, electrics only. (Electric navigation lights are essential: no others are remotely adequate. Electric engine starting is also desirable. And see Chapter Twelve on Navigation.)

Rigging and sail maintenance is not difficult, just absorbing. One will need, for sail repairs, a more substantial kit than those typically sold to the dilettante in Cowes. A yard or two of various weights of cloth to suit sails and awnings, and different weights of seaming thread on commercial-size reels. Twine for whipping, roping, grommeting and serving. Each of the crew to have their own palm to fit, and practise how to use it. I have not found stay-put sail-repair tape effective for even temporary repairs, possibly because it had been in the locker a long time before being used, though round-the-world racers have access to much better products.

We find it convenient to fix sail repairs of seams with strong parcel tape and then to sew over the taped seams. This makes the job much easier, the stitching perforates the tape, making it simple to rip off afterwards. We have also had success with a temporary repair by glueing a patch on both sides with Evostik contact adhesive.

If travelling far afield, take spare cordage. Not only is it a consumable item that must be replaced, but it is also an attractive commodity in less prosperous communities; the theft of all of a yacht's running rigging is by no means unknown and one should be able to replace the more vital items at least.

If your standing rigging is highly tuned, so that tension is critical, it is important to have some matching steel wire. Stainless steel wire is unobtainable in many places, and even when it is you cannot be sure exactly what you are getting: these steels differ quite a bit, and some are unsuitable for a salty environment.

Always use anhydrous lanolin for greasing shackles, rigging screws and other deck fittings. It is not only more waterproof than grease, but does not wash off easily, and is cheaper and less messy. Never use graphite grease in a steel or aluminium ship's fittings because it can produce local galvanic corrosion problems.

• *Maintenance reminder* •

As a logbook we use an A5 page-to-a-day diary. Those sold by English stationers are glued together and do not last too well, but on the Continent it is possible to get older-fashioned sewn and bound diaries. These will have the added advantage of giving Mediterranean holidays and local phone numbers, but will omit the metric conversion tables.

These diaries or logs also become maintenance reminders. Put items that are time-critical on their expected days. Normally it will be highly inconvenient to do that job when that day comes round, and when the page is turned the job gets forgotten. This likelihood can be reduced (though not eliminated) by having a bookmark. When an item crops up which cannot be done at once it is added to the list on the bookmark, eventually to be crossed off when done. I have a very large bookmark.

If you have no engine hour meter, then whenever you use engine or generator note the time run in the log and keep a cumulative total. I record it only to the nearest half-hour, trying to be consistent about rounding up or down as appropriate.

Even in the tropics, use antifreeze in the cooling water because it has good corrosion inhibiting properties, though it can be understandably hard to find.

Do not forget to keep your sextant lightly oiled, and attend to compass gimbals. Swing the compass yourself once a year to check for alterations in the deviation. If it is only a degree or so different just make a note on the card. If there are some large differences, or if the differences are clustered in the same quadrant, then check to see if you have left anything magnetic about or have moved or fitted something significantly metallic. If there is no simple explanation get a professional

Sometimes it is necessary to save time and effort – here we have hired a sand blaster for routine maintenance.

adjustment done. Note that after passing through a violent thunderstorm or if the ship is on a cardinal heading for a long period, the magnetic characteristics of a steel vessel can be altered quite a bit. Take an early opportunity of checking, but you should do that daily in any event. Such changes are normally not permanent.

If one of the crew is contemplating having a replacement hip or knee joint, make sure to specify to the surgeon that the metal parts must be non-magnetic. No joke!

HOMEWARD-BOUNDERS

Repair problems are best avoided by keeping things simple. What you cannot repair yourself with on-board materials and facilities is probably going to cause trouble sometime. Things do go wrong; even well-designed, well-made items break or fail for no apparent reason. Murphy's Law being certain in its effect, you can bet your life things will fail just when you need them. Here are a few examples of pre-planned jury-rigs that can be used to manage temporarily. We call them 'homeward-bounders':

- Bulldog clips for rigging or, better still, double throat wire grips (Davey & Co old catalogue number 1626) which do not cripple the wire. Keep quite a lot of the right sizes stowed in lanolin to keep them usable, and a few lengths of wire rope or short chain to bridge a gap. If a wire parts and you have no spare wire, make eyes with the clips and close the gap with a lot of turns of small cordage, which is better than one or two of larger.
- Carry a little impeller pump of the sort that can be used on an electric drill. I have used one when the cooling water pump on the generator failed, and for other less important jobs.
- Holes in rubber exhaust hose can be fixed with a short length (an inch or two is enough) of the right size steel pipe. Cut the hose, insert pipe, and secure with hose clips. Holes in a rigid exhaust are best closed by a hose clip over a soft leather patch (if wet exhaust), or over a Fearnought pad (if dry). On wet exhausts, heavy cloth and rubber are usable.
- Hose clips have a variety of unofficial uses – they do not merely stay round in shape, but they can be used to bind all sorts of things together.

Various advisory or regulatory bodies approve copper tube for diesel fuel lines. I think this is dangerous in a boat that gets a lot of use, for copper not only work-hardens by vibration and frequent change of shape, but also time-hardens when liquid is flowing through it. In either case it becomes brittle and breaks when it will cause most trouble. Bronze pipe would be fine, but I prefer the flexible woven metal type, which is not overly expensive. Metal-clad plastic will only protect against accidental physical damage, but it does not proof the tube against fire. But when your copper (approved) tube breaks, and it certainly will before the plastic, that can lead to fire, too. For this eventuality (the break, that is) keep some strong plastic tube and clips. If using the metal-covered flexible piping, make sure that the metal cover is in contact at each end to eliminate static electricity build-up. Recently we have come across approved flexible tubing for diesel oil. This will solve the problem (we have fitted it in *Hosanna*), but many boats will not be so fitted.

A frequent failure spot is a metal elbow in a wet exhaust system. Spares are very heavy, and they fail so often that one can get badly caught out. Look around lorry agencies for rubber cooling water elbows, which can be the right size. They might be cheaper, lighter and better fitted from the kick-off.

Steering gear fails from time to time; this problem is solvable by using the emergency tiller which you will have in the locker. The rudder shaft itself can break, leaving the rudder intact but swinging freely. As a precaution against this horrible event, arrange a small V-shaped notch (open downwards) near the top after edge of the rudder. It is easy to lower over the stern a bight of rope with a few overhand knots in it, or with a length of light chain (6mm section, say) in the

Jury rudder control, using a strong pre-fixed hook.

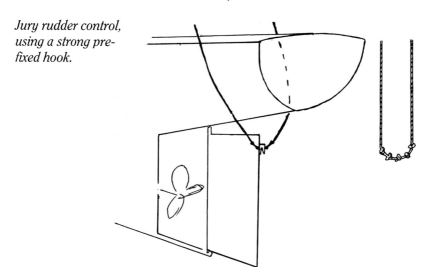

middle. With one end either side of the boat, pull gently up and the knots or the chain can be jammed into the V, thus getting the rudder under some sort of control without having to go over the side to do it.

SPARES AND TOOLS

Finally, here is a list of the spare parts I have needed over the past 25 years, which must indicate something. The tool list is somewhat longer than for normal cruising. If you become able to use all of these tools competently before you start you will be better off than I was at that point, for a lot of these have had to be added to my original outfit. Do not let the chores spoil the sailing.

SPARES USED IN BOTH *FARE WELL* AND *HOSANNA*

These were used in more than 25 years of continuous cruising. The number in parentheses is the number used where this is more than one.

ON DECK

Oil seals renewed on SL521 windlass (2).

Shockcord, various sizes, over 50 yards.

Cordage for sheets and lashings.

Shackles. I mostly use galvanised, and replace them when they rust. But stainless ones do fail, and of course the pins I lose never match the bows I drop at other times.

SL hatch stays (3).

Hatch handle.

Various hinges with brass pins (these are never strong enough).

Hatch sealing round the acrylic.

Winch handle.

Deck caulking. Rotator for towing log (dropped overboard).

IN THE ENGINE ROOM

Submersible bilge pumps (3); switches (1) for same.

Water Puppy washdown pump (2).

Godwin fresh-water pump shaft seal and bearing, also a new motor.

Float switches (7).

Air-pressure pump switches.

Sight-glass plastic tubing on FW and oil fuel tanks.

Fuel-oil tubing, olives, cocks, bits and pieces.

Exhaust rubber tubing, exhaust elbows.

Dozens of hoseclips, all sizes.

Water pump on refrigerator (2).

ON THE MAIN ENGINE

Flexible lube oil pipe, set of cooling water hoses, numerous filters, shaft gland packing.

ON THE GENERATOR PRIME MOVER

The Farymann needed: injector, water pumps (2), set of flexible mountings, fuel pipes, valves and valve gear.

The Petter needed: new cylinder heads (2), valve springs (7), new lube oil piping, water pumps (2), water pump impellers (3), set of flexible mountings, bleed screw on injection pump, injector, corrosion inhibiting anodes (22). A lot of blasphemy.

ELECTRICAL

Lucas AC5A alternator (3).

Lucas 440 regulator (6).

Lucas indicator bulb for above circuit (2).

Bosch alternator.

Auto voltage control for G&M 3kVA 230V alternator.

Transformer (1), rheostat, and bridge rectifiers (2) for G&M alternator.

Brushes for all motors.

Diodes in SL Shorepower rectifier (5).

Main batteries. Obviously, these will need changing from time to time.

Battery isolating switches (3).

Japanese battery changeover switches (2).

A large-scale rewiring following lightning strike.

Diodes for Sharp Autopilot (2).

Solenoid spool valve in Cetrek hydraulic pump.

Ammeter.

Many switches, sockets and plugs of all types. Fuses.

Dry batteries by the dozen. New torches.

Fluorescent tubes.

Bulbs – dozens, but especially the 24V 6W.

NAVIGATING INSTRUMENTS

Impeller assemblies for Walker Trident Mk 3 log (14!), and major repairs (3).

Wind instrument complete due to lightning strike.

Photo-transistor in anemometer. Vane blown off wind direction instrument – twice.

NAVIGATING INSTRUMENTS

Rotator and flywheel for Walker Cherub log.

Echosounders: various small repairs, 1 new instrument and 1 transducer (Seafarer) and one co-ax plug.

Radio receivers (2).

Pencil sharpener.

Magnets for compass correction; they rust away in time. (Watch this carefully if they are encased.)

DOMESTIC

Weights for pressure-cooker valve, and seal.

Sewing machine driving belt.

Tap washers.

Photo-electric cell for Perkins Mate cooker.

Sealing strip for hob of cooker.

Fire-cement for cooker furnace.

Lavac WC: spare seat seals (2), flap valves (2), joker valves (5). Tubing for WC installation. Lavac WC bowl (the aluminium casting disintegrated, but they don't make that type any more, sensible people).

Fire extinguishers

Some Tupperware.

Thermos flask.

A SPARES LIST FOR CONSIDERATION

FOR (EACH) ENGINE

Water hoses

Pump impellers

Any flexible pipe

Complete exhaust run

Filters

Pipe couplings and olives

Gaskets and seals

Mountings, if flexible

Valve springs

Plastic fuel pipe and clips

Hose clips – dozens

HP fuel pipes (from pump to injectors)

Spare belts

Duplicate flanges for hoses

Coupling bolts

Grease for stern tube

Automatic transmission fluid for gearbox (if appropriate)

Enough lube oil for one oil change.

ELECTRICAL

Electrical terminal strip

Crimp terminals

Alternator regulator warning lamp

Circuit breakers, fuses

Switches, sockets, plugs, light bulbs

Assorted resistors, capacitors, diodes, transistors – you may not be able to use them, but someone else might on your behalf.

Lucar connectors

Cable of all sizes

Motor brushes

OTHER

Spares kit for all pumps

Rubber sheet (2mm)(an old smooth hot-water bottle does nicely.)

Paint, brushes etc

Soft aluminium sheet (3mm), or copper in wooden boat

Threaded rod, nuts

Bits of plywood, timber

Sealing compound

Caulking

Stainless sheet (about 1.5mm)

Duct, and self-amalgamating tapes

ON DECK

Drive belt for windlass

Bolts, nuts for spreader roots

Shackles, thimbles etc

Canvas and thread

Cordage

Bulldog clips

Lanolin

Oar for dinghy (plus oarlocks, if of the loose type)

Flags and ensigns

Eyebolts

Clevis and cotter pins

Whipping twine

Shockcord and terminals

20ft of largest wire

20ft of smallest wire

Winch handle

Wooden plugs, assorted

Sail battens (if foolish enough to have them)

TOOL LIST

I did not start out with all these. Many have had to be added on the way, which tells one something.

SAWS

A general-purpose, medium tooth

Large hack and small hack

Coping (if jigsaw not carried) spare blades

HAMMERS

Large ball-peen

Claw

Chipping

CHISELS

1/4 and 3/4 inch firmer

Hard chisels

SCREWDRIVERS

For no. 4, 6, 8, slot-screws

Dumpy for no 8 slot-screws

Small and large crosshead

Dumpy crosshead

Very large slot

Angled slot, and crosshead, preferably ratchet

Percussion

FILES

Small triangular, round and half-round

Large, round and halfround,

Half-round wood rasp (the wood-butcher's *vade mecum*)

Thread-restoring files

CLAMPS

Assorted, including adjustable opening vice, or a Black & Decker Jobber or Workmate

ASSORTED

Bradawl

Bevel guage

Square

Small smoothing plane, rebating plane

Pliers: large, small pointed, and circlip

Spanners: ring or open tube according to choice

Socket set. Large and small adjustable. Pipe wrench

Large and small Mole wrench or Visegrip

TOOL LIST continued

ASSORTED	ELECTRIC TOOLS, AND TOOLS FOR ELECTRICAL WORK:	
Nut splitter	Two-speed drill up to 10mm	Multi-test meter to read
Stud removers	Jigsaw	0–25V DC, 0–250V AC,
Taps and dies	Orbital sander	0–10 ohms,
Hand drill	Small angle grinder (steel	0–100 ohms, and
Steel rule, calipers	boats)	0–1000 ohms
Allen keys	Soldering iron	Crimping tool
Punches, drifts	Wire clippers and strippers	Long jump leads (lorry
Sheet metal shears	Insulated screwdrivers (lots)	type, say about 20ft)
Oilstone, rough and	Pointed-nose small pliers	Short jump leads
smooth each side		Plenty of screws, bolts,
Dentist's probe		nuts, washers, friction
Long, angled, surgeon's		washers, self-taps, tacks,
forceps (the best		panel pins and nails to
dropped-item recovery		choice
tool)		
Funnels		

Aboard *Hosanna*, which followed *Fare Well*, our needs have been rather different. We fitted out *Hosanna* while living on board, and even while cruising, so we carried vastly more tools than one would need for maintenance. This did not matter much for *Hosanna* is the size of a small factory; there is a wealth of difference in maintaining a small yacht and a large barge. Most of it is a matter of strength, not only of the barge, but also of the crew.

Watch out you do not get a boat so large and heavy that she is beyond your resources, financial and physical. Laurel and I are 15 years older than when we bought *Hosanna*, and they are significant years. Maintaining *Hosanna* (displacing 60-odd tonnes) has been hard work, but we feel repaid by having lived and cruised widely in a damned good boat. We could not wholeheartedly recommend such an undertaking to anyone who has not had some experience of big boats.

Financially, the difference is not in proportion to her size because one can buy second-hand, or from commercial suppliers who do not demand the same markups as the yacht-chandlery trade, but that suggests knowing where to look, experience that takes time to acquire. One will use different tools and the work will be on a different scale, often involving far more physical strength, lifting things for instance.

The most important criteria are to marry one's comfort to one's financial circumstances, also to one's knowledge and physical ability, and lastly to a sense of joyous improvisation, problem solving, and being undaunted. If, however, you lack practical hands-on experience, gain it on something handier in size, and then work up.

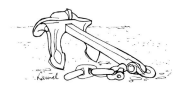

9 • Power

'.....some onely will burne and fume out a most stinking poyson smoake…'

There have been references to engines and power sources in various chapters, but I would like to pull some of this together to consider the question as a whole.

We once made a long cruise with a six-month-old baby in a wooden yacht with no engine and no electricity. There was no water tank, wash basin or galley come to that, nor were there any guardrails, lifelines, radio or loo. Instead of the latter there was a bucket marked 'for sanitary purposes only' in red paint. When we lent the boat to a foreigner who we thought spoke English, we were dismayed to find he had used this bucket for fresh water. He had read the bucket's legend and reasoned that the loo bucket would be marked 'for insanitary purposes only'. We thought it kinder not to disillusion him, but have wondered ever since about the claim that English is the most easily understood of languages.

That cruise was wildly successful, three adults and a baby enjoyed it immensely, but it was almost 50 years ago; expectations were not extreme, and you could sail (literally) into any Mediterranean harbour and never meet another yacht. The late Geoff Pack, a splendid sailor, was a great advocate of the simple life afloat: 'KISS', or 'Keep It Simple, Stupid', but even he expected a slightly higher standard of living when we discussed this with him in the 1990s.

An engine of some sort has become virtually a necessity. Before yacht harbours or marinas existed, a yacht would enter commercial harbours under sail and warp herself into a convenient berth with little effort. Nowadays many commercial harbours are closed to yachts altogether because there is a marina next door where they are supposed to go and pay for the privilege. And marinas tend to have rules forbidding yachts to meander about under sail because there are not only too many yachts, but too many yachtsmen who have never learnt to manoeuvre in a constricted space under sail.

Even those that have can get it wrong. Hal Roth, a renowned sailor who has sailed many times round the world, liked to berth engine-less. We were in Seville when he arrived. He jilled about waiting for the huge road bridge to swing open and close off traffic on the four-lane main highway. When it did, he tried to sail through, but found that he had to pass through in the lee of the bridge piers against a contrary current. As he was blanketted, he lost way. He remained poised motionless between the bridge abutments while half Spain fumed on the roads above. Finally, after about a quarter of an hour, he made it through, to resounding cheers, sounding of car horns, and possibly a firework display as well. He reached the berth, the usual stern-to affair.

He must have been unnerved by the bridge business. In the end it took the massed crews of the several yachts already in place to manhandle him bodily into the intended gap. It took more than half an hour. Not a pretty manoeuvre! If sailors like him can make such a horlicks, what chance have lesser mortals?

So, take advice: an auxiliary engine is now virtually essential.

ENGINES

There are some companies whose diesels may or may not be the best, but whose engines are found world-wide and whose service is first class. In my view, chief among these is Perkins, whose engines in one form or another are found everywhere in tractors, combine harvesters, trucks, buses and fishing boats. I have come across sheds in rural Calabria (there is an Italian saying, 'si trova niente in Calabria' 'one finds nothing in Calabria' and it's evidently not true) and huts in Africa piled high with every conceivable Perkins part. At every depot I have visited it has been, 'Yes, how many do you need?', and I have not found any other make of any other thing anywhere near this standard. If you add to this the fact that *Fare Well*'s Perkins 4236 engine did over 5000 hours without any major attention, you will understand my feelings.

In the bigger boats, General Motors and Caterpillar diesels do well, and service seems to be good. Gardner still hold the best reputation for sheer reliability, though the company is no longer the majestic affair it once was. In my opinion Ford suffer because there are so many differing marine conversions, not all of which are well done; and though spares for the engine itself are not too bad, the problems attaching to service of the marinising parts are great. I'm also aware that Fiat and Renault often have poor service away from their home ground. Mercedes have a good reputation, which seems not always to be borne out in practice; parts availability seems to depend on nearness to centres of prosperity.

My experience is that in the smaller ranges, Volvo have lost a lot of their one-time popularity because of poor spares availability and high prices. We have had two generators with Volvo 2002 prime movers, and I personally would never have a marine Volvo again. Twice bitten, more fool I. It required constant attention and more than its fair share of blasphemy, and thank heaven it has now been discontinued. Yanmar and Bukh seem to be popular. Farymann and Petter, whose engines are in use on so many agricultural pumps and farm generators, ought to have a good spares service for their marine versions, like Perkins, but I have been disappointed. Spares are hard to find anywhere for both engines, and even their local agents complain; one of them showed me his almost empty racks. He had been waiting months for valve springs. Engines of this type have been converted for

Wind-power is a useful energy – especially for airing bedding.

marine use and in Petter's case, the combination of aluminium cylinder head with raw water cooling together with a world-wide scarcity of the anodes essential for marine use was a perfect plan for trouble.

I refuse to discuss petrol engines at all in the context of yachts.

Beware of Gardner engines that have been reconditioned by backyard firms using poor parts and relying on the reputation of the basic engine to find buyers. Also beware when a good company is taken over by a bad one and the whole standard starts to fall.

If there is an engine already fitted in a yacht you are thinking of buying, then in addition to the broad views I have given, view with suspicion any product of a small company that is the wholly owned subsidiary of a major conglomerate holding company. The small company's managers may be competent and conscientious (though not necessarily: many of them are run by accountants) but in any case they are completely at the mercy of the management of their parent company, whose decisions will pay little attention to the interests of customers at the far end of an attenuated chain, but will affect such matters as spares availability and their overseas distribution.

Might I please appeal for someone to produce a range of marine diesels with all adjustments, controls and service points on one side and the top? It's not impossible.

By the year 2000, not a lot had changed. Perkins have decided to hive off their marine engines for adaption by other companies, and I am aware that the service has deteriorated in some parts of the world. They have also decided to produce small engines based on castings etc from other companies.

We, ourselves, in our big boat, have had a disaster with a Cummins engine. Though the French Cummins agent was excellent, I have to add this engine to Volvo on my personal avoidance list, not because it is badly made or because the service is bad, but because I find it far too complicated an engine for an amateur to self-maintain, and unless meticulously looked after it goes wrong stealthily. I want an engine I can abuse. Not seriously, you understand, but tolerant enough to be able to postpone maintenance until the time suits me and not the engine.

There are fewer slow-running, small diesel engines about now. The industry seems to think we are all obsessed by power/weight ratios and produce engines that give their horsepower by means of revolving at an ever-increasing rate. I am unhappy about this. My experience is that slow running diesels are the more tolerant, the easier to repair, especially in out-of-the-way places, and they do not give off that irritating high-pitched whine that characterises anything revolving at 4000rpm. For me the diesel is epitomised by those old engines like the Kromhout, the sort that revolved at 100 rpm, gave off a reassuring *thonk, thonk, thonk* sound, and blew smoke rings out of the exhaust. Simple (though energetic) starting and almost impossible to stop. Would run on anything including wheat flour. However, one has to compromise a little.

The Japanese market a range of high-revving diesels. With no expert knowledge, I recoil instinctively from them. They seem to me more suitable for high-speed runabout use rather than as auxiliary motors for sailing boats.

One reads about diesel fuel in backward places often being contaminated. I have never found it so, and suspect that water in the fuel so often written about comes from onboard sources, as it did on the only occasion when we suffered from this problem. But supply pipes should have very good water-trap type filters, preferably mounted in parallel, and each separated by cocks so that one can change one filter while the engine is running on the other. Other filters are needed in line, of course, preferably two. Carry a fair stock of filter elements, but change them frequently and in rotation, because they all have metal in them somewhere and this is liable to rust while in storage, thus rendering the filter element useless. We recommend Racor fuel filters; they are expensive but much better than any others we have come across, and fishermen swear by them.

If you have conventional filters, obtain from your engine's makers a world-wide list of equivalent elements and lubricating oils. Manufacturers do not like supplying such a list, and parrot cry that only their products are good enough for their engines. This is rubbish; they want to charge up to three times the proper price for an item with their name on, but that does not differ from the part manufacturer's model. Engine dealers like to sell, so if you are buying a new engine, get the list before you deal. They'll say they don't have the information: they lie. *Get it before you deal.* It is in any event impossible to obtain well-known brands in many places.

Make sure the fuel tank has a draw-off point above and clear of a sump. It should have an access big enough for a clenched fist, to enable the sump to be easily cleaned out. There should be a drain cock at the lowest point to drain off condensation which might gather over a cold spell.

Outboard motor (and all two-stroke) service is of a very variable standard. I think all companies appoint agents who are little more than salesmen, and mechanical competence varies from 0 to 100. The best I ever came across worked round behind Barclays Bank in Bequia, in the Grenadines. He was the only man who ever got our Evinrude working satisfactorily, and, sadly, he was getting on in years.

If possible, have all machinery in one compartment that you can get your body into. It is no joke having a diesel engine in pieces all over the living room floor, and it ought not to be necessary except perhaps in the smallest yachts. Nor should the machinery be fitted in like a three-dimensional jigsaw puzzle for this is a poor inducement to do maintenance. Ideally one should not have to remove A to work on B or vice versa. The engine space should be well ventilated for hot climates. We once had a fair amount of water down the engine room ventilator when laid well over in a storm, but it was an exception. Even so, it is as well to have flaps on the ventilators and, unlike me, remember to close them in bad weather.

There are several ways of arranging the exhaust. Most yachts now have a wet exhaust, where the heated cooling water is injected into the exhaust at the point where it leaves the manifold, and both water and cooled exhaust gases are blown out through the ship's side or transom. Because the gases are well cooled, it is possible to run the exhaust in re-inforced rubber tubing which builders find easier and simpler to install.

There are two main problems. If the engine is below the waterline, it is possible for the cooling water to syphon over and fill the system and engine cylinders with water. This can be embarrassing, and is best avoided by having an anti-syphon device. There are several ways of achieving this and which method you choose will depend on your particular requirements. If you have no experience of this problem, take local advice.

The other problem comes from the fact that the cooling water you blow out over the side is seawater. It is not desirable to cool engines with sea water because so many of them have dissimilar metals which corrode electrolytically in salt water. It is essential to cool marine engines with fresh water containing corrosion inhibitors such as diesel anti-freeze and then cool that fresh water with the sea water in a heat exchanger. (Anti-freeze in the tropics? Yes, it is a good idea.)

You will find various small diesels on the market which are cooled by sea water, a system known as direct cooling. Their makers will try to persuade you that sacrificial anodes solve the problem. They do not. They are sacrificed very much faster in warmer sea water; you do not have any ready means of checking what sacrifice they have made; they sometimes become difficult to extract when corroded; and often the right ones are impossible to obtain.

A third problem comes when navigating in water which contains large quantities of weed and/or silt which clog up the system. Jellyfish too have caused us some minor grief, as have plastic bags and a dead furry animal that I did not wish to get to know. If you are liable to spend time in such waters, then consider a different system.

Keel cooling, for example. We navigate *Hosanna* both at sea and in the canals and rivers. Generally our ratio of sea to canal is about 2 to 1, but a 2000-mile trip down the Danube has influenced that. She is a big boat, and instead of the usual big engine, we have three small ones. At sea we would use all three if we want any speed, on the rivers we use the outer two, and on the canals we use the centre engine only; it is very economical and is plenty powerful enough. The outer engines are sea-water cooled, but the centre engine is keel-cooled with a dry exhaust. Having the room, I opted for an extra large silencer or muffler, and then had it professionally lagged. The fresh cooling water is piped through the bottom into two long pipes fitted either side of the external keel. There is also a branch leading to the calorifier to give us hot water, but be careful: engine cooling water comes out at about 180°F, which is much too hot to wash your hands in.

The other alternative, a dry exhaust and air cooling, whether directly or via a water circulation and radiator is, I think, not wholly suitable for a boat bound for hot climates.

All the above considerations apply equally to diesel generator exhausts and cooling.

Hand cranking a diesel engine is not for the middle-aged and breathless, let alone the old and tired. It is heart-attack stuff. We once did that sort of thing to cars and lawn-mowers but modern cars do not even have starting handles and we have all got used to that. So our boat engines have electric starting, too, because it is easier. The battery enters the scene.

ELECTRICITY

Lead-acid, or nickel-alkaline batteries? The latter is the best by far, but its virtues are bought at a price. We have used many of the nickel-alkaline ones, second-hand from various sources of government surplus. A 20-year life is normal so they repay their very high cost. A big one aboard *Hosanna* is now 16 years old and is in perfect order. They take any amount of bad treatment and seem to resurrect themselves, with a little help. The electrolyte (potassium hydroxide) needed for their life-support is easier to store in a steel boat. But the cost of providing the ampere-hours that many fairly sophisticated boats need these days would be astronomical, about six times the cost of lead-acid batteries.

Lead-acid batteries come in different types. Starting batteries for engines are not suitable for running domestic electrical circuits, except in the very smallest of boats where having two separate batteries would be inconvenient. For most modern boats, it is best to have separate batteries for starting and domestic use, and these would be of two distinct types. The latter should be of the deep-cycle variety which withstand frequent discharging and charging. These are the type fitted to milk-floats and town delivery vans, and the batteries last much longer than starting batteries. *Hosanna* has a bank of them (they come in separate cells) made by Exide, that are now 12 years old. Like the nickel batteries, they do not come that cheap, but over time are a bargain. They cost (new) about twice as much as a starting battery.

I do not propose to go into details about how much battery power you need. There are excellent books on the market (or in the library) on direct current wiring for boats and it is a business that should be overseen by experts more proficient than I am. All I will say is that modern domestic and navigational equipment can need substantial battery power, and it is false economy to under-power the boat.

You can keep the batteries charged up in several ways. It is not a good idea, even for the simplest installation, to rely on the occasional use of the main engine. For larger installations with two or more batteries, a secondary charger is essential, and ideally one needs blocking diodes so that each battery will absorb a common charge, but not give off a common discharge, each battery being isolated on the discharge side to its own dedicated service. See a specialist book for a circuit diagram.

The special diesel generator is heavy, bulky and noisy. Admittedly they are getting less heavy, bulky and noisy, but nevertheless, like some husbands who fit this description, they are not comfortable bedfellows. We would only go down this road if the number of electrical appliances on board, and their consumption, were very substantial, and then I would suggest you consider making some of the appliances run on alternating current instead of 12 volt direct current, and having a diesel alternator. You are getting very substantial now, but with more and more marinas having 220-volt AC sockets, this approach has its virtues, even though the generators are expensive to run and are still heavy, bulky and noisy.

Windvanes are good in tradewind zones. We have written elsewhere about Bill's accident with a windvane (the idiot!), and we will spare him the shame of repeating it. They are dangerous beasts and need mounting high up and well out of reach of idiots and others, higher up than heavy gear like this should be on a small yacht. *Fare Well* had an Ampair, and it was excellent. It gave 5 amps at 24 volts in a force 4 wind. Its main problem was that it made too much power at winds of force 5 or above, when it would 'cut out' and then free-wheel. With no power to generate, the blades accelerated and whizzed round like aeroplane propellers, and made a hell of a din, a variable noise that it was difficult to get accustomed to.

Bill tried to couple a small alternator to the propeller shaft of the boat by way of a 10:1 geared pulley system to get a charge when sailing with the gearbox in neutral. It never worked out well. Churning up the oil in the gearbox absorbed so much of the power that there was not enough to power the alternator. If we could have had a mechanical clutch to physically separate the gearbox from the shaft, it might have been different.

• *Alternating current (AC)* •

Even if one does not have 240-volt generators it is worth considering a circuit powered from the DC batteries by either a rotary converter or an electronic one. It is easy to get 500 watts (or even more if you wish, but converter prices rise sharply with size), which can be used for a small food mixer as well as electric drills, sanders, blow-dryers, vacuum cleaners, soldering irons and many other things that ease the chores for permanent residents. Usually this type of appliance is on for a few minutes only, so the battery drain is small. In any event, a 240-volt AC circuit is desirable if one is going to spend a winter on shore power.

Do not rely on all countries having the same wiring practice. The UK system of Earth, Live and Neutral is good in principle, but foreign electricians often do not wire up three-pin sockets in a consistent way. Have twin fast circuit-breakers, one on each load-carrying wire of your shore power connection, and have a certain means of completely isolating the ship's AC generator when connected to shore supply. Also, do not rely on the third pin in shore connections being connected to earth; use a two-wire shore power cable and bond the earth connections of all your shipboard outlets to your own earth.

Some professional electricians recommend the use of an AC to AC transformer when on shore power abroad. This provides all the power you need, without any direct connection with shore terminals, and can be made to step up the Continental voltage, which is very slightly lower than the British 240 volts. Sometimes, at the outer end of a long marina pontoon the Continental voltage falls as low as 180, which is not good for your appliances. Of course, having your own transformer is safer, but I wonder whether the increase in safety is cost-effective. I think our method, with reasonable vigilance, is 99%: to improve that to 99.5% is not of sufficient significance.

In Europe generally the supply is 220 volts 50Hz, but, as we said above, voltage at the dockside sometimes falls as low as 180, especially in Italy where we know that a lot of people tap into the supply illegally with crocodile clips. In the USA the supply is generally 110 volts 60Hz, but it is possible with some shore sockets to get 220 volts by connecting up the pins in a particular way. Local knowledge is necessary, as the pilot books say, but Americans are very obliging. We found that all our 50Hz equipment worked without any noticeable ill effect on 60Hz, and I suspect that there is considerable tolerance in the design. Motors and clocks go faster: this is possibly what is meant by dynamic America.

HYDRAULICS

For boats over 40 feet, hydraulics systems are good for fittings such as power windlasses or even for sheet winches. With the coming of power-driven headsail furling/reefing gears that do not cost more than the boat, a hydraulic motor is best, for the motor has to be fitted at the worst possible place for anything electric: the very stemhead itself. Perhaps the electric motor itself can be sealed, though such seals are never totally reliable. Remember that the wiring has to reach the motor and pass through the forepeak and then a deck-fitting and is thus vulnerable.

It is also possible to have a hydraulic drive for the propeller shaft, and though these are not so power-efficient as a direct drive, they do allow the engine to be sited in a more convenient place. Opinions differ as to whether one needs to have a second hydraulic pump to drive auxiliary fittings (such as a windlass), but my own hydraulic adviser (Dick of Bure Marine Ltd), whose advice has been consistently good over many years, says in broad Norfolk that you dint orter muck about. Separate the systems and get the proper pump for the job because the extra cost isn't going to be that much.

SOLAR PANELS

Solar panels are getting cheaper but still have not got down to the price range which was once forecast for the end of the last century. What has happened is that the sizes and types available are more numerous. We have written about the need for good awnings, especially over the cockpit, and one should consider having a solid awning, plywood or something, which could then be covered in solar panels.

If your dinghy has an outboard with electrical starting, and these are becoming more common now, a mini solar panel for fixing in the dinghy is obtainable and this keeps the battery up when on passage, or when the dinghy has been on its davits for a long time.

Laurel

10 • Victualling, and Other Domestic Considerations

'Many suppose anything is good enough to serve men at sea'

THE GALLEY

A part from the heads, nothing will get more use on your boat than the galley. If you wish life aboard to be the peaceful and enjoyable experience we all hope for, it repays much thought and planning. You will not get it completely right to start with, but your first cruise will show up any design faults and mistakes in emphasis. These should be rectified. Even small inconveniences can become very irritating if encountered several times a day, and are intolerable in bad weather.

> *'The Cooke roome where they dresse the victual may bee placed*
> *in diverse parts of the shippe'*

Think of the following things:
Does the galley work at an angle of (say) 40° on both tacks? Will the lockers or cupboards open without depositing their contents on the floor? Is everything strong enough for the cook to hang on to, or fall against? Are the things that you need in bad weather easily and conveniently stowed? (If the pan you need is at the bottom of a pile of seven, Murphy's Law makes it certain that the 45° roll will come just as you have them all out on the floor to reach the one you want, which will be at the bottom of the pile.) Items in constant use should have prime space, closely followed by the mugs, bowls and stores needed in bad weather. Separate the stacked pans (especially if they are non-stick) with cardboard picnic plates to prevent noise and scratches. Drawers in the galley sometimes make more sense than cupboards or shelves, especially if they open fore and aft (ie construct the carcase athwartships: this goes for bookshelves, too). All need strong catches of some sort: drawers can have a vertical retaining bar, a swing catch, or be the lift-and-pull-out kind.

Magnetic catches are not usually strong enough against the G-force of heavy groceries and a big wave, though having said that my magnetic knife rack seems to hang on to its cargo in all weathers.

If the crew is small, it is of great benefit to have plates and cutlery conveniently to hand. A one-decker washing-up plate rack can be held in place on the drainer

Hosanna's *galley is very well-designed with a good range of shelving and racks and ample work surfaces.*
A combined gas and electric hob and microwave oven take care of the cooking.

with two strong hooks; I have found this to withstand even very violent motion, as does a deep cutlery drainer fixed to the wall, which holds the necessary knives, forks and much used kitchen tools.

• *Cookers* •

The kind of stove you choose to cook with needs some thought. Bill mentioned the different fuel options in Chapter Six in some detail; I need not repeat them here. Top-of-the-stove cooking is fine for holidays, but for living aboard you will want to cook as you did on shore, and you will need to bake bread, which means an oven and grill is desirable.

Mini-all-purpose ovens are available these days (see below). At the other extreme are cookers for big yachts, rather like Agas. They are very expensive, but wonderful; I had one in *Fare Well.* Mine ran on diesel and had the added advantage that the stainless steel bolster that covered it would take a folded sheet. This meant that if I folded the washing carefully and placed it, still a little damp, on the warm bolster, I could walk away and let the ironing do itself. The stove was not gimballed, but was mounted athwartships. (Its fiddles always prevented a serious loss of soup.) It heated the water too, and had a strong crash bar.

That model had become too expensive when we fitted out *Hosanna,* and for the same money we got an electric cooker, a mixed gas and electric hob, and (having the space) a microwave cooker, plus a generator to run them all. I no longer regret the exchange, though the ironing no longer does itself quite so satisfactorily.

Gas stoves have the great advantage of instant heat and adjustability. Both the diesel cooker and the coal stoves still to be found in older boats are hot to use in the tropics; cold lunches become the order of the day.

• *Microwave ovens* •

Many boats nowadays are thinking of installing microwave ovens, as I have done. Their advantages are: short cooking times, and therefore less power consumed; they do not heat up the galley in the tropics; and they fit into a small space. Though their output is measured as 600 watts, they will actually draw between 1000 and 1500 watts. They are now being made specially for yachts with a built-in inverter so that they may be used with battery power, otherwise an AC generator is needed. A drop-down door model, such as I began with, is best on a boat, but they are no longer on the market, so you must allow space for the sweep of the door sideways. In case you break the glass sheet or turntable (replacements are difficult to get and extremely expensive), take with you a suitable Pyrex dish as a spare. The best way of cooking in foul weather is in two-minute bursts, so you can see the handiness of a microwave. You can use it as a meatsafe if the weather is cool enough, and it's also an excellent place to put goodies away from pets or children – while they set or defrost, for example. The small all-purpose oven-grills with a hotplate on top, as mentioned above, are sometimes combined with a microwave oven. They are very convenient where space is limited, but their power consumption is as much or more than a full-sized electric oven, and, at nearly 3000 watts are more than small inexpensive generators can cope with. In my experience the combined microwave-grill works less efficiently than the two would as different items, and cooking for six on one of them I would find a headache. All this must be balanced against the saving of power and expense.

• *Other methods of cooking* •

Whatever you choose to cook on, have another method of cooking, just in case. An all-electric galley is no good if the power fails, and it is possible to run out of gas. I have described the split hob I have in *Hosanna*, with two gas burners and two electric plates (these hobs are domestic and now easily obtainable, and we found screw-down fiddles to marinise them). The saloon is heated by a wood stove, on which we often cooked our lunch while converting *Hosanna* in the boatyard, using an upturned biscuit tin on a trivet as a Dutch oven, if it wasn't stew. A small charcoal barbecue is not only wonderful for sunny anchorages, but can be a useful cooking back-up in good weather – or that old standby the single-burner Primus (the self-pricking one) or even a small Camping Gaz stove in case of dire need.

Remember that your stove (and you) may have to cook at a sharp angle, or even crashing up and down (I had the dubious satisfaction of knowing that my diesel stove on *Fare Well* would function at a 60° angle: we were stranded in this position for a day or more, so it was quite important at the time). You will therefore need well-designed, high fiddles to keep your pans in position on the stove in a seaway. In addition, check that water cascading down a hatch will not put out the stove and prevent its use in a storm, as has happened on some racing yachts. At a time when hot food is most needed, you will be glad that your stove is in a safe, dry spot, and that you can brace yourself to use it without a waterfall descending on your head.

• *The sink* •

The sink, as Bill has said, is best with natural drainage. This has been a help to us in emergencies, such as bailing out the engine room. Since sink and engine room hatch were close together on *Fare Well* it was easy with two of us to bail straight into the sink. When we were fighting an engine room fire it was possible to get water to it with a good deal of control, for the same reason. As regards one sink or two, while Don Street swears by a double sink, even if they are too small to wash large pans in (it does make an extra catch-all while working), I prefer one bigger one: if only because when baling it drained one bucket of bilge water before the next one arrived. Don is right to point out that small sinks save water, but this is achieved at sea by placing a plastic bowl in the larger sink, which has the added advantage of cushioning against breakages. I also get mad if the sink is too small to immerse a dinner plate.

A board that fits over the sink for extra workspace is commonplace now, but was not when we built *Fare Well*. We invented our own, wood on one side and Formica on the other. When not in use it slotted into a specially made groove alongside the stove. A separate one, smaller but thicker, is carried as a chopping block, and a cleaver goes with it, as meat and fish often come in their original state.

• *Equipment* •

Avoid the temptation to clutter precious workspace with domestic appliances that will not work without shore power. Think of the mechanical aids our grandmothers used, and if you want them handy create storage space for them. I would prefer to take such things as a hand mincer and coffee grinder (rather than bulky electric mixers or food processors too big for most galleys), a well-engineered hand beater and a wall tin-opener that will not rust in a few days. You will not, as on holiday, be either camping or eating out all the time, so be sure your equipment suits your style of cooking. If you are a dab hand at cakes, take your cake tins. I use the non-stick loaf tins, which I keep cushioned from scratches with paper towels or picnic plates and are still rust-free after several years' use at sea. If you are good at patés or potted tongue, take the containers you know to be the right size, and the piece of wood to weight them with. Take an elegant dish for your speciality: sometimes one wants to splash out, joining the neighbouring boat for a combined dinner; and a little style is a welcome change. Not that a salad for 20 people does not taste just as good from a plastic washbowl – take several, they have many uses.

Spend time looking for your favourite tools in stainless steel. It took me years to find a pair of stainless tongs, without which I cannot even boil an egg. It is much easier nowadays, when specialist kitchen shops offer a range of sturdy tools in stainless steel. Strong plastic can be a good alternative: sieves, ladles, and potato mashers come to mind, but strong is the operative word.

As well as my tongs, the things I would not be without are:

- A pressure cooker (miniature ones are available if you lack space).
- A wall-mounted can-opener is invaluable when fast sea stew is needed.
- A small spatula or butter spreader.
- A hamburger press (mine is plastic), in which you can make all kinds of chicken burgers, meat and/or vegetable patties, fish cakes and so on, as well as the obvious uses.
- A Bamix Magic Wand, see Appendix C the only electrical kitchen gadget that has been with me for 25 years. This is the neatest handheld mincer and beater I have ever come across. It consumes 100 watts on 240 volts AC, and used with a tall jar or jug will purée soup, beat cakes or chop vegetables. It was designed for the blind and is very easy to clean. Many other firms are making similar models.

You will need something to weigh and measure with.

- A set of stainless steel measuring cups are useful: I found the plastic ones too breakable.
- A polythene jug marked in centilitres has lasted till it is all but illegible. Fortunately these are cheap and readily available in the markets of Europe. I once thought a miniature diet scale would be great for weighing, but it was too small, too fragile, apt to capsize, and extremely unreliable. I go for: A compact battery-operated electronic scale; it takes no more space than a paperback, can be used with any container, and weighs in both kilos and pounds, which is essential when cruising. Mark One lasted eight years and is still working thanks to some dodgy soldering (ours).
- A minute timer, preferably the 24-hour kind with not too loud a tick, can be invaluable – not just for cooking but acting as spare alarm clock, reminding you of watch changes, weather forecasts and the noon sight. Fasten it firmly to a dry bulkhead, as landing in the washing-up bowl is not good for it.

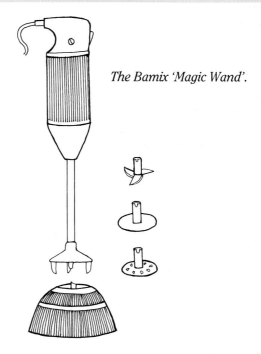

The Bamix 'Magic Wand'.

Consider your gadgets from this point of view: Do I use it a lot? If it is electric, is there a mechanical substitute? Is it robustly made, of a rust-free material? If not, can I be bothered to cosset it by building a special stowage? Is it reasonably resistant to going wrong, breaking or getting trodden on? Is there a simpler way of achieving the same result? (The company called *Lakeland*, see Appendix C, has a range of good stainless steel gadgets.)

Having said that, I would be the last person to discourage you from taking any beloved cookery device that you would be unhappy without. Be sure that it has a safe stowage, and try and protect it from the corrosive salt air.

Saucepans should be good quality, tall for their width, and have well-fitting lids. They should not deform if dropped, and have well-insulated handles. I have never regretted the stainless steel pans I bought for *Fare Well*, which after a quarter of a century of constant misuse are as good as new, bar one whose handle rivets have failed.

Apart from the pans already mentioned, you will need a frying pan. If you take only one, have it large, light and strong, unless you are addicted to cast iron. (Seriously, Bill interjects, you cannot have cast iron pans in a small yacht. It'd sink.) Lidded casseroles in good-quality enamel seem to last well, but the cheap ones chip too quickly. Stainless or aluminium dishes of various shapes and sizes are handy, as they have many uses either for cold food or in the oven.

• *Finding things that fit* •

This is tremendously important, and not just in the galley. Be sure to measure exactly the space available in your oven and get ovenware that fits well. It saves spills if the pans don't skid from side to side (most yacht ovens are too wide, imitating those on shore), and nothing is more irritating than finding that your two most used dishes don't quite fit side by side, or even one above the other. If you fit a drawer with a cutlery tray, make sure no space is wasted; even cutlery can be too large or too bulky.

Holders for this or that are not always the right size when you get abroad – we used to have to saw an inch off the end of Greek paper towel rolls; thank goodness they are now standardised.

One of your drawers should have an internal measurement of 33 centimetres by 8 centimetres high to take advantage of catering-size rolls of foil and food-wrap. Even kitchens ashore rarely allow for this.

• *Other ideas* •

I find the brown rustic ovenware that you can buy almost anywhere now can be used on calm days or in harbour. We have broken only one dish in ten years. Mine are mostly oblong, and the largest one fits the oven exactly and will do lasagne for ten or bake a huge fish.

We don't find it necessary to use plastic glasses. Arcoroc or Duralex, the sturdy French stemless ones, seem to bounce off most things except steel plate; we rarely break one.

On Don Street's *Iolaire* a huge aluminium pan is carried in case of lobsters. He says you can coil your dock ropes in it when not in use. We have one, but keep it in an inaccessible place with the large bowls that are required on such occasions inside it, since it is also useful for large quantities of rice and spaghetti.

Lightweight moulded wooden bowls and trays from the Far East are worth the space; they are unbreakable and last for ever. Wickerwork has a limited life, but is lightweight and cheap.

FARE WELL'S BASIC GALLEY EQUIPMENT

IN USE DAILY:

2 stainless steel saucepans
2 non-stick frying pans
Asbestos mats with handles
2 wooden spoons, 1 wooden 'turner'
Stainless steel tongs
Kitchen knives and cutting boards
Stainless steel measuring cups
Small spice jar containing salt and
  pepper mix (5:1).

IN USE WEEKLY:

Omelette pan
2 casseroles, enamel and lidded
Pressure cooker
Fireproof earthenware
Large and small stainless steel or plastic
  bowls and dishes
Assorted wicker baskets

Plastic bowls (for mixing, and rising bread
  in conjunction with a large plastic bag)
Potato masher, slotted spoon,ladle (with
  hook so it does not slip into the pan)
Wooden garlic masher (also pushes food
  into the mincer)
Wall or hand tin opener
Hand egg-beater
Bamix Magic Wand
Non-stick loaf tins
Stainless steel colander

**IN USE LESS OFTEN, BUT WORTH
THEIR SPACE:**

Hamburger press
Huge paella pan, also good for frying
  enormous fish
Huge pot for lobsters or rice/pasta
  for 20 people
Hand mincer

Hosanna's galley is as big as the kitchen in a London flat, but when we go back to a small yacht the above would still be on my list of basics. Before we leave the galley, let me remind you to find space for the now indispensable roll of paper towels, and for the teatowel and handtowel which otherwise are always on the floor among the spilt sugar, rice and onion skins. There should of course be a better place than the floor for such things, which brings us to:

• *Rubbish, garbage, trash and hygiene* •

As packaging gets more and more copious, our problems of rubbish increase. There is something to be said for unwrapping supermarket packets next to the supermarket skip, and giving them their boxes, paper, card and plastic straight back before humping the contents to your boat.

Some larger galleys have a free-standing bin just as you might find ashore, but this roams about in bad weather, and in smaller spaces it is probably better to have the kind that is fastened behind a cupboard door. The most convenient bin I have ever had either ashore or at sea is my present one, an exact copy of the one we had in *Fare Well*. It is fixed behind the door under the draining board to my left, the door drops forward on a chain just long enough to allow the bin lid to open automatically, and it is in exactly the right place to scrape plates into as you place them in the sink. It is lined with two used plastic bags, since one of them always has a hole in it. At sea you will use it only for plastic items, since when you are hundreds of miles from shore, decomposable rubbish has to be tossed overboard. Paper, card and food waste will disappear very quickly, into the maws of fish. Tins if punctured will sink and rapidly disintegrate, 2 miles down. We try not to throw plastic overboard anywhere. In harbour or near beaches and seashore, keep your rubbish and land it when you can, putting it in the appropriate containers if available. (It may, alas, yet end up in the sea, we have seen it dumped over a cliff by the local authority.)

If you have ever been woken at dawn by the relentless clonk of floating bottles along your hull, maddeningly loud and arhythmic (you are waiting not just for the second shoe to drop, but for the next nine green bottles), you will not, after a party, drop your bottles over the side to perform their *musique concrète* through the anchorage, waking more people than a change of wind among a ten-yacht raft-up. Bottles, if they have to be discarded overboard, are filled with sea water and sunk. Perhaps the only legitimate use for firearms on board is for potting other people's offending bottles and sinking them. (Some of these comments may offend certain eco-conscious readers, but the laws and requirements of environmentalism must be realistic. We find legislators do not take into account circumstances of which they have little knowledge, and our circumstances are in this category. In fact, there is a general exception for ships when offshore, in that they are not required to keep on board anything that might be a health hazard to the crew, and that makes sense. We all have to try not to take unreasonable advantage of it.)

The galley floor is best kept clear and clean. Your dinner will occasionally land on it:

> *Always clean your galley floors:*
> *The portion dropped there may be yours.*

You don't want to slip on a greasy floor either, so choose your flooring with care to be both non-slip and nice looking. It's hard to know if a soup-coloured floor is clean.

We have a rule that engine room dirt is not to be washed off in the galley sink. Bill disobeys it constantly, so I have to provide a sludge-and-rust coloured towel which he carefully avoids using. So any diesel puddings are his fault.

While I am ordinarily rather a slob at washing up, tending to leave it till I feel like it, I get more diligent if there are flies or wasps about. If there is nothing to attract them in the way of sticky surfaces and leftover food and water, there is nothing for them to wipe their filthy feet on. Sometimes they even go away.

• *Keeping your cool: refrigerators, iceboxes and other coolers* •

Fewer and fewer long-distance yachts nowadays travel with no means at all of cooling food. A refrigerator is both a boon and a tyranny; it makes a lot of difference to one's life, but it eats power. (See Chapter Six for comments on fuels.) Top-opening fridges make sense on a boat, but most of them have poky openings which make both access and cleaning difficult. Our top-opening fridge on *Fare Well* had two large lids, and wire baskets made to fit it, four at the top and four at the bottom. If we cared to use the extra power, the bottom would keep food frozen for a month or so. The fridge could be defrosted in about ten minutes with a hose as it drained into the engine room sump. Defrosting and cleaning was done as a combined operation, both of us working fast: remove the eight baskets, hose down the interior with fresh water, dry off and replace baskets. If the bottom was not full of frozen food, we put in a half-gallon container of sea water, frozen if possible (friendly fish markets will sometimes do this for you), to act as an extra cool bank.

This also helps in case of a power failure. In this dire event, do not open the cabinet, and try to increase the insulation by covering it with a sleeping bag or deck cushions while the failure lasts. After more than about 24 hours (given a tightly packed, well-frozen and well insulated mass) you may have to decide if a big cook-up is going to be necessary to save the food.

Iceboxes of the type that take a large block from the fish market are found in many yachts, and the ice lasts a surprisingly long time: ten to twelve days in the tropics and three to four weeks in cooler waters. Keep the ice as dry as possible by draining off any standing water. You should have no trouble finding ice, either in the Mediterranean or the West Indies, but it is heavy. Anywhere there is a fish market, there will be ice. If you can get half-gallon containers of sea water frozen for you, at the fish market or as is sometimes possible in the specialist freezer shops in the Med and the USA, you can pack your box with these and obtain a drier cold. In the Pacific, however, ice is harder to come by.

Ice cubes are worth a mention. The usual flat trays are of little use on a boat; they spill when you heel. For years I searched for a top-opening untippable ice cube maker. When the answer appeared it was, like all the best ideas, astonishingly simple, a compartmented disposable plastic bag, filled from the top and then tied off, which will fit good humouredly into odd corners of the freezer. My present packet of these is French, and contains ten sachets of 18 ice 'cushions'. This excellent idea is now available everywhere.

With no refrigerator or icebox we are back to Grandmother's meat safe, a wooden box with fly-screen panels which was placed somewhere dry and airy, and if possible cool. An insulated polythene cool box in a dry bilge can be effective. Other cooling methods are the sea water, which is often no cooler than the air, and the evaporation principle, used by earthenware butter and milk coolers. A cloth or muslin dipped in fresh water causes rapid cooling as the wind passes over it, as does the Osokool type of porous box with a well for cooling water. (This water should be fresh, as salt will clog the pores, but little is needed.)

MARKETING

This should be a pleasant experience, spiked occasionally with culture shock, and cushioned with coffee and cold drinks.

Those of our American friends who are used to the brown paper bags that go straight from the supermarket into the boot (trunk) of their car, will do well to

English Harbour, Antigua

acquire several capacious shopping bags. The ubiquitous string or nylon net bag of Europe is great for stowage on board but less good for bringing home the bacon, since sharp items protrude and bite the calves of the hapless marketer. The best sort of bag is something waterproof and shapeless with a drawstring top, which will subside into the inevitable pool of water in the bottom of the dinghy without disintegrating or soaking the contents. Such a bag can also be carried on the head, which is much better for your spine than hanging off-balance at the end of one arm. I often see yachties with rucksacks, another way to carry a heavy load safely. Europeans shopping in America, *per contra*, will soon realise that the paper bags, while ecologically sound, will not survive a soggy dinghy ride, and will take their own shopping bags with them to America where they can be difficult to find.

If you have room on board for a folding shopping trolley it will help with heavy items where delivery cannot be negotiated, though they are sometimes impossible to control over rough ground or beaches.

• *The joy of shopping* •

Entering a 'supermarket' on a Greek island, you will find a dim cave, smelling of wine, olives and sheep cheese. The shutters are closed to keep it cool. It is dark, the floor is uneven and the clutter is unbelievable. Only the owner knows where the lamp oil is, or what lies buried under the empty fruit crates, or how long he has had that dusty pile of rubber knickers for a previous generation of babies. (For today's babies, he has a rather less dusty pile of Pampers.)

Be careful how you step back or you will be caught behind the knees by the weighing machine that stands on the floor and end up sitting in an open sack of rice. The bolts of cloth on the shelf are brown, brown and black; there are innumerable battered boxes of coloured thread and large hanks of natural wool for weaving the local rugs. Wine is from the barrel, olives from the vat, and lamp oil from a drum: bring your own bottle. As it is several days since the last ferry, the vegetables are not what they were and the last of the fruit went this morning, but then you should have bought your produce on the day of the ferry, as everyone else does. However, there is wine, feta cheese and olives, and the bread that comes fresh every day, hot and redolent of the wood oven it was baked in. It makes shopping so easy when there is very little choice.

Compared with this, the supermarket in the Virgin Islands really was a supermarket. The packets and tins were on self-service shelves and showed signs of having been wiped over fairly recently. There was a great deal of strip lighting, though only a quarter of it was working. There were trolleys, some with a full complement of wheels, and there were a few baskets that did not snag your clothes with broken wires. Almost everything available in the USA was available here – tins a little bent and packets a bit battered by the long journey, and rather expensive, but here were your hominy grits, your canned chicken-and-dumplings, your Hershey bars and Betty Crocker cake mixes. (Was that a beetle in the cornflakes?) Local produce was tucked away at the back in coarse grey paper bags: the dried beans, cornmeal, black-eyed peas and delicious transparent tubes of split pea soup mix, like a miniature barber's pole of orange, yellow and green. Here too were the bottles of Hot Pepper Sauce, and a cold box for the sows' ears, pigs' tails and chicken gizzards. Were there beetles? Yes, some, but at least they would not be resistant to every known bug destroyer.

That supermarket was luxury itself compared with the one we found at Sulina, in ex-communist Romania. The shelves were almost bare, with about six packets each of staples such as flour, sugar, powdered milk, and huge bricks of soap. After the previous night's rainstorm the pasta section (all 2 feet of it) was flooded, and tin baths were strategically placed to catch the drips still coming through the roof. A few tins of tuna, carp and luncheon meat, plus locally made jam and honey, comprised the gourmet section. UHT milk was unknown, and there was no salt.

I find it all intensely interesting from one extreme to the other. I love to know what people eat, and how they cook it, and where better to find out than the covered markets of Europe or the Western world, wafted through with scents of fruit and spices, where the cries of the vendors are accompanied by the country tattle of chickens, goats and donkeys, and good food is to be had at low prices.

I get my heavy shopping over early: it's cooler. (In Yugoslavia and other ex-communist countries you may find everything sold by seven o'clock in the morning.) My 'donkey', who is only too anxious to leave, takes the load back to the boat, leaving me to the leisurely delights of tasting, chatting, balancing price with quality, and discovering new things. No one in a supermarket has time to chat as the market traders have. They will tell you how to prepare and cook unfamiliar things, that if you wait a week the peaches will be cheaper, that the market will be closed tomorrow for a fiesta, that the broad beans are new and tiny enough to be eaten raw with cheese. They will tell you how to clean squid, and never to boil endives. I discover treasures in obscure corners; I observe how things are bought and by what name; and what is in the cup-

The 'everything' shop. Meganisi

boards at the back of the stall. With a bit of luck I come home with something cheap and delicious for lunch, which is well deserved since everything has to be logged in and stowed somewhere first, a time-consuming chore.

Having done it, though, you can then go off to quiet bays and not worry about shopping for a while; only about trying the new recipe one of the market women gave you. The language of cooks and those who are interested in cooking is surprisingly easy to follow: if you don't know the word, a little mime helps. Before I learnt the Greek for eggs I had to act the hen admiring her product, which used to cause great merriment; perhaps life is less fun now that I know more words.

STOWAGE

'How the Ordnance should bee placed, and the goods stowed on a ship'

Stowage is a fine art. There are three requirements.

1 Your goods should be safe from breakage, beetles and bilge water.
2 They should be accessible.
3 You should be able to find what you want easily.

To take the last point first, I recall how Clement Freud, taken on to cook magnificent dishes for a long yacht race, prepared a splendid scheme of labelled lockers, a detailed inventory of every bit of food he had in them, and a delicious daily menu. Alas, immediately the stuff was delivered on the quay the ship had to leave. It was bundled in anywhere it would fit by the frantic crew and Freud lost all track of it, getting occasional nasty surprises during the trip.

Whether you keep an alphabetical 'where to find it' notebook, or a list of the contents of every locker and drawer taped just inside them, or have a phenomenal memory, it matters not as long as you can find what you want. A filing system by which everything beginning with, say, S, goes in the same place sounds alluring, but has practical drawbacks. One is that you get incompatible substances oddly mixed together, like soup, sandals and seizing wire; and the other is that of nomenclature: B for butterscotch, or S for sweets? B for Bandaid or P for plasters?

The Set Theory works well: stow like things together. It is logical, which helps other people to find things. Thus your paint locker is the logical place for solvents, brushes and sandpaper and discarded nylons for straining varnish. So the bosun's locker is for all sorts of nautical bits and pieces which do not fit into the come-in-handy box, which all cruisers know and love if not by that name.

We start with the heavy things, which ought to go near the bottom of the boat. That means the bilges.

Tins   You will read many an account, in books about world-girdling or Southern Ocean racing, of the tedious task of varnishing all the tins and painting on some sort of shorthand to indicate the contents. (This led to a friend of ours saving a tin of 'goose' for his birthday, only to find on opening it that it was gooseberries.) We do not do anything to our tins, other than group them by kind in different-coloured plastic bags. We then put them in the bilge, meat aft, fish forward, and vegetables amidships. A dry bilge should be the norm for cruising; if you have reason to believe that your labels will soak off, change to a drier boat. The plastic bags are merely to help separate a batch of tinned soups from the sort of tinned meat that goes with salad. There is also a bag with party delicacies in it, for birthdays and such. (The portion of the bilge which contains the sump, bilge pump and/or strum box must be kept free of anything which could clog the pump if the worst should happen. It is, therefore, a good place to put hard objects with no extraneous bits to float off, such as drums of antifouling or gallon jars of detergent, well wedged in against chafe.)

If you have room, large flower pots, trays and square plastic buckets make good separators, and the latter are always handy: we find we lose one plastic bucket per storm. Beer crates are also good, but too large for many boats.

Bottles   The bulk of these can stow in the bilge, too. If you get your duty-frees there may be quite a lot of them. We used to pack ours carefully with corrugated paper, but when we ran out of it we found that jamming them in head to tail between the coffer dams was just as effective: breakages are almost unknown, though a beer bottle once popped its crown cap due to excessive fizz.

Those bottles that you want handy to the saloon can be stored in cradles, on their sides as in a cellar, or behind a retaining bar, upright in circles cut to fit or an arrangement of pegs. All these restraints need to be at least 3 inches tall if you want to prevent clinkage when rolling.

Glasses   These go with bottles. They can go in similar circles, or be slotted into a holder if they are stemmed, or be packed fairly tightly into a drawer. The cheap French glasses will stack, but sometimes jam together unless separated by a leather tag. It is also possible to fit a bracket rather like a toothmug holder for glasses, and it's very good policy to have one to hold the helmsman's glass or mug in reach of the wheel. We find these holders equally good for jars of pencils and have them everywhere, with a circle of rubber or foam plastic at the bottom to prevent rattles.

Plastic containers   These should be of flexible polythene rather than the hard transparent acrylic, which breaks too easily. The lids should fit well (Tupperware has been a boon to yachtsmen) to keep out beetles and dampness, but a determined mouse can chew through them and a rat will be through in two bites. (Keep a cat.) Nevertheless, they are indispensable for dry stores such as flour, cereals, pasta, rice and all the things that cannot be left in their original paper or plastic bags. The heavy polythene used for 5-kilo bags of rice seems to be beetle proof, provided you protect them from chafe.

I have seen very impressive galley drawers built to fit their containers, all top-labelled and awesomely neat. My herb drawer is less orderly, as the jars and bottles are all different sizes and shapes; I've never known a serious cook who was able to stick with one brand of herbs and spices, ranged neatly in racks to fit as in the glossy magazines. We are not to be regimented like that. At least mine are all top-labelled and easy to find.

A combination of square and round shapes also means that you can get a jar out when you want it. This was not the case with a drawer I once saw packed tightly with square containers of the same height: it looked wonderful, but you could not get a finger in to lift a container out. This was not what I meant when I said everything must fit where it stows.

I find the pierced plastic storage baskets now on sale useful for things that are not used every day. All the curry and Chinese ingredients go in one, to be got out when needed; all cake and pudding things go in another, and so on. If you are very short of space, put your herbs and spices into the small self-sealing plastic envelopes that are sold for jewellery, labelling them carefully. They should then be kept in the dark, so a biscuit tin might be better for your collection than tupperware in this instance. Buy them as whole seeds and pods and they will keep much longer than ground ones.

A ready-use shelf near your stove should hold all the things that everyone needs constant access to, such as tea, coffee, cocoa, salt and sugar; it should also hold half a dozen tins of bad weather food (see Cooking in Bad Weather, on page 215).

In Spain, you can buy strong polythene milk containers with a double-sealed screw-on lid. I found these ideal for large quantities of wholemeal flour and the like – the 3- and 5-litre sizes suited me best. Being cylindrical, they stowed in the bilge and did not chafe as the squarish ones containing soft drinks or detergents did. We had supposed that the latter would stow beautifully in the bilge, and so they did, but after six months or so in close contact with their bedfellows they began to chafe and crack at the corners, and the resulting orange-flavoured foam was astonishingly hard to mop up. We still use such containers, but are much more careful about protecting them from chafe. Similar containers, round and square, are obtainable in Greece for storing olives.

Other points concerning storage   Remember that foil packets of instant mashed potato and dried soups and vegetables are irresistible to weevils, which can eat through the foil with ease: put all your packets into a lidded box. Cardboard boxes and packets are also not beetle proof, so put the contents into glass coffee jars, which though heavy seem very strong and we have not broken one yet. Take extra lids though: they do break. Cut out any instructions from the packet and tape them to the jar.

Oblong bins   The kind sold for cleaning materials can be screwed in suitable places such as the engine room. A shelf or bracket for them to stand on prevents them breaking away from the screws if they are used for heavy items. Ingenious use can also be made of flowerpot holders and deep sink tidies: for the brushes and scourers by the sink, and in the heads or shower for organising everyone's toilet gear. Stainless steel and plastic tool clips have many uses, from preventing the washing-up liquid falling in the sink to actually holding tools. We wish the stainless ones were to be found in a wider range of sizes.

Nets   Good for fruit and vegetables, since they are airy, and if strung horizontally help to minimise bruising. Net bags, hung from hooks so as to occupy those almost unusable spaces, can be used for a variety of awkward objects.

Cardboard boxes   These are not recommended. Some yachts will not even allow them on board long enough to unpack the groceries, but instead unload on the quay because they are believed to harbour cockroaches. While the cockroach, according to one of my authorities, is an innocent little creature and one of the few to whom no blame can be attached for carrying any disease, it breeds fast, is aesthetically unpleasing, and crunchy underfoot. (Chapter Seven will help you to deal with it.)

Other almost unusable spaces, such as behind linings, I have seen used to make little shelves for cassettes, or hidey-holes for insecticides and rat bait where the cat and the children can't get at them. Once, where there was a rather larger space, holes were cut in the lining and various brushes stuck through them, with their handles in the space behind.

Large shelves can be made more practical by the use of plastic baskets and bins; you can even colour-code them. They are good for sewing materials, the bulkier items of first aid (bandages, rolls of adhesive tape), and personal gear.

SHORT-TERM VICTUALLING

In previous editions we gave detailed lists, country by country, of what to buy where. It seems no longer necessary to go into so much detail, since shopping in Europe has evened out since the coming of the EU. You still won't get pork in

Muslim countries, ground ginger in Greece, soda water and Bramley apples in France, and anything left alone and natural in the USA. We then substituted a cost-of-living food basket which we thought more useful (now Appendix A), but I shall try to indicate here and there what was hard to find and what to store up with.

Some people prefer to do all the shopping at once, and hire a taxi or donkey to get it back to the ship. On the Intra-Coastal Waterway in the USA you can often borrow a 'courtesy car' to do this. In Europe, stores will sometimes deliver to the quay; it's worth asking.

• *Storing bread* •

Most Mediterranean bread is meant to be eaten the same day. If the baker takes the trouble to bake every day, he reasons that you should pay his bread the respect it deserves by buying it daily. Wrapped bread, which keeps a week, is looked upon with scorn and is only available in the larger centres. You can give your daily loaf a longer life, after you have enjoyed its first crusty day, by keeping it in a clean poly-thene bag, and thereafter placing a hunk of it for immediate eating in a lidded casserole in a moderate oven for a while. A damp tissue in the casserole helps. If you have a microwave, bread can be freshened by wrapping in damp tissue and giving it about 15 seconds. This needs a certain amount of judgement as you want the result to be close to fresh bread, not a dried-up rusk. When this has all gone, you will need crispbread or crackers, or bake your own bread. The long-keeping 'half-baked' loaves available in England and the USA are beginning to appear in the yachtier centres of Europe. The equivalent of *pain de campagne*, (country bread), in almost any European country, keeps three or four days.

• *Storing meat* •

Meat for a week is easy if you have a fridge. With the possible exception of France, Mediterranean butchers do not hang their meat and it benefits enormously from a sojourn in your fridge of at least four days, especially lamb or beef.

If you have no fridge or icebox and the weather is hot, take raw meat for one day (perhaps two if you have a cool spot for it), cooked meat for one more day, and cook up a double batch of meat in the pressure cooker which you put somewhere cool and do not open. (The manufacturers frown on this idea because the cooker is not hermetically sealed, but we find the contents keep a day or so and are free of dust and flies.)

• *Dairy products* •

Eggs and butter all keep well enough for a short cruise. Salt butter keeps better in normal conditions, but if you want to keep it in the freezer use unsalted butter. You will need a keeping kind of milk: condensed, powdered or UHT (Long Life); the same goes for cream if it is wanted. Enjoy good cheese; eat it quickly, its life is short even under the best conditions: 5° to 10° C and 85% humidity). Soft cheeses last a few days; semi-soft, such as Port Salut, St Nectaire and Provalone, will last a week or more; the harder cheeses, like Cheddar, Edam, and the mountain cheeses of France and Switzerland, will keep up to three weeks.

Even for a week, put biscuits, crackers or cookies in an airtight container. There is something horribly demoralising about soggy biscuits.

LONG-DISTANCE VICTUALLING

'Gammons of bacon, dried neat's tongues, Beefe packed up in vinegar . . . '

Long-distance here means long enough to cross an ocean, though the same considerations apply to a long cruise among the more backward or isolated communities where supplies may be difficult to get. We were more benighted going down the Danube, especially in the ex-communist countries, than we ever were in remote Greek islands or the West Indies. A month to six weeks should encompass most ocean passages if one takes the more practical routes between ports.

I suggest that you start by reading the previous section on short-distance victualling, as much that I have written there is also relevant to long distances. I then have merely to underline and expand, without repeating myself.

Not enough attention is paid, I believe, to food for long passages. The lad who airily assured me in Barbados that he and his all-male crew had crossed the Atlantic on beer and cornflakes was pulling my leg (I hope), but there is more than a grain of truth in what he said. I've seen the least experienced youngster sent off at the last minute to victual the ship with a hastily compiled list in which liquor had clearly been discussed at length, but which was vague as to kinds and quantities of other items. I have sometimes been spotted as a yachtswoman and asked for advice right there in the market a couple of hours before the hapless purchaser is due to depart. If the heavy shopping is done a day or so early, there is plenty of time to stow things properly and choose your fruit and vegetables with care. If you then get them back to the boat without bruising and stow gently, they should last well.

• *Discounts* •

If you are starting from England, explain to the manager of your local cash and carry that you need bulk stores for a long voyage, and you will usually be allowed to shop there on a once only basis. Lipton's in Gibraltar give a discount to long-distance cruisers if they spend more than a certain sum. It's worth a try.

• *Planning* •

Where do you start? Where do you begin when planning food for a long voyage? Some swear by Frederick M Gardner (see below); I went by multiplying a head count *times* meals *times* portions. On a normal cruising boat don't worry about a small surplus. On transatlantic crossings to the West Indies I am glad of the surplus remaining, as tinned and bottled stores are expensive and sometimes hard to find in the Windward Islands. While we try to live on local produce where we can, to do so in the West Indies would cause deprivation to the carnivorous males among the crew as steak dinners ashore are largely beyond our means. Luckily the omnipresence of chicken from the USA; frozen, fried or both, saves them from carnal famine.

• *How much do you need to take?* •

Carry food and water for twice the normal expected passage time, plus emergency provisions and water for a further ten days. You do not want to end up 'down to the last tin of corned beef and licking the dew off the deck', as one of our single-handed friends described his landfall. Mr Gardner's famous list, 'The Care and Feeding of a Yachtsman', lists items by weight and calls for $5^1/_2$lb of food per man per day, of which $14^1/_2$ oz was meat. To that he added a gallon of liquid per head per day for drinking.

So he expects four people for 40 days to consume *over a ton of food*. It takes a bit of organising, both to buy and stow. I studied this list with great interest before our first long ocean passage and came to the conclusion that our crew of three men and two very tiny women would consume rather less than that. No way can I eat nearly a pound of meat a day. So I decided to think in terms of the number of meals per day and the portions required, and to allow a bit extra each time in case of extreme hunger. My deliberations will be found further on and are easily modified for larger or smaller appetites.

• *What should you take?* •

Protein

After the first week if you are a carnivore you will have to rely on tinned meat and fish, with eggs, cheese, vegetable and nut proteins if you are not. Dried and preserved meats such as hams and whole salami in their infinite variety are a boon to yachtsmen as they should hang in the air anyway. How long will salami keep? In 1944 we returned to the house we had left in 1939. In the deserted larder we found, hanging lonely under a shelf, a forgotten salami, given to us by a grateful Czech at the outbreak of war. In that drear time of rationing we seized it with glee. It was used, slice by precious slice, in all kinds of ways; the smallest dice giving an exotic flavour: a bit chewy after all those years but still delicious. Take dried fruit, peanuts and peanut butter, powdered milk, wheatgerm and cheese to add a little more wham to your spam, and see the section on food-combining for further meatless protein.

• *Tinned goods* •

If you have no freezer you will need plenty of tins of meat. These should be solidly packed protein, not the kind that is full of gravy where you find only two walnut-sized lumps of gristle with difficulty by using a magnifying glass. Good tinned meat and fish is expensive, but is worth the money especially if you have no fridge. Good buys are corned beef, chopped pork, sausages (but why do most tin only the hot dog kind?), stewed steak, luncheon meat, ham and tongue, and, for special occasions, pheasant or grouse if you can run to it. Fray Bentos steak and kidney pie is good, and they make an excellent range of pie fillings: steak and onion, steak and mushroom, and steak and kidney, which are extremely popular with the crew, much better than the tinned steak and kidney puddings, where the duff was of doubtful consistency and the filling rather meagre. Also popular is the stewing steak from Ireland, brand-named Casserole, and Libby's Beef Stew. Newforge's Irish Stew tasted good, but we had to add more meat to it. Meatballs, which I thought would be great with spaghetti, turned out to be pasty and flavourless. I washed the gravy off them and replaced it with a good strong Italian ragu (spaghetti sauce) full of onion, tomato and basil, which made them more interesting. Nowadays I make better meatballs from tinned hamburgers when we get tired of them. French tins of cassoulet (gourmet pork and beans) are wonderfully ribsticking stuff; add some pork boiling sausage (vacuum packed, keeps well) to pep up the protein. I no longer give space to tins of spaghetti. The real thing is so much better, and almost as quick and easy, especially if you cheat and use ready-made sauces. The same goes for tinned soup (I make an exception for *Soupe de Poisson*); there is always something to make fresh soup from, even if it's potatoes, onions and milk, and a stock cube. There, too, is something worth its space: a variety of stock cubes of different flavours to add interest to soups, stews and risottos.

Tinned chicken is always a disappointment; it is too soft in texture and the flavour is changed. The best we found was the chicken and dumplings of the Southern USA. However, I carry a few small tins of chicken in jelly, to add variety and extra protein to bad-weather soups and risottos. I've recently seen tins of smoked chicken and turkey, which might be worth a try. Tinned patés are always a good idea, as are hams and tongues.

Vegetables that survive canning best are petit pois (tiny peas) haricot beans (get some of them *au naturel* rather than in tomato sauce, for a wider variety of uses), garbanzos (chick peas), spinach, sweetcorn, beetroot, celery (the texture is wrong but the flavour is good), tomatoes (very useful), lentils, green beans, broad beans and mushrooms (but dried mushrooms have better flavour and don't weigh so much).

In Spain, tinned cauliflower and brussels sprouts are available; we found them rather soft, but the cauliflower made quite good 'Crème du Barry' soup, and the sprouts, fried with onions, made an occasional change. Carrots are useful for a touch of colour, but fresh ones keep so well that I hardly ever need the tinned variety. We carry assorted tinned Chinese vegetables, but miss the crunchiness of the real thing.

Tinned fish is very handy in all varieties. Octopus and squid survive canning well, mussels taste tinny. Tinned kippers and salmon make good paté or kedgeree. Paella mixture (a small tin of mussels, squid and octopus available in Spain) can make a good fishermen's risotto as well. Pilchard-and-potato pie is good. Sardines make a delicious 'spaghetti con le sarde', while anchovies make a good spaghetti sauce when mixed with garlic, chilis and olive oil. Tuna is useful. Crabmeat is

BOLULU
RAFET USTANIN
YEMEKLERİ

HOTEL

BODRUM MARKET

ERİŞ TECİMEVİ

KONFORLU

BERBER

expensive, but put some in the treats bin: a tin will feed a good many people in a risotto or a seafood quiche.

Take a little tinned fruit; your fresh supplies ought to last well, but something like pineapple, raspberries or gooseberries can make a treat. Tinned fruit cake is worth taking, as it is time and fuel-consuming to cook. Other tinned goods that I find valuable are the small tins or jars of spaghetti sauce available in Italy in four flavours, or the less good and rather sweeter ones now available everywhere in Europe and the USA. We find tinned ravioli and spaghetti pretty soft and sweet compared with the real thing, but many crews love it. You can add more meat, fish or mushrooms to make a very satisfying meal, especially with wholemeal spaghetti.

Many of these tins can be used for cold lunches, perhaps accompanied by a cup of hot soup if the weather is cool, or a salad if it is hot.

• *Dried food, cereals, grains, pulses* •

These are particularly important to vegetarians. Grains, seeds, cereals and dried pasta will keep for at least a year. Grains and legumes add texture and crunch to tinned food and have a fresher taste. Dried haricot beans, split peas, lentils and chick peas are all good (in spite of the jokes), and all add protein to the diet. Fresh water is necessary to soak and cook them. Rice keeps indefinitely and is essential in my cooking, both white and brown, but the brown takes longer to cook (soak it for 24 hours first). Dried pasta of all kinds keeps splendidly as long as beetles are kept away; they love it too. Wholemeal pasta is available and makes a more wholesome food, but it does not taste the same. Burghul (also known as bulgar, burgoo, or cracked wheat) makes interesting pilaf and is a change from rice.

Muesli and similar mixtures keep better (six months: the nuts in it deteriorate first) than crisp breakfast cereals (like cornflakes, which sog very quickly and take up much more room). Note that nuts go off much quicker than dried fruit, so do not mix them in advance.

You will need bread flour, white and wholemeal, and ordinary flour, but take a tin of baking powder to make your own self-raising flour. Now here's a thing, can I find baking powder or cream of tartar in airtight tins these days? They are all in cardboard or plastic containers marked 'keep in a cool dry place'.

White flour, if kept dry and beetle-free, is good after a year. Wholemeal flour is supposed to last about six months because of the greater fat content, but in my experience is usable for much longer. Keep it in the dark. Wholemeal bread-mix is worth its space. Cake-mixes can be useful when time is short, but they keep less well than separate ingredients because the fat content spoils. Ready-mix packets, such as cake, pastry, scones and dumplings, have a shelf-life of about six months, but fatless ones, such as bread-mix and pancakes, keep about a year, and the bread-mix is usable for much longer if you refresh it with more easy-blend yeast.

Bread making   There are times when a loaf of really solid high-protein bread is worth a whole trayful of bridge rolls. Try this one:

HIGH PROTEIN BREAD

1 packet (10oz, (280g)) wholemeal bread-mix (Grannie Smith, McDougal's, etc) or use 10oz (280g) of wholemeal flour

Add to the dry mix:

$\frac{1}{3}$ cup wheatgerm (a generous $\frac{1}{2}$ oz) (This product does spoil rather quickly, unfortunately)

$\frac{1}{3}$ cup soya flour
$\frac{1}{3}$ cup instant powdered milk
$\frac{1}{2}$ tsp (or 1 sachet (6g)) instant dried easy-blend dried yeast if not using a bread-mix packet or if packet is past its use-by date

Stir into the 6fl oz (160ml) of handhot water you will use to mix the dough: 1 tbs of molasses, black treacle or dark honey. Add this liquid to the dry ingredients, mix well, and knead for five minutes. You won't need a bread tin if you then shape it into a bunloaf or cob. Put it on a greased baking tray; place it, tray and all, inside a large polythene roasting bag (take with you several of the turkey roasting size), secure the bag with a wire tie, and leave in a warm place to rise for an hour. Knock back and rise again, unless using a mix. Bake for 35 to 40 minutes at 425°F 220°C, till the bottom sounds hollow when tapped, and eat with enormous pleasure.

You will notice in the list of ingredients on the bread-mix packet *ascorbic acid*, (vitamin C). This is not to do you good, but to cut out one of the usual two rises. If you make your bread from scratch, you can cut out one rise by adding a crushed 50mg vitamin C tablet per 1.2kg (2lbs 8oz) of flour, or add a pinch of vitamin C powder for the recipe above. Vitamin C powder can be bought at a pharmacy.

DIE-HARD BREAD

You have no oven? Try this:

- After kneading the above recipe, shape it into a round and put it in your pressure cooker, gently warmed and well oiled. Cover with a damp cloth. When the dough has doubled in size remove the cloth, put the cooker over high heat for three minutes, with the lid on but the pressure valve open. Turn down the heat to as low as possible, using an asbestos mat or flame spreader if you have one, and cook, still with the pressure valve open, for 30 to 35 minutes. Turn the bread over and cook a further few minutes to brown the top. This really works, I've done it.

- Collect and take with you recipes for quickly made top-of-the-stove breads such as griddle scones, soda bread, bannocks and oatcakes. I have about 40 such recipes; they can be a life-saver when morale needs a boost.

Combining protein-rich grains and cereals   Meat, fish, eggs and chicken are 'complete proteins'. On long voyages among remote islands, such as the Antipodes – Red Sea run or across the Pacific, you can find your diet short of meat and fish. The same can apply if you cannot afford large quantities of tinned meat. You will therefore be short of protein, and will need to get it from other sources, as vegetarians do.

It is worth studying the following facts with care and in more detail than I have space to give here. (The Small Planet books listed in Appendix B will tell you more.) Certain grains, seeds and legumes, *when combined together* contain all the amino acids needed to make up a 'complete protein'. This explains why the poorer nations thrive on:

- rice with lentils
- cornmeal and kidney beans
- bulgar and chick peas
- barley and beans

And why even baked beans on (wholemeal) toast is a 'complete protein'. Take with you dried haricot beans, lentils (all colours), split peas, soya beans and soya flour, chick peas, butter beans, and peanut butter, and combine them with brown rice, bulgar, wholemeal grains and pasta, for nourishing pilafs and spaghetti dishes. Add cheese, or spoonfuls of powdered milk or wheatgerm, small pieces of meat or fish if you have them, and plenty of spice and flavour. These protein-rich mixtures get you out of trouble if the fresh food runs out, and are excellent dishes in their own right, extremely varied and tasty. Recipes will be found in Middle East and Indian cookbooks, so do not be lulled into substituting tins of baked beans in tomato sauce, which make everything taste of sweet ketchup. The pressure cooker makes short work of the dried vegetables, which can be cooked in stock or soup to add different flavours to suit whatever meaty morsels you have.

• *Sell-by Dates* •

On long voyages you will outsail many sell-by dates; don't panic – they are the manufacturer's get-out, and need not be regarded as written in stone. If it looks, smells and tastes all right, it probably is. The only things past their date that have made me really ill are walnuts. In England.

Yeast   Life is now easier with easy-blend dried yeast such as Harvest Gold or McDougal's, which keeps (they say) for nine months, longer in my experience. Sprinkle it in with the other dry ingredients.

• *AFD (air freeze-dried) foods* •

These are made in quite a few varieties now and keep very well. Apart from the dried soups you can get beef, chicken and shrimp curries, farmhouse stew, savoury mince and beef stroganoff, all kinds of rice dishes, and soya chunks for non-meateaters. They need fresh water to prepare and take time to cook. Their texture tends to be rather monotonous, but they have their place – especially for bulking out leftovers. It's worth reminding you that the average shipboard beetle gnashes its way through foil packets with disturbing ease, so keep them in a metal or plastic box, and be conscientious about putting the lid back. In Italy you can get an excellent freeze-dried mixture of about ten diced vegetables, intended for minestrone. There's an English equivalent, too. A handful of this in any soup or stew is good: you can also use the whole packet with a little salt pork, bacon, or boiling sausage and pasta, for a dish you can stand the spoon up in. While I stick to my freshly made soup when I can, I find a packet of asparagus or leek and potato soup can add body to a vegetable quiche.

Dried fish   This is always heavily salted. Throughout the Mediterranean and in parts of the West Indies you will see boxes of rough-looking sheets of cardboard, vaguely fish-shaped, light on one side and dark on the other. It is, in fact, fish; called bacalao, baccala, stockfish or salt cod. It keeps for ever if kept dry, and is very good when properly processed, but even if you get a preliminary amount of salt out by soaking it in sea water and then fresh, it still needs rivers of fresh water washing over it for 24 hours before it is edible, so it doesn't work at sea.

Dried mushrooms   These are a splendid idea: they have much more flavour than tinned ones. The French, Italians and the Chinese have very good ones; soak in a little warm water for 20 minutes.

Dried egg   I have mixed feelings about this. It's probably all right in cakes; otherwise use it to eke out the breakfast scramble or omelette. To make scrambled eggs entirely with dried eggs brings back too many wartime memories, but today's kids might like it, knowing that there are plenty of other things to eat and bacon or Bacon Grill (tinned) to go with it. Dried egg is not easy to find these days, except in bulk for commercial use.

Dried and salt meat   Whole salami has already been mentioned. If you have no fridge or icebox, a piece of smoked bacon will hang in an airy place, dusted with black pepper to keep the flies away. Hams are trickier, since the cut section dries a bit, but a leg of mountain ham we bought in Yugoslavia lasted all of a Mediterranean summer. It was heavily smoked and we hung it in a net inside greaseproof paper which was changed regularly. Similar hams are to be had in Spain, Italy and France. Vacuum-packed smoked and salted meats keep from six weeks to two months and are worth their space for snacks: so are sliced ham, prosciutto (Parma ham), sliced salami, and liver sausage. That valuable standby, boiling sausage, can be chopped and added to soups; the Dutch ones are excellent. Vacuum packs of bacon will keep a few weeks, but a large piece of smoked streaky bacon (*poitrine fumée* in France) will keep much longer and taste better: keep it like the ham, in greaseproof paper.

• *Dairy produce for long voyages* •

Long Life milk (UHT) and cream keep for five months, and we think it is nearer to fresh milk than either powdered or condensed; it is a matter of opinion. (We were amused to find that it arrived in the USA while we were there in 1982: hailed, of course, as 'new', when we'd had it in Europe several years!) A little of the instant powdered milk can be useful in many recipes: ie high-protein bread. Get the powder in plastic containers for best keeping. Long Life cream tastes better on tinned fruit than tinned cream, and is fine for cooking. Nothing beats fresh milk for cereals or just drinking, but I have yet to meet a cruising boat with a cow on board.

Cheese

Sad to say, cheese is a problem. It is best kept in a cool humid place such as the vegetable drawer of the fridge (not the freezer, which is ruination to cheese). Any soft or semi-soft cheeses will not survive the first week; say goodbye to Camembert and Brie after seven days. See also page 194 (Short Term Victualling) for further storage suggestions, Semi-soft cheeses (St Paulin, Tommes, St Nectaire, Wensleydale) will delight you for a week or so if you wrap them tightly with plastic wrap to exclude the air. Roquefort and other blues should be wrapped in a damp cloth and put in a plastic box, to keep a couple of weeks or more. The harder cheeses need careful selection and dedicated care for their well-being in order to last; Edam, Cheddar, Gruyère and similar are best in plastic wrap with frequent attention to prevent sweating and pare off mould. (Having said all that, I have had some success with a cheese-keeper made by Tefal (see Appendix 'Domestic' Websites) which humidifies the naked cheeses it contains; they last at least twice as long and the hard cheeses a great deal longer. However, the cheese-keeper is bulky and should be kept in the fridge.

If you can find a whole 'stoved' Edam cheese (Edam *étuvée*, available in France and the Low Countries), you are in luck, it keeps indefinitely. So do the granite-like Parmesan (in the piece) and Sbrinz, its Swiss equivalent, which will happily break your teeth after a round-the-world voyage. Some of the industrial cheeses, vacuum-packed or wrapped in foil, keep well until opened, such as Philadelphia and other cream cheeses: study the sell-by dates, and take boxes of small portions of wrapped processed cheese of various kinds for the night box. There are such things as tinned Camembert and Brie, made in Bavaria. If you keep them long enough you might have sufficiently forgotten what real cheese tastes like to find them amusing. Vacuum-packs of grated cheese are very useful on board, and keep for several months.

The only way to have yoghurt after a couple of weeks at sea is to make your own from a good Bulgarian culture.

• Eggs •

Fresh eggs need no refrigeration: indeed EU regulations make the chilling of eggs illegal. Buy your eggs from a hen personally known to you, along with her assurance that they are new laid, ie this morning's or, at a pinch, yesterday's. Do *not* wash them. It is not an old wive's tale that eggs should not be washed: it is illegal in the EU for eggs to be washed before packing. The reasons are: a new-laid egg is protected from bacteria by a film thoughtfully provided by the hen for the purpose; this film is removed by washing. Also, a dry egg is impermeable to bacteria but this impermeability breaks down if the shell becomes moist, and while the egg is wet germs can pass through the shell and set up premature spoilage. (In the USA, eggs are washed *and dried* at the packing stations under strictly monitored sanitary conditions.) In Europe, if you are fussy, you may gently brush off loose dirt and feathers, but leave any washing until just before you cook the egg.

It will now be clear to you why an egg that has been chilled should be avoided: on removal from the fridge condensation occurs, the shell becomes moist, and bacteria can enter: shortening the life of the egg.

Keep your eggs carefully packed (we found fibre egg-trays cut to fit square plastic buckets which we kept in the bilge were perfect) at a temperature of about 10°C/50°F; a cool dry bilge, for example, and they will keep for a month to five weeks with no further attention. On the average transatlantic crossing in either direction you should have no trouble.

How to deal with a bad egg   As this is now a rare event in Europe and the USA, I revive some forgotten tips. After four weeks, start to test your eggs in a glass of fresh water. If they sink they are fine. If they float with a bit of the shell above the water, have ready a clean yoghurt pot or other disposable container: avert the nose and break the egg into the pot. If it is bad, you will know at once. Do not pour it down the sink: unless you have a salt water pump at the sink you will waste too much water flushing away the smell. Just deep-six it over the side. If you are doubtful, you did use a clean pot, so the egg will be OK for well-flavoured omelettes or ginger cakes. If your egg is undecided whether to sink or float, it is probably not young enough to be a breakfast soft-boiled egg, and the whites may refuse to whip, but it will still be usable for most purposes. A flattened-out runny yolk or white means the egg is old, but not necessarily bad. Broken yolks also indicate a stale, but not necessarily bad, egg. No, you cannot test them in salt water because they would all float.

A new-laid egg (up to three days old) is very hard to peel when hard-boiled, and takes longest to cook, but you won't have that problem for long. If your journey is going to last longer than a month or five weeks, some of your eggs will need to be preserved. This is done by sealing the shell, either by putting the eggs in waterglass (a solution of sodium silicate obtainable these days only from very old-fashioned chemists) or smearing them with petroleum jelly (Vaseline). Make sure you get the odourless kind: eggs absorb smells and tastes very easily. In waterglass, the new-laid eggs that my mother put down in wartime kept for a year. After six to nine months you could not count on unbroken yolks, but otherwise they were great. Pacific and Indian Ocean voyagers are not the only ones who could use this method with benefit, eggs are scarce in some of the West Indian islands too. Eggs bought in less sophisticated places must be suspect. Very often the hens run free and the eggs are found in all sorts of places, and not necessarily on the same day (or week) of lay.

• *Fats and oils* •

Outside the fridge, salt butter keeps better than fresh sweet butter but it is harder to get in the Med and more expensive as it is usually imported. Keep all fats as cool as you can. Margarine keeps longer and melts less easily. Both are available tinned, but require a bit of tracking down. Learn to cook with olive oil, which keeps a year or more, like other cooking oils. Lard keeps very well indeed, more than a year. Packets of suet should be kept cool, and last about six months, or check the sell-by date.

• *Boil-in-the-bag and foil dinners* •

Some are very good indeed, though they are expensive and the portions are small. They have an inestimable value for no-fridge voyagers, as they have a long shelf life. They make good celebration food. Stowed so they do not chafe through, they last almost indefinitely. Chicken and duck in these packs are infinitely better than tinned.

In Italy a boiling sausage known as Cotechino or Zampone is put up in the same way. It can be boiled in the bag, and is excellent hearty food sliced and eaten with lentils, mushy peas and mashed potatoes. All these sealed packs can be boiled in sea water. Other sausages such as garlic and liver sausage, to be eaten cold, are appearing in the UK in long-life foil packs too; no need to refrigerate these.

• *Variety of foods* •

Do not rely on just one kind of food or one kind of cooking, even on a short trip. I heard recently of a racing crew almost succumbing to despair and famine; they had been furnished only with boil-in-the-bag meals, but the alcohol cooker that should have heated them was ruined by salt water in a storm. A single Sterno burner was all that remained to cook for ten people. Freeze-dried food is just as useless without the fresh water to mix it with, and even tins need an opener (carry two or three). As a last resort in storms you could take a few of the self-heating cans now available. They are very expensive, but in dire need you might feel a hot meal was worth the money. If you ring the changes with freeze-dried foods, tinned, vacuum-packed, salted, and good old long-keeping standbys like rice and dried pasta, with fresh bread, onions and potatoes, you probably won't even need vitamin tablets.

• *Other ways of preserving* •

Vacuum-packed bacon and cold meats keep very well in a fridge or icebox, as does paté. Even if you have no fridge there is a great deal of choice. Paté will keep for a month, potted in jars under a layer of butter to seal it. You can keep a brine crock (I use Tupperware with a well-fitting lid to prevent spills) and salt down pieces of pork, hocks, trotters, slabs of belly or tongues. If you leave them in the crock for three days they are mild enough to cook in the pressure cooker without previous soaking, and will then keep for up to two weeks in a cool dry spot, though my guess is that they will get eaten fairly rapidly. Not for nothing were the sailors of yore called 'salt horses'. A little practice in the ancient art of salting and pickling may stand you in very good stead if you wish to cruise in the wilder parts of the globe. Even in the Eastern Mediterranean and the north coast of Africa where the Muslim culture makes pork and *charcuterie* hard to find.

Bill and I became genuine salt horses on one Mediterranean cruise. I was looking for a tongue to salt before cruising eastwards, and in an Italian market allowed eagerness to overcome caution when I found one after a long search. I bore it back to the corner of the market where my 'donkey' was waiting with the heavy stuff. Beaming, I showed him my prize. He sighed, and pointed out the stall where I had bought it, where I could now plainly see the horse's head that adorned the sign. I had bought horse tongue. I pickled and cooked it just the same-it was excellent – we ate every bit with relish.

In the south-west of France they pot down goose and duck in the autumn; the meat is cooked gently in goose or duck fat, potted, and covered completely with the fat in stoneware jars. It keeps for a year in a cool larder. My food bug authority worries about this, so if you want to experiment make sure you get an authentic recipe and follow the instructions carefully. The dish is known as *confit d'oie* (goose) or *confit de canard* (duck). I made some to take with us when we left England: we ate it and survived. In French supermarkets this duck and goose confit are now available in tins or vacuum-packs which keep well.

Bottling Bottling jars are quite robust. I take a few containing Bramley apples, apple and blackberry, and gooseberries, since they used to be unavailable tinned. Supermarket apple sauce is woefully tasteless, and cooking apples are unknown even in Europe. On the Danube in Hungary I bottled red peppers which were pennies for a kilo, and marmalade oranges can be had merely for asking in most places where they grow.

• *What to put in the freezer* •

If you are fortunate enough to have a freezer, and still more fortunate to have one that works, pack it with the most solid meat available. It is a waste of space and energy to fill it with bone, gristle and other bulky inedibles. Choose cuts with a minimum of bone or none, and reduce chickens to legs (or thighs and drumsticks) and boned breasts. Put them into packs of the number of portions needed for a meal. Do the same with chunks of stewing beef or lamb: you will be very glad at sea that you took the trouble to remove all the fat and gristle and to pack it in convenient meal-sized portions. Chops, whether pork or lamb, should be parcelled according to crew numbers, or in packs of two, enabling you to add small amounts of protein to rice or pasta dishes. Shrimps are good packed in small amounts to add to fish soup, paella or risotto; even a 100g (4oz) is handy sometimes. Fillets or steaks of cod or haddock make a change if the fishing is not going well. Hamburgers can be made into meatballs, or cottage pie; get the best quality you can. The same goes for mince; get really good quality and put up in meal-sized parcels which reflect the number in the crew. Keep a careful record of what is in the freezer, where it is approximately (baskets help, or different-coloured bags), and cross it off the list as consumed.

I would grudge freezer space for prepared dishes, vegetables (except spinach and green beans) puddings and junk food such as pizza, but you might not agree. Morale is a funny thing – if you feel that frozen doughnuts or Black Forest gateau might at some point do the trick, don't let me dissuade you! In the freezer sweet butter will keep for six to eight weeks, salt butter rather less. (The reverse is true outside the fridge.) Margarine or low-fat spread keeps longer than butter.

• *The care and treatment of sick vegetables* •

There is no reason why you cannot eat fresh vegetables from the Canaries to Barbados, or the West Indies back to Europe. Oddly enough, this will be more difficult coming east from the Americas or going across the Pacific, for it has little to do with the length of the journey.

It has everything to do with whether your fruit and vegetables have been wounded in the chill-room of the supermarket, or killed in the gas chambers of the commercial fruit merchants. If they have, then for keeping purposes they are not worth a damn, as you must have noticed. Regrettably since we first wrote 15 years ago, things have deteriorated further, and it is now very hard indeed in the Western world to buy genuinely fresh vegetables that have not been chilled.

You have only to compare the potato clamp at the frosty field's edge, the onions drying from hooks in the barn, the apples laid neatly on the attic floor to keep all winter (and what a memorable smell that was for the children!), the pumpkins stacked on the outhouse roof in bright orange rows, and the pomegranates and persimmons left on the tree to burn like lanterns in the autumn night, as used to be common (and still is where life is simple), with the expected life of the produce you bought this morning at the supermarket. If you don't put that cucumber in the fridge at once it will dissolve into a pint of greenish water by morning. The lettuce has suffered already in the car. The cabbage and oranges may last till the weekend. Not much else will.

Chilling kills fruit and vegetables. They die of hypothermia. Buy them straight off the tree, out of the ground or off the vine, from the farm or market (but never from the supermarket of the Western world). Choose them with the care you would give to selecting your next child from the orphanage, carry them gently without bruising them, and cradle them like babies in a cool and airy spot. If you wash them at all (to rid them of slugs or beetle eggs) dry them with great care and thoroughness to prevent mould. Unlike babies, you go through the whole lot daily and throw any doubtful ones overboard. We kept our main stock of fruit and vegetables in the dinghy under a canvas cover raised over the oars to give a through-draught; it was easy to check them over.

As almost any packet of fresh fruit and veg from the supermarket says 'keep refrigerated' you'd need a refrigerator as big as a double-decker bus. Recently I have been using Stay-Fresh bags , intended to keep your vegetables and fruit fresh for much longer. You are supposed to keep them in the fridge, but I have been experimenting with keeping them in the dinghy, as one does. The results are quite encouraging, and I now use them for celery, carrots, whole green and red peppers, and such (see Appendix C).

• *Fruit and vegetables: how long do they keep?* •

East-to-west Atlantic crossings, November to March You will be buying your stores in a Mediterranean climate, in the markets of Spain or Portugal, the Canaries or Madeira. Quality and variety are excellent and prices are low.

- *Will last six months*: pumpkin (if you do not pierce the skin); potatoes and onions, kept loose or in nets; lemons wrapped in foil.
- *Will last a month or more*: carrots, Jerusalem artichokes and parsnips buried in earth or sand. (These last three I now put in a Stay-Fresh bag.) Citrus fruits, cooking and eating apples, which are best kept on fibre trays (you can get these from a fruit farm or some supermarkets; the hollows protect the fruit and prevent them touching if one goes mildewed.) Tomatoes, if you choose them hard and all shades of green, and wrap them separately in paper towels or newspaper (but not foil because the acid in tomatoes eats through it), and put in a cool dark place on fibre trays as above. Check daily, eat the reddest, and throw out any squashy ones.
- *Will last about three weeks if the skins are undamaged*: melons, cucumber, marrow (do not pierce), avocado pears, hard white cabbage (kept loose).
- *Will last two weeks*: kept in Stay-Fresh bags: whole green peppers, celery, leeks, Romaine and iceberg lettuce, fresh figs, courgettes (if the flower has not dried off the end they are particularly subject to mould).
- *Will last ten days*: aubergine, globe artichokes, pineapple, cauliflower, green beans. The *big* Romaine and iceberg lettuces keep especially well. Soft fruit, floppy lettuce, grapes, green runner beans. Mushrooms seem to keep best if kept separated in open fibre egg-boxes. They dry and shrink a little, but are edible for about a week.
- *Eat first and fast*: soft fruit, spinach and broccoli (a Stay-Fresh bag extends its life by a couple of days only), spring greens, watercress, Dutch lettuce, and anything slightly damaged.

The above times are based on choosing undamaged fruit and vegetables checked for wild life, and picking them over daily for signs of decay. The Stay-Fresh bags need checking at intervals; if they contain too much moisture blot them (and their contents) with kitchen tissue before replacing the produce and sealing tightly. The bags may be washed and re-used several times. The above probably sounds like a lot of work, but fresh food on a long crossing really is worth some trouble, and if it's like most of our voyages you'll be glad of something to pass the time. For vegetarians, this advice will be essential.

Despite all I've said about chilling produce, if you like chilled salad, and you have a fridge or icebox, it is of course permissible to chill all these things just before serving. After all, you have to kill a chicken before eating it.

West-to-east crossings, in May to August: You will be buying your produce in the

West Indies, North America or Bermuda. For the USA or Bermuda, the notes on European shopping apply, with some alterations for the change in season. You will have to 'think seasonal' to avoid chilled produce. Remember: get it out of the ground or off the tree (or from under the hen).

Bermuda is a special case; you will find it harder to follow the rule that a chilled vegetable is a dead vegetable, because a large proportion of green stuff and fruit is chilled and imported from the USA for immediate consumption. At great expense, I might add. Never mind, it's only 18 days to the Azores where everything is cheap and fresh.

The West Indies have some unfamiliar edibles worth describing. The large variety of roots (yams, eddoes, tannia, dasheen) keep well for months in a dry place. Yams and sweet potatoes are big enough to have doubtful pieces excised: use the mutilated ones first. Sweet cassava can be kept buried the same way as carrots and artichokes. (It is the bitter cassava from which the poisonous juice must be extracted; it is mostly used for laundry starch.) Pawpaw should be bought green, when it can be used as a vegetable until it turns golden, then it is eaten as a fruit after a week to ten days. Coconuts have a long life: while they come to no harm from a bump or two, it is worth stowing them securely or they crash around the boat like cannonballs.

Mangoes keep about a week. The huge bananas known as plantains are only for cooking; as they are very starchy you can treat them like potato. Breadfruit has the same function and keeps well. It grows on one of the most beautiful trees in the Caribbean. Christophene, in appearance like a pale green knobbly pear but a better keeper, cooks like a crisp marrow. Aubergine is often called melongene or eggplant.

The bunch of bananas that is the badge of all long-distance cruisers in the West Indies, hanging somewhere in the rigging, is something else. Even if you put a few 'hands' in the dark and cool to slow the ripening, you will still have to eat them fast when their time comes. You will need recipes for banana bread, banana curry, banana milkshake, banana cake, banana pudding, fried bananas and rum-buttered bananas, just for a start. They will cost you about a penny each, if you shop right. Be sure you hang them the wrong way up, which is actually the right way up (ends suggestively uppermost).

• *Other items you might need* •

The best way to remember every item you will need is to imagine your way through a day, from the moment you rise till the time you go to bed, and write down every thing you eat or use. Thus you will not forget the toilet roll, can-openers, matches, washing-up brush, tartar sauce or salt. Then do it again going through events that crop up only weekly or monthly. (Yes, ladies, don't forget those; or your pills either.) As Captain John Smith reminds us, at sea: '. . . there is neither Ale house, Taverne, nor Inne to burne a faggot in, neither Grocer, Poulterie, Apothecary nor Butcher's shop.'

TRANSATLANTIC FOOD

My thinking went thus:

Meat for five people for supper for five weeks, using up the frozen meat first.

SUPPER

First two weeks: Day 1, Hamburgers. Day 2, Chicken. Day 3, Tinned. Day 4, Pork chops. Day 5, Steaks. Day 6, Party night, Day 7, Rice or spaghetti.

Following three weeks: Day 1, Tins. Day 2, AFD Curry. Day 3, Tins. Day 4, Steak-and-kidney. Day 5, Rice or spaghetti. Day 6, Party night. Day 7, Tins.

To my great astonishment we caught a fish, so one night we ate that. Party night food had been thought of, and was tinned pheasant or frozen duck (Bill's birthday), or national dishes mostly Chinese or Italian.

LUNCH

These were bread (home-made when the bought bread gave up after the thirteenth day) and cold meats, galantines and pâtés, salami, etc with salad as long as it lasted (till the nineteenth day), cheese and fruit. If it was a cold day, we added hot soup.

BREAKFAST

Very important, after everyone had done at least one and maybe two night watches. We used combinations of eggs, bacon, porridge, sausage and beans, bacon grill, and kippers, plus toast and marmalade, and hot drinks. Cereal bars of fruit, nuts and honey make wonderful emergency breakfasts.

NIGHT WATCH FOOD

Sweet biscuits, chocolate bars, cheese portions, wholemeal crackers, nuts and raisins, dried figs, fruit cake.

WHAT WE CARRIED

For five people. We already had on board pickles, jams, sauces, salt and pepper, stock cubes and other staples bought in Italy, France, Spain and Gibraltar.

TINNED MEAT	SIZE	TINS		SIZE	TINS
Hot dogs/frankfurters	15 oz	6	Meatballs	15 oz	8
Stewing steak	15 oz	18	Irish stew	15 oz	12
Breast of chicken	3½ oz	6	Sausages	15 oz	6
Corned beef	7 oz	12	Roast beef	7 oz	7
Bacon grill	7 oz	4	Roast pork	7 oz	7
Bacon grill	12 oz	6	Roast lamb	7 oz	4
Tongue	1 lb	6	Pie fillings	(15 oz)	
Ham	1 lb	3	Steak and Kidney		6
Steak-and-kidney pie	15 oz	2	Steak and mushroom		6
Steak and kidney pud	15 oz	6	Steak and onion		6
Steak and kidney pud	7 oz	12			

TRANSATLANTIC FOOD continued

TINNED FISH

Kippers		9	Crab	7 oz	6
Prawns/shrimps	7 oz	15	Mussels	3¹/₂ oz	3
Pilchards	15 oz	15	Oysters	7 oz	2
Salmon	7 oz	7	Sardines		12
Squid	7 oz	3	Paella Mix	3¹/₂ oz	2
Tuna	7 oz	6	Anchovies		2
Chopped clams	15 oz	2	Herring Roes		2

OTHER TINS

Chopped pork	7 oz	6	Fabada (Spanish pork and beans)		1
Pork and beans	7 oz	6	Paella	15 oz	2
Sausage and beans	7 oz	6	Ravioli	30 oz	3
Pheasant	15 oz	1	Cassoulet	2 lb	1
Game pie filling	15 oz	1	Fruit cake	2 lb	1
Chinese goose	7 oz	2	Soups	15 oz	12
Liver pâté	3¹/₂ oz	2	Oatmeal	500 g	1
Pâté de campagne		3	Spaghetti sauce (Bolognese)		6
Sweet biscuits	3 lb	1	Spaghetti sauce (Matriciana)		6
Biscuits for cheese	3 lb	1	Spaghetti sauce (clams)		6
Spaghetti sauce (mushroom)		6			

TINNED VEGETABLES

Pelati (tomatoes)	15 oz	12	Brussel sprouts	15 oz	12
Pease pudding	7 oz	7	Ratatouille	20 oz	2
Mushrooms	7 oz	9		15 oz	3
Leeks	5 oz	2	Red peppers	7 oz	5
Cauliflower	15 oz	7	Garden peas	15 oz	8
Spinach	15 oz	7	Petit pois	12 oz	4
Celery	15 oz	4	Water chestnuts	7 oz	2
Beans, green	15 oz	5	Bamboo shoots	7 oz	2
Haricot beans (natural)	15 oz	12	Bean sprouts	7 oz	6
Macedoine (mixed veg)	15 oz	6	Curried beans	7 oz	4
Butter beans	15 oz	3	Heinz beans	15 oz	3
Beetroot	7 oz	2	Carrots	15 oz	5
Broad beans	5 oz	2	Sweetcorn	10 oz	12
Chick peas	15 oz	3	Red cabbage	15 oz	2
New potatoes	15 oz	12	Lentils	15 oz	4

TINNED FRUIT

Pineapple	15 oz	3	Peaches, large		3
	7 oz	4	Raspberries	15 oz	4
Pears, large		3	Fruit salad, large		3

TINNED PUDDINGS

Syrup sponge	8	Jam sponge	2
Chocolate sponge	2		

TRANSATLANTIC FOOD continued

FROZEN

2 Large pizzas	5 Steaks
10 Loin of pork chops	1lb Chicken pieces
2¼ lb Chicken breast	1 Duck
24 Beefburgers	

IN FOIL

Cotechino (sausage)	Chicken curry, 12 portions
Minestrone	

PERISHABLES

		2 kg Green tomatoes	2 kg Cucumbers
10 kg Potatoes	10 kg Onions	1 kg Green beans	1 kg Carrots
2 Cauliflowers	4 Cabbages	1 kg Lemons	
6 Aubergines	1 kg Green peppers	3 kg (10) Grapefruit	
1½ kg Courgettes	10 Avocados		
3 kg Sweet apples	3 kg Acid apples	6 Large white loaves	6 Large wrapped
4 kg Oranges	4 kg Green bananas	12 Bread rolls	wholemeal
3 Melons	1 kg Red tomatoes		loaves

FRESH GROCERIES

3 lb Streaky bacon	16 lb Butter 5 x 7oz
2 lb Vacuum packed bacon	3 lb Turkey galantine (whole)
3 lb 5oz Garlic sausage (whole)	2 lb Ham
1½ lb Liver sausage	1 Pork boiling ring
2½ lb Cheddar cheese	1½ lb Double Gloucester cheese
2 boxes Cheese portions	8 dozen Eggs
36 bars Bournville chocolate	36 bars Kit-Kat chocolate
2 pkts Crispbread	Nuts and raisins 24 small packets
Wholemeal crackers in packets of 4 x 24	

DRY GOODS

Plain flour	2 kg	Tea bags	250
Wholemeal flour	8 x 3.3 lb	Dumpling mix	½ lb
Rice	2 x 5 lb	Batter mix	6 pkts
Spaghetti	10 lb	Dried yeast	1 tin
Chinese noodles	4 pkts	Instant-blend dried yeast	3 pkts
Sugar	8 kg	Paper towels	6 x 2 rolls
Long Life milk	36 litres	Toilet rolls	6 x 2 rolls
Long Life cream	12 pkts	Nescafe	1½ lbs

DRINKS

Beer	144 cans	Orange squash	½ gal
Lemon and lime squash	½ gal	Wine	40 litres

TRANSATLANTIC FOOD continued

WHAT WE ACTUALLY USED (23 DAYS)

All the beer! All the fresh vegetables, and the following number of tins:

Ham	1	Pheasant	1	Lentils	1
Steak-and-kidney	2	Tongue	1	Brussels sprouts	2
Steak-and-onion	2	Roast beef	3	Bean sprouts	1
Steak-and-mushroom	2	Roast lamb	3	Pease pudding	3
Chicken breast	1	Crab	1	Mushrooms	3
bacon grill	3	Salmon	2	Bamboo shoots	1
Meatballs	1	Kippers	3	Fabada (Bean stew)	1
Stewing steak	1	Prawns	1	Haricot beans	3
Sausages	2	Soups	6	Pelati (tomatoes)	2
Sausage-and-beans	4	Ravioli	2	Water chestnuts	1
Irish stew	5	Spaghetti sauce	6	Potatoes	1
Game pie filling	1	Cream	1	Heinz beans	1
Chopped pork	1	Jam sponge	1	Raspberries	2
Corned beef	2	Carrots	1	Pears	1
Chicken supreme	2	Peas	4		

We had 2 dozen eggs left, fresh fruit (oranges, lemons and grapefruit), and plenty of useful basic stores which stood us in good stead in the West Indies.

When we were within four days of Barbados the beer ration (jealously watched by the men) went up from one can a day to two, and then, to their great joy, to three.

DEEP-SEA COOKING

SONG OF A SEA COOK

I think what pleasant thoughts I can
While bending o'er the frying pan
But truth to tell, I'm ill at ease:
It's hard to cook in seas like these.
But break the eggs and stir the pot
And try to be what you are not:
A cook with stomach not upset
Who hasn't lost her breakfast yet.
Why do they always ask for more
When half the stew is on the floor?
How can they eat so heartily
When I can't even drink my tea?
But peel the spuds and cook some duff
(Three pounds of flour should be enough)
They'll eat like the proverbial horse
Even if served with Diesel sauce.

• *Cooking in bad weather* •

'. . . give every messe a quarter can of beere and a basket of bread to stay their stomacks til the kettle be boyled . . .'

If you are the sort of cook that most of us are, fine on deck but subject to sickness down below unless horizontal, you have to develop a method if you are not to starve yourself while feeding the crew.

One method is to bring all the ingredients up on deck, in one or more washing-up bowls, and do the preparation up in the fresh air. This is suitable for put-together meals like salad and sandwiches. Enlist help and it will be done fast, but half of it will be eaten prematurely.

A variation of this is the do-it-yourself buffet. Again washing-up bowls are used, to avoid everything landing on the floor of the cockpit. You cannot, of course, lay things out nicely on a plate, so recourse is made to smaller bowls and boxes with lids. Larger ones can contain potato or tomato salad, smaller ones sliced meat and salami, or tuna transferred from the tin. This is where I would use paper plates on the wicker plate-holders available in the USA, or wicker breadbaskets, which save washing up.

At some point in the day, however, you will have to serve something hot, since that is what is really popular in bad weather: a steaming pot of something rib-sticking such as soup, stew or risotto.

For this I have a second method based on one-minute dashes to the galley, interspersed with fresh air up on deck until it is time for the next dash. (An extractor fan in the galley also helps.) There is no need for gourmet cooking under these conditions. Your crew will be more than grateful for that simple dish known to all sailors under various names such as lobscouse, slumgullion, potmess: in fact, Sea Stew.

Force 8 stew

Choose a moment when you are feeling particularly strong, and make your first dash. Bad-weather stores should be handy in the galley, so if you also have a wall tin-opener it will take you no time at all to put in a large deep pan: one tin of meat, (Veggies will substitute chick peas, or beans, or soya chunks.)one tin of vegetables, one tin of soup, and one tin of drained potatoes. (It does not seem to matter what kind any of these are, the result is invariably excellent, though some mixtures you may discover to be more favourite than others.) Light the stove and put the pan on, with lid. A pressure cooker is deep and works well – even without the lid. This mixture is very thick, and at intervals further dashes will be required to prevent it burning and to turn the whole mass over with a wooden spoon. When the entire contents are gently bubbling, serve in large mugs to three people.

This is the most delicious food you will ever have had if you are cold, wet and hungry. Starch seems to be needed for queasy stomachs to work on, so risottos and spaghettis are also good, but they are a little more time-consuming to cook – say 15 minutes instead of 10.

Force 6 stew, by the way, is made with fresh vegetables and potatoes instead of tinned ones, as the cook should be feeling stronger. Veg cleaning and preparation can be done on deck, using helpers, but watch your knives don't get chucked overboard with the peelings. Anyone who is too sick to eat Sea Stew should be encouraged to eat at least some wholemeal crackers, and if you boil a kettle for a hot drink try the sufferer with bouillon or Bovril, which may go down better than tea or coffee. It is good to give the stomach something to work on: we find porridge and brown sugar very heartening too.

Another bad weather recipe

We lay just inside the pierhead at Bastia in Corsica at the day's end in howling wind. In sailed a tiny yacht with storm jib and close-reefed main, towing a 40-foot charter yacht. There seemed to be no one aboard the charter boat so Bill went to help. As they came alongside a tiny girl swung her huge tow round to us, released it, and allowed us to berth the charter yacht stern-to while she, the skipper, finished berthing herself. There were four seasick Germans in a charter boat she had rescued who had done nothing to help her or themselves, but were quick to dash ashore and up to the restaurant. We invited her and her student crew on board for a drink: Bill wanted to say 'well done' to Anne-Marie of the famous Breton sailing school at Glenan on her magnificent seamanship. Let alone his penchant for five-foot girls.

Anne-Marie agreed with us that in such weather it was best to stay with our boats, and that we could happily eat together, having much in common. At that moment a great gust tore the German boat's inflated dinghy from its fixings on board and carried it across the bay. Anne-Marie sighed, and with immense aplomb went off in her dinghy to get it back. When she returned and had made it fast properly, she cooked one of the best bad weather dishes we've ever had. What a girl!

Anne-Marie's Patates au Lard   A Breton sailor's dish. All you need is a pressure cooker, one Spanish onion per person, lots of potatoes, and a big hunk of poitrine fumé, (smoked belly of pork). Onions and meat in the bottom, then the potatoes. No water – the onions and pork bathe the potatoes in delicious juices which make the gravy. Pressure-cook it for 7 to 10 minutes. Food for the gods. And goddesses.

During Hurricane Alberto we had hot food the first day (eggs for breakfast with oatcakes and coffee, soup for lunch with fruit cake, and Sea Stew for supper). Then water got into the batteries and for the only time in ten years the stove would not light and we had cold food that day. The following day Bill got some of the batteries going again, and as the huge seas were beginning to subside we celebrated with an enormous lunch of T-bone steaks and tinned raspberries and cream. Gosh, it was good.

Once the alarms of the first day of the hurricane were over we drank a lot of coffee, some of it laced with brandy.

On the 'cold' day we had rum punch, which boosted morale without confusing the brain too much, and ate apples and chocolate and fruit cake, with the occasional ham sandwich.

It is noticeable that people who normally spurn puddings and cakes and sugary drinks, such as all three of us, turned in a time of worry and crisis to sweeter food and drinks. We were also immensely hungry, perhaps partly because it was hard to sleep through the noise and violent motion.

This brings us to:

OTHER USEFUL WAYS TO COPE WITH BAD WEATHER WHEN COOKING

- Use a damp sponge cloth or dish towel on the table or worktop to anchor plates and mugs.
- Pour drinks out fore and aft, not athwartships: who holds, also pours. Don't fill saucepans or mugs too full.
- Hand things up to the cockpit in a wicker breadbasket for each person. This will take a mug of stew, bread, implements, and an apple or tomato.
- Mugs are better than bowls, which are better than plates.
- There should be somewhere the helmsman can put a drink safely, without it ending up on the deck.
- The high-friction Dycem plastic sheet, which we call 'Sticky blue', can be cut to fit any surface. It has been so successful in preventing spills that we have been able to dispense with fiddles except on the cooking stove. A similar product called Scootguard is available (Address in Appendix C 'Domestic Websites'.)
- Used and empty utensils should be put straight into the sink ready to wash up, so they do not roll underfoot and get broken.

• *Night watch food (the nightbox)* •

Night watches consume a lot of energy and, except in pilotage waters, they can also be very boring. You can count on the night watch losing all sense of morality and burrowing like alley cats in a dustbin through the cook's precious stores. If you do not want your menus totally disarranged, and large desserts intended for tomorrow to disappear without trace, you *must* provide a tempting and adequate night box. A large Tupperware bread bin might just be big enough.

It should contain both sweet and savoury items, such as dried fruit and nuts, cheese (wrapped portions are handiest), wholemeal crackers, chocolate bars and boiled sweets, cereal bars (a sort of solid muesli, available on the diet and health shelves of the supermarket; they keep a year and make excellent bad-weather breakfasts); fruit cake and biscuits. If you are on a long passage where fresh fruit is limited, make it crystal clear whether fruit is allowed as an extra or counts as part of the daily ration, since it is impossible to satisfy a three-apple-a-watch person with the stores carried on a small boat. Some yachts fill vacuum flasks with soup and coffee for the night watch, others (if the autopilot is working well) find that the watchman gets a welcome break by making his own hot drink.

Drinks and nibbles on deck as we celebrated Fare Well's *first 25,000 miles at sea.*

• *Food for morale* •

'And after a storme, when poor men are all wet, few of those but wil tell you a little Sacke or Aqua Vitae is much better to keepe them in health than a little small beere or cold water, although it be sweet'

When morale is low, break out some treat or delicacy: a tin of Dundee cake or shortbread, tins of boeuf bourguignon, cassoulet or smoked salmon pate. If the weather is fine and spirits need to be raised, pancakes, drop scones or new rolls with honey all do wonders.

Find an excuse for a party: celebrate (or commiserate) something: the best day's run or the worst, 500 miles, 1000 miles, the day we saw the whale; and get everyone to help with the best dinner you can manage. Give a prize for the most inventive costume or headgear, or the best limerick. I always keep a bag of small presents on board. Whenever I see anything small and attractive ashore, I add it to the bag. Thus one can always cope with an unexpected birthday or find a suitable prize. You can also run a sweepstake on the noon-to-noon run.

WATER

*Skip will not let me wash my hair
Nor yet my grubby underwear;
'The water's getting low,' he shrieks,
'We've just enough for ten more weeks.'*

Water, the lack of it, and where to get it, occupies the mind of cruising people a great deal. The habit of being mean with it must become second nature. If you run to the luxury of hot water, you cannot allow the tap to run hot without saving the cold water that comes out first. On our boat this is done by having a jug of the right capacity kept in the head: when the jug is full, the water will be hot and the jug of cold can (and must) be used elsewhere, in the kettle for instance.

'. . . a little pumpe made of a Cane, a little peece of hollow wood . . . to pumpe the Beere or water out of the Caske, for at sea wee use no taps'

Small toddlers love pumping water and turning on taps. So, unfortunately, do guests. Make sure that the water is not frittered away without your knowledge; a press-and-release tap would help, being harder for a toddler or guest to use than a Whale pump or a foot-button.

Have plenty of buckets. One cannot have too many, as one always seems to lose one (plus a doormat) in every storm. Then when it tips it down in the West Indies or the Pacific, you can fill your buckets and have a water frolic. Some people can plug their cockpit drains and turn it into a huge swimming bath.

If you are really short of water it is possible, indeed desirable, to use fresh water twice. First, where hygiene is essential, such as washing oneself or the dishes. Having done that, the resulting water, according to its state, may then be used for the galley floor, or engine room overalls. Hair needs a lot of rinsing, but the water used is usually still clean enough, if a bit soapy, to wash clothes in. Judgement has to be used here. To shore-people who have water to wash cars with, this must seem rather revolting. (We did say that the life is not all pâté and champagne.) I can assure you that Bill, coming up from the engine room with filthy hands, is quite glad of leftover washing-up water to get the worst off. All galleys should have a salt water tap, if only for firefighting!

A very refreshing gambit that takes a minimum amount of fresh water goes like this: heat a cupful of water to boiling point and put it in the bottom of a warmed jug. Hold your face over the jug, under a towel as if you were inhaling balsam. Your face will be nicely steamed. Wipe off the grime and salt with a tissue and hand the jug to the next person in the queue, reheating the water as necessary.

Water that has been used to boil potatoes or pasta can be used for soups or freeze-dried food, but go easy on the salt. Water drained from tinned vegetables can be used for the same purposes or to boil potatoes.

Water became even more desperate in a submarine on 40-day patrol in Bill's time in the Navy. No washing was allowed at all except that there was a bucket of sea water and nearby one solitary bucket of fresh for 60 men for a week. One washed dirty hands in the sea water, then rinsed them in the fresh, which gradually turned into diesel soup. Long passages can lead to similar problems in a yacht without adequate water tanks and to an inevitably smelly crew. Submariners say one gets used to it because everyone smells the same. Submariners' wives say they can identify their husbands in the dark by the smell of diesel. As long as it is their own submariner climbing into bed, not someone else's.

• *Can you cook in sea water?* •

To illustrate an important point: once in Yugoslavia we went on a Club Mediterranée sailing barbecue, the first of the season, which was going to be done in style, huge amounts of meat with rice and spaghetti cooked on a remote beach. Everyone helped. Well, nearly everyone. Some of the men went off to taste the wine at the local tavern 3 kilometres away, and returned disgusted. 'One has drunk a wine of the most execrable,' said a tired Frenchman, 'and one has spat all the way home.' He began to wash his mouth out with wine from the huge jars we had brought with us. 'Which one is the water to cook the rice?' I asked, looking towards the jars. 'That's all wine,' said the organiser, 'one will use sea water.' 'Have you done this before?' I enquired with some doubt. He brushed my worries aside with superb confidence: what do the English know about cooking? So we duly cooked rice and pasta for 40 people in sea water. Both were so salty as to be totally inedible, and I have since found that the same thing happens with potatoes. You cannot cook vegetables in pure sea water. Not in the Mediterranean, anyway.

I have done some tests, and find that 5% of sea water makes it quite salty enough. That is 1 part in 20, or 1 fluid ounce of sea water to 1 imperial pint of fresh. You would have to be pretty desperate for that to make any difference.

• *Washing at sea* •

Washing machines are not often carried by the long-distance cruiser. There is a small simple plastic washing machine that I have seen on live-aboard yachts, which seems to please its owners, being light but solidly made. It is on the market in France for about £80. As these machines don't heat the water, they don't use much power – but they do use a lot of water, which is probably why I have seen them in use only in marinas or close to a dockside tap.

A hand-operated one is sometimes available from UK mail order catalogues for about £30. Laundromats are rare in the Med; smaller boats do their washing on the quayside.

When water is pretty short, as it always is on long-distance cruises, the time comes when the skipper's shorts are sufficiently redolent to be capable of independent movement and will come when you whistle; with the embarrassing affection of an elderly and appallingly smelly dog. Now is the time to consider washing

 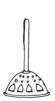  

Washday ancient and modern: Greek wash board, a copper posher, a wooden 'milking stool' dolly, an all-plastic clothes peg.

in salt water. Any strong liquid detergent will wash satisfactorily. If it is choppy, put the clothes in a tub and let them slop around with the motion of the boat doing much of the work for you. You must get the salt out by a rinse in fresh water; otherwise your clothes will be stiff, the salt will attract moisture so that they never fully dry, and you could end up (particularly with tight jeans) with a painful skin rash caused by chafe, or worse, 'gunnel bum' (salt water sores).

In places where it rains, such as an east-to-west Atlantic crossing, it pays to see a shower coming and get out the clothes and buckets to benefit from it. To get oneself and the clothes one is wearing thoroughly soaked in fresh water can be very refreshing, and is usually an occasion for much hilarity and splashing about. The west-to-east crossing is considerably colder and normally contra-indicates such skylarks, but it would depend on the degree of desperation.

Acquire an old-fashioned washboard and that useful article known as a dolly or posher. Washboards are still found anywhere there are no washing machines, such as the Greek islands and the West Indies. The dolly is rarer, but it is not hard to make one of the milking stool variety illustrated. If you were used, on shore, to a washing machine and a tumble dryer, you will be surprised and pleased at how much longer your clothes last when you wash by hand, provided of course you don't lose them overboard when you've pegged them out to dry.

Before I learnt the art of clothes-pegging I lost overboard two good towels, a pillowcase and a woollen jersey. All sank to the bottom with extraordinary rapidity before we could seize the net. Spring-clip pegs, I learnt, are not strong enough. Lead the washing line across the wind if possible, and use pegs that have no metal parts to rust, the old-fashioned gypsy peg or the all-plastic ones made by Hozelock (see Appendix C). Turn the clothes inside out (the strong sun will fade them quickly otherwise) and peg them firmly in such a way that they parachute across the wind. Lead the line through arms, legs or belt loops if you can. They will dry in no time. Bring them in while still a little damp, fold carefully, and stack in a warm place. As they finish drying, they will 'iron' themselves with no further attention.

PRACTICAL HINTS FOR BOATWIVES AND SHIPS' HUSBANDS
• *The WC and shower compartment* •

Sea water used for flushing the loo causes scale to form. Putting some vinegar in the bowl from time to time, especially if you are leaving the boat for a few days, helps to minimise this, as does a daily sprinkle with washing up liquid. An occasional cautious catharsis with the delightfully named Greek product 'Drastico' (hydrochloric acid as far as I can make out) is abhorred by the loo manufacturers, but works absolute wonders.

The second most important habit to acquire (the first being not to waste water) is to put nothing down the loo that could lead to a blockage. It helps everyone to remember this if there is a separate lidded bin for hairballs, cigarette ends, matchsticks, dental floss and even more unmentionable items. If your taste is for waggish notices on brass plates, now is your chance to let rip. Otherwise a simple green cross painted on the lid will indicate its use to most people. It will not stop children from poking about in there to see what it contains, but that all comes under the heading of a broad education. My children learnt a lot that way.

• *Thoughts about the accommodation* •

Which is what the yacht brokers call your living space. We find we need safe places for spectacles these days. Pockets for them – and indeed for anything that needs to be readily to hand, such as seasickness pills, sunscreen cream, finger plasters, bottle openers and so on – can be made from felt, leather, fabric or any suitable material, and screwed or stuck to the linings or cockpit in strategic places. Doublesided sticky pads can be used to fix not only these but digital clocks, perpetual calendars, navigating gimmicks, and even pictures and photographs if they are not too heavy. Fewer screwholes keep up the resale value!

You might doubt that magnetic racks would be of any use at sea. We have one for kitchen knives and one for small tools. Only the big carving knife and the heavy ratchet screwdriver get jerked loose by a choppy sea: they are fine for smaller items. Don't site magnetic racks near a compass, it goes without saying.

Stow seaboots upside down on dowels of suitable length. This not only helps them to dry but prevents them from filling up with rubbish and dead wasps.

Keep a bag of plastic foam offcuts to stifle any clinks and bumps that can disturb your sleep in choppy seas: cassettes, bottles and glasses are the worst offenders.

A cylinder type vacuum cleaner has many uses apart from the obvious one. Ours helped us to build the boat. It was second-hand even then and has swallowed everything from wood shavings through nails and screws to lumps of rubbery caulking compound, drilling swarf, rust chippings and grinding dust. Put together backwards it can be used as a heavy-duty blow-dryer for newly painted areas, or even damp bilges if you should be so unlucky. We are thinking of coarse painting, naturally. We would not blow dust and flies on the sort of paint and varnish where dogs must not sneeze and cats must not tread. There are now some battery-driven vacuum cleaners that are worth their space for light duties: crumbs, fluff, loose dust, even dead insects if they are small ones. Nowadays there are vacuum cleaners that suck up water. They can be used instead of a bilge pump on occasions; the nozzle can reach awkward corners which might have got waterlogged.

Few cottons and canvases can stand up to sea water and hot sun, but lining your curtains with heavy cotton prolongs their lives. Cockpit and deck cushions are usually vinyl covered, which lasts well but sticks to bare skin. Most people make loose cotton covers and accept that they will need replacing frequently. It's worth it not to find your thighs securely stuck to the cushions in hot weather.

A practical thought: you can buy sticky labels in the form of little coloured circles. Get several different colours, and use them to match plugs with sockets, so that a red spot plug fits a red spot socket. Or use them to highlight important electronic buttons that the designers try to hide from us by camouflage and incomprehensible icons: charcoal on charcoal seems to be flavour of the month.

DUTY FREES

Not only have the rules changed considerably, but duty-free stores are more difficult to get. We are not talking about the rip-off 'duty-frees' on the cross-Channel ferries, no cheaper than Continental supermarkets, and recently ended. The real article is available if you are bound for a destination outside the EU, and will cut your booze costs considerably. The difficulty is to find a bonded warehouse at all, let alone one who will deign to supply a dozen cases to a yacht, instead of a truck-load to a ferry. When we did find a willing supplier we found that procedures were now much simpler. No longer was our booze embarked under the eagle eye of the Revenue men and sealed with lead excise seals. The paperwork was done, and the goods came on board just before sailing, and we pushed off from Southampton bound for Istanbul. The further your destination and the larger your crew, the more you are allowed. No cheating, we did actually get to Istanbul. It just took us a year or so. Cheers!

AND FINALLY: THE PLEASURE OF IT ALL

Two occasions I shall miss dreadfully if I ever come ashore. One is the impromptu cruising barbecue, on a beach perhaps, with half a dozen dinghies hauled up on the shingle, and the yachts nodding at anchor a short swim away. The fire is already crackling under many and different grids and grills, bring your own meat, fish or veggieburgers, something to drink, and 'a dish for the table' that everyone can share. The meal lingers langorously and deliciously into the warm afternoon with chat and laughter, memorable days.

The other is of wonderful meals for two after a good day at sea, not in themselves so Epicurian, were it not for the beauty of the day, the good temper of the sea, the satisfaction in our progress, and the sharpness of our hunger. With such a sauce, anything tastes good.

11 • Misadventures

'. . . some accident that requires the help of all hands . . .
which in most voyages doth happen'

CRIME

There are two sorts of relevant crime: those committed by yachtsmen and those against yachtsmen, with the occasional merger of the two.

One of the features of long-cruising is its suitability as a way of life for the criminal who is either retired or resting. It is sad that in recent years the professional criminal has become aware of this: sad because inevitably the processes of identifying, tracking and arresting them will impinge on the freedoms of the cruising yachtie.

When only a small number of retired criminals were involved, the forces of international law and order did little, for attempts to track individuals would have been inordinately expensive. The occasional cigarette smuggler was arrested, but there was no great international co-operation for one country was not over-concerned about another's smuggling problems. But the alarming increase of narcotic abuse has brought yachtsmen into notice.

• *Drug smuggling* •

Drug smuggling is of two broad types: the highly professional operations of organised crime, and the more casual, small-scale activities of individuals. The 'casual' smuggler is of any nationality and can operate anywhere, though there is much activity close to the USA. The US authorities try hard, but they have a very difficult problem because of their closeness to some very anarchistic small states.

Yachtsmen in the Caribbean become aware that Mr A, who was paid crew on the charter boat *XYZ* in 1990, appears in 1991 as the owner of a Swan 65. No one checks on his sudden wealth; his boat is registered behind nominees in a British colony, and he is all set for a life of comfort. And a major contribution to his ability to enjoy the fruits of his dirty enterprise is made by the British government through its laws on colonial banking, company registration and ship registration.

These laws become a major factor in the activities of organised crime, and not only in its drug smuggling mode. Most of the hard-drug traffic in the Mediterranean and Caribbean happens under the Red Ensign and there is no doubt that the British flag is falling into disrepute, to the inevitable disadvantage of British yachtsmen in general. Ownership of these yachts is vested in companies set up in Jersey, Guernsey or Gibraltar; the shares are held in the names of nominees, often living in Sark; the yachts are registered not only in these places but also in Southampton or London.

Laundering the proceeds takes place in many ways, but one is by buying and selling these yachts through certain brokers in the South of France, the transactions passing through banks in all the financially rotten parts of the world, ie Switzerland, Liechtenstein, Luxembourg and the Channel Islands. A significant blow could be struck against organised crime by closing the secrecy loophole of company and ship registration in the Channel Islands and other British colonies. And our national ensign would enjoy a better respect.

• *Pilfering* •

That apart, most crime perpetrated by yachtsmen is petty, and typically against their fellows. French yachtsmen in the Caribbean have a poor reputation. This is hard on those pleasant, honest froggies who wish to enjoy civilised cruising; and in the Med, for example, these are more typical. What seems to have happened in the Caribbean is that many young Frenchmen set out to build cheap steel yachts to follow their heroes, Moitessier and Tabarly. Hard-chine hulls could be seen building in the most unlikely rural sites all over France. Armed with kilos of pasta, and vin de table, they sailed for the palm trees with stars in their eyes and empty pockets.

And the money ran out. Jobs were not to be had. To return costs money, to go on to the South Seas costs money, and it was easy to nick Zodiacs, which are untraceable. Though this activity is largely laid at the door of the French, others – including the locals – are not above it. Given the fragmentation of the islands into dozens of small states, there is little that can be done; the criminal can keep on the move.

So far as crime against the yachtie is concerned, the wanderer is at the mercy of the petty pilferer. It is impossible to live in tropical heat and turn one's boat into a fortress. Fortunately there are few places where pilfering is a serious problem, for the more primitive the culture the more likely the inhabitant will have strong conceptions of hospitality and a lack of covetousness. Most of us try to steer clear of big cities.

Theft in big cities

From the experiences of ourselves and friends, I think it unwise to leave a boat unwatched, even for short periods, in open harbours in big cities. By open harbours I mean those where there are no dock gates with police or Customs men controlling entry by the public. Typical among open harbours where care is needed are Barcelona, Baltimore (USA), Brindisi, Marseilles and Palermo, but there are many others. Most yacht marinas in or near a city are targets for thieves, especially where they are open to public access, such as Antibes and others along the Riviera. This leads to boats in these marinas being fitted with alarms, and sleepless nights for all crews living aboard when these things go off semi-continuously. In some countries, notably Italy where dishonesty is part of the culture in big cities, there is a very fierce desire to protect the property which a person has, even if he stole it from

These Sunsail boats had been propped up on oil drums. This is very bad practice and should not have been done.

someone else in the first place. Marinas in Italy have more positive security systems, sometimes leading to a prison camp mentality. One near Rome was surrounded by a double chain-link fence, with vicious dogs running unleashed between them. There was only one gate, double locked, and a scrutiny before entry that stopped just short of body-searching. There was a conscientious armed night patrol but, in spite of all this, thieves arrived by water one night and stripped several boats of their electronics. This marina, unlike some, welcomed live-aboards as reliable watchmen who actually paid the marina, not vice versa, for the privilege of keeping watch.

If you leave your boat unwatched, locking up becomes necessary. Doors and hatches in sea -going craft are generally stoutly made and good locks can be fitted. But these are not necessarily the whole answer because thieves are often adept at undoing them. It is worthwhile devising a complex door or hatch opening system that is apparently contrary to logic. We know of one case where such an entrance to a boat was attacked and battered without the raiders gaining entry, even though it had not been locked.

For our own part, we had until recently lost little to the pilferer, which indicates that people probably worry too much. The total over many years was a teak-handled knife, a tape recorder that we left on deck while we were ashore, and two fenders which might have been badly made fast and, of all things, a steel derrick. Our total financial loss was probably less than the cost of a good lock. Until this year, that is, when we returned to England for a major refit in an east coast port. Vandals raided *Hosanna* three times in 60 days. Twice we were on board at the time and Bill fought one of them, a teenager, and almost managed to throw him over the side into the tideway, but this was just after the case of the unfortunate farmer who killed a burglar. Fortunately, our intruders ran away. Another time, though, while Laurel was undergoing her own major refit, we were properly done over and thousands of pounds of wanton damage was done and goods stolen. The sad thing was that the Norfolk Police could do nothing against teenagers. The English provinces, once so civilised, are now part of the anarchic jungle of woolly pink do-gooderie. Note that we still steer clear of cities.

Unfortunately one can no longer rely on scrupulous honesty anywhere in Europe. We have even had a length of hose and a fender stolen in a Greek island, something unthinkable 20 years ago.

One point to watch in regard to petty theft abroad: it does not always pay to report it. Ask around to see what experience others in your spot have had. Your chances of getting your property back are virtually nil, but to report it is to involve oneself with officialdom, and sometimes to have one's freedom of movement restrained. As a final indignity, in many countries the local Customs will assess you, the loser, as having imported the item and charge you duty on it, effectively multiplying your loss. This unfair and unreasonable insult is the clincher.

Stolen inflatables and other theft

The most common stolen artifact is an inflatable dinghy, with or without out-board motor. There seems to be a world-wide market for these items. *The Financial Times* should list them under 'Commodities' with the day's buying and selling prices: 'The Zodiac market moved narrowly today with a fair supply from St Lucia which found ready buyers. Avons were in steady demand and gained £40. Metzeler lost ground in early trading with a large batch of nearly new from Palermo, but recovered later to close the day £20 lower.'

Normally inflatables are cut adrift from the parent yacht during the night. Old West Indies hands hoist their dinghies in at night, or else reeve wire painters, but these are difficult to make really secure to an inflatable. The ease with which they can be stolen and then hidden for later disposal is an important factor in the choice of which type of tender to carry.

Liferafts are occasionally taken, for their cost is substantial, but as they are more easily traced they do not find such a ready market.

Running rigging and on-deck gear is sometimes stripped from a yacht. In Brindisi this can be done by real experts while the crew are sleeping below. Brindisi is a bad port for theft, with pilfering both by local urchins and by the swarms of hitch-hikers waiting to embark on the ferries for Greece. The fact that Corfu suffers from thieves is due not so much to Greek dishonesty but almost entirely to young tourists. But it is in Italy that thieves have real chutzpah. At Palermo, thieves who had been locating the dinghy they wanted, found to their dismay that the owners had chained it to the stern davits. They stole the davits too.

There is also an active market in whole yachts, mostly confined to those in quantity production, which are less easily distinguished one from another. The liability of having a particular type of yacht stolen is in direct proportion to its ready resale: so it does not necessarily pay to buy yachts with high resale values.

In Antibes the yacht next to us, a German-owned *Amel,* was visited over several days by an overalled young man in a battered van, who did certain work aboard, and this aroused no suspicions. Nor was anyone alerted when the yacht sailed, ostensibly to the boatyard for slipping. It was by chance that a friend of the owner (who was at that time home in Germany) saw the yacht in Palma and went to greet his chum. He was an alert man, suspected something was wrong, phoned his friend, and brought in the police. The thief was arrested, and it subsequently transpired that he had selected the yacht some time before and had negotiated a series of West Indian charters for her before actually committing the theft.

Other points about theft

Theft of all types is endemic in the French and Italian Rivieras, and in or near any large Italian or Spanish town. Be wary in Athens, Egypt, and to a lesser extent Tunisia and Morocco, and the touristy parts of Portugal.

In tiny places like Bequia one would be visited by a lot of native people, very friendly for the most part, some begging, some selling, but fundamentally law-abiding.

PLACES WHERE THEFT IS VIRTUALLY UNKNOWN

- The rural areas of Greece and Turkey.
- The more isolated and rural areas of southern Italy (away from tourist centres).
- The Canary Islands (away from tourist centres).
- The Azores except for Punta Delgada.
- The out-islands in the Bahamas.
- The rural parts of Yugoslavia.

In all other areas, unless you have local knowledge to the contrary, assume that tourism has brought those that prey upon it. If you have any doubts about a place, you can leave or take precautions. There is no call for paranoia, just observe a little, ask a little, get to know the local feeling. It pays to take at least elementary precautions against petty theft.

WHAT PRECAUTIONS?

- Do not display ostentatious wealth ashore. Even modest possessions by North American or European standards are wealth beyond dreams for many people. To them, possessing a yacht of any kind means you are a millionaire, even if you built it from scrap with your bare hands.
- Do not leave dinghies in the water, or leave boarding ladders down, or ropes and fenders overside while at anchor overnight.
- Do not sleep on deck if you are seriously worried about a place. Fasten hatches and large openings in a half-closed position that will allow ventilation but not admit an intruder.
- Take reasonable care, but do not reduce yourself to a fortress mentality all the time.

• *Piracy* •

Many are concerned about piracy, which is the taking of a vessel or the robbery of crew, cargo or equipment on the high seas, ie away from harbour. This crime has been much played up by the press, particularly in the USA with respect to piracy in the Caribbean, to the level of mild paranoia. In the chandlery at Bahia Mar, Fort Lauderdale, I waited to be served while an American bought a rifle, a sub-machine gun, and two pistols for about $1200. While they were being gift-wrapped I enquired where he was bound with such an arsenal and was told the Virgin Islands. I observed that he would be better off without them, which led to a frostiness on the part of the shopkeeper, who furnished many such armouries.

From which, you may gather, we do not travel armed. In my experience firearms are a positive liability; or to put it another way, gun-toting yachties have more problems from carrying weapons than the unarmed get by not. Now, after our experiences in England, we wonder whether we are right after all. I suspect I would have used a gun had I possessed one – but I certainly would not have wanted to end up in prison like the farmer I mentioned earlier. Clearly the firearms issue is something each of us has to work out for himself.

• *To arm, or not to arm?* •

'To be a good gunner, you must learn it by practice'

Consider the question of how to use these weapons. Guns are killing weapons. It is no use having one unless you are prepared, instantly and without stopping to think, to point it at someone and fire to kill. The typical handgun is a very inaccurate weapon, and cannot be used to wound without seriously hurting. It is only possible to pump bullets in the general direction of the target and hope one of them will do sufficient damage to stop an assailant, if it is in fact an assailant. A rifle is not a close-quarters weapon (unless it has a bayonet: God help us) and is designed for comparatively accurate longer-range work. Anyone with any experience of naval gunnery will know of the great problems attaching to sighting from a platform moving randomly in three dimensions, such as a yacht. Skilled naval gunners with complex control gear hardly ever hit anything: what chance has an excited amateur?

All these weapons must be kept clean, lightly oiled, and ready for instant use if they are to be effective. In many ports they must be declared, probably landed under police control, and collected again before sailing. There are heavy penalties for transgressions of firearm laws, which differ from place to place so that one is never sure what they will be.

In real life one is also faced with the problem of identifying an assailant as such. An American yachtsman (it is almost always Americans who get into trouble with guns) panicked and shot dead one of the crew of a Spanish trawler near Alboran. The trawler was approaching to swap fish for foreign cigarettes, a common practice at that time. That trigger-happy yachtsman became a sadder jailbird.

So how do you tell if the boat approaching is friendly or vicious? Do you shoot

anyway? Hardly. And do you think that if they are real pirates they will be unprepared for your rather limited self-defence? They'll be ready, and they'll blast the hell out of you at the first shot, or ram you. The only people you will discourage by arms will be friendly ones.

We once went into Aghios Andreas Bay at the southern end of Ithaca to find an American ketch the sole occupant. No doubt he was irritated at having his solitude spoiled, but the situation hardly called for his appearance on deck with a shotgun, telling us to get out of the bay as it was only big enough for one. It is the impulsive exploitation of the enhancement of power given by a weapon that is so dangerous in the hands of a person who is temporarily, or even partially, unstable. What did we do in Ithaca? We told him to grow up, and anchored. He became quite friendly later. This story, which we have related from time to time, recently came back to us in sketchy form as having happened to someone else. I hope there are not two gun-toting nuts around the Ionian Sea.

I believe that the very ownership of a weapon fosters paranoia. If already of that tendency, it becomes more accentuated and even dangerous. I hope I get over my own current feeling of paranoia, but it has to be faced that if the forces of law and order fail, the citizen is tempted to defend himself as best he can. Boathooks aren't a bad weapon.

• *Murder and violence* •

This probably happens oftener at sea among a dissident crew than in harbour by persons unknown. What about attacks in harbour? These do happen. Whereas we have no personal knowledge of any authentic example of piracy, we do know of people who have suffered personal injury in harbour. It is necessary to consider whether these incidents would have been prevented with firearms. They all concerned intruders boarding a yacht. At least one of the yachts carried arms but the victim had no chance of using them. Two of the three cases were murders, in St Vincent and in Port of Spain, Trinidad. That in Friendship Bay, Bequia, was almost murder. Two of the yachts were American, one was British. It is impossible to be sure, but I believe that the mere possession of firearms would not have altered the outcome of any of these cases, where the murderers had been able to get to close quarters before being observed.

Do not make too much of these terrible events. They are deplorable, but probably less common than if you stayed at home. The St Vincent government did not appear to investigate this crime with any energy whatsoever. Trinidad did at least produce and sentence a culprit.

The whole thing is a question of prudence once again. Nothing will eliminate robbery and/or violence. But in places where it is known to occur, then some vigilance will reduce both its probability and its impact. Port of Spain is a big commercial port and not a noticeably congenial place for a yacht (though nowadays it seems to be getting better).

ACCIDENTS

'Master, let us breathe and refresh a little, and sling a man overboard to stop the leakes.'

Not all damage to boat or person is caused by a criminal. Mishaps happen. In our experience most collisions between craft are trivial, most are clearly defined as to fault, and in most cases the defaulter makes amends instantly and without quibble. Three times we have suffered damage while made fast. Once in Boulogne from a member of the Royal Motor Yacht Club, who departed shouting 'Sorry, old man' and never answered our letter asking for the cost of a new starboard light.

Twice by Italians who volunteered compensation and paid in full.

The problem is that chasing compensation in foreign countries, in foreign languages and via post is a most unrewarding and frustrating pastime. Better to do a modest deal *on the spot* while the other fellow's conscience is still troubling him, than to hold out for full and complete indemnity. Most yachtsmen are decent types, thank God, long may it last.

Major damage is a different matter. Here insurance is a very definite help, for even if the perpetrators cannot be traced or brought to book, underwriters can be expected to settle in the terms of the policy, or even a little more in some cases.

If you commit the damage yourself, to another vessel or a person, then you will probably appreciate being insured. This is a mischance all the more likely as yachting centres get more crowded and increasing numbers of novices take to the sea with certificates obtained at evening classes, fondly believing they are competent. To sail without good third party cover is foolhardy and anti-social, especially as more people new to the sport bring a motor-car mentality to sea with them. One must also remember the fortune that many modern yachts represent in money terms, and the high cost of repairs.

• *Personal accidents* •

Minor damage to the person is discussed in Chapter Fifteen, which is about treatment that is totally within on-board resources. But one can have major accidents or mishaps that require surgery or hospital treatment, and though this cannot be considered a minor matter it will have to go in that chapter too, together with some comments on health insurance.

Not all accidents to the person happen on board, or even to your own crew. Everyman's mishap diminisheth me, to bastardise a good quotation. We once had a difficult time helping fellow British yachties with problems when a singlehanded yachtsman was killed in a motor accident in Italy. The British Consul at Florence was unhelpful and discourteous.

Laurel and I frequently travel about together in little excursions from our ship, and it is always a possibility that an accident to one would involve the other too. Such accidents do not have to be fatal to be bothersome to strangers. And the problems ensuing, if temporary neighbours whom you have only met the day before, or local officials, have to trace your relatives, are so great that some small precaution should be taken.

Each cruising yacht should display close to the main hatch a small, semi-permanent notice saying, 'In case of urgency or difficulty, contact ...'. One should also leave a will in a place of safety, and in the case of couples (because the likelihood of both dying at the same time is greater than for shore-dwellers) consult a lawyer about whether special clauses should cover this. If so, draw up compatible wills.

On a less gloomy note, it is a good idea to have a square foot or so of surface, close to the main hatch, painted in blackboard paint. We leave messages on it in chalk, or at appropriate moments write up announcements of pure joy.

ACCIDENTS AT SEA: THE LEGAL POSITION

I have mentioned already the obligation to go to the assistance of a vessel in distress. This is detailed in Section 6 of the (British) Maritime Conventions Act of 1911, the terms of which will have been enacted by all nations signatory to the Convention.

We are *obliged*, so far as we can without danger to our own vessel, to render assistance to every person (even if such a person be a subject of a foreign State at war with Her Majesty) who is found at sea in danger of being lost. Failure to do so is a misdemeanour. This is further amplified by the Merchant Shipping (Safety Convention) Act 1949, which should be read. (It is too long and detailed to include here: copies can be had from Her Majesty's Stationery Office.) The procedure for dealing with casualties on board is in Section 73 of the Merchant Shipping Act 1970. Casualties (and note that the ship herself can be a casualty) must be reported to the Department of Transport as soon as possible, and in any case not later than 24 hours after arrival at the next port. The report should contain a description of the incident, give details of injuries to personnel and damage to the ship, the name and official number of the ship, her position, next port of call and ETA, and should go to any DTp Marine Office, or to the Marine Coastguard Agency at Southampton.

• *Births, deaths and marriages* •

Also coming under 'accidents' we have Births, Deaths and Marriages at Sea. The law covering deaths is given in the Merchant Shipping (Returns of Births and Deaths) Regulations 1979. A Master is required to make a return of births in a ship, or of deaths in or from a ship. It should be made as soon as practicable (but within six months) to either a Marine Superintendent in the UK, a British Consular Office in foreign countries, or the equivalent of a Marine Superintendent in a Commonwealth country. There will also be local procedures if a body is landed at a port (the Regulations warn), but the UK regulations apply whether or not the body is landed, buried at sea, or not recovered.

The official record of a birth or death is in the register entry made by the Registrar following the receipt of such a return from a Master.

Marriages on board have a legal basis only when conducted by an authorized person, and when the ship is in the territory covered by that person's authority, and the official record would be held under the law of that territory. A British shipmaster is not, and never has been, an authorized person, and there is no UK machinery for recording marriages at sea. An entry in a log book is not, of itself, legal evidence of a marriage. Sorry, Captain.

There is no legal obligation to recover a body sighted at sea, because of the dangers of capsizing, disease etc, but sightings should be reported to the nearest authorities. Do so by radio, if possible. If reporting by person, the report in a foreign country should be made to the British Consul in the hope of avoiding local problems. That is the official position; there must always be a strong incentive not to sight bodies at sea.

If wrecked, the yachtsman is normally not entitled to be treated as a shipwrecked mariner for the purpose of free repatriation, and anyone in this unfortunate difficulty would be treated by a Consul as a normal distressed British subject. And God help them if my experience of British Consuls is anything to go by.

It is worth noting that while on the high seas a British registered ship is considered an extension of British Law, but once she enters the territorial waters of another state the situation is not so clear, particularly if citizens of that state or their property are affected.

LOSS OF SKIPPER

A particular disaster that worries a lot of wives, mates and less experienced members of a crew of two, is the loss of the skipper, whether permanently overboard or temporarily through injury or sickness while at sea. Such a worry justifies a word or two. It indicates a lack of confidence that, if justified, needs attention.

The crew must be able to handle the craft, even if only under power or with reduced sail. Even for a novice this is not so impossible as it might seem, especially when needs must. Some people are afraid to discuss this, particularly wives with their husbands, but it is worth making the effort because the conclusions will never be forgotten.

There are a few simple precautions to be taken. In times past, in big ships it was normal for the radio room to be given the ship's position every watch so that in emergency they had an approximate position always at hand. (This problem has eased considerably with DSC radio.) In a yacht I always plot the position at least once every four hours in the oceans, and at least every two in soundings, whether by fix or DR. I always have in the ready drawer charts for diversionary ports to which I might have to go for some emergency, and my plan for the voyage lists some of them. Because Laurel is the Met Officer she is always aware of wind patterns and the weather; because she often works out a sight alongside me, she knows how to do it; and because I insist she uses the VHF from time to time she is not nervous on the radio (and a lot of people are). She is not so hot on engineering but she can start, stop and use the engine.

One of the useful things to have on deck in the event of a man overboard is a moderate length (50 metres, say) of light floating rope, about 8mm diameter. This will not get in the screw, and given two circumstances: that manoeuvring is difficult and the victim is conscious, it is possible to come close enough and turn so that the rope is brought across the victim. If the yacht can be stopped, it is possible to haul him alongside. The rope should have a metre-long loop at the end, but the person should not normally be towed. Better to let the rope go from on board, and to pick it up again, if you have too much way on. There are some commercial kits which perform the above function: they are not expensive and have the right sort of fittings.

I believe in use of the engine in recovery. My experience is that even when running under spinnaker, the engine at full astern will not destroy steerage way

Taking the opportunity of a fair day's sailing to dry out after an Atlantic storm.

and will save valuable yards while the sail is being furled: a point of importance for short-handed crews. But beware of trailing cordage when furling.

Loss of anyone at sea is a terrible disaster. Its effect and the awful fear of it can be mitigated by a discussion and decisions of what to do if the disaster happens. That is probably enough to make sure it never does.

INTERNAL DAMAGE TO THE YACHT

Even with good care and maintenance, things do go wrong in ways that are dangerous. I once had a shaft coupling disintegrate off Ushant. It had been badly machined by someone I was entitled to expect to do it well, and the chatter of the bad fit destroyed the metal. The shaft dropped back leaving a 2-inch diameter hole. One of my crew on that occasion was a professional cabinet maker: I have never seen a wooden plug made so fast, but it took a lot of getting in against the water pressure. It could not be put in the outer end. The lesson I drew from this was to have ready-made plugs for all the openings in the hull.

Perhaps the most frightening possibility is fire, particularly at sea. We had one and I was fortunate in having been trained in ship firefighting. The experience is instructive. I had fitted a ventilating fan above the batteries, and the exhaust side had Tannoy brand ducting secured by clips supplied by the manufacturers. The ducting consisted of a wire spiral thinly covered by plastic. In the compartment there was a deckhead-mounted Noxfire automatic extinguisher.

At about 0330 when somewhere north-west of Corsica (we always have a bad time round there), sailing in a very rough sea at the tail end of a gale, Laurel, who was on watch, called me to say there was a smell of burning. I opened the hatch to the engine room and found the whole space full of flame and smoke. I shut the hatch; the fire was clearly beyond the capacity of extinguishers and I naturally thought that the automatic one had gone off but had failed to cope. In fact, it never did go off.

After some time I managed to get the fire under control using a very fine spray of sea water. As the smoke cleared I saw the cause. The ducting had fallen out of the clips, which were clearly not adequate for the extra strains of violent motion in bad weather (a feature that is distressingly common in items designed by whizz-kids who have never had a wet shirt). The ducting had dropped on to the battery terminals, rolled about, and soon worn away its thin plastic coating; the wire had shorted across the terminals, igniting everything nearby, helped by the contents of a plastic can of paraffin that I had been idiot enough to stow there.

LESSONS LEARNT

(Some of them I knew already, but needed a reminder.)

- Cheap and flimsy fastenings just will not cope with the violent movement of a small boat in bad seas.
- Contrary to popular advice, it is a good precaution to cover batteries, but the covers must permit the passage of gases. A strong plastic mesh would be effective.
- Paraffin and cans of any fuel, particularly in plastic containers, should be on deck.
- Automatic extinguishers, even when in date, cannot be relied on and are therefore not worth the money though your insurers may insist on one.
- Butyl insulated wiring, specified by Lloyd's as being fire resistant, burns as merrily as other, less expensive, plastics but is more difficult to extinguish.
- Our thick-walled plastic diesel fuel lines did not ignite or melt, even though damaged. This may be because the engine was running and the tubing was cooled by the flow of oil in it.
- The sort of fire extinguishers that can be carried in a small craft, while adequate for a minor outbreak in the early stages, cannot cope with a serious blaze.
- Crew cruising a lot need to have actual experience of putting out electrical (the most frequent cause) and fuel fires using only a water spray. Not a jet, but a spray of as fine droplets as one can get. It is cheap and effective, but it is a definite skill which the long-cruising yachtsman should acquire.
- Boiled batteries do not work.
- The mess from a fire is horrible, and hard to clean up.
- We were in more physical danger from the fumes of burning plastic battery cases, wiring insulation etc than we were from heat and flames.

BRIEF COMMENTS ON FIGHTING FIRES IN SMALL CRAFT

'Captain, we are fowle on each other and the shippe is on fire'

• *The nature of fire* •

To start, a fire needs three essential elements: fuel, oxygen and a source of heat. I think that for our purpose we can ignore some of the more esoteric chemical fires which the full-time fireman may have to deal with, and consider the simpler ones. In a yacht there are fuels galore for a fire: diesel oil, plastic linings, foam upholstery, the resin in fibreglass, paints, wood, cooking fat and gas to name the more obvious ones.

Heat is necessary in two ways: the fuel has to be raised to its ignition temperature, below which it will not burn. This varies with the material, and for some is remarkably low. In addition a source of heat has to be applied (even if momentarily) at a temperature known as the flash point and this triggers the flame. This also varies with the material and again can be quite a low temperature.

To extinguish a fire, break the triangle of fuel, oxygen and heat. One can remove the fuel, cut off the supply of oxygen or lower the temperature of whatever is burning, or preferably do a combination of these. Even if the flames are put out, if the temperature of the fuel is not lowered below its ignition temperature, the fire can re-start.

We remove the fuel by, for example, throwing it overboard. Very effective, but sometimes not practicable. We can remove the oxygen by smothering the fire, with a fire blanket or foam, for instance. We can cool the fuel with water or certain chemicals.

• *Fire extinguishers* •

These are essentially for first aid. They are useful and necessary to provide a very quick means of dealing with minor outbreaks which have been detected in the early stages. Of course they are also helpful even with major fires, for in these circumstances every little helps.

Given that their chief effectiveness is against small fires, one should choose extinguishers that do not themselves cause a great deal of damage, inconvenience or mess. In every case where I have seen a dry powder extinguisher used on a small fire, it has caused more mess and damage than the fire. This experience cannot be extrapolated indefinitely because the fire, if unchecked, would obviously have gone on to cause a great deal of damage, but it does contain a lesson.

One should also get an extinguisher that is easy to use. Instructions to beat the top on the floor, shake for a minute, then point away from the fire for five seconds are too complex to remember, and far too difficult to absorb if on the edge of panic.

Extinguishers with certain chemicals are dangerous to the user. Carbon tetrachloride (Pyrene) is a close and poisonous relative of chloroform, and must not be inhaled for any length of time, especially if there is any alcohol in the body. There are extinguishers loaded with Halene or Halon, an inert gas similar to the freon used in refrigerators. We used it when careless welding in the engine room of *Hosanna* set alight some rags soaked in spilled diesel oil. It was extremely effective; only one squirt was required. It is, however, supposed to affect the ozone layer several miles up, and has been banned due to 'Green' pressure. The gas is much heavier than air; no one has yet explained how it gets up to the ozone layer since it does not rise! Yes, I know all about the Brownian diffusion of gases, but that does not apply in a centrifuge, and the earth's atmosphere is just that. Most professional firefighters are angry that Halon has been banned, and none more so than those at sea, because the ban is unnecessary. When used on a fire Halon undergoes an endothermic reaction: it absorbs heat from outside itself, thus cooling the fuel as well as depriving it of oxygen. It becomes a completely harmless substance after this and does not affect the ozone layer. At sea we cannot use copious quantities of water and Halon is so far and away the best product that to deprive us of it for an unproven theory is to endanger the lives of seamen. It discredits the whole Green movement.

Carbon dioxide is the best alternative for use in a boat at present. It is a heavy gas and does no damage. Because of weight it does not leak away from the boat, as it would do in a caravan, for example. It is effective against fat fires in the galley. It is possible to use some of the contents on a small fire and still have the remainder usable if you are unlucky enough to have another; a very important point at sea where replacements are unobtainable. Like Halon, it works on all oil fires, but, unlike Halon, it does not cool the fuel, so after putting out the flames that has to be done. The failure to cool means that CO_2 is not so good for dealing with fires in carbonaceous or solid materials, unless some other method of cooling is subsequently used. It replaces oxygen, so you need to watch out you can go on breathing.

Foam extinguishers are really only for oil and petrol fires. They make a horrible mess and do not cool effectively. They need a certain skill to be fully effective and are probably not really suitable for small yachts.

Automatic extinguishers usually work by having a fusible plug which melts in heat, or by having an electronic actuator which senses smoke. I have known the former go off by accident, and also to fail to go off, but I have never heard of a case on a boat where they went off as promised. In my view they are a snare and a delusion and are best avoided, though surveyors, who must find something to grumble about in every yacht they survey, are keen to recommend them in insurance surveys. (So far, in more than a dozen insurance surveys, the number of idiot recommendations exceeds the sensible ones by a proportion of three to one.) I have no field experience of the other type in action, but I mistrust electronics in small craft. I have rather more faith in my wife's nose.

So, what sort do I have? I still have five Halon extinguishers and I am unashamed because I value my skin. I do not let out the gas in a cavalier or casual fashion. I would only use them if I were to be in desperate need and I assure you that in those circumstances only a suicidal nincompoop would worry about the ozone layer. They are easy to see if up to pressure and ready to work. One must be sure to renew them according to the makers' recommendations and it is now difficult to replenish Halon extinguishers. In my professional career I fought two serious fires at sea, and have spent much of my life since thinking about the problems. I am going to repeat that I disapprove strongly of the banning of Halon as a result of 'Green' pressure. If ever a cross-Channel ferry takes fire, lack of Halon will cost many lives. Shore-based firefighters have alternative techniques not available to the ship-firefighter and Halon should be permitted for use *at sea*. When offshore, and with no outside help available, the seaman is *entitled* to use the very best material available: undoubtedly Halon. To forbid its use at sea is tantamount to sentencing seamen to death. Let's be Green, yes, but let us also be merciful to those in peril.

Any other firefighting materials? Yes, a fire blanket is worth keeping, both to smother a small fire or to use as a means of removing burning material. It's cheap and has nothing to go wrong. But remember a blanket does not cool the fuel: this must still be done, and very quickly.

Sprinkler systems, which ought really to be called spray systems, are worth installing in large yachts, especially in machinery spaces when it may not always be possible to get in to fight a fire. They give off a spray of minute droplets of water, usually sea water. As their effect is not carefully aimed they do a fair amount of devastation, particularly to furnishings, so in my view are not recommended for automatic use, when they could be expected to go off unasked. For an automatic system in the engine room I would prefer Halon or carbon dioxide, but remember that engines cannot run on it. If the access is down a hatch, do not go leaping gaily down when the fire is out. There will be no oxygen for you to breathe, and maybe toxic smoke as well. Again the burning material will not be cooled, and could therefore re-ignite if the gas is dispersed.

• *Big fires* •

We define this as a fire beyond the capacity of your handheld extinguishers. It may not be large, but perhaps it is intense and soon could be large. In a yacht there is only one firefighting material available in sufficient quantities: water. You are surrounded by it, but to succeed you must use it skilfully. Water can be used against almost any type of fire if used well.

Fire Brigades occasionally deal with ship fires in port. Soon there are dozens of 3-inch hoses snaking aboard, and before long the weight of water in the vessel either sinks her or destroys her hydrostatic stability by creating free surface which capsizes her in her berth. (The Bootle Fire Brigade hit the jackpot in 1953 with the *Empress of Canada*.) It certainly puts the fire out, which enables the firemen to call it a success. It usually writes off the ship, puts a busy berth out of action, and may cause more financial damage than letting the fire burn itself out.

At sea one is rather obsessed with preserving the ship, so make sure every bit of water let into her will be used to the maximum advantage. The jet of water used so dramatically on fires in buildings has a point in enabling firemen to get water to the seat of a blaze they could not otherwise reach. It also blasts apart solid material and cools it. In its place, it is the right way of doing things. In a ship, and especially in a small ship, it is very seldom the right way. Notice I do not say 'never' or 'always': there is no such conception in firefighting.

Water serves the important purpose of cooling. Its most effective way of doing this is not by conducting heat away but by evaporating, which uses up a very large amount of heat energy. In most circumstances, therefore, it pays to deliver the water in an ideal form for instant evaporation: this is as a very fine spray.

A fine spray also acts as a sort of curtain. As the fire uses oxygen, it draws in more air and feeds itself. The spray curtain, though not a complete screen, reduces the flow of air to the fire. As the water droplets evaporate efficiently they turn almost instantly to steam which, because it has many times the volume of the water it came from, helps to create a quite effective barrier to air.

Jets of sea water conduct electricity well. A perfect spray of fine droplets, because the droplets are separate from each other, will not conduct. In practice, of course, a spray is never perfect, but I have taken part in experiments showing that a fine spray of sea water can approach to 75cm away from a high-voltage source without the nozzle giving more than a mild tingle to a person holding it with bare, wet hands. It is not for repetition with backyard lash-ups: it is potentially a very dangerous thing to do and the experiments were very carefully controlled, but it demonstrates that in the presence of low-powered electrics it is acceptable as a firefighting method.

To sum up, a fine spray can be used effectively against any likely fire aboard a yacht. Ideally the spray should be under pressure: it can be pumped by hand using a galley pump. If enough pressure is obtainable the JetSpray hose 'gun' used aboard many boats for washing down decks and paintwork is good. If pressure is low, then a shower fitting is better than nothing. A rose from a watering can is good, but a rarity aboard a yacht. Rather than chuck buckets of water over a small fire (which can actually help it spread) I have found that dribbling water from a sponge can be more effective.

How do you use a spray? The spray's weakest effect is against solid materials. In this case use it to drench the burning items and to keep wet the adjacent area. Even when the flames are out, continue cooling until the surfaces stay wet. If in doubt remove charred matter with a knife or coarse rasp and cool again because it might still be very hot inside.

• *Galley fires* •

Of course Halon, CO_2 or the fire blanket are best used first. One must also cut off the supply of fuel to the stove. A lot depends on the state of a fat fire. If it is entirely inside a saucepan (and one should endeavour always to use deep cooking utensils in a boat) put a lid on it and cool the pot down. Don't let any water get in the fat or it will spatter explosively. If the fat has spilled and spread, then we have an oil fire.

• *Electrical fires* •

There is not really any such thing: electricity provides the initiating heat and flash point and it is other matter that burns. The problem is usually that the electricity goes on supplying a source of great heat, which hinders attempts to extinguish the fire and also constitutes a hazard.

Usually the trigger of the fire is a short-circuit, which may or may not be arcing and therefore may not be easy to see. Try to identify the problem point and cut off the power to it. Smoke can prevent one from being able to see, so this is not always by any means easy. It is possible to use a spray curtain to contain the smoke to some extent, enabling one to see the seat of the fire. Apart from the regenerative potential of a continuing short-circuit, this type of fire usually turns into one of the others. A particular problem is that when plastic electrical insulation burns it gives off poisonous fumes.

• *Oil fires* •

If the area of oil that is burning is large, use the fine spray curtain as if one was holding an umbrella against a very strong wind, and slowly sweep the surface of the oil to try to reduce the burning area and to 'gather' the burning part into an ever-decreasing area. Do not leave any burning patches behind; go back and sweep again, slowly. You are both cooling it and reducing the oxygen supply. You will not succeed quickly. Try not to use more water than the fire is evaporating. If the oil is sloshing about in a moving boat this can be helpful because it is assisting cooling somewhat, but it does make containment with the spray more difficult. If there is a lot of oil (and water) in the bilge try to pump it out; ecology comes a poor second just now. The oil, even if hot, is unlikely to cause problems in the pump. If more oil is actually leaking into the fire it is important to cut the leak off as soon as possible, so it may be necessary to concentrate on cooling the site where the isolating cocks are situated before tackling the main blaze.

• *Smoke* •

Many of the comforts of modern life produce toxic smoke when they burn, for example fabrics, upholstery and mattresses, plastic linings. Others produce carboniferous smoke which is not necessarily poisonous but which stops us breathing. Incomplete combustion can produce carbon monoxide, which is poisonous. Sea water mixed with battery acid gives off chlorine, which is deadly as well as choking.

Some of these toxic gases are lighter than air, and in fire conditions, when they are hot, most can be expected to rise. Under most conditions it pays to approach fires giving off smoke by keeping as near the deck as possible. Wet cloth over mouth and nostrils will filter particles, but will not stop most toxic gases. It hardly seems worth lumbering up a boat with breathing apparatus, but if necessary, it may be possible to improvise with a diving face mask and some tubing.

All this is easy at a firefighting school. The important thing about actual firefighting, when every fire is different, is to be aware of the principles, to know the methods (and if possible to have exercised their use), and then to use your intelligence. The tradition of rushing to a fire is a very good one, but on arrival do not go mad and waste your resources. A few seconds to determine the nature of the fire and to plan the battle will be amply repaid.

The point at which you call for outside help depends on what help is available, what means you have to call it, and the relationship of the fire to your resources. If in doubt about your ability to cope and help is available, take a moment to call it.

Most port authorities insist on a Fire Brigade being called, because they have an obligation to protect other vessels. They usually have power to tow away a burning ship to a safe berth and similar draconian rights. In these circumstances, ie in port, you must summon help, but unless the fire is beyond your control remember you are still in command of the ship.

Before you set sail (I refrain from saying before you burn your boats); find, if you can, a Fire Brigade that has a specialised ship-firefighting team. There are not many of them, but Kent is one. I am sure that one of the Fire Officers would spare a moment to let you exercise with extinguishers. Getting the feel of the equipment in advance is a powerful advantage.

IN CASE OF FIRE
- Call the whole crew.
- Get to the fire quickly, but calmly.
- Determine the generative centre of the fire.
- Assess the dangers of toxic gases and take precautions.
- Cut off any outside supply of fuel, or potential fuel.
- Select your firefighting apparatus.
- Attack the generative centre if it can be reached. If not, determine your route to it.
- Keep on until flames are out.
- Thoroughly cool the previously burning material.
- Check at frequent intervals afterwards that you have not overlooked any hot spots that are smouldering.

'The fire is out, God be thanked'

DISMASTING

Other mishaps to the yacht involve the loss of mast, and canvas. We carry enough spare or alternate sails to get by, perhaps less efficiently but nevertheless practically, if some are blown out.

Loss of a mast is more serious, and is best dealt with by getting them strong enough at the start. The extra cost will probably be less than the excess on one's insurance policy. Cruising boats should not go around with the bendy fishing rods sported by the racing folk. It helps to have a two-masted rig too, but only if there is no triatic stay. (I am not sure triatic stays contribute very much anyway.)

What to do if you lose a mast is very well covered in salty books on seamanship. Racing yachtsmen write about it frequently in magazines, but mostly they have large crews of gorillas to heft spars about. All the more reason for the cruising man to consider his double-strength masts and rigging, and then double again to be on the safe side.

Yes, I have been dismasted. Twice. Once while racing, and once in *Hosanna*, and both in almost exactly the same place off the Kentish Knock Light Vessel. Racing, we were grossly over-canvassed and deserved it. *Hosanna*'s solid wood foremast had rotted round a knot under the paint, and the vibrations of motoring (yes!) into a short, steep sea brought it all down. At 0400 of course. Laurel steered while I managed to get all 400 kilos of it back inboard, and we continued south to Ramsgate. We have a galvanised steel mast now. No mucking about.

Bill starts the clearing up process after we lost Hosanna's *foremast.*

LIGHTNING

During the talks we have given we have been surprised at the interest shown in lightning at sea.. *Fare Well* was struck once, and Bill was struck once before in a small warship; it is one of those very rare sea-going experiences which seems to fascinate everyone.

A while ago *Yachting Monthly* had a correspondence on what policy to adopt when entering a violent thunderstorm, and one writer advocated donning rubber gloves and boots. Bill, being rather a rude sort of sailor, wrote in, suggesting that someone had forgotten to include a condom. The then Editor, Des Sleightholme, doyen of yachting wits, wrote back that he felt the comment a little ripe for the readership, and finished with the following:

> *The lightning flashed, the thunder crashed,*
> *The mate of the watch turned pale,*
> *For St Elmo's fire struck his rubber attire*
> *The moment he touched the rail.*

It is St Elmo's fire that one is more likely to encounter, especially in a steel boat. In a GRP boat or a wooden one, there is a lot to be said for having a bond between the sea water and the top of the mast. Of course the standing rigging does this if the mast is not metal, the only link required being between the chainplates and the water. The reason for such a bond is to keep the electric current flow on the outside of the boat.

Thunderstorms in the tropics, and also in the Med, can be very much more violent than we in temperate zones are used to. We once counted 42 lightning flashes within one random minute. In these circumstances it is obvious that there is a huge potential difference between the atmosphere and the sea.

It is only when this difference is unable to disperse peacefully that it runs riot and strikes. During a night thunderstorm one will often see St Elmo's fire (a brilliant display from the masthead looking like a 'sparkler' type of firework). This discharge is helping to prevent the violently damaging strike.

I was on deck both times when struck, and it was difficult to assess exactly what was happening. Both times there was an enormous display, several metres across, of St Elmo's fire at the masthead, and it went on some time. In *Fare Well* (then in the Gulf Stream) the sparking increased rapidly in intensity as I watched. I felt the sensation usually described as one's 'hair standing on end', even though I was wearing a cap. It was an extraordinarily strong sensation. It developed into a feeling of being lifted off the ground a few inches, of stopping breathing, of being held by the back of the neck like a rabbit, of being absolutely unable to move at all. Those below felt nothing.

During this time I was aware that the sparking at the masthead had turned into a brilliant ball of light about 7 metres in diameter, and that the rigging was glowing white.

Suddenly, as if by throwing a switch, it all turned off. I fell to the deck in a state of shock, and all the fire and sparks at the masthead disappeared. Notice that I have given no time-scale for these events. I was not aware of any sensation of time passing. It is possible the whole sequence took place in a second, it might have taken ten or twenty; I have no idea.

What was the damage to a steel boat?

To me personally, nothing that a good breakfast could not put right. There are few things that do not yield to a good breakfast. The problem was: no breakfast yet. The only interior part of the boat affected was the wiring, which suggests to me that the current flowed in the skin of the boat (the Faraday box effect) and set up a strong magnetic field that induced current into some, but not all, of the wiring. It must have done so at great speed, for in some cases the wire had melted before the fuse had blown. Generally wires melted or insulation blew open at sharp corners, and the damage took the form of a directional blast along the wire. It was as if the current had a linear momentum and could not negotiate the tight bend, mounted the banking, and left the track like a racing car.

Some physicists I have discussed this with deny that such an effect is possible, but I have seen it, and I have found one scientist who says there is some evidence that very violent flashes of current have what he called a 'plasma effect'. Well now.

Question: Was that a strike or a very bad attack of St Elmo? Answer: Who knows? Next question: What can one do about it? Answer: Nothing more than I said above.

If it was just very bad St Elmo, then in the thunderstorm going on at that time, it suggests to me that a good electrical path up to the top of the mast, together with a good area of conductor in the water (we had recently had a spectacular grounding in coral which had taken a lot of paint off our keel), inhibits a strike by organising a very effective discharge. If it was a proper strike, then compared with the devastated condition of both wooden and GRP boats that have been struck (all I have seen have taken fire), I cannot help feeling that a boat built of a good conducting material has advantages for the tropics.

What else was damaged? All the electronic fittings on the mainmast were blown apart, but to my amazement I found that some of the instruments themselves (those which had been switched off) survived the blow. All the electronics on the mizzen mast, including the Decca radar, survived. Our radio sets all survived (they were switched off, and their aerial plugs removed: my practice in storms). Several electric motors did not. The stator coils in the generator had to be re-energised.

As for the standing rigging, it appeared to be undamaged, possibly because the current was flowing over the surface rather than inside the wire, and of course the wire was soaking wet in the heavy rain, which may have cooled it. It survived several more years of use and abuse.

There was one other important effect which does not go under the heading of damage. The whole ship became highly magnetised and the compass was wildly in error. Fortunately we had logged the direction of the swell a couple of hours before the storm, so we had an angular reference. Without that, in completely overcast conditions and 400 miles from land, we would have had absolutely no idea of which way to go.

It turned out the compass deviation was about 90° to start with, but within an hour this had fallen to 35°. A week later it was about 15°, but it took three months to fall below 15°. It never did return to its former state; after about six months we adjusted the magnets to remove the last couple of degrees.

It wasn't much fun clearing up the mess, but it was a fascinating intellectual exercise trying to sort it all out. All in all I feel there is not enough objective evidence in existence to justify any heavy expenditure on this problem. One can, however, take the simple precautions I outlined at the start. At least they won't do any harm. And keep the log up to date!

• *Emergencies outside the boat* •

These are emergencies which can lead to the abandonment of the enterprise, its interruption, or a temporary trip home for one of the crew. Illness of a close relative, for example. It really is impossible to give advice to cover so many different problems in so many possible places, and at widely varying times. We have only had to make two out-of-routine or emergency trips home in 25 years, one from a Greek island, and one, half-expected; from southern France.

I would counsel maintaining a contingency fund of cash on board to cover both fares and additional costs that will be entailed in such an event, if there is any chance of it occurring. It is possible that a real family emergency while cruising the South Pacific could be ruinous (see Chapter Three).

• *Back up and outside help* •

There are those who worry about disasters, that they might be unable to cope. I think most of us have worries of this nature to some extent; it is natural. And if it induces an atmosphere of prudence and care it is a productive worry. To set sail with a literally careless abandon is dangerous and childish, and it is not macho because real men *care*.

Some get over their nervousness by a decision to make their first ocean crossing in company with an organisation like the Atlantic Rally for Cruisers (ARC) or on a round-the-world jolly organised by, say, the RAFYC. It's a free world and there are those for whom the sociability and jollity, combined with inevitable outbreaks of competitive spirit, are welcome enough to attract them. But I would not say that organisations such as the ARC enhance security or are able to provide *effective* support in case of trouble at sea.

In the first place, the Atlantic crossing itself from the Canaries to the Windward Islands is unlikely to be other than a comparatively safe voyage. The voyage to the Canaries before you start your crossing is far more difficult and dangerous; and thus more appropriate for a passage in company.

In spite of all the aids to communication, all the chatty radio nets, boats inevitably disperse on a long voyage and end up miles apart. Finding another yacht in distress is not easy; one's range of vision from deck level is only a few miles and yachts are not equipped with direction finding equipment. Even with the ARC, you cannot rely on outside help coming quickly, if at all. For ocean cruising you must have an attitude of independence, of self-reliance, of self-confidence. The ARC may be ideal for those 'doing the triangle' (Europe– Caribbean –Bermuda–Europe, all in one year starting in October), but if you have longer distances in your sights, we think, and it is only an opinion after all, that you should start as independently as you will have to go on.

THE PANIC BAG

Having advised that a good rigid dinghy is in many respects better than an inflatable liferaft, I have to remind you that the latter does have a survival pack of sorts on board. Therefore, if you use a rigid dinghy as a lifeboat, you should have a pack to help you survive. We call ours the panic bag. Some people object to the use of the word *panic*, saying that it is the last thing one should be aware of in this circumstance, but I disagree. Actually using the word reminds one of the danger of panic, and inhibits its formation.

Ours consists of two bags: the First Panic Bag, which is kept in the dinghy on passage, and the Second, which is kept reasonably handy for grabbing if there is time. For those with an inflatable liferaft, it might be worth comparing my lists with the contents of the provided survival kit, and making up a bag to contain the difference. (You cannot check the raft's pre-packed supplies: they aren't always as promised.)

Our lists are based on consultation with a survivor friend, and also my own 600 ocean miles in an open boat.

THE FIRST PANIC BAG (for 2 people)

4 x 8 pints water in opaque plastic bottles	Tweezers	300-foot codline
2 strong drinking cups (Melaware)	Small compass, mirror	Fishing line, spoons, hooks
4 red flares, 4 orange smoke day markers	Needles and thread	Greek-style foul-hooks for fishing
Torch, spare bulb, spare batteries	Cotton wool	Greek 7-pronged harpoon head (a barbed miniature
200 multivitamin pills in plastic jar	Small bottle TCP antiseptic	Poseidon's fork)
100 Horlicks tablets	Tube of antibiotic cream	Gaff for fishing
1 lb boiled sweets	100 tablets broad spectrum antibiotic	Set of small chartlets in a plastic bag
Swiss Army knife, dinner knife, spoon	Tube of sunscreen ointment	Survival type solar still (RAF surplus type)
	Seasick pills	
	Sponge (bailer is already in dinghy)	
	2 small hand towels	
	2 'space blankets'	

THE SECOND PANIC BAG (for 2 people)

2 inflatable cushions	Candles, matches in screw-top jar	Cereal bars in waterproof container
2 single blankets	Araldite (epoxy glue)	Can-opener
2 wool sweaters	More boiled sweets	2 pairs sunglasses
3 square yards 4oz canvas	4 more pints water	Bucket
Some fresh lemons in foil	More sunscreen ointment	2 sun hats
2 parachute flares	8 assorted tins of food	
Small funnel		

Items which deteriorate must be replaced when time-expired. And let's hope that, like us, you get a quarter of a century of cruising and never have to use your bag.

12 • Navigation

'If you don't know where you are going you will probably end up somewhere else.' – PETER AND HULL, *The Peter Principle*

Navigation at sea has changed dramatically since we wrote the first edition 15 years ago. There have been attempts by professionals to reclassify it as a science, but I, though a professional, make no such claim. To me, navigation is a practical craft, not even an art. Science (the very word comes from *scientia*) is a 'thinking thing' but navigation is doing, achieving, arriving. During the war, emblazoned above the map at Operations HQ, our aim was defined: 'The safe and timely arrival of the convoy'. That is what navigation is concerned with. That, and nothing else, defines it. The safe and timely arrival of our ship.

But science matters. We use it. We now navigate almost entirely using science as a tool channelled through technology. It is still possible to use the old-fashioned, pre-science method (Back to Basics), but to do so these days reminds us of a three-legged race. It can be fun on occasions like the primary school sports day, perhaps because it needs certain rarely used skills; but for safe and timely arrival, Basics are neither good enough nor convenient.

Since we first wrote, the coming of the satellite-based Global Positioning System (GPS) has revolutionised navigation. It has taken out much of the old niceties of judgement as well as many of the chores. It has reduced doubt, the old bugbear of the navigator. Even the tyro can know instantly where he is with a degree of accuracy that was unbelievable not so long ago, and he can know it with complete confidence. It has changed the entire philosophy of the way we navigate, and oddly enough we have gone back to the philosophy that helped the primitive navigator. We now use dynamic navigation instead of static. This makes it much easier for the novice, since nobody need now be worried about his lack of advanced knowledge and technique.

Some basic knowledge is, however, still desirable. For a start it is necessary to read the GPS users' guides. Electronic instruction booklets have come a long way since the days when they seemed to be written by quasi-literate Japanese Sumo wrestlers choosing English words at random. However, they still suffer from a major defect: they are all written by people who already know how to use the device, just as signposts are erected at road junctions by people who already know the route. Signposts should be positioned by drivers who have never been that way before, and user handbooks should be written by someone who *had* to learn how to use the machine the hard way, from scratch.

Laurel was astonished to find how difficult it was even to switch on the little Garmin, for instance, since the handbook doesn't explain sufficiently clearly that it requires two fingers on two different buttons simultaneously. She could be heard muttering mutinously that she could think of another two-fingered gesture, and to whom she should aim it.

To have a chance of understanding the GPS handbook you have to know what the words and the acronyms mean. The navigation world is littered profusely with groups of letters that are ambiguous except to the experts (and even to some of them). It is also littered with words that do not mean what the layman knows them to mean through his general education. Unfortunately there is no known dictionary of navigational terms and acronyms, nor could there be, for the damned things change with each edition of the *RIN Journal*. Do not despair. It's all a bit like using a computer: a little common sense goes a long way.

There is more awareness nowadays of your ship's latitude and longitude, which is how the GPS receiver tells you your position. One should still teach oneself familiarity with the shape of the earth and facility with the measurements upon it; that is to say, the way latitude and longitude are drawn upon the earth's surface, the relationship of latitude to longitude, and which is which.

One should be aware that, because the earth is not an exact sphere, a degree of latitude (and thus also a nautical mile) varies in length by a small amount as latitude increases, and at the same time a degree of longitude varies rather more with changes in latitude. One should be aware of great circles, of the projections used for drawing charts, and the symbols used by the chart-makers.

Tides are important to navigators, and so are currents. (Do not confuse the two. The expression 'tidal current' is a nonsense: tidal streams and currents might feel the same but are quite different phenomena.) GPS cannot help you to judge tidal streams (except by observation), nor can it tell you whether there is sufficient water under your keel. GPS knows nothing about the sea; on that subject you know far more than it does. Just as a clock will tell you the time, it's still up to you to get to the station to catch your train. Your GPS will help to navigate for seamen, landsmen and airmen equally (indeed ours often tells us that *Hosanna* is flying at an altitude of 36 metres) and, if you let it, it will happily tell you exactly which rock you have just hit. If your charts are outdated and drawn to an old datum so that they are not GPS compatible, you may experience, as we did in the Ukraine, the odd sensation of finding that your boat is apparently in Ismaila railway station a mile to the north, instead of safely afloat in the northern arm of the wide Danube delta as our senses told us we were.

What has changed about the technique of navigation is that we used to be obsessed with knowing where we were as precisely as possible, and then we projected ourselves towards the destination, carefully checking our position at intervals on the way to see if we were still going safely. A recent seminar at the Royal Institute of Navigation had all the wiseacres busy getting trendy about the GPS having come to stay, but all except the man from the world of fast motor boats (who I believe was once an airman) were still discussing the problem in terms of 'where am I, and how do I get to where I want to go?' They are right that navigation is changing, but they hadn't realised how. Two breaths after you have noted your position, 'where am I now' is already past history.

To use GPS effectively we do the reverse: we choose our destination and let the machine tell us how to get there by reading off the course to steer. Except in the case of Man Overboard, it doesn't much matter where you are at this moment. We need to check with the chart to make sure the course to steer is safe because, if not supervised, the GPS will cheerfully carry you over a projecting reef, or even into the railway station if that were possible. So you check *back* from the destination (which can be an interim waypoint) along the reciprocal of the course to steer and make sure that the proposed track is clear of all danger. Then all that is required in order to get to the waypoint safely is to stay on that track. The machine itself will tell you if you are on track and you can adjust the course steered to keep it so. It will even keep you on track automatically by interfacing with an autopilot so as to allow you to rest, and give you an alarm call just before you arrive at your destination. It will automatically solve those troublesome triangles of velocity caused by tidal streams and it will compensate for leeway. This way you are more concerned with distance to go, than with distance made good. Easy peasy then! But what if something goes wrong?

Never forget that the most trying part of seamanship is coping with the nautically unexpected:

- GPS will not prevent you being run down by a supertanker, but in the sophisticated world you can also interface with your radar and get a warning about that too.
- Do not choose waypoints that are physical objects, such as buoys. You will end up hitting them if you are not careful.
- In bad visibility, beware of using waypoints from a book of standard waypoints. Other people may be doing exactly the same thing and you'll all end up ramming each other.

The Yachtmaster syllabus and its examiners presuppose that GPS fails about twice in every watch. Of course as instructor/examiners charging fees for both aspects of what they do, they have every inducement to make you believe that it does just that. Then they can teach you all about Old Navigation, which is what they all really like doing anyway, just as I do, not only because that is what we all had to learn when we were young, but also because it can be made so complicated that the fees can be higher. (It does seem that teachers of navigation, and I have been one myself, enjoy making the subject over-complicated.) Am I being unduly cynical? Perhaps, but not much.

We ourselves do a lot of seatime and in the last 15 years of heavy use have never known GPS fail. Uncle Sam, who has the on/off switch under his control, did turn it off without warning once during the Gulf War, but not for long. Being a military provision, he was entitled to do that, just as he was entitled to downgrade the signal for civilian use. But with the elapse of time it has changed from being a military tool

*Bill keeps his hand in with the 'old system' and takes a sun sight off Bermuda.
Although we are happy to use GPS, it is reassuring to know that if the electronics
ever fail us, we will still know where we are.*

available out of charity, to become a public utility of almost vital importance world-wide. Downgrading has finished; the system is wonderfully accurate; and there are more than enough satellites to give a thoroughly reliable service. It is far more reliable than any lighthouse, indeed than any other piece of navigational equipment.

And yet, it would be imprudent to go to sea with insufficient knowledge of how to cope with some navigational disasters, however unlikely. You'd feel a right Charlie in mid-ocean calling up a passing ship (How? With no electricity?) and asking, 'Which way is Barbados?'

Well, we know people have done just that, but it doesn't look very good in your logbook, does it? Cuts down the barstool boasting a bit. We still feel that Mary

Blewitt's classic book on navigation (see Appendix B) is worth study to know something of the basics. It has the merit of being succinct, unlike some of its more recent rivals.

I, Bill, qualified in navigation in the old system. Not the old system that is nowadays called the old system, but the system before that when one heaved an armed lead (a weight with tallow pressed into its bottom so that you could bring a portion of the sea bottom to the surface and examine, and even taste it), and talked in terms of compass points instead of degrees. A time when charts were handed down from father to son, and grandson. When I remember those days I am rather glad to have GPS and be shot of the old system, let alone the even older system. There is too much sentimentality about the sea in general. The good old days were not always so good.

Now, what about the ship's gear? Doesn't electricity frequently fail on board a small yacht?

The answer nowadays is 'not often', or at least 'not altogether'. In our early days of cruising back in the 1940s and 1950s, we sailed with neither electricity nor engine. Both were justifiably considered unreliable, and in those simple days unnecessary. We placed oil navigation lights at night, used oil lamps in the cabin, and cooked on a Primus stove. Here, too, there has been a revolution. Those writers of sailing books who draw slavishly on previous classic tomes, will go on repeating the hackneyed advice that electrics are unreliable at sea in small boats. We have been living aboard for 25 years now, have sailed many thousand miles, and only once, after being struck by lightning and rolled over in a hurricane (see *Heavy Weather Sailing* by Peter Bruce), were we without electricity because the batteries turned on their sides, and then only for about 12 hours before I improvised a battery and got a generator going again. Getting struck by lightning and/or being rolled over is rare, rare, rare. Most small-boat GPS sets have a facility for dry battery operation as a back-up. (Keep a few spare batteries in a watertight container and renew them from time to time.)

And if your autopilot, radar, GPS or whatever does go wrong, try the simplest remedy first:

* Is everything still properly plugged in? • Has it got power?
* Could it be a fuse?

Sometimes the failure is a purely mechanical one. We had an echo sounder that traced onto paper, as the old barograph used to. (We had one of those too.) When it stopped, we imagined dire inoperable tangles in its electronic interior, but Laurel noticed that the stylus had got bent. When straightened, it continued on its merry way. (How had it got bent? Bill wanted to know, but has never had an answer.)

Laurel suggested that here I should append a list of all the things that could go wrong. I thought about it, but realised that even if the list contained a million items, the next thing to go wrong in any boat would not be on it. The gremlins have an infinite capacity for causing unexpected mischief. Indeed, that is some of the charm of sailing: coping with surprises. Keeps you firmly in youthful middle age.

CHARTS

Paper charts are still necessary in normal navigation. Not long ago, I boarded an 8,000-ton, Cyprus-registered, refrigerated cargo ship bound for New York, 5,000 odd miles away. The Master had on board only four charts. One was for the area round Nantucket Light Vessel where he expected to pick up a pilot to enter harbour and he presumed the pilot would know the way. Another was of the Straits of Gibraltar. Between those two, he would navigate across the Atlantic by traverse table (trigonometric navigation tables, now rather old hat, before the old, old system), knowing there were no intervening dangers. The shipowners expected the Captain to buy his own charts: Scrooge isn't even in the running for the meanness of shipowners, a fact that is relevant to the poor standard of big ship watchkeeping nowadays. (Don't always blame the watchkeeper: the poor guy is doing the work once done by three or more men and he is often overworked while on watch.)

You wouldn't navigate on insufficient or inadequate charts. Well, would you?

The problem is that charts are now very expensive, largely due to the cost of metrication, of surveying the ocean to increased depths for the benefit of the oil industry, and the virtual disappearance of the Royal Navy as chart users.

Civilians used to get Admiralty charts at bargain, give-away prices. No longer! A complete outfit of charts for a world cruise nowadays might well cost £6000, with the associated pilot books on top of that. An outfit for cruising the Med in a yacht would cost over £1500. Add 15% on to that for pilot books. We have mentioned earlier the weight and volume of all that paper, a big factor if cruising in a small yacht.

One is supposed to keep charts and books (NAVPUBS) corrected up to date. I tried doing this (while typing, the computer first coughed up 'tired' instead of 'tried': it understands! Both words are true). Two factors told against my best intentions. One of these was the difficulty of getting weekly Notices to Mariners in out-of-the-way places. The other was the not unreasonable desire to enjoy some quality sailing time. It is worth recalling that as a Royal Naval Navigating Officer with a chart folio the size of *Hosanna*'s (470 charts), I had the full-time assistance of a specially trained rating (a Navigating Officer's Yeoman) and often the part-time help of a Midshipman too. We estimate that correcting 470 charts requires over 250 expert man/hours per annum.

We have solved the problem to our own satisfaction by using Admiralty Sailing Directions, or pilot books as they are popularly called. Once dismissed as useless for small craft, they are much better now than they used to be (not all things change for the worse) and there are periodic supplements to warn of major changes. These enable one to be aware of possible chart corrections that one has missed. I never use a chart without consulting the latest supplement. Now, in early 2001, I have just heard that Notices to Mariners are available on-line. In April 2001 the service is being improved to search for data more quickly. This is marvellous, and we have all been waiting for it (see Appendix C).

One should now be able to flag all the notices that refer to charts you possess and save them in a file. Delete the rest. Every time you want to use a chart, call up the relevant notices and see if they affect what you wish to do. I think there is now no longer any need to correct physically all one's charts.

However, if you want to keep your nice new chart folio conscientiously corrected (and I am sure there will be lots of old navigators ordering you to go on doing just that), then you will need to keep careful record of what you do and what is still to be done. Each correction gives you the number of the previous correction, so that it is possible to check back that you have done the lot. And each correction that you do should be noted in the left-hand foot-margin of the chart. The problems arise when there is a new edition of a chart and corrections to the old are no longer published. You may well be finding the old chart quite satisfactory for yachting purposes and see no reason to buy the new edition.

This leads to the habit of using out-of-date charts, and the fact that the vast majority (probably nearly 100%) of yachtsmen cruising offshore uses old, second-hand, and probably officially cancelled charts. One can get the latter from generous Merchant and Royal Naval Officers (they would otherwise be thrown away). Many yachts use second-hand charts, often third-hand or even more well thumbed than that. We did originally get all ours new (some donated by a grateful sovereign before I retired), but by now some of these are verging on the antique. There is an active market in second-hand charts. And for the really impecunious, there is the photocopier.

All this is officially *very bad practice*, and in the case of photocopying British charts, it is illegal for copyright reasons. We will not digress onto the evils of the laws governing Crown Copyright as exploited by the Hydrographer of the Navy. Such laws once lost us 13 colonies. It is an old hobby-horse of mine and I should not be encouraged. The alternative is:

• *Electronic charting* •

Computers and laptops

This is worth considering now that hardware can be bought second-hand quite cheaply if you are prepared to settle for last year's model. 'Computer fairs' abound selling re-vamped trade-ins from major companies.

It is possible to get an outfit of charts digitised onto a CD and view these on a colour laptop or (much better) a PC. The charts are synthesised and digitised (ugh) from British Admiralty or US Government charts in such a way that the program can change scale when required and show less or more data and symbols with change of scale. One can thus outline a passage plan on screen at small scale, move to a medium scale to select waypoints simply by clicking on them (which also transfers them to the GPS receiver), and then going to large scale to check for detail on the track which is drawn in for you.

The computer-generated system will show your present position on the screen as (typically) a moving red cross, and you can check its progress continually, or relax and let it tell you if a pre-set alarm sounds as you approach either a danger or your destination. In bigger ships, there is a programmed Collision Avoidance

Although the prime use of radar is for collision avoidance, it is also a very useful navigation aid.

System, which works out the best avoiding action to take. Always providing the radar detects the other ship in the first place.

These systems have the advantage that the difference in chart datum and the actual geography, which can be as much as one and a half miles on certain old charts, can be ironed out by reconciling radar and GPS. Such differences can make old charts a bit of a menace with GPS unless you use an additional check such as radar or a visual fix.

Two electronic charting systems that I have experimented with are the Tsunamis system and the Dutch Chartworx system. These have many common features and differ only in detail. One buys the program and also buys a folio of electronic charts, which comes on a CD. It is possible to get corrections for the charts you have bought by downloading from the internet, when all your charts will be instantly updated for you (at a cost). This is to me the main advantage of the service, though the corrections are not cheap (typically between 10% and 25% of the original cost of the charts).

The disadvantages are the fact that no matter which scale you choose, the display is limited to a computer screen in size and there is much compression and overload in data, despite some ingenious layering facilities. Also a laptop screen, even with the best TFT display, (you should not consider anything less for this purpose), is hard to read in bright daylight. The program tells you more than you need to know, though you do have the facility to filter some information out. It would take much practice to become familiar with all that the programs can do, much of which would be of little value to the typical yachtsman. The cost saving *vis-à-vis* conventional charts is not that marvellous, largely owing to the excessive royalties demanded by the Hydrographer, a factor which is badly holding up development of electronic charting for small craft. (Hobby-horse again, sorry.)

An additional disadvantage and extra cost is due to the rapid obsolescence of computer hardware. We sailed on one long cruise with a computer, MS/DOS and $5^{1}/_{4}$-inch floppies. By the time we returned, one could buy nothing new that was compatible with this: by that time it was Windows 3.11 and $3^{1}/_{2}$-inch floppies. After another cruise, throw that lot away: things now come only on CD for Windows 98 or later. Already the geeks and nerds are moving on again, holding us to ransom. As a computer on board is there to do other things besides navigation, this is a factor to be reckoned with.

However, the CD system, once one is a registered customer, allows one to download charts via e-mail. This could be a marvellous boon in out-of-the-way places because chart agents are few and far between away from the glitzy fashionable yachting centres.

Electronic chart plotter

The use of the dedicated chart plotter into which you can load 'cards', each having a modest number of charts on it, solves the rapid obsolescence problem for it has only this one use. Provided the cards continue to be available in the long term, this may be the most economical system for the yachtie, though a round-the-world set of cards might be uneconomic compared with the CD system. On the other hand, the typical plotter screen size is so small that one gets the impression of navigating on postage stamps. (Regard that as the moaning of a paper chart man, who likes to spread out a few square yards of the stuff, lovingly branded with cocoa rings, biscuit crumbs, paw prints, and even the odd smear of blood. He then stands back and admires it as some might do a painting in a picture gallery.)

Generally, yachties do not buy large-scale harbour plans in chart form, since they get this information in specialist yachtsmen's guides that naturally concentrate on the needs of small craft both in terms of navigation, suitable harbours, and recreation ashore. I get the impression that the chosen charts in folios more appropriately meet big-ship requirements. Presumably the directors of these companies are ex-Merchant Navy people who are now too busy to do much active yacht cruising. Poor chaps. These electronic chart companies (and I do not differentiate) should investigate more closely just what spread of charts a yachtsman needs.

If you decide to go for electronic charting (and beware: officially, it is only to be used as a back-up to paper charts, but that is frankly a Luddite official caution and will change), then you will have to study the different systems on offer, and make your own cost/benefit analysis. This is a field that changes almost daily. I cannot predict what will be best by the time I've written this paragraph, let alone by the time the book is published.

Nevertheless, *electronic charting is the future*, and for anyone starting now from scratch, it would repay some perseverance, both on the part of the provider and the user. It is easier to grow up with a new system as it develops rather than have to change to it when one has become entrenched in one's ways.

• *Back up* •

What happens if your computer crashes at sea? This is far more likely than an electrical failure and it has to be reckoned with. If you have to have a back-up laptop to back up the first, you are starting to lose the cost-saving advantages over paper charts.

In our view one will still need the back-up, at least, of some smaller scale paper charts sufficient to approach a coast in the event of problems involving milliamps. One would also need yachtsmen's guides to the harbours. The cost advantage of electronic charting recedes still further, as guides are expensive. It is time Imray and Adlard Coles started marketing electronic versions of their yachtsmen's guides. It shouldn't be that difficult.

Yachtsmen's guides are now available for just about everywhere and are generally to a high standard of reliability. Of particular merit are the publications of the RCC Pilotage Foundation, usually in co-operation with one of the well-known publishers. What does differentiate one guide from another is not so much the detail as the coverage. An example of two guides by the same author will illustrate without (I hope) causing offence by comparison between authors. Rod Heikell's guide to the Aegean Sea is the definitive work for that sea. One has to pick nits to find fault with it (other than its high cost). By contrast, the same author's guide to the Indian Ocean is less good, not because the entries themselves are poor, but because the coverage is too thin to merit the claim implicit in the title. I spent some time examining this guide to check on the ports and anchorages I once surveyed and cruised, but found virtually none of them in it. Two things though: it is the only Indian Ocean guide we are aware of, and there is no doubt that future editions will improve the coverage.

ASTRO NAVIGATION AS A BACK-UP

Should one, in the new millennium, learn astro-navigation before cruising the ocean? I stick my neck out and say: 'Desirable but not essential.' We are both aware of the sextants carried by yachts that never see the light of day from one year's end to the next and exist on board like ballast in an overloaded boat. Also, astro-navigation in a small boat has practical difficulties and only becomes reliable and accurate enough if it is practised assiduously as a pianist practises the piano. As a generalisation, if visibility is good and you cannot see land, you have no need to worry. If visibility is good and you can see land, then you don't have much need for astro-navigation anyway. If visibility were poor, you probably wouldn't be able to use your sextant and you might be worried. (It is said that there are only two sorts of navigators: those who sh*t if they can't see land, and those who sh*t if they can.)

• *The compass* •

Continuous use of GPS tends to make one careless, and one of the things one gets careless about is compass deviation. If you do not have back-up navigation methods there is one little area of expertise that we would commend to the ocean sailor, and that is to acquire some knowledge of magnetism, both the earth's magnetism and ship's magnetism which can be permanent, temporary, or (much more awkwardly) sub-permanent. One should understand how they interrelate as one moves about the globe. Navigation by DED-reckoning requires directional accuracy. Good compass adjusters are getting hard to find and it is not only steel boat skippers who need to watch this. We have seen some considerable misconceptions paraded from time to time in yachting magazines – for example, an eminent yachtmaster examiner stating that because a wrench had been left close to a compass for even a little while, it would permanently affect the deviation. It wouldn't. If it is removed, the deviation returns quickly to its former state.

Mary Blewitt's book (see Appendix) has a good chapter on compass adjustment that says it all – far better than we could do. The compass should be checked frequently. A warship checks the compass every watch, and though that is hardly necessary for a small yacht, to make a regular daily duty of it is no bad thing. Remember that the influence of the earth's magnetic field that you feel will change as you voyage north/south and the change can be significant. Enough to make it necessary to relocate your compensating magnets. Obvious as it seems, one of the most important precautions is to make sure that nothing that might change the magnetic field that the compass works in is fitted, placed or left close enough to the compass to affect the deviation. So obvious that it is often overlooked. Don't put steel tools near the compass, check your seaman's knife, your sun-glasses, false teeth, hip-replacements, surgical pins, bottle openers, enamel mugs and tins of anchovies at cocktail time; many of these are magnetic. Check that your personal stereo has no effect; some do, it seems. There is another thing to remember: with time and a salt atmosphere, your correcting magnets will corrode. Even those encased in copper will do so, and when they have corroded their effect will have virtually disappeared. If on a long voyage, take some spares and keep them warm and dry (and well away from the compass). Copper bracelets containing magnets are the current fad for arthritis sufferers. These must not be worn near a compass.

Cost of electronic charts

An aspect of cost is the way electronic charts are packaged for sale. They come in standard folios, which cover areas that seem to bear little relationship to the needs of the cruising yachtsman. For example, the complete Med folio in the Tsunamis system, all or nothing, costs £2754. This is rather more than a carefully selected folio of equivalent Admiralty paper charts, but the typical yachtie does not need such a complete folio. For example, the Hydrographer has over 4000 charts in his world-wide catalogue, but a circumnavigation in a yacht can be safely accomplished with less than 500.

I wanted next to give a rough comparison between Chartworx and Tsunamis, and I did much work trying to find a basis for a cost comparison for a typical yachtie folio. The only conclusion I came to is that both companies need to get their marketing acts in order. There is a mass of information available on CD and in leaflets and booklets, but one has not got the time to plough through this much chaff to find the relevant information for comparison purposes.

What I will try to give is some idea of those items which seem to me to be comparable. Be cautious about them as it is not always clear that one is comparing like with like, but it will provide some approximate basis for comparison. Chartworx do not help by pricing some things in guilders or euros, and others in dollars. Tsunamis do not help by failing to identify the sources of their charts.

CHARTWORX

- The program (*TheMap 10*, elementary and basic) 100 Nguilders (about £30, or $45).
- Individual charts vary between $14.95 and $24.95 which is far from helpful. We presume the more expensive ones are the UKHO charts.
- Folio of the whole Mediterranean: Ng3120 (say £900 or $1320).
- Update price: 50% of original price (could be cheaper by two-year contract) (based on October 2000 prices).

TSUNAMIS

- The program (*Coastal*, the most basic) £100, Tides and currents, £100 extra.
- Individual charts: US charts £8.00 ($12); UKHO charts £18.00 ($26).
- Folio of the whole Mediterranean: £2754 or $4000.
- Update price: 10% of original price (based on October 2000 prices).

PRICES OF PAPER CHARTS (AUGUST 2001)

- US charts (no standard price): $9 to $16; UKHO charts £15.65.
- Both countries offer a world-wide coverage.
- British charts are on far better paper, and fold to a standard size, while US charts are apparently printed on toilet paper and fold all over the place.
- On the whole, it is easier to obtain British charts, except within the USA.
- Do not forget the publishers of yachtsmen's charts. These charts are often good and cheap.
- In out-of-the-way places check the chart you buy locally. It might not be up to date.
- US Government charts are available in England to order from Kelvin Hughes (see Appendix).
- Sometimes charts produced by the local country are better and cheaper, as in Turkey. Check this out locally.

(*Stop Press*: The Hydrographer has recently announced a 40% price reduction for his ARCS 'Skipper' raster scan charts, with an updating service by CD. A folio of

10 costs £70, but you would need to have a program to run them. One such is PC Maritime's Navmaster, but I have no experience of it.)

The above data is given in good faith. Every figure comes from company literature, so if there are errors (and I am sure the companies will say there are, and for which I apologise) I think they will be errors due to comparing slightly different products, so be sure to check up before you deal. I am grateful to Kelvin Hughes for their help on this subject (address in Appendix).

QUALIFICATIONS

A problem for the long-cruise navigator is that many of the techniques he will, or ought to, use are not those dealt with in most courses in Britain or the USA. In Britain the chief aim of most courses is to fit the student for the Yachtmaster's Certificate in one of its forms. These naturally have a home-waters emphasis, and this applies equally to the Offshore and Ocean syllabi.

In my opinion, the navigational content of the RYA Yachtmaster qualification is about as relevant to today's navigation as that of Vasco da Gama, and the rate of change in the use of science in the craft of navigation is frightening, even to professionals. With serious consideration being given to unmanned 100,000 tonne bulk carriers (not in my lifetime, I hope), and proposals to change the collision regulations to suit computer-navigated ships, yachtsmen will have to do something to keep abreast of developments. Even if they do not use them, the other guy may be doing so.

Further inadequacies of the RYA syllabi concern the problems associated with waters that are inadequately surveyed, ill-provided with marks and lights, with meagre tidal data, and where the expected, conventional and prudent arrangements for keeping up to date are not available. I regret to say that although the Hydrographer of the Navy is beginning to consider the requirements of his yachting customers (who in some parts of the globe constitute the majority of users), this consideration applies so far only to home waters. He is still publishing new charts of overseas areas that are, from a small craft point of view, very much worse than the old ones. For example, BA1703 (Majorca and Minorca) is a poor job compared with 1317 which it replaced, and not only because the scale was reduced from 1:193,000 to 1:300,000. The whole field of navigational data is an ergonomic nightmare: it was never planned, it just grew piecemeal, and is badly in need of a complete review. The trouble is that the professionals are so familiar with the present chaos that they will resist change.

PRECAUTIONS

There is an underlying precept of navigation and that is prudence. Don't get taken by surprise and avoid doing anything that will cause you to be surprised. Now let us have a look at one or two dangerous points that we know affect yachtsmen.

There is an old saying, 'Outward bound, don't run aground'. This means that if you are going to be at sea on a 20-day passage it is not worth cutting across a dangerous sandbank when leaving harbour, just to save ten minutes. But people do it! A yacht inside us at Ramsgate got us up at 0400 in order to catch the tide and sail for the Caribbean. When we followed him four hours later we found him stuck on a sandbank just off the pierhead, and, though tempted, we did not have the heart to leave him there.

Even in sight of land the sextant can be a lot of use if you are familiar and easy in its use. I use mine for vertical danger angles or for obtaining the ranges of mountains or lighthouses using Lecky's Tables. It is a very fast method and much less trouble than switching on radar, but the tables are now out of print.

In bad weather, when maybe you or the crew are feeling unwell, take especial care. One French destroyer I served in had notices plastered round the ship saying '*Valeur et Discipline*'. Whether such notices achieve anything depends, I suppose, on those to whom they are addressed, but if you are the sort that responds to exhortation then stick them up.

If you do lose your electronics and are not sure of your position, then, however miserable and seasick you may feel, *do not put the ship on a course that could be dangerous*, as you would be that much less able to cope with an emergency should one arise. Even if it means standing off in discomfort, that is better than the Shipwrecked Mariners' Hostel, supposing one exists. Do not cry for help because you are miserable: go out to sea where you will be safe as long as the ship remains seaworthy.

IF YOU GET LOST

This is particularly relevant to making a landfall, and is a branch of navigation that is insufficiently treated in textbooks, perhaps because professionals either do not get lost so do not know how to cope or, more likely, do not wish their fellows to know that they have been lost. There have been several occasions when I have not known where I was, so here goes.

First, remember that if any navigator without GPS happens to be exactly where he thinks he is, it is purely accidental. This is true. Old navigation is not an exact science, it is a craft in which judgement plays a very important part. All systems and aids contain the possibility of errors and all human beings make them. What makes someone a professional is being aware of the possible or likely errors in the method he uses and subconsciously being completely aware of the degree of reliability of his position. In theory, this is complex mathematics, but there are plenty of practical wrinkles. It is impossible to give complete, generalised counsel for all cases of being lost – there are too many variables. Long before getting into this state, keep charts and pilot books up to date; that can make it a lot easier to get out of it.

If you are clearly well offshore, you do not have an urgent problem. You have a problem, it is true, but it is too early to start worrying. Provided weather conditions are reasonable and the shore is not a lee to a very strong wind, approach it. The problem may even solve itself. We will not discuss night-time. My advice with a doubtful position close to land by night or in bad visibility is to b***** off out to sea and wait till conditions improve. You will recall that in the great storm of October 2000, the cross-Channel ferries did not try to berth in Dover, but remained outside the harbour (admittedly in the partial shelter of Deal Bay) until the weather improved. However costly and uncomfortable, that was prudence.

If, having raised the shore, you cannot identify any feature or find your chosen haven, then you still have a problem. If it is a question of visibility, wait and stand off. But if the weather is fair, and if the coast is not a dead lee with known or suspected offlying unmarked dangers, then approach it cautiously at an angle. I, personally, would go downwind in such a situation, but know of competent friends who would do the opposite. It may be something to do with whether you describe a bottle as half full or half empty: I always believe things will improve. Reasons for approaching downwind at an angle to the coast are:

- If one does come across a danger one has more scope for hauling clear very quickly. To do so going upwind puts limits on one's manoeuvrability without tacking, which is not always the work of a minute when short-handed.
- One changes one's position faster. If landmarks are not distinguishable in one place, then get somewhere else as soon as reasonably possible.
- The motion will be less, making observation and chartwork easier.

• *Where are you NOT?* •

In this process there is the advisability of changing one's outlook. You do not know where you are, but there are plenty of places where you know you are *not*. Start eliminating: huge areas go at once. The length of time since your last known position should give you a radius of possibility, and even if you had lost your compass, for example, I am sure you would have been able to have found an approximate direction. It is probable that the unknown area that you are in is quite small.

Inspect all the relevant large-scale charts and the pilot books for any features. There may be reference to a chimney or radio mast. Unless you are very unlucky and they have just been demolished, you can cross off those bits of coast within their visibility distance. And so on. Things will narrow down. Is part of the coast hilly, or swampy with offlying banks? Are there soundings? Are there ships in sight? Are they on courses that might converge at a point? If so, they are almost certainly going to or from a port; that is a position line of sorts, and I once found Colombo that way, though this is the first time I have ever confessed it.

Don't forget the simple things. Is there a river estuary? This often brings discoloured water as well as a lot of floating rubbish. (If approaching Italy you will see many floating plastic bags, and you can recover a few to see the address of the shops printed on them; known in the trade as 'bag of buns navigation'.)

This general problem does not always follow ocean crossings. We once headed for Majorca after being hove-to for a time. Approaching at right angles to a coast with many similar features is almost as bad as approaching a coast without any at all. This was a virtual cliff of high-rise buildings. After studying the chart, I called up to Laurel, who was on watch, 'I think we're either off Cape X or Cape Y', 'It's Cape X,' she said, looking through binoculars. 'How do you know. . . ?' 'That building with the red balconies has a sign that says the Cape X Hotel.'

We once drifted in the little yacht *Phoenix* which had no engine and contained our six-month-old daughter for two full days in the Malta Channel, completely blanketed by thick fog. At the end of this I had only a vague idea where I was, plus or minus 50 miles, but as the fog began to clear one evening I saw over the horizon the signs of fireworks. Someone had given me a Roman Catholic calendar that had the saints' days on it. It took only a moment to identify which parish church was busy beating the hell out of the devil for its patronal festival, and then I had quite a reasonable position line.

Once at night well off a coast I saw what appeared to be the loom of a lighthouse where none should be. (The loom of a light is the beam in the sky when the light itself is out of sight below the horizon.) It was oddly irregular. In fact, it was a busy main road with a sharp rising bend and the beams were the headlights of cars going round it. Jokes about navigating by road maps are out of place: not all valuable information is published by the Hydrographer. For another example: nautical charts do not show the flight paths of aircraft. With a low fog it is very useful to be able to pinpoint where aircraft turn for a final approach; this is helpful off the mouths of the Tiber, near Fiumicino Airport, among many other places.

Ferry timetables can be of value. Apart from being a rare potential fixing aid, the ABC shipping guide helps one to avoid these tracks, for ferries are notorious for being inconsiderately driven.

INLAND WATERS

Those readers not contemplating oceans, but who are more interested in the world's inland waters, should be on their guard, for the whole system of licensing both ships and captains is in process of change. Why should they be exempt, everything else is changing?

We have a situation where the Collision Regulations (Colregs), which have been agreed by treaty, and are legally binding on all states, and which apply as a basis in all waters navigable by sea-going vessels (see Reg 1(b)), have been disturbed by a United Nations Congress which proposed alterations to be applicable to Europe only. These European regulations (SIGNI) have no international standing, not being subject to treaty status, but have nevertheless been implemented by certain countries, notably France. To confuse matters further, the French call these rules CEVNI, as they don't like anything written in any language but their own. Speaking to the acknowledged world expert on this subject at the International

Maritime University at Malmö in Sweden, I was told that the matter would have to be regularised, but that the European Commissioner for Transport was not exactly being very industrious about it. Nobody had told him anyway! Well, I did, but I do not hold out any great hopes of anything being done because nobody will take on the French. After all, the original Monsieur Chauvin was French.

In the circumstances, get whatever certificates you can. Make a collection of them, overload your boat with the nasty little pieces of paper. When you are asked to produce your qualification by a gendarme who does not know one end of a boat from the other, shower him with bureaucratic confetti. We feel that not only the RYA and the Maritime Coastguard Agency should issue certificates, but also each yacht club, the Dutch Barge Association (whose certificates for English members should sow complete confusion throughout Europe), and perhaps the RSPCA should certify British pets as competent ships' cats. (I am getting carried away again.)

Fishermans houses
Gowra Bay.

HYDROGRAPHERS AGAIN

Another word or two about the Hydrographer in charge of BA charts. I am critical
of the organisation, occasionally of the design or printing of charts, but the standard of surveying is generally excellent and has been so, given the instruments
available, for a long time. There are few serious errors on charts, and I am scepti-
cal when I hear someone say (and it happens quite frequently) that they ran
aground because the chart was wrong. Mostly they were not where they thought
they were. But things do change, and at an alarmingly increasing rate, while the
Hydrographer cannot keep survey ships up every little by-water. If you do come
across a change, or an error which you are sure is an error, then drop a line to the
Hydrographer. It is called an H note, and a blank form is found at the back of all
Supplements to Admiralty Pilot Books. This form should be used if you can, for it

is a reminder of the background details that H would like to know. You may be a novice, but if you are off the beaten track you may be the first to report something that may save a ship; you are keeping up the standard of charting and helping to keep down costs.

Remember that navigating is not a mystery any more. There are many techniques that will come with experience, but the cautious novice, exercising common sense and using intelligently the little knowledge he already has, will get by and gently learn more. It is an old axiom that there are old navigators and bold navigators, but no old and bold navigators. *Prudence* is the word.

SINGLE-HANDED SAILING

Being empassioned by the love of the freedom that one gets by going offshore in one's own boat, I ought to be an ardent advocate of singlehanding. I suppose that, sitting in an armchair, I am – or at least of the freedom to do it if you so wish.

Where my theory gives way is in the practice. As an amateur, I can ask, 'Why not?' As a professional, I know why not. I remember crossing the track of a singlehanded race during the night in a big ship and I was petrified that I might hit one of them. Small chance, perhaps, but by no means impossible, and one does get 'give-way' situations well offshore. Even if the singlehander were showing lights, how would I know whether he or I had right of way? Also, one can only rely on seeing a yacht at 3 miles. If what you see is a single white light, (an overtaking light) then it is some time before you know what you are coming up with, and remember that boats under windvane *can* alter course, and such alterations can be very confusing.

The obligation to keep a watch is clear. Rule 5 says: 'Every vessel shall at all times maintain a proper look-out by sight and hearing . . . .' The word is *shall*, not 'should', nor 'ought to', or 'it would be nice if'. And it is followed by *at all times*, which means what it says, not 'sometimes', nor 'when I can', or 'if I feel like it'.

Special or specious pleading about cat-napping just will not wash. Very careful evaluation by specialists in sleep patterns have demonstrated without any doubt that efficiency falls off to an unacceptable degree after about 36 hours unless one gets proper sleep. Most ocean-going singlehanders are risking the lives of others, and relying on others to help them when, inevitably, things go wrong. I admire the courage, endurance and sailing skills of those who, for example, brave alone the Southern Ocean, which I have sailed and know; the Vendée Globe competitors, for example. But the number of them that have retired after a collision or had to be rescued shows the folly of it all.

Perhaps there is scope for the singlehander who combines his love of solitude with common sense, if he limits the port-to-port length of his voyages. From experience I know that if one prepares oneself sensibly, then one can make a 36-hour passage without needing sleep. One cannot cross oceans like that, but one can get about, and be prudent.

13 • Communications

'What cheere mates, is all well?'

We did not have a special chapter on communications in the original edition because at that time the typical yachtie's only problem was how to organise mail drops, and could be dealt with in one paragraph. A secondary need was to understand telephone systems that had not progressed far since Mr Bell had first rung himself up. (Question: If you are the one who invents the telephone, who is there to call?). We still found places where the local telephone worked by turning a handle to call the exchange and the local shopkeeper timed one's call with a turnip watch. We fried or froze in glass boxes far from our boat, and wore our pockets through with kilos of loose change.

In many places marine VHF was not much used. We had been invited to dinner on board a German yacht and in the meantime a full gale blew up and we could not get ashore from *Fare Well* to get to the rendezvous. We had to wrap a message in a plastic bag, together with a spare steel nut to weight it, and throw it across to the other boat; basic communication equivalent to the cleft stick.

In the West Indies we found marine VHF used everywhere as a standard local telephone service; one could summon a taxi or reserve a table at the local restaurant by VHF. The coming of mobile phones has helped those islands with a poor terrestrial phone service. Unfortunately the islands have chosen the less-efficient American system, but the necessity of servicing so many tourists has led to the local mobile phones being easy to obtain. Try the local office of Cable and Wireless for a start.

Becoming a radio amateur is easy out there: during the hurricane season, the radio hams are a vital and inexpensive lifeline and local governments want as many people as possible to be qualified.

What a lot has changed within a mere 15 years! Nowadays communications is much discussed among yachties before they set out, though we have to say it does pale a little in importance as that rhapsodic do-nothing condition known as *dolce fa niente* sets in. We even discuss nowadays the prospect of people going on working for a living (!) from aboard their yacht while cruising. We have to say that to us this seems to negate the very essence of the live-aboard life, which is to be free of ties and independent of calendar and clock. Writing is not a proper job and doesn't count. That's right, isn't it?

Getting mail, as we have said, isn't easy in some places. The job of co-ordinating and forwarding your snail mail as you move on is complex and, if done well, takes a lot of trouble on someone's part. Sent too soon and *Poste Restante* sends it back, *restante* being a relative term. Sent too late and you have to wait until it arrives and you miss the monsoon or whatever. If you have a relative willing to undertake this chore, well and good; at least in return they get to hear from you from time to time.

There are those who will do this chore for a fee plus expenses. This is not unreasonable, especially as some such will also act as your agent for getting spares. One of these agencies works under the title of Ship to Shore, (e-mail: michelle@shiptoshore.co.uk). We are not familiar with it, but have heard no complaints from the Ocean Cruising Club members who have used it.

Nowadays, most people think in terms of radio or telephone, internet and e-mail. We disclaim being able to write from depths of experience, though we have used radio and telephone a fair bit, and e-mail too, though in the latter case we are only on the edge of knowledge. What we will try to do here is filter through some of the advice we have received on the subject and see if, partially sighted, we can give the totally blind a lead, well aware that by the time this goes into print it will be out of date.

RADIO FOR SHIP'S USE

In the marine VHF band, there are big changes afoot. GMDSS and Digital Selective Calling (DSC) have arrived, and from May 2001 the old-fashioned VHF sets will no longer be available. What we have to face is that the whole world of marine radio is in flux. In fact, most of it has already changed dramatically and it is only for small pleasure craft that a longer 'run-in' time has been allowed. For the moment, for small craft, the old and new system will run side by side *in some parts of the world*.

The problem is that though the IMO has ordered the change, it has left individual countries to implement it according to their perceived needs, provided the change is made before 2005. Some countries have jumped the gun. Others, with a large fleet of pleasure yachts, have allowed the maximum change-over time because yachtsmen have votes (though sometimes you feel the politicians are unaware of the fact).

The principle of the new system is that the radio equipment that must be carried by *big ships* (over 300 tonnes) will depend not on their size, but on where they navigate. Typically the equipment will be expensive and, for most ships, I feel it is way over the top.

One feature is that each transmitter will have a unique, built-in, callsign which will be held on a central data-base. (Rather like micro-chipping your cat.) Each transmitter must also be connected to the GPS, so that if it makes a distress call, the system will know by the callsign who it is, and by GPS where they are. The system is already in being and the false alarms are running at a ridiculous rate owing to the usual electronic introductory glitches. Nothing can go wrong, can go wrong, can go wrong - - - -.

GMDSS will affect yachtsmen by providing a search and rescue organisation which will be more effective and less expensive than heretofore. Even if, like us, you do not want the search and rescue people to bloodhound after you without your say-so, you may get involved whether you like it or not. ('Ve hev vays of getting you rescued!') It will also affect all VHF coastwise radio traffic, which most of us use, and so we must read all about it.

We do not carry HF transmitters, preferring to look after ourselves on the Arthur Ransome principle: 'If not duffers, won't drown. If duffers, better drowned'. Others may not feel so purist.

Yachts will have to have only a VHF version of this, which will also use DSC calling. Channel 70 will be the distress channel and chat on this channel is forbidden. Channel 16 will eventually cease to be used for distress, but for the moment most ships will continue to keep watch on it.

Clearly it will be advisable, if starting out in a fresh boat, to go straight to the new system, which is not cheap. You will need to obtain a new GMDSS certificate to allow you to use it. Yes, you have guessed; a whole new legislative ball-game is in play. Though the practical requirements to operate the VHF part of this system are very few, the syllabus itself goes on and on, enabling the sailing schools to run long courses on the subject so that they can charge unjustifiably fat fees before giving you that piece of paper. In passing, it is worth noting that when VHF first started way back in the 1940s – it was called TBS – Talk Between Ships – and there was no licence requirement. It was assumed that anyone competent to keep watch at sea should be able to cope, as we now do with mobile phones. Ho, ho, ho, that was too easy. The bureaucrats moved in. The licence fee just covers the costs of giving you the document.

You will need that piece of paper. Some official in some country somewhere is bound to have been trained in the awkward squad, and will ask you for it just because you've got up his nose.

If you want to mug up on GMDSS, there is a dense book called *Understanding GMDSS* by Tetley and Calcutt, published by Arnold/Hodder Headline, price about £30. This will tell you more than you need to know about the subject, so at that price it might be as well to borrow it from the library.

Lesser and more manageable details (but still rather too many for most of us) are available from an excellent Australian website and also from ICS electronics, who made the first small transceiver on the market that I have found (see Appendix C for websites).

Note that DSC will apply to marine HF as well as VHF.

Our freedoms are rapidly disappearing. We need a certificate now just to steer our little boats, which must pass CE regulations that put up their price.

We need a certificate to talk to each other at sea, and ask for assistance.

Soon we shall need a certificate to say that we are responsible enough as citizens to allow us to own a boat at all.

We'd never get one.

HAM RADIO

This is also something on which I have to take advice, for though I passed my licence exam years ago in expectation, I do not own an HF transceiver and have never used Ham radio.

The British Government has never liked the idea of allowing citizens to exploit a new invention, especially if it has military potential. Marconi's research was financed by the Royal Navy, and it was considered best for the nation if its relationship with the Royal Navy was one of abject adoration. Do not concern your pretty little heads with what My Lords of the Admiralty are up to. Wireless will do the masses no good. Radio waves soften the spine and rot your teeth. Leave it to the professionals.

So the rules for using that band of the radio spectrum which more enlightened countries set aside for the use of amateur radio enthusiasts (the nerds and geeks of their time) were made as difficult as possible by the British Government to limit the use of the radio by amateurs.

This attitude has persisted to this day. Though all form of morse transmission has ceased among professionals, it is still a significant part of becoming a radio amateur. Britain was virtually the last nation on earth, after even the Soviet Union, to permit Citizen's Band (CB) radio. The attitude persists in the exams for the use of VHF for yachtsmen, which are made unnecessarily complicated. The system is simpler than trying to use a mobile phone on the internet for which no exam is needed, and in any event, the exam and its licence has not succeeded in preventing abuse of the airwaves every fine weekend in the Solent.

So why bother becoming a radio Ham? As a last resort you could use it for distress calls. But the new GMDSS, which will be compulsory by 2005, will cope with all that far more efficiently.

Ham radio is for social use. It can be used for 'patching in' to a country's domestic telephone service, thus making an international call at the cost of a local call, but in Britain we are not allowed to do that (see above). US citizens are, and it hasn't caused rioting in the streets.

I once asked the RYA to suggest to the licensing authority that there should be a special simplified, limited qualification for cruising yachtsmen to allow them to use only the established 'maritime mobile nets' and only when outside territorial waters. They were not interested, even though it would have been a major service to cruising yachties.

The inevitable outcome is that some yachties broadcast while unlicensed. They are deemed radio pirates and are liable to prosecution if caught, but with a modicum of prudence and cunning there is little likelihood. Licensed amateurs are prohibited from communicating with the 'pirates', but in practice have a hard job checking them because many pirates 'borrow' real call signs from someone of the same name.

If you are interested in this activity, then it is much better to be licensed, but do try to get your licence while still living ashore. Most places in Britain have amateur radio clubs whose members are usually delighted to help, and there are sometimes courses at evening classes. More information on amateur radio can be obtained from the Radio Society of Great Britain, Lambda House, Cranbourne Road, Potters Bar, Herts. EN6 3JN. The Secretary of State for Trade and Industry also produces an excellent booklet on the subject, but I would try the other sources first.

Amateur radio is used for chatting to other Hams, relaying useful information that is not available in the public domain, and for keeping in touch generally. In each area Hams set up a radio net at a given time on a given frequency and chat among themselves. It is a sort of informal social club. These are known as Maritime Mobile Nets. The expression 'maritime mobile' has other uses too, in certain official areas, so beware.

We have got together a list of the nets that we have come across in the last couple of years. There does not seem to be any co-ordinating body for this activity (some say Thank God), so the list is not guaranteed to be either complete or totally up to date. These things change. But there should be enough here for you to find an entrée. All times are GMT.

Net	Frequency kc/s	Time
Baja California	7238	1600
California to Caribbean	14285	2300 Mon
Caribbean MM	7241	1100
Caribbean	7158	0000
Confusion !!	14305	1900 Mon-Fri
Maritime Emergency Net	14310	0400
	14303	1800
Waterway (USA)	7268	1245
	14290	2130
Transatlantic	21400	1300
UK MM	14303	0800 & 1800
Gulf Coast Hurricane	3935	0100
Pacific Indian Ocean	21407	0100
Pacific Seafarers	14313	0200
South African MM	14320	0630
Mediterranean MM	14300	0900
Canary Islands MM	7080	0900
Young Ladies Emergency Net	14332	1200
SE Asia Net	14320	1200
Caribbean Weather Net	3185	2230

Note that frequencies may change because of changes in propagating conditions in the ionosphere.

Carrier pigeons are practical only from ship to shore. They may lose track of where *you* are, but they could wing home to Dagmar Terrace.

E-MAIL

Our sources for in-depth comment about this are Hugh Marriott (RCC) at the time of writing, half-way round the world; and Ron Bollay of Santa Barbara, USA. Ron was living in a boat years before we were and brought up three boys on board. One of them is now chairman of a quoted Artificial Intelligence company.

My sources are not responsible for errors; they will be ours due to misinterpretation of what they have told us.

Hugh says there is little excuse for not being on e-mail, and we endorse that. It's not that difficult in essence, but there are several ways of doing it and which one you choose depends on what you want to get out of it and how much you have to spend. Yachting is like that.

How much time will you spend in harbour? Of course you do not yet know, but even the most mile-hungry reckon to be at sea on only one-third of the days in a year. If you will be making short passages of less than 500 miles, or four days, say, then you can rely on shore facilities for your e-mail. If you frequently undertake long passages, say 1000 miles or over, it will boil down to whether you will want to communicate while on passage.

E-mail services are now so good that one can actually run a business from on board the yacht, but beware: the costs of having on-call quality service will be high. One of the major problems of onboard e-mail is that it is difficult to achieve a fast baud rate (the speed at which data is transferred) and difficult to ensure thoroughly reliable radio contact cheaply.

The table opposite, devised by Hugh Marriott and originally printed in *Yachting Monthly* in September 2000, gives the options more clearly than any other that we have seen, and certainly better than anything we could devise. He has gone to great trouble to show a comparison of how much it might cost to send a message of a standard length. You cannot accurately forecast the cost of *hardware*; you can spend as much as you like, but it is perfectly possible to send and receive e-mail fast enough with a 486 black and white computer. These are available second-hand at give-away prices. For laptops, you pay a bit more, but again a used 486 with one of the cheaper HPA displays will only cost about £150. We print the table with permission.

To help you make a decision as to which option might suit you best, we ask some questions:

- What sort of e-mail will you be sending or receiving? Simple short text, long text, or graphics?
- How often do you wish to send/receive? Daily, weekly, or occasionally?
- Will you carry a computer on board?
- How much are you prepared to spend on hardware?
- Which is more important to you: economy or efficiency?
- Would complex or large antennae be suitable for your yacht?
- What sort of passages do you tend to make? Oceanic or short hop, or mixed?
- Do you intend to have an HF radio transceiver anyway?

To help you get more data, we give some websites in Appendix C under the heading 'Communications'.

Location	Means	Transmission	Own computer	Equipment required	World wide	Restrictions	Likely cost per printed page
Ashore	Cyber café	Telephone landline	No	None	Yes*	None	50p charged by time
Ashore	Marina phone	Telephone landline	Yes	Modem and telephone cable	Yes*	None	25p (charged by time
Ashore	PocketMail	Telephone landline	No	JVC HC-E100 PocketMail device	Yes*	Acoustic modem, doesn't work with digital phones. Short messages	Say £5, as all calls have to be made through the USA
Onboard	Mobile phone	Mobile phone	Yes	Modem for mobile phone, or email-enabled mobile phone	Yes*	None	£2.50
Onboard	Inmarsat Mini-M	Satellite	Yes	KVH Tracphone 25, Thrane & Thrane or similar	No	None	£7.50
Onboard	Inmarsat C	Satellite	Yes	Thrane&Thrane Trimble, plus modem	Yes	None	£37**
Onboard	Magellan GSC 100	Satellite	No	Magellan GSC 100 handheld satcom device/ GPS	Yes	2000 character max length, no attachments*** Small keyboard	£12 (charges are monthly for 10 short messages)
Onboard	PinOak	Marine HF radio	Yes	SSB and modem	Yes	Text only, no attachments, not always 24hr service	£3.75
Onboard	Globe wireless	Marine HF radio	Yes	SSB and modem	Yes	Text only, no attachments,	£14
Onboard	SailMail	Marine HF radio	Yes	SSB or ham radio and modem	No	Text only, no attachments; 10 mins a day; messages up to 5 Kb in length	£2.50
Onboard	SeaMail & CruiseMail	Marine HF radio	Yes	SSB or ham radio and modem	No	Text only, no attachments, messages up to 5 Kb in length	£2.50
Onboard	Ham e-mail	Ham radio	Yes	Ham radio and modem	Yes	Text only, no attachments; no business e-mails	Free

* But you have to get to the cyber café or telephone landline first or, if you're using a mobile phone, it has to be within sight of a mobile telephone shore antenna.
** The charge is one cent US per character which may not sound a lot, but is.
*** One A4 page off my printer contains 1000 words, or 5600 characters, or 5.6Kb. The Magellan can send 35% of this in one message.

14 • Social Life and Entertainment

. . then all the rest may do what they will til midnight'

Entertainment might seem an odd subject for those to whom sailing itself is an entertainment, but when sailing the vessel from one place to another is the main occupation, some forms of diversion are needed.

Reading is the most obvious. People used to books cannot easily manage without. There are no libraries available to the wanderer, so one has to have reference volumes to taste. Most yachts carry a paperback library comprised of those loved books which one keeps to read over and over again, and also those less loved books that are enjoyable once and are then swapped with other yachts for similar works.

Swapping paperbacks is a continuing process. It is sad that British and American paperback publishers now use a form of unsewn binding that falls apart. To bind reference books in this way is little short of fraud, and they are certainly unfit for the purpose for which they are sold. Many yachting centres have second-hand bookshops, where your nearly new paperbacks may be swapped for a fee.

Nowadays there are internet bookstores which will deliver world-wide. We note a few in Appendix C. The trouble is that you still have to wait for them to arrive by post, so you can take advantage only where you have a good postal 'drop'; *Poste Restante* is not usually reliable enough.

More and more reference books are becoming available on CD for use in computers. This is a very good way of carrying a reference library in a boat, for it saves enormously on space and weight. Much navigational data is available this way now. It costs a lot, though.

Apart from reading, games are played rather more by the typical yachtie than by his land-dwelling friends. A lot of chess is played. Some, including me, play computer chess, but it is not the same as playing with real people. One soon learns the weaknesses of the program, and finds after a time that one is not so much playing chess as outwitting a computer program. The computer goes on failing because it is a totally obedient moron and will never learn. Real people spring surprises.

Draughts (or checkers) and backgammon (or tavla) are played a lot. We are occasionally asked to play bridge, but as we do not play we are unaware of the extent to which it is enjoyed. I think not much, but then I never thought of it as a game for the sort of people who enjoy sailing.

A very popular game is Scrabble. There are certain difficulties playing it with American friends owing to their inability to spell. We solved the problem by using the *Shorter Oxford Dictionary* when aboard *Fare Well*, and *Webster's* when in their boat, but they had the worst of it because *Webster's* is kind enough to have both American and English spellings.

Bridge and Scrabble can be got for playing against a computer. I find computer Scrabble unsatisfactory owing to there being no choice of dictionary. It uses *Chambers*, which has some extraordinary words in it and omits ordinary ones.

The Royal Cruising Club has a song book, and at a suitable time aboard their boats the skipper may hand them round like hymn books so that the anchorage resounds with song. The accompanying instrument for sailors' songs has traditionally been portable and easily stowed: a pipe, concertina or harmonica. Later a fiddle came in. Then, of all things, the yacht piano, which solved the ballast problem I suppose. Now we have electronic keyboards (where will it end?) and guitars. The traditional Spanish guitar, of thin wood put together with non-waterproof glue, has minimal aptitude for life in a yacht, but innumerable boats have one, occupying a lot of valuable space.

We have the obligatory guitar. Someone should invent one, the inside of which can be used as a locker. Not content with the guitar, Laurel bought a dulcimer kit in the USA and amused herself building it while coming back over the Atlantic. I hope there are no double bass kits.

HOBBIES

Sailors of old did not have a lot of spare time, but they had various diversions including decorative knotting (macramé), knitting, scrimshaw and some wood-carving. These are all enjoyable pastimes today, though real whales' teeth are getting as scarce as hens'. These pastimes all have the virtue of taking up little space, and when well done the products can be sold.

The first problem is that more and more of the old seafaring hobbies are condemned as environmentally unfriendly (to whose environment is not clear), and are therefore banned by landlubber legislators. The next problem is that many well practised shoreside hobbies do not translate to the sea-going life. Collecting is difficult because of space and the importance of protecting vulnerable and valuable items from sea damage – postage stamps and books, for example. I have not heard of anyone actually having a model railway in a yacht, but I expect one exists somewhere. I sometimes wish I had an old-fashioned Meccano set.

Almost any art or craft, except possibly stained glass, fresco painting, mosaic and monumental masonry, can be practised, and cloth crafts are particularly appropriate. Laurel once did patchwork; she says it is an occupation which can be done in any corner at any time and is easy to put down or take up. Let your imagination run along those lines and do as you will. Take any special tools and spares with you, for they are sometimes unavailable or hard to trace.

We made our own music afloat; Laurel even made her own instrument to play it on – she bought a dulcimer kit in the USA.

One of the chief entertainments while cruising is the social life, meeting and getting to know other yachties or passers-by. One sometimes does not have much in common with the people in the next boat, except the sea and common experiences, but one learns a lot.

When on our own, the radio is valuable. It is wise to keep track of world events; you do not want to arrive somewhere in the middle of a *coup d'etat*. The BBC World Service has regular news broadcasts, mainly political in nature, and it seems to concentrate on the Third World as if the other two do not matter. Its entertainment is not so hot, but this is not its prime function.

The broadcast frequencies for any area vary during the day, and also from month to month as they have trouble from sunspots or human interference. A magazine, which used to be called *London Calling,* but which now changes its name with every change of controller, is published by the BBC, which gives a lot of programme information, and there is a monthly sheet listing frequencies in use. Both these can be got from the BBC World Service, Bush House, Strand, London WC2B 4PH. Other shortwave radio reception varies with locality and time. It has recently been announced that the BBC World Service is to move from

Bush House, probably to Broadcasting House, but in April 2001 was still at the above address. The website is in Appendix C.

Local national and provincial radio is heavily dependent on taste. In the West Indies one gets reggae morning, noon and night. In Europe all countries have an approximate equivalent to the BBC Home Services, and most countries have a programme with cultural leanings. France Musique is excellent because its announcers have almost perfect diction which is a great help in learning the language. (How foreigners get on trying to learn English from the BBC who seem to employ only Glaswegians and Geordies, I cannot imagine.)

Turkey and Greece both have cultural Third Programmes. The Greek one was excellent, but its former director is out of favour politically. Now the service is obtainable only near Athens and is musically less interesting, seeming to consist of interminable readings of avant-garde poetry. The Turkish programme put out a lot of trad jazz when I last heard it.

Radio in Italy is chaos. Everyone seems to start their own station, mostly to broadcast rock music and advertisements, and they are so unregulated that frequencies overlap. Some transmitters are so poorly modulated that the marine distress frequencies are affected, but no one bothers. Near Rome there is Canale 5 which has non-stop classical music all day, and is very good when not subject to interference.

In the USA the radio situation is a pale copy of the Italian; much the same in principle, but with some order superimposed, though not much is apparent to the outsider. For those with mental pretensions above the moronic there is Public Radio, which we thought good in quality and not only because they sometimes use BBC material.

The best domestic radios are those with digital tuning with 'save' buttons. There are several on the market. We carry a JVC multi-system miniature television set, which works everywhere except France. I like to pretend it is for watching weather forecasts, which are often more easily absorbed if one can see a synoptic chart. But television is also an effective language teacher. By watching children's programmes, one gets talk in a simple vocabulary with simple grammar, usually spoken slowly and clearly. (*The Teletubbies* are an exception.) Advertisements can be in simple language, and repeat phrases over and over again, with pictures. This can be a great help. There is not much entertainment from television abroad. One finds an occasional piece of excellence that is relevant to us, the foreigners, but not often.

Now there is satellite TV. The commercial programmes cannot be obtained legally as the companies insist on a telephone connection and tell us they will not license their special receiving decoders for use in boats. However; it is possible to get pirate decoders through various shady gentlemen who advertise in papers like *Exchange and Mart*, or *Loot*. We have not been down this road ourselves, not being tele-addicts.

There are some fee-free broadcasts by satellite. The gear can be obtained from any retailer and installed yourself, though they will tell you it cannot and offer to do so for a large fee. The problem in a yacht is pointing the antenna in the right direction and keeping it there. The boats alongside us as I write have mounted their winter antennae on poles fixed to the piling.

Last week, our omni-directional TV antenna blew off the foremasthead in a gale and fell over the side. I recovered it, decanted the sea water from it and from its co-ax connectors, and propped it on a boathook secured to the guardrails. It worked better than ever, thus destroying some of my more secure beliefs in electronic technology and UHF propagation.

In the Med, in winter, one finds lots of opportunities to swop videos, and in the more populous centres, where there are land-lubberly ex-pats, there are usually places to buy English language videos. One should be careful about video recording and playing: recorders/players must be compatible with the TV set you have on board and the local system. Multi-system video recorders are available, but at a hell of a price.

Multi-standard terrestrial television sets are available. We have just bought a 14-inch Grundig which will receive everywhere, including France, but not of course that awkward country in the Western Hemisphere. For the USA, we found that a British set would receive the picture but not the sound. As a temporary expedient we bought and placed next to the TV, a little radio set tuned to the TV frequencies intended for those who cannot miss the latest soap. Even when out walking.

YACHT CLUBS

Talk of social life leads us to consider clubs and associations of interest to the long-cruising yachtsman. There is a tendency not to belong to clubs. We are thus exceptions, though we question just what benefit we get from some. Loyalty dies hard.

We have to consider this mainly from a British point of view, as we know less about other countries' clubs than citizens of those countries. It is likely that the generalities we make about British clubs will apply to all.

Clubs (other than local ones) which help the cruising yachtie are:

- *The Royal Cruising Club*, the most senior of them all. Its membership is limited in number and very mutually supportive, but not at all snobbish. Its members really do get about the world, and tend to be well informed.

- *The Cruising Association*. After being nearly asleep for some time, it is now much more active. It has an excellent clubhouse in London with charts and information for consultation by those planning a voyage. We meet many members, who display creditable levels of skill.

- *The Little Ship Club* has also been kissed by Prince Charming and is now wide awake, and extending its influence. For the long-cruiser it possesses the asset of having premises with comparatively cheap bunks right in the centre of London. When one has sold up, a base can come in handy. It also has excellent courses for those wishing to improve their skills. Sadly, it is a little expensive for those living near London.

- *The Royal Naval Sailing Association* is a very active club (it started and organised the Whitbread Race for example), and has a fantastic spread of Hon Local Officers world-wide, almost all of whom are superior in every respect to those attached to imitating clubs. Though supposedly for serving or retired Navy, Reserves, and those associated with the Navy, these qualifications are so loose that virtually anyone can join.

- *The Ocean Cruising Club* is a classless, and somewhat international club for those cruising the oceans. Qualification is a port-to-port voyage exceeding 1000 miles in a small yacht. It is run by people more interested in sailing than administration, but that seems to be improving. It does disseminate a lot of valuable information through its magazine *Flying Fish,* and constitutes the second largest batch of members that we meet in harbour and on the high seas. It ought to offer Apprentice membership.

- *The Seven Seas Cruising Association* is run from the USA and is specifically for live-aboards. All members are Commodores, and we find the sensation that all are Chiefs without there being any Indians rather eccentric. One ceases to be eligible if one moves ashore, even for short periods, and that is a good idea. The membership qualification is loose, so that one finds a high proportion of live-aboards are house-boat dwellers on the US east coast waterways. A very friendly lot.

We were once in favour of a club for European live-aboards, but were nervous of initiating anything that would either fail because all the membership were so busy sailing that there was no administration, or alternatively it would, like so many clubs, end up by administering itself into the position of taking in its own expensive washing, thus achieving nothing at great expense.

For many years I was a personal member of the Royal Yachting Association (I joined the then Yacht Racing Association in 1948), but I got very disenchanted, especially when I discovered that many of its policies are actually detrimental to the interests of the long-term cruiser. The Secretary General in 1984 told me that long-distance cruisers are a minority and they couldn't be bothered with them, but so are ocean racers, Olympic helmsmen, and indeed most types of sailors when you classify them. The yachting fraternity is a collection of minorities.

I found that most long-term cruisers did not feel quite so strongly as I did about the RYA, possibly because they have not involved themselves. But general opinion is that the RYA has no relevance if you are out of British waters. One must give the RYA its due and say that it has been very helpful to yachtsmen in the major changes of VAT legislation in the EU, and it is the only body capable of seeing through the nightmare of European compulsory qualifications. I have therefore rejoined. I liked President Johnson's saying about a protesting aide: 'Better if he's inside the tent pissing out, than outside pissing in.'

MAGAZINES

I suppose it is fair for authors to review yachting magazines, because they do review our books (we hope!). But doing so imposes the duty of being fair.

No yachting publication specialises in matters of interest to long-cruising folk, though various journals have periods of temporary enthusiasm, which have become longer as they realise we are a bigger group than they at first thought. The American *Cruising World* is probably the most consistent. It is well produced, and is probably the nearest to a truly international yachting magazine. British magazines are more inward looking, perhaps a little parochial, but there are some brilliant contributions from time to time. Other countries have some good magazines too; the French and Scandinavian ones are very good, but parochial in their turn: as we said, there isn't a truly international magazine, and there is perhaps a lack.

The main problem with magazines is getting them. With their weight of advertising they cost the earth to post, and are little found in bookstalls overseas, even in established yachting centres. The problem is that the advertisements are often rather valuable and informative, except for double-page spreads of motor cars and property for sale. Somehow, we wish the advertisement print could be smaller, and the layout tighter, to save weight on board boats. We might then buy more of them!

FLAGS AND THINGS

If there is one thing that the old guard keep banging on about, it is so-called flag etiquette. People who write for the RYA or pontificate in club journals on this subject seem never to have left Cowes, or else believe that no one else in the world goes sailing other than 'English gentlemen'. In the real live world, Britain now comes some way down the list of countries where yachting is popular: the amount of boats actually under way in some parts of the world greatly exceeds our own backyard fleets. We are no longer entitled to be the arbiters of taste in such a matter, because etiquette is, by definition, the generally accepted code of behaviour and these days the traditional British code is no longer the generally accepted one. Now I am very fond of flags, but I have come to accept that the old traditional etiquette has had its day. Here is the situation as I see it:

Legally, a British ship has only to show an ensign on entering or leaving a foreign port (Merchant Shipping Act 1894). The ensign she may use is also laid down, and the Royal Navy is supposed to, but no longer does, police this. In addition, a lot of countries expect to have their ensign displayed by visiting vessels, and in some cases (Turkey is one) the courtesy ensign is a legal requirement.

I have said that etiquette is the 'generally accepted code of behaviour', so that if one belongs to a club or association which expects its members to conform, that is a reason for conforming. It is, in any event, economical to lower the ensign at

Fare Well *in Vathy, Meganisi for the Feast of St Bissarion. Apart from the masthead dressing lines, the hoists from each upper spreader are the courtesy ensigns of all the countries we have visited, 23 in all. Note the precautionary use of two anchors, the prevailing wind in the harbour coming from the port beam.*

night when nobody can see it, because they cost quite a lot, and soon wear out if left flying all the time.

An exception could be appropriate in Mediterranean ports when one is lying stern-to the main town quay which is well lit, and on which the local population is taking their evening stroll. I like to have the ensign on a good-sized staff, so that I can dip it to warships (usually with no response; it seems to be a courtesy that has died nowadays), and also to half-mast it on occasions such as the funeral of the mother of the taverna keeper on the other side of the quay. If one half-masts an ensign, one also must half-mast the courtesy ensign, do not forget.

Courtesy ensigns by tradition were flown at the foremasthead. In yachts this was traditionally kept for the club burgee, but nowadays few cruising yachts belong to clubs, and if they do they usually fly the burgee at the port crosstrees. The starboard crosstrees are then for the courtesy ensign. This is because mastheads are now often cluttered with electronic decorations. There are some clubs that insist their burgee *must* be flown only at the masthead, and it is

A common Continental method of flying an ensign in a ketch. It is both practical and sensible. Sometimes the downhaul of the halyard is inside the tubular fitting.

interesting that for those that wish to, the masthead can be so arranged as to permit this.

Many smaller yachts have their ensign tied to the standing backstay, where it stays until it rots. This is almost the current etiquette, so if you do the same no one is likely to notice. But it does add to the cost of living, and it seems to me desirable to have some sort of halyard so that when one remembers one can haul the flag down to prolong its active life.

International Code flags are a waste of money, unless you wish to dress ship for a celebration. You will need flag Q on arrival in some countries, though no longer within the European countries, unless coming from outside the EU. Apart from that, most flags carried will be courtesy ensigns, which have become a bit of a nuisance since so many former colonies have become jealous little republics.

The best way of dealing with the problem of multiple courtesy ensigns, since they are so expensive, is to follow our previously given advice and carry a sewing machine and a couple of yards of material of each of the primary colours, plus some different-coloured fabric-marking crayons (Vogart is a trade name of a suitable brand) to do the intricate bits without which no modern flag seems to be complete. If possible, arrive in a country with its courtesy ensign hoisted. Try not to be mean with size; flags are generally hoisted high and can look very tiny, which hardly seems a courtesy. In some places yachtsmen have been fined for having a tatty courtesy ensign; this raises several thoughts about what is a courtesy, and to whom.

Recently the whole question of flag etiquette has come under debate in the journal of the RNSA. The fact that old-and-bold naval officers are at last questioning an outmoded practice should augur well for a change in the position.

• *Dressing ship* •

It is a present-day nautical convention to hoist strings of decorative flags between mastheads and down to stem and stern in order to celebrate various occasions. Not many observe it, except a few British and Dutch with the odd American or German. We do it because I am a flag nut and think it looks good, but we do not do it for those rather formal occasions laid down by the Admiralty. We did it at Meganisi in Greece where we were staying at the time of the Feast of Saint Bissarion, the local patron. It is an island of merchant navy men, and several called by to thank us for the courtesy. It all helps to make the yachtie more welcome.

We once did it on Trafalgar Day while in France, and a French Naval Captain observed 'This is a good day for the France.' '*Comment?*' we replied, a little surprised. 'Well, we shot Nelson that day, and if we had not, we might well now be a British colony.' Everyone enjoys a sense of humour; we made another friend.

The usual form for dressing lines is to alternate the flags of the code with the pennants and substitutes. The order does not really matter – just make a colourful show.

Our dressing occasions are: the birthdays of crew, Trafalgar Day, St George's Day, Christmas Day, New Year's Day (when we also hoist a full string of courtesy ensigns for the past year, known as one's brag-line), plus any special dates for the country or port we are visiting.

HOW TO BE A POPULAR YACHTIE

The considerations that apply to flag etiquette apply also to yacht etiquette – the arbiters are no longer those elderly blimps from Cowes or the New York Yacht Club who have for so long arrogantly imposed their values on Anglo-American yachting. The arbiters now are the people who actually sail, and they comprise many nationalities. The form nowadays can be summed up:

- Cause the minimum inconvenience to other yachts' crews.
- Help another yacht berthing close by you.
- Give assistance willingly, and without legal haggling, to anyone in difficulties.

These three tenets are obvious to most people who want to sail. In more detail, certain usages have grown up around them, and I will give those I have noticed. If I have missed any, then I apologise to whomever I have offended.

Diesel generators   Their use is growing, and it has to be faced that many yachts have them and need them. In general, most confine generating to the forenoon. There is a growing tendency for a second run in the dog watches, between about 1600 and 1800, which is not so nice, but tolerable. In port, you should not run generators before 0830, between 1230 and 1600, or after 1900 unless you want to incur the justifiable wrath of your neighbours.

By 1997 the use of generators at *all* hours had become more common. Charter yachts are likely to run their air-conditioning 24 hours a day, and even among the smaller yachts the practice is on the increase. There is a law in Greece forbidding the running of noisy machinery anywhere between 1400 and 1700, the better to further the *Ipnos*, or afternoon sleep. We suggest this should be observed in boats, extended to include the late evening and night-time. At anchor, when yachts are some distance apart, the convention can be relaxed, particularly if it is windy, but in close anchorages such as Bequia or Union Island it ought to be observed.

Dinghies In Europe, dinghies left ashore are inviolable. You should make yours fast on a long painter so that it can be shoved to one side to allow others to get alongside to land. In areas where Americans abound, and particularly where their racing circuses congregate, the unsolicited borrowing of dinghies is not uncommon. Americans seem to tolerate this noxious practice, which is generally anathema to our older civilization. Either take precautions or be surprised.

Anchors Be particularly careful when berthing bows or stern to a quay not to lay your anchor cable(s) across others. In many places it cannot be avoided, however. The first to arrive at Navpaktos, in the Gulf of Corinth, is obliged to be the last to leave; the centre of this tiny harbour resembles a diagram for a multi-part Matthew Walker knot, tied in cable. A great deal of tolerance is needed.

Untangling foul anchors is an example of the willingness of yachties to help each other. Usually anyone with a dinghy down will paddle out to do his stuff. Greek yachtsmen are particularly good about this. If you are moored stern- or bows-to with the usual taut cable, and someone fouls it when weighing, you have an obligation to respond to reasonable requests from the fouler, who is probably in the best position to know how he is foul. He will probably ask you to give him some slack, for a yacht without a power windlass is unlikely to be able to haul a tight chain to the surface so that he can unhook his anchor. Even if he has power, if he hauls up a tight cable he is likely to haul up your anchor with it, so some slack is usually desirable. If wind conditions are troublesome run your engine at modest revs to hold your stern off the quay. If you are the fouler, and haul out the anchor of a berthed boat, try to re-lay it as close to its original position as possible.

One does *not* buoy anchors in a busy port; the chaos if all did so can be imagined. If you are worried about foul anchors use a trip line taken back to your bow. In an open anchorage, an anchor buoy can be of help to another yacht in avoiding anchoring too close because sometimes one's cable lies in a curve on the bottom. In a crowded anchorage it is a help to a newcomer shaping up near you to tell him how much cable you are lying to. It is the responsibility of the late-comer to keep clear of those already anchored, and this continues unless the first-comer changes the state by veering or shortening cable, or by letting go another anchor.

The last to haul or the last to veer,
He's the one who must keep clear.

Berthing   It is usual to help with the ropes of a yacht berthing next to you. In the Med, where harbours are often crowded, it is anti-social to berth alongside the quay. There are exceptions, such as Poros in the Aegean, or Khalkis, but for special reasons. Anyone berthing in this way has to be prepared for others to berth alongside them without any ceremony. In the Azores, Bermuda, Baltic and some Canaries harbours, yachts sometimes lie alongside six or more abreast. Outside yachts (other than tiddlers) must have breastropes to the quay, and springs to their neighbours. Utmost co-operation is needed, and is usually forthcoming to a measure that breeds friendships.

The old convention of always crossing over the foredeck of a neighbour is gone: many voyagers now have a proper sleeping cabin in the fore part of the yacht, and in warm climates often a wide-open hatch. It is proper to enquire (by day) how you should cross, and the responder should also pass on the information he has already got from yachts inside him.

Footwear   The real seaman wears deck shoes because he knows that stubbed toes can be debilitating, and also that quaysides are often fouled by disease-ridden dogs. Dilettante yachtsmen who spend more time polishing their yachts than sailing them have an elaborate ritual of donning or doffing shoes like a crowd of Japanese at a temple. But you cannot expect an outside crew to take off their boots just because you bagged the inside berth. Face the fact that if the deck of your yacht will not stand up to deck shoes it is not fit for its purpose. (A little small grit is very good for teak; it roughens it, improves its nonslip qualities.) On the other hand, the shoe wearer has an obligation to see that his shoes are clean.

Smoking   Do as you like in your own boat, but in harbour do not throw cigarette ends overboard. Many yachts put their dinghies down in harbour, and it's too easy to start a fire in one.

Garbage   The French and Italians tend to leave plastic bags of garbage on the quay, thereby encouraging rats, stray dogs and cats, and incurring the wrath and disrespect of others who mostly look for the garbage skip. This is often full, when there is nothing to be done except to leave the garbage alongside it. In the Caribbean and elsewhere, pay no heed to little boys who paddle out to your anchorage and offer to dispose of your garbage for a fee. They will rummage through it for anything of interest, and then leave the rest on that pretty little beach where you wanted to swim.

Quiet   Quiet times vary from place to place. Some are still beating at 0300. A few miles away, at another port, the inhabitants will all be asleep by 2230. Local people may well welcome the income from tourism, but do not want to pay too high a price for it. Ascertain and respect the local convention.

Helping   There is a tradition of helping others with navigation information. Where they are otherwise unobtainable, charts etc are loaned for photocopying. Linguists pass on the weather reports, and any yacht who has been in the port more than a few days should pass on the whereabouts of sources of essentials (water, or gas bottles) or even non-essentials that are particularly interesting.

CRUISING IN COMPANY

It had (truly) never occurred to me, Bill, that anyone would be seriously nervous about an Atlantic crossing in the tradewind belt. It first came up when we invited a relative to come over with us in *Fare Well* in 1982. He brought his wife, a lovely lady, an experienced sailor, and a valuable member of the crew.

Halfway over, she appeared on deck with a face of thunder, and her shame-faced spouse was clearly in for some rough handling. It transpired that the only way he had been able to get her across the Atlantic was to tell her that we were making a short trip round the Canaries. She had been shanghaied! It was a calm voyage; the only rough bit had been between Gibraltar and Tenerife, running before a wild Levanter (east wind).

Given that sort of feeling, we should have expected that someone would propose a trans-Atlantic voyage in company. Jimmy Cornell, an experienced ocean sailor, started the series of Atlantic Rallies for Cruisers (the ARC) which, backed by *Yachting World*, have been a great success, and have pleased many people. We mentioned this briefly in the chapter on safety matters, but it is important enough for other aspects of it to crop up again.

The ARC series would not suit us, because we like to be on our own at sea. We like to pick our ports of departure and arrival, and the organisers changed the latter from Barbados, which was a sensible arrival port, to a very commercial marina in St Lucia, which we think is not. We also do not have the spare cash for the substantial fee (when last we heard – 1995 – it was up to £400 per boat plus about £30 per person in the crew). We also do not feel personally happy with the competitive atmosphere (prizes for the first boat and so on) that has grown up. Those caveats are our own personal views, and the fact that so many have enjoyed the experience indicates that there are many yachtsmen who welcome Jimmy's founding initiative. He has given pleasure to many. If you feel you would like that way of cruising watch *Yachting World* for details.

There are other cruising 'rallies'. One runs from Hampton, Virginia to Bermuda and Tortola, but we have no details. There have been others on a 'round the world' basis, making several stops en route. These latter do attract some criticism. They are expensive, and the folk are in holiday mode. They call in at well-known yachtie stops, and quite frankly spoil things for the independent

Ships that pass…we meet, raft up and have a party before sailing on.

yachtie. We have met Australian and New Zealand boats which have arrived in the Med quite angry about these yachting circuses, which are quite different to the ARC. This latter goes from one port directly to another and causes no bother elsewhere.

We have to face it that yachting in all its forms has expanded greatly over the past 50 years. Many coastal yacht clubs and marinas are full; almost the only yachting still with growth potential is the long-haul cruising world. It is all going to get more and more crowded as more and more countries take up yachting. Wait until it really catches on in Japan: it's starting to.

15 • Health and Welfare at Sea

'The Chirurgeon is to be exempted from all duty but to attend the sicke and cure the wounded; and good care would be had he have a certificate from the Barber-Chirurgeon's Halls of his sufficiency . . . for which neglect hath beene the losse of many a man's life'

Nowhere is it more obvious than on a long-distance cruise that sickness is more a state of mind than of body. Most cruising people find that as the pace of life slows to 5 knots on average and the world shrinks to the size of their boat, many bodily ills dwindle and disappear. It's years since either of us had a cold. On the other hand, you have a better chance of doing yourself a minor injury on a boat of cruising size than might be the case if you had stuck to golf and lawnmowers.

Consequently, while you need no longer exempt your Chirurgeon from all other duty, it would be well, as Captain John Smith points out, that he have a certificate; nowadays from the Red Cross or St John's Ambulance Brigade, at least. It has to be said that the Red Cross and St John's courses are neither heroic nor practical enough for the long-distance cruiser. Even if we have access to advice by radio, we are likely to need practical skills such as giving injections, administering a drip, stitching wounds, and the control of pain and infection. When we first wrote about this, many doctors in the British Isles still had a deep-seated mistrust of allowing any Tom, Dick or Harriet to acquire such paramedical skills or even read about them, though in the USA there was a crash course (the Intensive Survey of Medical Emergency Care) designed by a doctor/sailor. So in the first edition we wrote that there were no medical courses in the UK for long-distance yachtsmen.

However, since we persuaded *Yachting Monthly* that our idea for a Long Distance Cruising Symposium would be feasible and popular (an event which we organised with the Editor and the much-missed Geoff Pack, daringly including in the programme Practical First Aid at Sea), the scene has gradually changed, though we think there is still a need for more and better. That very first cruising seminar in 1987 was a runaway success, and the herald of many look-alikes; they are now commonplace. Even the RYA now runs them, complete with a talk on 'First Aid at Sea'. With luck you can catch Professor Noel Dilly's talk on the subject, riveting, useful, and hilarious.

Years ago, when there were no such courses, the only one Laurel could find was the Ship Captain's Medical Course, which was obviously not intended for yachtsmen. She duly attended the Lowestoft Nautical College, a woman among the assembled ships' captains and mates, and found the course wonderfully reassuring.

The medical course is based on the *Ship Captain's Medical Guide* (known as The Book) which all British merchant ships are required to carry on board, as we did ourselves. We always carried a copy for long cruises in *Fare Well* and latterly in *Hosanna*, and found it very useful in emergencies. Embarking on our travels again after swapping boats, I felt I wanted some practical knowledge to add to the drugs and equipment which we had carried in *Fare Well*. It was all very well having the stuff on board, but did I know how to use it all? No, I did not.

Many people ask how we cope with sickness or accidents at sea. The only response that we can make is: 'As best we can, it doesn't happen often.' One knows that help is not within reach, and that the High Street surgery is 4 000 miles away. When the crunch comes you are your own barefoot doctor – you, with the worried look and the shaking hands. I ought, I felt, to be able to give an injection, and take a stitch-in-time with a suturing needle.

So I, Laurel, enrolled on the three-day course, and began badly. I was ten minutes late, and already I'd missed the whole of 'Preparing a Cabin for a Patient' and half of 'Vital Signs'. Yes, the course was dense and intense. There were six of us, four Merchant Navy Officers, and two yachtswomen, Caroline of *Heartsease* and me. We went at the pace of a motorcycle scramble. The breathless speed made us reel. We learned how to take blood pressure, record temperature, pulse and breathing, how to test urine and why. (Nurses in the old days used to taste it to find what was in it, said Rosie SRN, our Mentor, thank God we now use Labstix.)

We did Observation of Specimens, and Care of Bed Patients; we learned to face the enema, and to give rectal infusions (to fight the Demon Dehydration, the killer in many and varied diseases and conditions). We learned how to cope with Malaria, we saw a slide cassette on Heat Exhaustion and Heat Stroke.

Fortified by lunch, I then discovered more than I care to know about Sexually Transmitted Diseases. This lecture was beautifully sung by a Welsh doctor, who accompanied it with extraordinary slides. He began *pianissimo* with the diseases we'd all heard of, went into a fugue of oddities that were new to some of us (the males usually), and ended up with a threnody on AIDS.

We then pelted through Poisons, including many gases that were relevant to the cargoes of Shipmasters, but not very likely on a yacht.

We roared past Resuscitation, hurtled through Haemorrhage, and halted for a while for Hypothermia (something that anyone who goes boating on the lake ought to know about, let alone long-distance cruisers).

We galloped past Gallstones, shot through Surgical Emergencies, were mesmerised by Mental Illness and Myocardial Infarction (which up to then we had called heart attack).

We were petrified by Palpation of the Abdomen, bemused by Bodies (disposal of) and bothered by Burial at Sea.

And all the time Caroline and I would ask: 'But suppose you haven't got room on your boat for all that apparatus/equipment/vast array of drugs?'

Improvisation can save your bacon, as I well know, and Rosie often assured us with examples.

I remembered once leaving Port Mahon (on a Friday of course) when Bill was freeing the anchor from a heavy rope encrusted with barnacles, when a huge fish-hook caught deep in the pad of his middle finger. My first action had to be taking the strain off the rope, and therefore the finger. The second was to check that the boat was still safely anchored. The third was to sit down and think a bit.

'Push the hook through the skin (if no vital organ is endangered), nip off the barb, and withdraw', said the first aid book. But they hadn't seen stainless steel Spanish fish-hooks; they're more like something you find at the butcher's, with a whole ox hanging from it. Which was not far from the truth, as I pointed out to the skipper at the time: he was not amused.

A brief effort to obey the first aid book with the aid of bolt cutters threatened to amputate the finger and was quickly abandoned for a Stanley knife, 'sterilised' with brandy.

Both patient and 'doctor' then drank some of the brandy (not recommended in The Book) and, shaking like leaves, cut out the hook, which was baited with something slithery that looked very evil. I wish I knew what, as the wound healed clean and with great rapidity, and we might have made a fortune selling it to a drug company. Observe that it never occurred to us to row ashore and find a doctor. One loses the habit.

I also recalled putting the skipper's neck in traction with a handy billy and a 7-kilo gas bottle over a pulley, and under 'Burns' in the appropriate section you will find an ingenious use for the rain gauge.

Back to the course. In two and a half crammed days we learned to stitch gaping

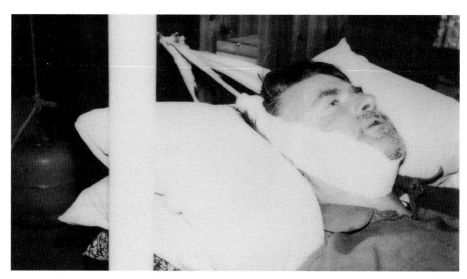

Bill's neck in traction with the aid of a 7-kilo gas bottle over a pulley.

wounds in surprisingly resistant foam rubber (very like the real thing, said Rosie) and not to put our unsterilised finger on the knot. Knowledge of stitching I could have used on a couple of occasions for small wounds.

We learned to inject oranges. We learned to approach the plastic model of Resusci-Annie with confidence, despite her lying on the floor with her lungs exposed and a feral grin on her face. Her bared rubber teeth looked as if they could bite you if she didn't care for your technique, or your aftershave. I added the Brooke Airway to our first aid list.

When it came to exam time on the third afternoon, we all regurgitated sufficient material (some of it only half digested) to pass; Caroline and I were the first women to do so at Lowestoft who were not Shipmasters.

What did all that make me? Certainly not the Doc. But next time something happened, I had a modicum of confidence to add to common sense. I hoped to reassure my victim that my panicky search through 'The Book' would bring help and relief. Raising morale is my strong point. Even without the brandy. And I was more determined than ever to harp (to the point of boring my readers) on *Prevention* of accidents and illness at sea. Stop it happening, and you don't have to treat it.

It is to be hoped that you will have gone to sea in a state of good health, as far as can be ascertained by check-ups and dental work before you go. So cherish this happy state of affairs by thinking 'prevention' rather than 'cure'. Catch it before it happens. Eliminate the chances of sickness and bodily damage to your uttermost. Since this attitude goes hand in hand with the watchfulness that every good seaman cultivates, the quicker it becomes second nature to you the sooner, paradoxically, you can relax and enjoy your cruise. By 'looking for trouble' you are avoiding it!

FINDING HELP WHERE YOU NEED IT

At sea you are dependent on who may be within call. Advice may be available by radio: a call of 'Pan Pan Medico' should produce results if any doctor is monitoring, or any merchant ship or shore station picks up your call.

If you are within reach of land, English-speaking doctors who have been properly trained may be found world-wide by joining IAMAT, the International Association for Medical Assistance to Travellers, a non-profit-making organisation. Otherwise there is MASTA (Medical Advisory Services for Travellers Abroad), a world-wide advisory health service for travellers. Approved by (and next door to) the London School of Hygiene and Tropical Medicine, they will tailor a Health Brief to your individual requirements (from £9 to £30 according to the number of countries you will visit), with details of all inoculations required, information, and a list of medical items to take with you, and up-to-date 'health newsflashes' from all over the world, via their computer bank. Long-distance yachtsmen would need the more comprehensive service, which could be very good value. They also run a health insurance scheme. Forms are available at branches of Boot's, chemists, or direct from MASTA. Addresses and websites for all these will be found in Appendix C, together with other extremely useful sites with detailed (free) medical advice for travellers, including updates on what plague is endemic where and what inoculations to get. The doctor's surgery by cyber-café has arrived; you can describe your symptoms and receive reassurance and advice.

HEALTH INSURANCE

Be sure to take with you form E111, duly filled in and signed, for reciprocal health agreements in Europe. It is included in the excellent booklet D. o. H *Health Advice for Travellers*, available at post offices, (also see website in Appendix C.).

Though health insurance is a luxury if cruising the waters of EU member states (generally, the health service of anywhere in the EU is better than the British, and we can say that from experience) it is another matter in the rest of the world where all medicine may be private. When we first wrote it was impossible to get world-wide continuous cover. It is still not easy. It is necessary to shop around to get quotes. Big companies are not interested because their underwriting is geared to mass processing. Smaller ones have insufficiently large books to be able to spread the risk, and the remainder blow hot or cold depending on the way their risks are spread. Quotes can even vary from month to month.

All medical insurance is expensive, and usually excludes what diseases and conditions you are most likely to get. We made the decision long ago to do without it. Over 25 years we have paid for the usual small accidents, visits to surgeries and dentists, and two major operations. We are still ahead of the game, and healthy for our age.

As people in Britain have no idea what their health or their drugs cost, it's worth knowing that a visit to a doctor in France costs 120 francs, and for that he will do minor surgery, stitches or lancing a boil for example. This is about £11, and is not very much, as I pointed out to a doctor in France, having just taken the cat to the vet and been charged twice that. If your form E111 is in order you will get that money back. You will also get money back for prescriptions and surgical procedures, though sometimes only a proportion of it.

In the USA they will take your credit cards before allowing your suffering body into the hospital; this is where you may need insurance, though we have always managed without.

Three points:

- Get a policy with a watertight repatriation clause.
- Insurance for the USA will be expensive, though cheaper if taken out in the USA.
- For EU countries, don't forget form E111.

WHEN YOU GO

Take with you 'The Book', and/or *The First Aid Manual* published by the Red Cross and St John's Ambulance Association.

If you have room consider taking the following books:

1 A copy of the *BNF* (British National Formulary) which gives comprehensive information about drugs – very useful abroad. A polite request to the prescription counter of any large pharmacy usually produces an old copy, as it is a bi-annual publication.

2 *Where there is No Dentist* and *Where there is no Doctor* (Specify International or African editions) from TALC, address in Appendix C. What was the difference between the International and the African edition? I asked the young man who answered the phone, thinking different bugs and diseases. 'The pictures,' he said. Of course.

There follows, in alphabetical order, not the first aid advice you will get from the above books and websites, and other helplines specially conceived for yachtsmen, but a useful list of preventive measures, which is less often come across.

• *Preventative measures* •

AIDS and STDs

It used to be sailors who spread Sexually Transmitted Diseases (STDs). Now that everyone travels, it is the tourists and the businessmen who spread the plague. Doesn't stop sailors catching it, though.

- Take the obvious precautions, and a long hard look at new and sexy friends.
- Carry condoms with you at all times, you never know whom you might meet. We met Uffa Fox in the breakfast room on our honeymoon; he wished us a warm good morning, prepared to sneeze mightily, and scattered condoms like confetti as he drew out his handkerchief. This was 1952; he had the right idea, but best not keep them with your handkerchief. We gave a lift to a young man in Corfu, desperate to catch the next plane out. Matter of serious illness in the family. 'A close relative?' we asked sympathetically. 'It's me,' he said, 'I've got the clap.'
- Remember that condoms have a limited shelf life, and are hard to find in remote places. Buy them where you can be sure of the quality – we are sure the tale of rubber workers in Catholic countries pricking every tenth condom with a pin to re-establish God's little lottery is not true, but you get the drift. Give them a balloon or water test if you are uncertain. Fun and educational for all the family. If bought loose and wholesale, it helps to shake a little talcum among them, to preserve the *preservatifs*.
- Consider asking your doctor for an AIDS kit if you intend going to certain parts of the world where AIDS is especially rife. Thus if you had to go ashore for any kind of treatment you would take with you your own syringes, needles, blood-giving set, sterile swabs and plasma. (MASTA, see Appendix, has information on this.)
- Avoid accidents needing blood transfusions, and don't go in for tattooing or piercing in dodgy places, both bodily and geographical.
- Carry a Brooke airway and surgical gloves, for giving first aid.

Appendicitis

This is the great bugaboo that once frightened everyone. Many transatlantic yachtsmen used to have an 'elective appendectomy' in order to avoid any possibility of trouble. This would need to be discussed with your doctor. We feel that nowadays hospitals take away the disease you came in with and give you several new ones in exchange: this is even acknowledged by the medical profession in a fearsome Greek-derived term: *Nokosogeneric* (meaning arising in the hospital) disease. Stay out of hospital and stay healthy, we say. However, it is a worry. We know of no one who has died of peritonitis at sea since the 1960s: it seems that modern antibiotics can hold the situation until help is at hand.

Births

(For prevention see also under *AIDS above.)*

It is *very* difficult to get any kind of contraceptives in large areas of the world. To be safe, take a good supply with you, and have several different methods in case you run out.

Lady, if you are seasick to the point of vomiting, or have even a short attack of diarrhoea, or vomiting, or both, the effectiveness of your contraceptive pill could be endangered. Talk to your doctor before you go about the possible effect on your sort of pill: it might be necessary to use a supplementary method for the rest of that cycle.

Bites

For mosquitoes see *Malaria* below, and Chapter Seven on pests.

Fleas   Repellants such as Deet should work for all biting insects. The drill for fleas is to undress in the bath, shaking every item of clothing so that the little beast lands in the water (it will be obvious that a shower stall doesn't work quite as well). I miss the Keatings powder that one shook among the sheets in the good old pre-war days when one picked up fleas on the bus, at Saturday cinema, and in Woolworth's. It even smelt nice, though it felt a bit sandy. I suspect some veterinary flea-powders are similar. Ask.

Animal bites see *Rabies* below.

Ticks   Ticks can give you or your pets nasty diseases; the only good use for a lit cigarette is to encourage ticks to drop off. Otherwise ether works, but see Chapter Seven on pets and pests.

Bodily damage

A yacht is made of hard and unyielding substances, which in bad weather get up and hit you, causing bruises, cuts, concussion, cracked ribs or broken bones. The old salts used to say: One hand for yourself, and one for the King.

A yacht big enough to go cruising in is under the sway of enormous forces. If something breaks or casts loose it can cause serious damage to people or boat. Part of seamanship, therefore, is learning how to approach and tame your tiger, whether it be a flogging sail or twin boom, with the minimum of danger:

- Learn the motion of your boat: when she may jerk or spin, as in a gybe all-standing or the wash of a big ship, or a sudden squall.
- Make sure that handholds are numerous, in the right place, and that these and anything that can be used as such are *strong enough*. We have seen (for instance), tables on production boats that collapsed into matchwood when crashed into by a 7-stone weakling.
- Expect the Captain to warn you, if at all possible, that a big wave or jerk may be coming.
- Climbing the mast at sea should be attempted only in dire necessity.
- The deck of a yacht is never smooth. It is dotted with cleats, rings, bitts, upstands, screwplates and deadeyes, all waiting to bite your feet.
- Wear good deck shoes to protect your feet from damage, as well as for traction. Bare feet are fine in harbour or at anchor, but get your shoes on for manoeuvres. Shipboard work often cannot wait while you hop around holding your toe and yelling.
- Use preventers and guys to limit the swing of spars, and prevent gybing. Again prevention is better than cure, so check halyards for weaknesses, ropes for chafe, wire for kinks and broken strands (the latter are a constant source of lacerated fingers), replace bent shackle pins, and tape up protruding split pins or enclose them neatly in plastic tube.
- If the weather threatens, shorten sail early to lessen the forces you have to control. Even a handkerchief of canvas in a force 8 can bat around like a tin roof in a hurricane, and a rope can assume the murderous quality of an iron bar wielded by a maniac.

Listen to the flotilla. They believe that nothing can hurt them: after all, what could possibly happen on two weeks' holiday?

'I'm coming in a bit fast: stick your foot out and hold her off, will you, Harry?' The luckless Harry tries to stop 5 tons of fast-moving boat in zero seconds: oh dear, he's hurt his foot. But Dad is very busy at the other end:

'Maude, can you let a bit more anchor line out? What? No more? Well tie another rope to it then – be quick, I can't quite reach the quay. HOLD ON! What did you let go for? Stop crying, it's only a rope burn. Fred, take a line ashore, will you. No, I can't seem to get any nearer, we've run out of anchor line: can't you jump it?'

Fred, challenged, jumps at the precise moment when the cleated anchor line brings the boat up short. He is lucky if he is precipitated into the water rather than onto the rough concrete quay, which will result in numerous cuts and abrasions if not worse. The same abrupt halt has probably thrown Mum against the cockpit coaming, a frequent cause of cracked ribs. All it needs now is for Sandra to stub her bare toe against a cleat and, on leaving, for Susan to jam her fingers in the anchor cable roller and Dad to get a hernia heaving up the anchor, unaware in all the excitement that the ferry has come in and laid several hundredweight of chain across it. We have watched all these things happen, and a lot more, but not all to one boat, at one time, mercifully.

A few more hints:

- Don't fill a bucket of water from the sea if you are sailing fast. Even at 5 knots the jerk can almost dislocate your shoulder.
- So can an unexpected gybe if you are holding the mainsheet in your hand. 'Never cleat the mainsheet' goes back to our dinghy days: it is not valid for bigger boats.
- Anchor chain can crush fingers or hands: I have a healthy respect for ours. On *Fare Well* it was very heavy. I kept my hands well away from it by looping a short length of codline through the links when I needed to move it: this could be let go instantly if the cable began to run out unexpectedly, or even cleated up to stop it if you were quick.
- Release with care those dinky little elastic sail gaskets with a plastic knob at each end, or they will snap back and knock your teeth out and probably break your glasses as well.
- Finally, wearing a lifejacket can save you a few bruises, as will a padded jacket with integral buoyancy.

Body odour

This delicate matter must be mentioned, since the chronic water shortage on board often prevents normal bathing and showering:

- Be aware that your clothing affects your smell. Man-made fibres all engender smells in the smalls after a couple of hours. Cotton, wool and linen may be worn for much longer before they need washing. You may decide that the easy-care qualities of polyester/cotton mixtures are worthwhile, but you will have to wash them more often, thus using more water.
- Canvas shoes and trainers need washing whenever you have access to a shoreside hose, otherwise the smell can become intense enough to glow in the dark; leather deck shoes are more expensive, but kinder to plates and mates.
- Personal hygiene can be assisted by moistened wipes. Do not use those saved from restaurants in the interests of economy on anything except your hands: I shudder to think of the effect of the lemon-flavoured variety on tender portions of the anatomy. There are specially made ones for this purpose such as Bidette and Femfresh. A huge box of baby wipes is worth a great many baths. For women, throwaway pantyliners are a godsend; one wishes there was a male equivalent, a sort of paper jockstrap. My greatest contribution to cruising is probably the discovery that the Debutante brand plastic bowl (withstands boiling water and is graduated in pints and litres) fits exactly into the Lavac bowl to form a bidet. I was so excited by this discovery that I bought a second plastic bowl, but the first one has lasted ten years without breaking.

Bill is under the delusion that underarm deodorants are effective. Overuse can cause dermatitis.

Breaking nails

You need strong short nails at sea. There are preparations to paint on and strengthen them, but you can also 'eat' them strong by including plenty of gelatine in the diet: eat straight jelly (Jello) cubes if you like, or dishes in aspic such as *oeufs en gelée*, brawn or pig's trotters, oxtail. Wearing gloves can spare you damage: not the delicate little pair from the Yotte Shoppe which expose your finger ends (in our experience one of the most vulnerable and easily damaged part of the body), but a strong leather or plastic-palmed pair. The yellow ones sold for bargees in European waterways prevent injury either when dealing with wire rope, or that popular French mooring system called the *Pendille*, where you pick up a fixed rope between the quay and a mooring buoy, and slide it through your hands to bring it to the forward anchor winch to make fast. As the rope spends a lot of time in the water, it is covered with coral and small, sharp crustacea. Those on shore can be heard tittering as you lacerate your hands and bleed into the scuppers. A pack of false nails takes little room for those who fancy a little silent boasting among well-groomed people ashore.

Burns and scalds

Every cook must evolve his or her own way of coping with hot pans in a choppy sea. Some advocate seats and straps in the galley, but I prefer to be free to leap aside. With good fiddles it is not the pans that move, it is their contents, so it makes a lot of sense to have deep, tall pans, with well-fitting lids, and not to fill them too full. Pressure cookers are excellent because the lid stays on. A wide-based kettle with a whistle closing the spout keeps boiling water in the right place. You need a safe place to put a hot pan down where it will not slide, and insulated pan and pot handles. A large cover-all apron of tough plastic will protect you from splashes.

Should you be unlucky enough to sustain a burn or scald, it is important to prevent dehydration. When Bill accidentally barbecued me four hours away from civilisation, we were acutely conscious of this. Following instructions in the *Ship Captain's Medical Guide*, he fed me lemon squash with a little salt in it, half a pint every half-hour, and measured my output in the rain gauge, driving the boat at maximum speed all the time, I should point out. He also radioed ahead for assistance. On arrival (at an eastern Mediterranean port with a hospital) we had waiting for us on the quay willing hands to help Bill berth, a French doctor, an English doctor, an English nursing sister, and an American nurse (all live-aboards or on holiday in yachts). All of them advised us not to go near the hospital, and were delighted with Bill's lemonade, now satisfactorily coming through me every five minutes, and tickled by the rain gauge idea. With such good care, the burns on thighs, arms and hands healed in no time. I convalesced in the cockpit on a clean sheet.

Other crew members can get burnt if you have an onboard barbecue (usually the kind that gimbals on a stern rail). At anchor, smoke and sparks blow harmlessly

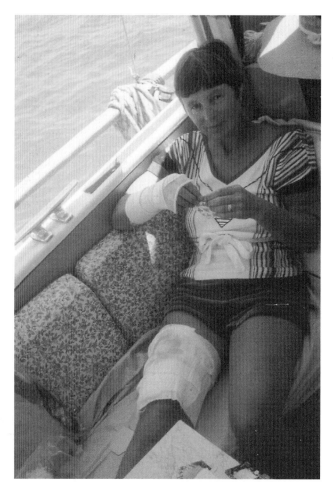

Sometimes you have to treat your own injuries: Laurel recovers from being barbecued by Bill.

away aft, but moored to the quay it pays to study the wind direction. We know of two cases of burns caused by thoughtless use of methylated spirit: firelighters are much safer. We keep a fire extinguisher and a fire blanket near the cooking stove in case of galley fires. (Firefighting in yachts is covered in Chapter Eleven.)

Ciguatera poisoning

This is caused by eating fish from coral reefs near the Equator. It manifests not only with the usual food poisoning symptoms, nausea, vomiting and diarrhoea, but can also produce tingling and numbness in the fingers, toes, lips and tongue; joint and muscle pains, weakness and cramps; fatigue, fainting and headaches; and itching made worse by alcohol. To confuse the issue even more, any or all of these symptoms may be present, and they may be so slight as to be barely noticed, or severe enough to include breathing difficulties. Some sources say the death rate (mostly from breathing difficulties) is 2–3%, others 1%; still others say that it could be less as the milder cases are not reported.

In by far the majority of cases, unpleasant as these symptoms are they will go away in time, though muscular weakness may persist for quite a while.

Ciguatoxin is found in a small organism that attaches to the algae on certain coral reefs, where it is eaten by small fish. These are then eaten by larger fish, and as the food chain gets longer the toxin is concentrated until in the larger predatory fish it becomes a danger to those who eat it.

Distribution   This is the hard part, as the distribution of the affected reefs is sporadic and capricious: it is not yet understood what factors make some reefs harbour the organism, and others (though quite close by) not. So while one can say with truth that ciguatera is present in reefs in the Pacific, Japan, Queensland, the Great Barrier Reef and the Caribbean, that is not the whole story. North of Antigua in the Caribbean, ciguatera is present in some reefs. To the south, the Windward Islands and the Grenadines are free of it. French Polynesia is widely affected, Raratonga is not.

What is certain, in all the myth and rumour which abounds on this subject, is that the local fishermen, be they Polynesian, Caribbean or Floridans, know with fair exactitude which reef and which fish species to avoid. They will also volunteer much folklore on testing fish for poison, ranging from cooking it with a silver coin (which turns black if the fish is toxic) to trying it out on the mother-in-law. No reliance can be placed on these methods, as only very sophisticated laboratory tests can detect whether the fish is affected. Neither heating nor canning destroys the effects of the toxin. So what to do?

Local knowledge from a reliable source is vital. If in any doubt, do not eat the larger predatory fish: grouper, barracuda, emperor, sailfish etc. (One source describes over 10 kilos as large.) Do not eat moray eel. Do not eat the roe, liver or other offal, especially from large fish.

Research is going on in Queensland, Tahiti, Japan and Hawaii, among other places, to establish accurate tests for ciguatera in fish, and one such is now available. It's not cheap, and has a limited shelf life, but if you catch big fish in affected areas you might find it useful. (See Appendix.)

Colds
Just go to sea. The virus disappears after a week to ten days, and you will catch no more colds until you visit the next supermarket.

Cystitis
Cystitis is a urinary tract infection. If you are subject to this, make sure you drink a lot of water, wear cotton next to the skin, and take your favourite remedy with you.

Dental problems
Some old Salt Horses, chiefly from the New World, used to suggest having all your teeth out before a long cruise. This seems to us a draconian solution, especially as our teeth seem to last much better nowadays. It should suffice to ensure that you are 'dentally fit' before you leave. Tell your dentist your plans, and he will be careful to miss nothing.

Thereafter, look after your teeth. I will not insult your intelligence by telling you how, since we are all over-exposed to dental hygiene. Here are some thoughts that might not occur to you, however:

- If you wear dentures, take them out if you feel seasick; they are all too easily chundered overboard. Of course, you will take a spare set in case of accidents.
- Take a dental first aid kit, (see Appendix C), which should contain a temporary filling mixture, and cement to repair bridgework, or even broken teeth. The designer of such a kit recounts the dreadful story of a woman who tried to replace her front crowns with superglue, all that was obtainable in the remote island where she found herself. The glue engendered intense heat as it set, causing unimaginable pain and damage.
- Lost fillings may be temporarily replaced by Granny's remedy: equal parts of oil of cloves and powdered zinc oxide. Mix this well, and work it into the well-dried cavity. It will set in about a quarter of an hour, and last until you can get it seen to.
- Oil of cloves on cottonwool is a harmless localised painkiller.

Departure stress

Leaving home and friends can be grievous. Husbands and lovers could help a lot by trying to understand how serious a bereavement this is; the male has no roots, it seems, certainly not the ones who go to sea, and feels less pain on upheaval. The tumbleweed male should allow plenty of time for his partner to adjust to transplantation (in the gardening sense). Unlike plants, this will be worst before the actual uprooting; on sailing day the relief will be balm to everyone's pain but the weeks or even months before you go will be hard.

Bereavement is a sense of loss, of people and things that are loved and respected. It is not necessary for the people to actually die, or the things to be destroyed for you to feel bereft; bereavement is also caused by leaving treasures behind, whether human, animal, abstractions or objects. Bereavement is something to be reckoned with. It is a very germane consideration. Men come up against it with a jolt when they unexpectedly lose their jobs. Some people suffer severely from bereavement when they retire, and grieve for their lost jobs and status. If they have no absorbing hobby they can die of despair. In the same way, women will grieve for family, friends and the house they leave behind.

Happy are they who are encouraged and comforted while they work their way through this painful stage. Grief is extremely hard work, and very time-consuming for the person undergoing it; and the support group will need great patience. He will need to check the urge to say: 'Aren't you making rather a meal of this?' or 'Dear, oh dear, you are going on a bit.' Of course she is. That is how she will work through it.

Diseases, avoidable

'They fall sicke of one disease or another . . .'

Unless there are positive medical objections, it makes sense to acquire vaccination, immunisation, and inoculation against smallpox, tetanus and typhoid (TAB).

Some parts of the world will not allow entry without an International Certificate of Vaccination, against smallpox and/or yellow fever.

It may also be advisable, according to where you intend to travel, to have shots against cholera and polio, and gamma globulin shots against hepatitis and some other viral infections. Babies should have the triple vaccine (diphtheria, whooping cough and tetanus) unless your doctor advises otherwise. It is not considered advisable for babies under nine months to have yellow fever shots, but you may insist, in writing. Children should have the triple vaccine, plus immunisation against polio.

Discuss with your doctor the advisability or otherwise of all these precautions, and whether to include shots against tuberculosis and German measles for your children. Tuberculosis is making a disturbing comeback, and the vaccine BCG is in short supply, as is that for yellow fever. Discuss whether you should do something about malaria, the increase of which is causing concern.

Detailed lists are available in a leaflet from your local Department of Health and Social Security, and the Department of Health website. The Scottish NHS site is especially good. Try also the Hospital for Tropical Diseases and MASTA (Medical Advisory Services for Travellers); whose websites will be found in Appendix C.

Ear itch

Many people get this infuriating complaint when swimming. Ear plugs or a good bathing cap are the obvious answer. Otosporin (on prescription) seems to work.

Eye damage

Whether you wear glasses or not, have your eyes tested before departure. You will need good sight by night as well as day, and if glasses help, wear them. Tell the optician your plans and discuss with him whether the lightness and toughness of plastic lenses outweighs their tendency to scratches. Take spare pairs (and your prescription) with you. Keep them on with chain, elastic or string: whatever suits you. Do not keep them in a breast pocket: I have seen many a pair of specs go to the bottom of the sea as their owner bent over a rail; otherwise they fall down a hatchway and get broken. Fix a steel tag to them and you might get them back with a Sea Searcher magnet: we have rescued not only spectacles but keys, fountain pens, bolts and wing nuts, fish traps and bicycles with this. Many spectacle wearers are bothered by sea spray. A motor cycle visor helps; it can be tilted up for long, clear vision and cleaned off without the salt crystals scratching your prescription glasses.

When using the sextant for sunsights, be extra careful not to glimpse the sun directly through the telescope. This is easy to do on days when the sun is fitful. It can burn the retina, causing irreversible damage which may not be noticed at the time. Professional seamen seldom wear sunglasses, preferring to train their eyebrows to jut like yardbrooms and to observe the world through slitted eyes. Nonetheless, Polaroids can be helpful if you are looking up-sun. If bright reflections give you headaches, add a broad-brimmed hat or an eye shade.

There's nothing that drives you out of your senses
Like constantly losing your contact lenses.

Talk to your optician about the advisability or otherwise of using these at sea, and ask him to check for colour blindness, which would preclude unsupervised night watchkeeping. Eyes are priceless: guard them well.

Falls

Much of what was said under Bodily Damage is equally valid for falls. Apart from damage to fingers from tools, we observe falling to be the major cause of damage to yachtsmen, resulting in a wide variety of lesions, from bruises and scrapes to the very common cracked ribs, through broken bones of all kinds up to skull and vertebral fractures.

Good handholds and the right shoes go a long way in avoiding these injuries. In weather when the ship's motion is very jerky, clip on and hold on, and only move when necessary.

Bill and I hold opposite views about cockpit cushions: I like plenty of them to cushion me when I get thrown off balance; Bill thinks there are too many, as he falls over them if they get dislodged.

A padded coat or lifejacket can save bruises to the upper part of the body. I sometimes inflate my pilot jacket a little to enable me to bounce off hard edges.

Your steering or helmsman's seat should be difficult to fall out of, as well as comfortable to sit in.

Mop, ah, mop those spills away,
Before you crack your vertebrae.

Flip-flops are for wearing ashore only. They are highly dangerous. We knew a paraplegic who acquired his injury by catching the rung of a ladder between his toes and the sole of his flip-flops. He fell 30 feet.

Peeing over the side in a rough sea is an excellent way to fall overboard, however alluring it might be not to have to go below. There is evidence to show that attacks of faintness (known as vagal inhibition, chaps) can occur during this process, which make it even more dangerous. How about constructing a 'pig's ear' as the Navy calls it? Make a funnel from the top of a plastic bottle: an opaque one for aesthetic preference; attach it firmly to a length of hose which will reach over the side, then hang the business end within reach of the cockpit. A little ingenuity with the design of the funnel even allows us disadvantaged females to use it, instead of getting our bottoms splashed by the rollicking seas in the toilet bowl.

Heat exhaustion

This is nothing to do with sunstroke; it is caused by working in hot humid conditions. The danger arises with temperatures of over 27°C, (80°F), combined with high relative humidity. Increasing bad temper and bolshiness on the part of a normally co-operative crew is an indicator. A sufferer will be cool, sweaty, and pale. Prevention is a question of allowing the cook a heavier hand with the salt, and plying the crew with anchovies and highly seasoned salami. Keep cool and stay in the shade if possible. Stokers in the Navy used to be given pints of salty lemonade to prevent heat exhaustion.

Heatstroke, sunstroke
More catastrophic, but less common than heat exhaustion. The sufferer will not be sweating, and become very hot. Acclimatise yourself gently to hot weather and strong sun. Wear light clothing and a hat. Stay in the shade and keep decks and crew cool with buckets of sea water. Drink plenty of fresh water and don't be mean with the salt.

Herpes (cold sores)
Avoid sun on the lips, as it excites the herpes virus into action. So does wind, dryness, and a raised body temperature. Wear a shady hat, and use a sunscreen or lipsalve. We find Zovirax ointment effective.

Hypothermia
'Not so much as a cloth to shift him, shaking with cold'

In our young days, something vaguely termed 'suffering from exposure' attacked mountaineers, fell walkers, and shipwreck survivors. Old people and babies died, too, in their homes. After years of study and research, it is now called hypothermia and is recognised as a killer. Not only in cold climates, take note. It is now suggested that yachtsmen at risk, whether in the water or in a liferaft, actually succumb to hypothermia more often than drowning. If they are in the water, it is hypothermia which probably causes them to drown.

Since this is at present the most likely cause of death at sea, know the enemy. Hypothermia is a serious loss of heat from the deep areas of the body. If the inner body temperature falls below 32°C (87°F) the prospects are not good. Your clinical thermometer is no use for these deep body temperatures, which are caused by heat being leached away from the body without being replaced. This can happen when immersed in cold or even cool water, when exposed to wind without proper clothing, or, as in the case of the very old and the very young, through malfunctioning of the body's heat regulators.

The time it takes to get into this condition is idiosyncratic; if you are strong and physically fit – even, dare one say, fat – you will last longer than someone of smaller build who is equally fit. Well-covered people have an initial advantage as they store more heat, but lose their edge when they tire more rapidly and become exhausted. Children cool faster than adults. Cold water leaches the heat away faster than cold dry air, and wind chills you very fast.

Prevention Your sailing clothes are important. They should protect you from wet and wind, and have some insulating (air-retentive) properties. The former is provided by waterproof foul weather gear, and the latter by wearing under it anything that will trap air, such as a knitted garment, or a foam lining. Those furry garments – sometimes called polar suits – trap the air in the pile, and are comfortable. However, as they are of man-made fibres, a woollen jersey over them is a good idea, as wet wool is a better insulator than wet nylon and actually generates a little heat.

Even on a warm night, a sudden strong wind can chill you rapidly. It is as well to have a windproof jacket and a woolly hat handy. Preventing loss of heat from the head (20% heat loss is through the scalp), hands and toes becomes important in colder climates, and there is no substitute for wool. Wet nylon socks will not keep you warm, but having said that, once you get to survival level, anything is better than nothing.

SIGNS TO WATCH FOR

- The person may not realise that he is dangerously cold.
- He may be shivering. (This is beneficial, as it generates heat.)
- He may be awkward and clumsy, and his movements and speech be very slow.
- His mind may feel like porridge, and a state of lethargy can set in, preventing self-help.

THINGS TO DO

- If you suspect hypothermia, prevent further heat loss.
- Remove the person from the water or wind.
- Get him below. If possible, replace wet clothes with dry ones; otherwise, wrap him in a foil space blanket.
- Cover the head with a woolly hat, and mouth and nose with a closely wound scarf to prevent heat loss from the lungs.
- *Do not leave him alone*, as he is capable of irrational behaviour, including removing all his clothes.
- Encourage a little activity if he is not exhausted. If he is conscious, give hot, sweet, drinks, but *no alcohol*, which causes central heat loss and a dangerous fall in the blood sugar.

It is much more important to *prevent further heat loss* than to try artificial warming by means of hot water bottles or baths, as this can bring the heat to the body surface at the expense of the deep organs. If the sufferer can get into a *warm* bath without help, it is safe for him to have one.

Survival in the water   Stay with the boat or wreckage. Float, don't swim. Swimming dissipates heat. If you are not alone, cluster with the others, try to roll into a ball to reduce the heat loss from your body.

Infantile diarrhoea

This is probably the most dangerous thing that could happen to your baby or toddler, apart from severe sunburn. The baby becomes progressively dehydrated until he is seriously ill. To combat dehydration in children (and adults as well if need be) you can obtain a double-ended plastic spoon which has been developed for Third World mothers. Salt goes in one end of the spoon, and sugar in the other, and both are stirred into a glass of boiled water until dissolved. One glass for a child, and two for adults, is taken after every attack of diarrhoea. This cheap and simple device has saved more lives than kidney machines. The address to send for the spoon is in Appendix C, but if you encounter any difficulties here are the quantities: ½ teaspoon salt, 2 level tablespoons sugar or honey, *dissolved in a litre of boiled water.* (Dissolving is important because your body cannot use the salt otherwise.) Alternatively, ask your chemist for Dioralyte sachets, a ready-made mixture of sodium chloride (salt), potassium chloride, soda bicarbonate and glucose, for mixing with 200cc (7 fluid ounces) water. They will be more expensive than the salt and sugar mixture, but can be used even for tiny babies.

Legionnaire's disease

This risk is present if the boat is left for a few months, when plastic water tanks and pipes encourage the growth of the *Legionella* bacteria, which are then spread in a fine droplet spray from the shower. After a spell of disuse, clean empty water tanks and pipes with chlorine, then flush through thoroughly with plenty of fresh water before refilling.

Low morale

'For when a man is ill or at the point of death, I would know whether a dish of buttered rice with a little Cynamon, ginger and sugar . . . bee not better . . . than salt fishe . . .'

Sooner or later the time comes when nothing goes well, and everyone feels low and grouchy. I have said earlier that food and drink are important: now is the time to break out something special for the next meal. In the meantime, splice the mainbrace or have a coffee with some rum in it, or eat a whole candy bar.

The aftermath of bad experiences takes its toll of all the crew, not always in the same way. Some talk a lot, some do not talk at all. Some sleep at once, some cannot sleep. Some are elated because it is over; others worry in case it happens again. All need comfort and reassurance. What we sailors have known about for years and dealt with by simple humanity has now a fancy name – post-traumatic stress disorder – and become the province ashore of professional counsellors. These do nothing that tact, understanding, and mutual support from your mates cannot do as well or better. Talk it all through, as often as is needed. A recognition that it takes different people different ways is at the heart of everyone's recovery.

If we found it hard to sleep after an exhausting (even frightening) experience, a tablet of Serene or Kwells was an effective calmer. If something stronger was needed, 5mg of diazepam usually did the trick, without fogging our heads in the morning, as stronger tranquillisers are apt to do. Usually, however, our best practice after such events was to talk the shock away for an hour or two over a stiff brandy or gin, to cut the adrenalin. When we felt sufficiently unwound, we went to bed and usually slept like logs.

Morale on board is a delicate flower. It has to be nurtured and tended with care. We have met yachts where it seems to have broken down completely: everyone moving well away from each other in a heavy silence, speaking to us and other strangers without looking at us, in tones that are too loud. Someone is often crying down below; and you can bet she will be the first to recover.

I have said something already about mutual support between skipper and crew. This must extend, gentlemen, to allowing your ladies a good cry, after an exhausting or terrifying experience. Most women are immensely strong mentally and can also call on more physical strength than might be thought, if need be. They will do whatever is necessary, beyond what you could have hoped for. They will fight fires, pump valiantly, bail like demons, staunch the blood, and hang on to the uttermost.

They will cope, beyond the point of pain and exhaustion, like the human beings they are. When there is no more to be done, they are likely to burst into tears. Men react indignantly to this. They feel it as a reflection on their actions; but crying is no more a criticism of him than his heartfelt swearing at a sulky generator is a reflection on her. What is more, tears are as beneficial as a cold beer on a sweltering day. Better, since there is some evidence to show that a natural anaesthetic is released into the brain when someone cries. No wonder it is such a relief. Try crying a bit more, chaps: it's good for you.

> *After the storm is over*
> *Indulge in a real good cry,*
> *Swallow a whisky and water*
> *And dinner with lots of pie.*
> *Comforting words should be spoken*
> *Helping you sleep till morn,*
> *Harmony need not be broken*
> *After the storm.*

Malaria

This dreadful disease is caused by the bite of certain mosquitoes. It is on the increase and must be taken seriously. We are collecting more and more evidence that shows that taking tablets of brewer's yeast alters the taste of your blood to the point where mosquitoes say 'Yuk, gross', and cease to bite you.

There are pills to prevent malaria. You must start them well in advance, and continue after you leave the area known to be infested. IAMAT, previously mentioned, and MASTA, and the Department of Health, have good information. Unfortunately malaria is becoming resistant to the present range of remedies. See also Chapter Seven on pests, but the following preventative measures should be taken.

Avoid mosquito bites, either by burning pastilles or coils, using sprays or creams when awake and active, or when asleep, a mosquito net. In the evenings wear long-sleeved shirts and trousers tucked into socks. Proof your portholes with gauze. And take your preventative pills rigorously, starting well before, and continuing well after your visit, following instructions implicitly.

Malnutrition and deficiency diseases

Most ocean passages last less than a month, so it is unlikely that you are going to stagger ashore with beriberi or pellagra at the end of your voyage, especially if you paid attention to the chapter on victualling. However, multivitamin pills take up no space at all and might be useful. One of the really long passages is that made by cruisers from Australia and New Zealand, who come across the Indian Ocean and up the Red Sea to the Mediterranean. The time for this is the dry north-east monsoon, which means that fresh water is critically short and hard to replace. We have seen these folk arrive in the Mediterranean in poor shape, skinny (easily remedied), but with salt-water boils and ulcers that are hard to heal. The protein-rich cereal mixtures in Chapter Ten (victualling) could help to prevent these. For the boils (gunnel bum), see *Skin trouble* below.

Noxious diseases of all kinds

Your life will be changing completely. Would it be so hard to use this opportunity to stop smoking? Apart from the good effect it will have on your health and finances (and you will not find low-tar and filter tips in the remoter areas), smoking in the confined space below decks of a small yacht is literally nauseating and conducive to seasickness. Think about it.

Rabies

Get your ship's cat or dog vaccinated (see Chapter Seven), and in areas where rabies is endemic warn the children not to pet animals they may find ashore.

Animal bites must be treated seriously in any country where rabies is a possibility. Try to educate your children out of the pretty pussy mindset, and to treat all animals, wild or domesticated, warily and with great respect: look, but don't touch. If bitten, even if you have been vaccinated against rabies, seek medical help. In the meantime clean the wound as best you can with cetrimide or alcohol – gin or vodka will do.

Seasickness

This can spoil your enjoyment of (anyway) the first two days of your voyage. There is much that can be done to minimise its likelihood and shorten its duration. You could be one of those who are never ill at all, or one of the unfortunates who are very sick indeed for a long time.

It is a comfort to know that on a long voyage the large majority of people are over the worst on the second day. Thereafter a sensible regime will prevent its recurrence, even in rough seas, unless prolonged galley or engine room work are attempted.

To cut seasickness down to a minimum:

- Don't go to sea with a hangover.
- Go into a rough sea with the stomach warm and comfortably full of something fairly stodgy: stew with lots of potatoes, pilaf, pasta or porridge.
- Have an extra jersey handy; it is important not to get chilled and you might not want to go below for it. Best start off too warm; you can always discard.
- Try not to get too tired. Do whatever is necessary, and rest between tasks, up on deck if you can.
- Spell the helmsman, drive a bit. Drivers are seldom sick.

Preventatives　The most effective drug, statistically, is hyoscine hydrobromide. The stronger pills need a prescription; milder ones are available over the counter – such as Kwells (tablets) or Scopoderm-TTS (skin patches) which are better if you are likely to vomit. Avomine (promethazine theoclate) (now that dramamine has been discontinued) is almost as good; it is a question of finding out what suits you and taking it at least half an hour before it is likely to be needed. Sea Legs (meclozine) may be taken the night before sailing. Stugeron, Marzine, (both cinnarizine) and Valoid (cyclizine) are less likely to make you drowsy, and are therefore less useful as mild sedatives. None of these drugs should be accompanied by alcohol, which is anyway not a good idea in bad weather.

> *When storms begin*
> *Lay off the gin.*

Some people find pressure wristbands, working on the acupuncture theory, to be very effective.

If you can, keep eating. If you cannot face real food, nibble dry crackers or crispbread, and have an occasional sweet fizzy drink: a swallow or two of beer is surprisingly good, ginger ale not far behind; it's the fizz that counts.

As a last resort, lie down, for'd if running before the wind or aft if going to windward. (This takes one set of the semi-circular canals in your ear out of action, and so you feel less giddy.)

> *Take in time your seasick pill*
> *Otherwise you will be ill.*
> *Tummy warm and full of food*
> *Helps to keep you feeling good.*
> *Too much booze the night before*
> *Makes you toss your cookies more.*
> *Cold your body, head and toes,*
> *Overboard your breakfast goes.*
> *Nibble, nibble all the day*
> *To hold your queasy tum at bay;*
> *A gill of beer or ginger ale*
> *Will stay your stomach through the gale.*
> *Should you feel that death is near,*
> *Lying down you'll feel less queer.*

Skin trouble

Ulcers and boils (gunnel bum, in the racing world) are caused by constant contact with salt water, such as occurs on the long run from Australia up to the Red Sea. With water so desperately short, none can be spared for washing to remove the salt from the skin.

It would be well worth taking a large quantity of wet wipes: even one a day would get some of the salt off. Paper underpants make a lot of sense, too. Cocoa butter is soothing, and speeds healing. Multivitamin pills also help healing; a good diet is even better (see Chapter Ten).

Stomach upsets

'. . . And then if their Victuals be putrified it indangers all'

Assuming that you have had your TAB shots, get further immunity by eating and drinking locally. Take the normal precautions of washing or peeling fruit and vegetables just before you eat them. Boiling the water we have not found necessary anywhere, but with a small baby you may feel it essential, or if you yourself are susceptible and worried about the water source. Purifying tablets are available, both for large and small quantities of water. Most are based on chlorine. Small water filters are available for travellers.

Since a chronic water shortage leads to skimping the washing up, it is sensible to have two separate chopping boards. Keep one strictly for raw meat, fish or chicken and stow its appropriate knife with it. The other is for cooked meat, bread and cleaned raw vegetables for salads. It too has its own knife.

Stomach disorders are usually caused by one of the Fs: food, flies or faeces, so keep the first clean and cool, murder the second mercilessly (see Chapter Seven), and don't skimp the personal hygiene and hand washing: use medicated wipes if shortage of water is a problem. Keep some in the heads, with a bin for used ones.

We ran into trouble with stomach disorders on our return from the USA, when we visited Tangier. We had obviously lost our resistance in the two years we had spent in the ultra-sanitised States, and Tangier is not a good place to be sensitive in. We suffered somewhat, but our Mediterranean immunity soon re-established itself.

Remember that alcohol is a great bug killer. 'Take a little wine, for thy stomach's sake, and thine often infirmities,' as St Paul advised St Timothy. Our eminent authority states that 'a little wine' can be reckoned as up to half a litre a day!

Stress

You have gone to a great deal of trouble to leave stress behind. Make sure that you also leave behind such lingering habits of the old life as hurrying to get somewhere, working from morning till night, or putting the engine on merely because it is faster. There will be quite enough to challenge you in the months ahead without looking for extra work. Use the lazy windless days to store well-being and energy, as well as learning how to cope when the weather turns foul, things go wrong, and everyone is needed to the utmost. This is certain to happen, even if you neither girdle the earth nor round Cape Horn. If you do decide that you want to do these heroic things, beware that a sense of compulsion does not creep in, and with it a loss of that carefree feeling that you are doing what you want and not what you must. That is not the way of laid-back cruising. Nor is the driving urge to 'get your ticket punched', as we have heard circumnavigation and crossing the Atlantic described: trying to do this in a limited time probably causes as much pointless hassle as staying in the cut-throat world of business or fighting for your job ashore.

The way to circumnavigate or cruise without stress is to have no time limit and do it almost by accident, strolling from island to island and continent to continent.

> *Blue sky and green water pour into your mind;*
> *The balm of the world, landsman's daughter,*
> *You sought so long to find.*

Sunburn

Millions of words of warning are printed every year, yet one sees the boiled-lobster effect wherever there is a bit of sun and wind. Patience and a good sunscreen lotion are all that is required; you cannot get a deep-water suntan in three days, you will merely have your skin crispy-broiled. Take a total sunblock cream: apart from prevention it can alleviate even a nasty sunburn. Protect noses, lips, bald pates and the tops of your feet. If you stayed in the shade for a fortnight in hot sunny weather, you would still achieve a pleasant tan and no burns. Conversely you can burn even on a cloudy day

Sun is not always beneficial. Even with a good protective tan you can get skin cancer, which is on the increase. This is less likely if you are black, lucky thing.

Thrush (vaginal candidiasis)

This distressing complaint can be discouraged by wearing loose-fitting cotton (never man-made fibres) next to the skin. The contraceptive pill can predispose you to thrush. Take with you something to cope with it, like Canestan.

Water contamination

To prevent:

- Do not let the water hose fall in the dock.
- Keep the hose clean and protected. (It will last much longer if you don't leave it in strong sunlight, though this can give you a wonderful hot shower.)
- Before you top up, direct a jet at the tap or standpipe to clean it: shore people can be very careless where they walk their dogs.
- 30 grains of stabilised chloride of lime to 100 gallons of water will destroy all organisms in it, but so will a little alcohol in your drinking glass and it tastes better.

Worms

(See Chapter Seven.) If you are interested in *herbal remedies*, try 2–3 cloves of fresh garlic bulb, or ¹/₂ teasp of the juice. Or, to eliminate roundworms and threadworms, and paralyse tapeworms: steep shredded pomegranate bark in a tightly closed container, reduce by half, and take 4oz followed by a purgative. Better to use modern remedies such as Pripsen, which do not require purgatives afterwards.

THE MEDICINE CHEST

'. . . *Also that his chest be well furnished bothe for Physicke and Chirurgery and so near as may be proper for the clime you go for*'

Here follows a list of what we took (after much discussion with our doctor and other authorities); what we used it for; and whether we used it at all. In the 25 years since our first departure many improvements and discoveries have been made, so I also give an update and a list of additions that we found necessary. (POM indicates a 'prescription only medicine'. Ampoules are for injections.

WHAT WE TOOK AND USED

(POM) Ampicillin: Broad-spectrum antibiotic. *Update*: (POM) Amoxil.
Aspirin tablets, soluble: headache and colds, minor aches.
Cream of magnesia: Indigestion. *Update*: Aludrox.
Burrow's Solution: Still available as aluminium acetate lotion, for fungus infections. *Update*: Canesten cream.
Chloramine tablets: For water purifying. *Update*: Sterotabs, Katadyn Micropur.
(POM) Diazepam 5mg capsules: Tranquilliser (for sleeping in severe storms when nothing can be done but wait.)
(POM) Hyoscine hydrobromide (Scopolamine): For seasickness.
Kaolin and morphine mixture: BP: 'Concrete mixture', for diarrhoea.
Kwells tablets: Useful as a mild sedative as well as seasickness.
Multivitamin tablets: To prevent deficiency diseases.
Paracetamol capsules: For headache, toothache, colds, etc.
(POM) Tetracycline tablets: Broad-spectrum antibiotic

LATER WE ALSO ADDED:

(POM) Distalgesic tablets: For moderate to severe pain. *Update*: (POM) Dihydrocodeine.
Nurofen for flu, rheumatic aches, toothache.
(POM) Scopoderm-TTS: hyoscine hydrobromide skin patches.
Stugeron (cinnarizine): For seasickness.
(POM) Tetanus vaccine.
(POM) Xylocaine cream: Local anaesthetic.

WHAT WE TOOK BUT NEVER USED

(POM) Adrenaline ampoules: 1:10000: Shock or severe drug reaction.
(POM) Atropine: Narcotic, relaxes gastro-intestinal tract. *Update*: (POM) ProBanthine.
(POM) Benzedrine, 4 tablets: For emergencies requiring short-term prolongation of alertness.
(POM) Benadryl Antihistamine: For allergic reactions. *Update*: Triludan.
Codeine: Now withdrawn from sale. See paracetamol above.
(POM) Decadron: Severe allergies, shock and venom. *Update*: Piriton.
(POM) Diazepam ampoules: Potent tranquilliser.
Dioralyte powder: Against dehydration.
Gelusil tablets: Antacid. *Update*: Aludrox tablets.
(POM) Lasix: Diuretic, for use after near drowning in salt water.
(POM) Lomotil: For severe diarrhoea.
(POM) Naprosyn tablets: Muscular and skeletal pain (eg discs).
(POM) Nitrazepam, 5mg capsules: Sleeping tablets.
(POM) Penicillin VK tablets: Antibiotic. *Update*: (POM) Magnapen.
(POM) Pethidine ampoules: Narcotic for pain relief.
(POM) Septrin tablets: For those allergic to penicillin. *Update*: methoprim.
Senokot tablets: constipation. A rare condition, we found.
(POM) Xylocaine ampoules: Local anaesthetic.

As you see, about one-third of this list was never used in 25 years of travel from the USA to Turkey, from Calais to the Ukraine. The more heroic measures were there if they were needed, kept in a locked drawer. We were told later that we would have been justified in using one of the narcotic pain-killing ampoules on one occasion, but it was run-of-the-mill remedies we mostly needed: antibiotics, paracetamol, kaolin and morphine mixture and mild painkillers. As it should be.

• *Before you go* •

Thorough discussion with a qualified person will be necessary, not only because you will need prescriptions (and not necessarily on the NHS either), but also an explanation of how and when to use these things.

THE FIRST AID KIT

Whatever container you keep this in, it ought to be fairly near the cockpit (which tends to become the casualty centre) and easily accessible. A list of the whereabouts of more bulky items (large dressings, bandages, and the applicators for the larger sizes of tubegauze, for example) should be stuck into the lid or otherwise firmly attached.

List One is what we took when we started; List Two contains later additions due either to increasing age or experience (POM means we needed a prescription).

LIST ONE

(WHAT WE TOOK AND USED)

Acriflavin ointment: For burns.

Adhesive dressing strip and Elastoplast (finger plasters): We use hundreds of these. The waterproof ones don't seem to stick as well as the fabric ones.

Anti-sting cream: Mosquito bites, wasp and jellyfish stings.

(POM) Aureomycin ointment: Antibacterial, for cuts and abrasions.

Calamine cream: Minor skin itch, and sunburn.

Clinical thermometer. (see Fever Tester, in List Two).

Cotton wool

Crepe bandages: Can be washed and reused.

Butterfly sutures: Never successful, as the victim was always sweating and no matter how much we swabbed they would not stick.

Eye bath: For washing out foreign bodies with saline solution.

Fisherman's Friend: Rubbing ointment (no, not the pastilles!) for sprains, wrenches and muscle pain.

(POM) Furacin ointment: Antibacterial, for burns or wounds.

Golden Eye ointment (withdrawn, see *Neobacrin*.)

Mercurochrome stick: Used like iodine, stays on better in sea water.

(POM) Neobacrin eye ointment.

(POM) Nystan ointment: Thrush and athlete's foot. *Update*: Canesten cream.

Roll of adhesive plaster (tape): The Bandaid type from the USA came unstuck within ten minutes: we were glad to get back to Elastoplast.

Safety pins.

Scissors and tweezers: *never to be taken away and used elsewhere!* (Have a separate set in the lifeboat bag.)

Sterile packs of wound dressings in several sizes.

TCP antiseptic liquid: For disinfecting minor cuts.

Tubegauze bandages and applicators, in four sizes from toes to torsos. We used only the two smaller sizes. A particularly neat form of bandage.

We took a gross of disposable hypodermic syringes, with needles. We have never used them, and today's suspicious world being what it is, we recently took them to a pharmacy for safe disposal.

LIST TWO

(THINGS WE ADDED LATER AND WERE USEFUL)

Aerosol burn spray: Now kept near the stove.

Cicatrin: Antibiotic powder for wounds. Less painful to apply than ointments.

Fever Tester: A temperature-sensitive plastic film applied to the forehead; takes up no room, is unbreakable, but cannot be used rectally. There are several kinds of plastic thermometers nowadays.

Ice Pak: A once-only shake-and-apply ice pack for bad bruises. No need to store in the fridge. We got ours in the USA, but similar products are now obtainable in the UK. We now use a freezing spray which can be reused many times (Urgofroid, made in France). If you have a freezer there is nothing better than a pack of frozen peas for bruises and sprains, administered externally, of course.

LIST TWO continued

Low voltage electric blanket: For aches, flu, and general misery.
Nobecutane spray: Forms a sterile plastic coating over wounds or burns.
Oil of cloves and zinc oxide powder: for temporary tooth filling.
Sterile burn dressings: Sofra tulle, Opsite etc.

WERE ADDED BUT NEVER USED

A Brooke Airway, for resuscitation.
Disposable mini enemas (Microlax).
Disposable scalpels: After the fishhook episode.
Fluorescein stain: For finding damage to cornea.
Labstix: For testing urine.
Prepacked sutures, already attached to needle. For closing wounds.
Rectal thermometer (blue bulb): For measuring hypothermia.

Murphy's Law being what it is, since we got the scalpels and sutures we
have not required them again.

May you also never need what you have prudently taken with you.

16 • Cruising Grounds

'One to the top to look out for lande'

This chapter is devoted to cruising grounds we like and have cruised fairly recently and the best routes between them. Though tempted, we have avoided going back too far on our nostalgia tack. Things have changed too fast, and not only the places themselves.

There are nowadays many more live-aboards than there were (some people blame us for that, but they cannot be serious) and there is no doubt that some traditional cruising grounds have become more crowded. Very often we, long-distance live-aboard cruisers, 'discover' a wonderful cruising ground that is well detached from commerce, only to find that, eventually, an airstrip is built, and the charter yacht industry moves in, flying dozens of crews out for short holidays in locally based yachts. You can't fight this. It's difficult even to grumble, though we do so now and then. But the two forms of yachting are not wholly compatible.

The short-term charter sailor crams into his fortnight as much activity as he can. He is in holiday spending mode. And he spends in a concentrated manner. The long-term cruiser is less frenetic, more careful with his money which has to last. The charter parties raise prices, their operators negotiate special concessions for berthing and so on, and inevitably the yachtie moves on to discover somewhere else where the vandals of industrial yachting will inevitably follow.

And as the number of live-aboards also increases, we are getting significantly more adventurous. One has only to read such publications as *Roving Commissions* (the annual journal of the Royal Cruising Club) to see the extraordinary places to which some yachties go. Would you believe one couple spending two years in the Antarctic Circle? Someone else seeking out the North West Passage round Canada? A voyage from Britain to the Arctic Circle and then from the White Sea to the Black Sea through the Russian Rivers?

Cruising grounds, did we say? The world is the live-aboard's cruising ground.

However, most people contemplating this life have a palm tree in the vision somewhere, so I will start with the warm weather and palm trees par excellence:

THE WEST INDIES

We begin our overview at Trinidad, close to the South American shore, and include the Windward Islands, the Leewards, Dominican Republic, Haiti, Puerto Rico, Cuba, Jamaica and a few smaller units. Most have a mixed colonial history, and the main population is of African descent from slaves. Some islands are very poor with unstable or uncertain economies; others have become more prosperous by exploiting tourism.

To nautical tourists such as ourselves, there is a pull towards the Windward Islands (the Grenadines, St Vincent, St Lucia, and Martinique) and afterwards to the more diffuse Leewards; Dominica round to the Virgins. The parts farther west, Puerto Rico to Cuba, once less attractive for political reasons, are beginning to offer scope for visits, and even the central American isthmus, once best avoided except for the brave, is beginning to be cruised again. There are also the islands off the coast of South America from Trinidad to Curaçao, the smaller of which are becoming more popular; though being downwind of the main group they are not so convenient to cruise.

The major fly in the ointment for the private cruising yacht in this whole area is the large fleet of bare-boat charter yachts. Some are private craft let out on the occasional charter and these are no problem: the difficulties arise from what we call industrial chartering. The boats are often badly equipped, badly maintained, and too often badly sailed. The usual customers are Americans. The USA probably has more private cruising yachts than the rest of the world put together and probably more competent yachtsmen to sail them. In the same proportions, she has also more boorish idiots, and it seems that many of these holiday in a bare-boat in the Caribbean.

Search and rescue facilities in this area are scant and these charterers, used at home to nannying by the US Coast Guard, put out a scandalous number of distress calls, many for trivial reasons and others for want of elementary prudence. All vessels are bound by law to answer distress calls. Sadly, the professional, crewed, charter yachts have been driven to ignoring these calls, judging 99% of them to be frivolous. Tough on anyone in real trouble!

In addition, the bare-boat fleets have established bases which reserve for their exclusive use facilities which were once available to all. Either that or they charge discriminatory rates for private boats that are not acceptable to live-aboards. People on a three-week holiday from a very prosperous country can outbid longer-term visitors for the scarce resources, bringing high prices, the main benefits of which go to external investors and do not reach the local people. Local politicians should remember that the local tourism that keeps their islands solvent was started by private yachtsmen, and it is ungrateful deliberately to squeeze them out.

The pleasures of the area outweigh the minor irritations. There are wonderful anchorages and beaches, and the sailing between is excellent and free of great danger from December to May. We found, almost without exception, the local people friendly, extrovert and cheerful, the officials good-humoured and courteous. Generally, the poorer the community, the nicer the people and officials, and it was in the more prosperous Virgin Islands that we found the only examples of rudeness, and even those were not too bad.

Formalities are generally not irksome. Almost every island is a separate sovereign state, so that a lot of clearing and entering has to be done and a lot of expensive courtesy ensigns carried. Most islands make a modest entry charge, and some yachtsmen resent this because harbours tend to be open anchorages; but considering that the islands are poor, such a charge is hard to find unreasonable.

The cost of living in the islands is based on the US dollar (apart from the French islands, which are heavily subsidised by France). Much of the foodstuff is imported from the USA, often by air, so that these items are expensive except the ubiquitous frozen chicken. Stocking up in Martinique with its Galllic attitude to the importance of food is a pleasure after months in the wilderness, since apart from the wealthier, more developed islands, up-market foods are hard to find. Yacht chandleries have improved except in the more backward islands, but they are not cheap. Repairs can be undertaken at Antigua and Grenada, where there are boatyards with reasonable craftsmen, slipways, and berths with electricity for a self-refit.

Mail from Britain or the USA to the islands is generally good, mobile phone services are good and the international telephone service is improving. Flights are good and frequent but heavily booked at Christmas, New Year and Easter. Air freight is recommended for parcels. European flights go regularly to Antigua, Barbados, Grenada, Trinidad and the French islands; and the smaller inter-island services are busy and efficient, if sometimes hair-raising. Landing on Union Island or St Bart's is not for the faint-hearted.

Montserrat Air Lines used to run a well-ordered air ambulance service that was welcome because medical services on many islands are not very sophisticated, but the erupting volcano on the island has put a stop to that and many other businesses. It is as well to have medical insurance with a repatriation clause in the West Indies because hospital facilities in the islands are limited.

Diesel fuel is conveniently obtained in only a few places, but as the wind is so reliable, pleasant and free, diesel does not loom large in most people's minds. The most convenient points that I found were at Grenada (St George's), Martinique, English Harbour and St Thomas. If a really large amount of fuel is needed, go to Venezuela, where it is extremely cheap.

The weather is pleasant during the winter. The temperatures are moderated by the trade wind, which is usually about force 4 but does rise occasionally especially in certain channels. The most I recorded in one winter was force 6 off Kick 'em Jenny, near Grenada, where the seas were also unusually disturbed. Vulcanologists are now predicting a volcanic eruption in this area. It rains every few days, usually a sharp shower which should be used for topping up tanks, for fresh water is not easy to get in quantity. During this season hurricanes hardly hever happen.

In summer the weather is not so pleasant, but to compensate there are fewer tourists. It is hotter, wetter, a bit more capricious, and hurricanes do happen though they are not by any means an everyday event. The old rhyme tells you when they start:

'June too soon,
July by and by,
August you must,
September remember,
October it's over.'

Do not rely too much on this doggerel: we were damaged in Hurricane Alberto on 18 June, 1982, farther north, off Bermuda. If you are in the Caribbean there is a wealth of local knowledge of hurricane holes in which to get secure and what precautions to take. These matters are out of the scope of this book; my hurricane experiences (two) have both been well offshore; the best place to be, we think. It is quite another thing close to land. Well out to sea the winds are steadier, the seas tend to be longer, lower (except in the dangerous semi-circle of a tropical storm) and more predictable. The rise in sea level caused by the extraordinarily low atmospheric pressure is scarcely noticeable deep-sea; a rise that builds up as it approaches shallower water and causes the celebrated tidal wave (which is not tidal at all).

Charts and Navigational Publications are hard to get. For electronic or technical repairs, I found English Harbour the only worthwhile centre. Most services can be contacted on VHF. In fact, in the West Indies, almost everyone can be contacted on VHF: Sam Taxi, the scuba shops, the restaurants, and even hairdressers (callsign: *teeny weenie sweenie* or some such); some restaurants make a general call on channel 16 to inform all stations that their menu for tonight is on Channel 68, and bookings can also be taken thus. The radio is seldom silent, but on the whole, the system functions very well: it is because everyone uses the radio that one finds it useful in a way not possible in over-regulated Europe or the USA. The radio discipline is better than on Long Island Sound or in the Solent on a weekend.

As one goes farther west, the cruising gets less congenial. Big money dominates the Virgin Islands scene, marinas are found, and sophistication brings higher prices. By the time you reach St Thomas, you are in an American city and the supermarkets are well stocked, but the people lack the good manners of the poorer islands, and crime rates are higher. The welcome is often still good, but there is something missing.

The US Navy makes a nuisance of itself exercising north of Puerto Rico. Cuba used to be off-limits for British insurers, but I expect this is changing. I have not been to Jamaica recently, but have heard reports that it is not currently advisable. One reads alarmist articles in magazines about piracy, violence and robbery (see Chapter Eleven).

If one needs to leave a boat, say for an emergency visit home, the marina in St George's, Grenada, has good security; alternatively, there are facilities in English Harbour. Up-market marinas, at up-market prices, exist in Antigua, Tortilla, St Thomas and St Lucia.

CHRISTMAS IN THE WINDWARD ISLANDS

We lay at anchor in the big sheltered bay of a small island. An occasional sharp blow from the wrong direction needed prudence to watch neighbouring yachts keenly in case their crew were ashore when we all changed places like the cross-over sequence in a barn dance. Mostly, however, the weather was warm and lazy; we rowed ashore daily for brown loaves freshly baked in a wood shingled cabin. A covey of boys would 'watch your dinghy, man' for a copper or two if, instead of hauling it up the beach at the Frangipani, you hitched it to the wooden staithe that led on to the open space where, if anything was for sale, it would be sold. Had someone killed a pig, landed some bonefish, or brought in some vegetables? Apart from this when-it-happens-man market, there were round this space a small, simple grocery store not much bigger than a garage, an everything-shop mainly for tourists, and a tiny Barclays Bank. The Frangipani was a restaurant-bar kept by the Prime Minister with a few rooms to stay in and a sandy dance floor by the beach. It was also the yachtie's mail drop, which gave us an excellent excuse, 'just going for the mail....' There was a complex of chalets for tourists farther round the bay. That was about it.

If you wanted serious Christmas shopping you took the schooner to the big island, a wet and windy passage lasting an hour and a half. You went early, and were back by 1330, offloaded all the packages, boxes and parcels for the grocery store and the bar. Frozen chicken took its chance in the hold with everything else, and was slightly defrosted when it arrived, to be refrozen as quickly as possible in the store's minute freezer. Nobody suffered from eating it.

Dark came at six. After a carol procession in dinghies round the fleet, singing in about six languages, the lamplight gold against the velvet-blue star-sprinkled sky, we rowed ashore in shorts on Christmas Eve for rum punch, barbecued New York strip steak, and a jump-up to the island's steel band.

• *Now, how do you get there from Europe?* •

For a European, the first problem to be faced is getting away. If I say that a voyage direct to North America or the West Indies is contrary to the spirit of the casual wanderer, I think most readers will by now know what I mean. So, we rule out 30 days of beating westward into the winds of a series of depressions. This means that the first stage of a transatlantic voyage is south; not necessarily to Gibraltar, but in that direction.

This is also the open-sea route to the Mediterranean. There are other ways of getting there, and they will be mentioned under inland water routes. For the moment, then, let us look at a passage to Gibraltar, or its vicinity.

• *The Bay of Biscay* •

Your first challenge (if you choose to accept it). It is a sad fact of geography that the first ocean crossing which northern Europeans make on setting out is the Bay, a difficult stretch of water for sailing vessels. A sad fact also that if you, a new cruiser climbing a learning curve, are plucked out of trouble by helicopter, your 15 minutes of fame will be attended by castigation, condemnation, little respect

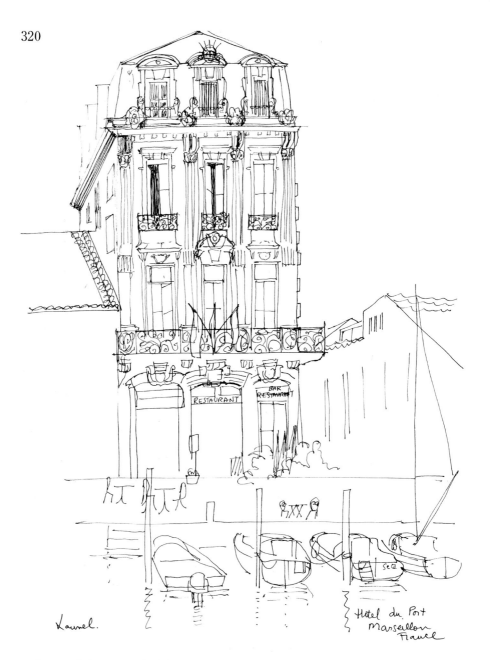

Laurel.

Hôtel du Port
Marseillan
France

and a week later, total oblivion. On the other hand, a racing yachtsman whose Southern Ocean rescue involves expenditure in megamillions, is treated as a hero and there will be a book and a film. It seems hard.

The reputation of the Bay of Biscay stems from the depressions that are characteristic of its weather patterns, causing strong westerly winds which blow craft into the Bay. With a long gale, or a series of short ones in quick succession, the average yacht has difficulty not only in getting out of the bay, but also in surviving the gale itself, for room to manoeuvre gets steadily less and less the more one is embayed. Further into the Bay it shallows, making the seas steeper and more dangerous, and the last part of a typical gale has the wind from the north-west: the worst possible sector.

Old sailing captains leaving the English Channel in weather other than a set-fair anti-cyclone would steer west until longitude 8° west, when they would turn south. It took longer, but that way they stood a fair chance of not becoming a statistic. It seems to us that cruising yachts manned by small inexperienced crews should think of doing just that. Top quality yachts manned by experienced gorillas do as they please, but families, especially with children, should play safe at the beginning of their world cruise.

An alternative is to coast to Cork in Ireland, getting gradually accustomed to the life and having shelter to run to, and then start from there. They're lovely people in Cork, and it's well worth a visit.

In any event, keep well outside the Ushant traffic separation scheme and special tanker channel; it is better to double Ushant out of range of the light. You should do so even if the separation scheme were not in operation, because if bad weather comes the wind is more likely to be west than any other, and it will almost certainly be accompanied by a current pushing a vessel into the bay.

Above all, be prudent.

I would pass down the Portuguese coast well out to sea, out of sight of land, and only close the coast near Cape St Vincent. This headland has a traffic separation scheme round it, which is of doubtful necessity and a hazard of itself. Sailing vessels should round this cape very close to with an easterly wind, in which case they are obliged to foul the badly planned north-bound lane, though there is seldom very much traffic. With a north-westerly wind, which is the most likely, it is well to stay offshore out of the way of the north-bound traffic. Keep a good offing if bound for Gibraltar in order to avoid the banks, for though there is depth for a yacht the seas can be very unpleasant there.

The distance from Falmouth to Gibraltar is 1080 miles, and from Cork it is 1098 miles. Most cruising boats average between 100 and 130 miles per day. We had our best day's run ever in *Fare Well* south-bound some 30 miles off the Portuguese coast, logging 190 miles with only 37 square metres of canvas set. We still took 12 days for the passage because we were hove-to for 48 hours in a Bay of Biscay storm.

• *West-bound across the Atlantic* •

Go south until the butter melts, then turn right; there is not much more to it. If leaving Gibraltar, it is better to wait for a Levanter (east wind), but that often brings poor weather generally. If coming from the north, it pays usually to keep well out and one can sometimes carry the Portuguese trades almost down to the Canary Islands.

Most yachts call at the Canaries, a good place to store ship before a crossing, and it can be quite a social scene there in November. The tradewind belt moves north in winter, and it is better to wait for it to establish itself up to 15°N or so, which usually happens during November. The wind increases, and by January is much stronger. If going to the Caribbean for a long stay, it might be worth spending a couple of months in the Canaries, or making a diversion via the Cape Verde Islands.

Only freak weather should disturb the easy tedium of the transatlantic passage. The occasional squall enables everyone to strip off and have a free shower, but make sure there is enough rain to wash the soap off before putting it on. For the nervous or extremely social, there is the ARC (Atlantic Rally for Cruisers).

THE BAHAMAS

Moving north-westwards from the Caribbean Islands, one comes to the Bahamas, another independent ex-British colony. It was peopled largely by loyalists from the revolting American colonies about 1778 and these white people with their black slaves were the forebears of many of the present inhabitants. In the north, the Abacos, much of the populace are so firmly nonconformist that you might imagine you were in Scotland. You might, but it would be difficult, for the weather and scenery are very different. The Bahamas are flat, palm-clad, sandy islands set on a series of broad shallow banks penetrated by the odd deep-water tongue of ocean. The local industries are tourism and drug dealing, but the latter is a closed shop and the participation of amateurs from outside is much resented and dangerous. It can still be dangerous if you innocently see something you shouldn't; be very tactful, and rather shortsighted.

The southern islands are more remote and less densely populated, with scope for some very quiet cruising, though provisions take some looking for. The northern islands are close to Florida and have large numbers of shorter-term visitors. There is a bay called No Name Bay south of Miami which we selected as a good dawn jumping-off place for a day sail to the Bahamas: so did half a hundred others. The Florida Channel between that state and the Bahamas is one of the busiest waterways in the world, with some very long commercial multi-barge tows using it, and it merits some care when crossing, especially at night.

The Bahamas are islands where souvenirs are few and an artist/craftsman could earn a bit, but the cost of living, being so dependent on nearby Florida, is high.

These islands ought to be prosperous. The currency is at par with the US dollar, but there are local notes in circulation, as well as American ones. The officials are pleasant, courteous, but not noticeably industrious or efficient. Communications are good with Florida, and then from Miami are excellent. Mail and telephone services seemed to be good. The banking system, where it is of British or Canadian origin, is above average.

The other sort of banks, the coral ones, require care. Paradoxically, the *old* British charts are the best. One of these, no 1496, was engraved in 1844 with the last new edition in 1907 and its detail is first class. I occupied myself for some time with checking several of the areas of the banks, and though there were some differences I would say that if used with a little prudence and common sense, this chart is infinitely preferably to the US chart of recent publication. But any chart cannot cope unaided. The latest supplement to the British Admiralty pilots should be carried, but even better are some of the recently published yachtsmen's guides. The chart kits published in Needham, Massachusetts by the Better Boating Association are a good investment and based on US government charts. They are cheap, too.

Care should be taken when using GPS in conjunction with older charts. We don't have to emphasise this, do we?

There are several places to leave a yacht in the Bahamas, but none of them are ideal and many are over-expensive. Unless one's departure is very urgent (in which case Marsh Harbour suggests itself), it would be better to head for Florida, a short trip away. There one finds every possible facility.

• *North-bound from the Caribbean* •

If bound for Florida it is better to go south of the Bahamas Islands. There are some doubts about the surveys east of the Bahamas; ever since a flag officer of the Royal Cruising Club was wrecked there, the charts have been assumed to be wrong.

Seriously, though, there have been quite a few yachts lost in those parts; one should think carefully before closing the low-lying banks. Whether the charts are wrong, or there are unrecorded strong currents, I do not know; nor, I suspect, does anyone else yet. It is not one of the most important bits of ocean.

If bound for the Bermudas, it is as well to start from east of Puerto Rico to be reasonably expectant of a reach. There are no problems. The Bermudas are well lit and clear of off-lying dangers to the south.

Heading to the USA from the Bermudas ought not to be difficult, though we once took 12 days for the 630 miles. We know from bitter experience that this is a passage where one should take a lot of care about the weather. Excellent forecasts are broadcast from Portsmouth, Virginia, by voice on SSB, and some of them are in English. The others are in what my American friend called 'Dixie'.

One of the important features of these forecasts is the relaying of the positions of the edges of the Gulf Stream. This ocean-going river flows at up to 3 knots in this part of the world and makes a lot of difference to a yacht's course made good. The edges are well defined: the northern edge particularly can be recognised with some exactitude by observing the sea-water temperature, which will fall several degrees in a few hours when bound northwards out of the stream and this is a method of getting a position line. Because of the current, very nasty seas can build up when the wind is north-east and gales from this quadrant can be dangerous.

Watch out for fog in the colder waters approaching the New England coast even in high summer. As soon as possible get the local weather forecasts from the special coastal VHF stations. Also, beware of shipping bound to or from New York. There are off-lying dangers near the New England coast so do your homework first and carefully. Take note that by some administrative lunacy, the offshore buoys off Nantucket that would be so useful for a position check in bad weather all have the same light characteristic: flashing white, every 4 seconds.

If having left Bermuda northwards you are tempted to return for any reason, then consider very carefully before doing so. The offlying reefs to the north-west of the islands are dangerous; and very dangerous in bad weather, being poorly lit and comparatively steep-to.

THE EAST COAST OF THE USA

There are many people who spend their lives cruising the Intra-Coastal Waterway between Chesapeake Bay and the Florida Keys. The Chesapeake is a bay of great size, which can get rough on occasions but has many delightful places to visit. Washington has been largely rebuilt by the industrious natives since my ancestors burnt it; Annapolis, is the home of the US Naval Academy; Jamestown, St Michael's, Oxford and Cambridge: some of these places are as delightful as their prototypical English towns. The Waterway extends right down to the Florida Keys, a string of islands connected by a causeway, extending round into the Gulf of Mexico.

The Intra-Coastal Waterway extends north of the Chesapeake, as far as New York (where one can moor in the middle of Manhattan for less than the price of a hotel room), but the depths on this section are not sufficient for most sea-going sailing craft.

It is superfluous to say much about the USA. The natives are friendly: however terrifying they may be as tourists, on their home ground they are charming, hospitable hosts, generous and efficient, with a vast and constant appetite for apparently tasteless food. But the country changes. The west shore of the Chesapeake, close to Washington, is rich, sophisticated and comparatively crowded. Progressing southward through the backwoods (literally) of South Carolina or Georgia, one finds people of less material wealth, and many of those at the supermarket checkouts are on welfare.

The Waterway country is evocative of the Norfolk Broads on a vast scale, with trees, reeds, herons, bitterns, flat country, estuaries and a similar state of mind among the local people. It is sometimes a long way between settlements; there are remote anchorages, quiet and beautiful, oysters for the gathering, and strong tides. There are many bridges. Those that open do so efficiently and the fixed ones have a minimum high-water clearance of 65 feet (except for one at Miami, which can be avoided by a short hop at sea).

There is only one lock; at Great Bridge in Virginia. The water in the Waterway is spread very wide, but thin. A draught of 2 metres (6 feet 6 inches) is pushing the limit, and one must expect to touch bottom occasionally, especially near the southernmost inlets.

Provisioning is often difficult as in most US communities all the stores are now in out-of-town shopping malls. For this reason, most isolated marinas have a (sometimes rather battered) 'courtesy car' which one may borrow free for local use.

The bigger yachting centres are crowded and made hideous by speeding waterhogs in fast powerboats; which makes the southern part of Florida's waters less attractive. But there are plenty of good marinas where one can leave a boat to do some touring, and good facilities everywhere for hauling out and refitting.

US marinas are different from those we have become accustomed to in Europe. The mega-marina does exist, of course, and is much better run than its European counterpart, but the typical US marina is a comparatively small family affair, often with only 30 to 50 berths, sometimes a little scruffy, but almost always with a real, friendly welcome.

The climate is surprising. In winter, southern Florida is pleasant, but from St Augustine northward expect some very cold spells. It can be bitterly cold in North Carolina. In Summer, the whole area is hot and humid and has the world's biggest and hungriest mosquitoes. Spring and Autumn are delightful.

US officials vary. We found Customs Officers everywhere to be courteous, helpful and on the ball. The immigration people were appallingly aggressive. Visas are no longer necessary for British citizens. US Customs will give the yacht a cruising permit on arrival, valid for six months, and though some states will renew this or extend it, others will not (South Carolina is one). Only yachts registered in countries with some mysterious reciprocal arrangement will be granted this permit, and it is difficult to get a definitive list. Britain is on it, so is France, but apparently Belgium is not. Yachts without a cruising permit have the chore of entering and clearing outwards in every state. Even with a permit, the obligation is to report by telephone every time one moors at an accessible place. In some states, the Customs have a toll-free number for this purpose which is very considerate for the US public phones are bad. European mobile phones do not work, and it is difficult to get a US one without a permanent residence, though cheapish pre-paid ones are available. We are familiar with this feeling world-wide: of being persons of no fixed abode. Live-aboard yachtsmen, whose boats may well be far more valuable than a house, often have no credit rating and are seen as vagrants, travellers, chicken-stealers, and only a short way off being responsible for all the looting, pillage and rape reported to the local police. But let's not get carried away on *that* hobby-horse.

Do not fall into the trap of regarding US Customs or the US Coast Guard as merely benevolent nannies to the large number of incompetent skippers who crash from mishap to ineptitude on the coast. There is massive drug smuggling through the creeks and inlets of the Intra-Coastal, and the Waterway is well patrolled. The Coast Guard, though apparently staffed entirely by teenagers, is enthusiastic and on the alert. They run the rescue service, maintain navigation marks, and keep watch on Channel 16 and also on 22A, which foreign vessels do not have. The US Coast Guard seemed to be permanently confused about our failure to reply on this channel. Note that several VHF channels have different user designations in the USA.

Buoyage is different, adhering to IALA system B. It would be, wouldn't it?

The electricity supplied from shore in most marinas is another oddity. Voltage is 110 volts and is rare, using alternating current of 60 cycles instead of 50.

The regulations against pollution are strict, and in the case of yacht heads and holding tanks, are so draconian as to be unenforceable. There being no pump-out stations, ordinary marine heads may be used at sea. I understand the whole situation is under review, when some of the ecological over-enthusiasm may be tempered with realism. On the Great Lakes, and in the canals and lakes north of New York where there is little outlet of water to the sea, the situation is different and the laws are enforced with vigour. There, marine heads may not be discharged overboard.

A brief word about the north, though these waters are not really our province as the sailing season is so short. Cruising the New England coast is delightful, though it does require alertness and good navigation because of the strong tidal streams and the frequency of fog. Navigation marks are good and facilities are excellent. In fact, the whole of the US coast is good cruising, and the people badly need to meet a few foreigners.

SUMMER IN RHODE ISLAND

We arrived in the dead of night, battered from the hurricane we had been through a week before, just north of Bermuda. We felt our way towards America in thick fog. The Coast Guard plane that had been sent out to find us had flown north/south at our request, to give us a compass check. That was after we'd told him we needed no assistance, but which way was America, please, as our compass had been shot in the lightning strike which unkindly followed the hurricane, and the sky had been too overcast to take sights. The fog hid the light of the harbour of refuge at Point Judith till we were only a mile or two away. We crept in, and with utmost thankfulness dropped anchor at two in the morning.

When we woke we found ourselves surrounded by lobster pots, and had some difficulty getting out, now we knew they were there. Newport was dressed overall, bands playing and crowded with people, all waving. 'Nice welcome,' we said. Then we found ourselves in the middle of the start of the America's Cup, so it wasn't for us after all.

There could be no doubt about the welcome that we got at Avondale when we brought our crew Nora home next day. We would be there for months repairing our wounded boat, and were never wanting for company, loan of a car or a television, entertainment, or a hot dish supper.

• *East-bound over the Atlantic* •

The most common route is via the Bermudas and the Azores. The passage to Bermuda poses few difficulties that we have not already discussed in the reverse direction. From Bermuda head north-east until the latitude of 40°N is reached, then steer along the parallel until a couple of days or so west of the Azores. The popular time for this voyage is May/June and then the weather will not be hot: often it is jersey weather all the way, and the winds can be variable and sometimes irritatingly light. There is always a chance of some strong winds, but most of the severe depressions should pass well to the north. (I do not guarantee that.)

Shipping is mostly light especially compared with the yacht traffic in May or June when something like 150 yachts arrive in the Azores each month from the west. The Azores is an easy landfall and a very impressive one after some 18 days at sea. Nevertheless, sailors have missed them completely; I do not know how, but they have. The welcome is good and the living is cheap. From the Azores, going on to Gibraltar, Portugal or the English Channel presents no special problems in the summer months.

THE MEDITERRANEAN SEA

The Med is a wholly different cruising ground to those we have already discussed. History, good food and scenic beauty, rather than the quality of the sailing, are the chief attractions. Generally, navigation in small craft is not congenial to most people in December to March, and should be indulged with caution also in November and April. It is around the equinoxes that conditions become especially capricious, and quite like British weather. Depressions that come in from the Atlantic are deflected at the last minute, and forecasts become unreliable. In high summer, the weather is usually dry and stable. Winds over much of the Med are characteristically light and variable then, though there are places where usable winds are good.

Within the Med, routeing is simple. There are a few caution-worthy spots. When crossing the Gulf of Lions check not only the weather forecast but also that you know the bad weather signs (see Admiralty Pilot, *Mediterranean*, Vol 2). Watch the Bonifacio Strait in rough weather for it seems to act as a funnel to the predominant westerly wind. Off Cape Corse, the weather is always bad and I usually suffer damage to either myself or the yacht. This last is, I think, a purely personal affair, but you never know.

Sometimes there is thick fog in the Sicilian and Malta Channels. They are both encumbered with shipping and fishing boats, and good watchkeeping is required. One occasionally gets very strong westerly winds in Spring or Autumn, with seas that can damage even big ships, and the east-going current can be strong in both.

The Straits of Messina is one of the few in the Mediterranean with a very strong tidal stream. I have personally measured 6 knots at springs. Consult the Admiralty Pilot (the tidal information is based on Gibraltar), and try to go through with a fair tide. Scylla and Charybdis, the whirlpools, may be seen, but since the earthquake in 1783 are no longer as menacing as heretofore, and one can sail right through the vortices, even at springs, with no ill effects other than being rotated a bit. In strong wind-against-tide conditions, however, a small yacht could find itself in trouble. There is a strict traffic control scheme in operation: one must have a motor ready for use, and keep watch on VHF. The ferries are frequent, arrogant, and difficult to cope with as they leave the port of Villa San Giovanni at full speed.

In the Aegean, the Summer (etesian) wind, often called by its Turkish name *meltemi*, can blow for several months from between north-west and north-east, sometimes reaching gale force, when ferry and even air services are interrupted. It is not so much wind strength that causes problems to the small-craft navigator in the Med; there is often a very short, steep sea with it, and it is this which does the damage and causes acute discomfort.

Navigation of the Dardanelles is only difficult because of the volume of traffic, particularly large Russian ships. There is often a strong south-going current. One's passage is controlled with all the strictness expected of air traffic control. One must report on VHF to each station as one approaches, and be passed on from one controller to the next. Language English; very efficient.

We have often cruised the Med in winter, and we have not been alone. There are always a few antipodean boats coming up through Suez, and some of these are on a limited-time world cruise, so that they do not want to lay up for long. They form the nucleus of winter cruisers, and we have had some good social times out of season, sharing offbeat moorings with some very congenial fellow wanderers. This is what it is all about.

We do not think we need to go into the Mediterranean countries in detail because, since writing the original edition, there are now many good guides. (I hesitate, as a one-time professional, to call some of them 'pilots', but that is letting my prejudices hang out.) We will confine our comments to generalisations that are relevant to live-aboards.

The welcome for live-aboards has changed somewhat over the past few years, but the increase in our numbers is not the reason for the cooler welcome. Where we live-aboards have pioneered yachting tourism in parts of the Med, others have followed us into the less well known places. Easily accessible cruising grounds, such as the Riviera, have always been overcrowded and expensive.

For many years the difficulties of private yachting for short periods, such as are available to the ordinary family who have to work for a living, were such as to limit the number of yachts. This changed with the flotillas, which frankly saturated the more congenial places such as the Ionian Islands. These holidaymakers, who were not always well behaved, changed the local culture during the Summer. Tavernas changed their style, their menu, their service, and their prices. People on a short-term holiday have, as we have said, money to burn. But it was the sheer numbers that tried to crowd into tiny little ports with no regard for local feelings that caused the problems. A few local people have profited, but many have seen their home villages spoiled for no personal gain. And so the yachtsman as a class has become unwelcome in some places, or at least not as welcome as was once the case.

Laurel.

SPRING IN THE IONIAN

In the little harbour of Vathi in Meganisi one Easter weekend, the local people prepared to enjoy their celebrations, which are as important to them as Christmas is to Nordic communities. There were two live-aboard yachts there, a German boat and ourselves, both of us long known to local families. We had been invited into the church, where Laurel helped to polish the brasses soon to emerge from the black shrouds of Lent, and Bill watched a young lad being coaxed to pass on hands and knees beneath the epitaphios that stood in the midst of the church, to bring him good fortune for the coming year. The epitaphios, a symbolic bier decorated with flowers symbolising the crucifixion, is processed around the harbour on Good Friday. This is the solemn climax to a long and bitter fast, during the 42 days of which many will eat only pulses, seeds and bread, no meat, fish, cheese or eggs – not even olive oil. The butcher goes on holiday.

In the midst of the procession, two separate flotillas arrived unexpectedly. The local population of about a hundred, marking the last days of a rigorous and austere Lent, was overwhelmed by a noisy invasion of about the same number, their shouts drowning the plainsong and their skimpy holiday clothes looking crude and tasteless beside the decorous black of the worshippers. The flotilla leaders were outrageously unsympathetic, encouraging their punters to push their way in to photograph the procession.

After dark, Judas is burnt in effigy, spouting fireworks. Of course, this is like Guy Fawkes, fun for everybody, and the flotillas were welcome to join in. The taverna owners and staff, however, were unable to do so; they had not yet opened for the season, they had had no advance warning, and were frantically rushing around organising a scratch meal for an unwelcome and demanding group.

The hordes left for elsewhere next morning, and the island enjoyed Easter in peace. At midnight, the cry of 'Christos anesti!' went up in complete darkness. A match flared in the church, the altar lamp was lit, and from it candle after candle lit and twinkled, one person to another becoming a rivulet of light spreading round the harbour and up the hill, as folk reached home and the windows lit up. If you can get your candle home alight, and mark a cross in smoke on your door, your year will be good. As the church was on the quay, we didn't have far to go.

Next morning we were invited to share kokkoretsi and scarlet eggs for Easter breakfast, and help spit-roast the lamb for later in the day. As we turned the spit, the villagers told us that they might ask the harbour to be closed to flotillas for Easter the next year.

The situation has been compounded by the growth of the bare-boat charter fleet. It is sad that the standard of seamanship of a significant proportion of boat charterers is low enough to endanger other boats, and their nautical manners such as to render peaceable anchorages no longer congenial.

While it is true that certain centres pose comparative overcrowding problems for those of us who were lucky enough to enjoy the Med in its uncrowded days when it was much cheaper to live there than now, it is noticeable that the new-comer is still as enchanted by the life as we have been. So the harbours of the Balearics are overcrowded but, apart from the very high season, there is still pleasure to be had. Likewise in Greece.

A picturesque quayside mooring for Hosanna *in the old town of Nauplion, Greece.*

We know of certain places in high season where the charterers do not get to. These are not necessarily as beautiful or convenient as the better-known spots, but they are often hospitable and cheaper. No, we will not publish a list of our own secret places, but if you take to this life, and go to the Med for a long stay, you will find them. During the winters, when yachties foregather, word gets round. We are a strong, but friendly, union.

The cost of living has risen in the popular cruising grounds. Mainly this is due to the common market, the EEC or the EU.

> *It escapes no blame*
> *By changing its name.*

Things have not necessarily been all for the better as Brussels has come to the poorer parts of the Med. There has been, it is true, massive hand outs to backward communities, but in the best Med. tradition, these have often created a few millionaires, rather than benefiting the whole population. With Brussels has come more imports: marvellous! You can now buy packets of Krokkiweet on the tiniest island, but with it has come elaborate packaging of everything, therefore much more rubbish, and higher prices.

Whereas prices in Greece and Turkey were once much the same, since Greece has been in the EU her prices have risen to a much higher level. Nowadays the cheaper places are the less sophisticated non-EU countries, such as Turkey and North Africa. In the latter case it is as well not to visit Algeria owing to their tendency to kill foreigners to teach them a lesson, or Libya, which is completely unreliable. (Though that may be about to change.) Egypt is also not wholly secure, but Tunisia and Morocco will give you a good welcome, though the climate is desperately hot in summer. Check current unrest with the Foreign Office.

The Dalmatian coast of ex-Yugoslavia is getting back to normal. The boats returning are mostly German. Alone of the northern yachting countries, Germany is close enough to ex-Yugoslavia for people to pour over the Brenner pass for a long weekend provided the boat is in Croatia. So, most of the berth-holders in Croatia are Bavarians.

Military matters cannot be ignored further east. Insurers prefer yachts to keep west of longitude 33°E unless an extra premium is paid. This puts a strain on visiting Israel and Syria. All is not exactly rosy west of this meridian, though the current Greek government is making an effort to bury the hatchet with Turkey. (Each country sent teams to help in each other's earthquakes recently.) There is hope here for better things, but the Cyprus situation looks as far as ever from resolution. If there is one lesson Greeks have been slow to learn, it is that they cannot push Turkey too far, because if they do: Wham!

The people of Cyprus are still suffering from this misapprehension. As neutral observers (and one of us was once occupied with security here), we find right on both sides, but no sign of any willingness to compromise. It is a situation where innocent yachts can get involved as the military deliberately try to harass each other, and helicopters dance like dragonflies in the hot air, with less innocence. However, we were there recently and heard of no mishaps to yachts.

• *Wintering* •

The Med climate is cold on winter nights, even if sunny at lunchtime. Greatcoat weather in places, and at times. Most people like to find a good, cheap, safe berth to endure it. Many try to find work, and this is possible within the EU countries for EU citizens. Most have maintenance to do, perhaps a short trip back to the homeland to see how Mum is or the grandchildren are getting on. An extension of a previously mentioned problem is that many of the best winter berths are nowadays filled with laid-up bare-boats, most of which finish their season early enough to occupy the more congenial and safer parts of the harbour, doing nothing for the local economy for months on end. Further secure berths are pre-empted by those yachties who have given up all pretence to cruise anymore and who have taken a job ashore and use their boats only as fixed houseboats (this last is a noticeable product of the relaxation of restrictive labour laws within the EU).

More and more general harbours are using EU subsidies to turn themselves into up-market (comparatively speaking) marinas which, in Greece at any rate, charge local boats a preferential rate at the expense of the foreign tourist, for the attraction of whom the EU money was originally intended.

But one gets by. The chosen wintering ports change. And it has to be admitted that there is a type of live-aboard who does foul the communal nest. Most of us tend to overlap onto the quay a bit, even if only temporarily while repairing something, for all live-aboard boats are encumbered. Some turn the quay into a junkyard. Others fall ill and cannot readily move on, or run out of funds and owe money, leading to their boat going rapidly downhill; as a class we have our share of personal disasters, and there is no welfare system to come and help.

In 1995–6, many boats left Greek waters for Tunisia and Turkey, where they were made welcome. Greece had introduced an exorbitant scale of charges which led to open harassment by their Port Police (I have already referred to the incident of painting the guardrails). Though the worst effects were later ameliorated, many found that a winter in Tunisia was a lot cheaper; the weather as well as the welcome was warmer.

WINTER IN THE ARGOLIS PENINSULA

We are in a huge sheltered bay, on one side is a long quay, partly occupied by fishing boats and the tourist caiques laid up till next season. In the middle of the bay dozens of yachts are anchored, most of them stripped for the winter and laid up till spring. There's room at the quay for eight or ten yachts which have crews on board. Some of these earn a little by working for the local boatyard on the boats laid up. We see each other daily, often in the local store, or at the post office (a portakabin on the quay), sometimes aboard each other's boats – casually, for the day temperature is pleasantly warm and there is work going on. The tourist shops have closed till spring, and so have many of the bars and restaurants, but Manoli's one-storey taverna under galvanised roofing never closes. On Sundays that's where we meet at lunchtime. We sit outside if it is sunny, Manoli clucks and tsks because he thinks it's too cold, and we have to bring the chairs out ourselves. Tough, us northerners. We are English, Scots, German, and Dutch. We swap stories and info. Some of the local ex-pats join in, the boatier sort. We drink Amstel beer or Manoli's homemade wine (at a price that the British can only dream about; the taste is something else, and has to be acquired). Invitations for the coming week are given and exchanged, a midday barbecue is feasible, a run to the local county town, or even to Athens, in someone's car. We eat *patatas tiganitas*, (fries, the best in the country, Manoli says) and plates of *marithaki* (large whitebait). Our lunch, most of it liquid, costs us about 80p a head ($1.20), pretty affordable, that. Home, then for the more energetic, a walk round the bay with a dog, perhaps. For us, back on board for a feet-up until dusk when we might need to light a driftwood fire as the sun goes down. There are no foreign newspapers in winter; we entertain ourselves with a book of crosswords, a paperback from the last swap session, and music from Greek Radio 3.

DOCUMENTATION

We have been taken to task by some readers of the first edition who had not yet set off deep cruising, for saying little about this subject, and several people at the early cruising symposiums, which we initiated, were clearly troubled by it.

There is a simple reason why we said nothing about it. Apart from the ex-communist bloc countries, documentation has never given us any real bother and we didn't think the subject merited space. Now we can say that it merits less space than ever, especially in the Med, where EU citizens can cruise about EU countries' waters with almost no formalities at all, rather in the same way that Americans can cruise from state to state in the USA.

Having said that, in November 2000 there appeared on the internet (ybw forum) last night a message from a yachtsman called Henry, saying that he had been obliged to take out a transit log in Greece, a document which has been dead for some time. Dead, but it appears it won't lie down. He was issued with a document called 'private pleasure yacht permission for stay and maritime traffic'. His boat is 10 metres LOA, and this document (valid for three years) cost him 20,000 drachmas, and then another 10,000 (£1 = approximately 500 drachmas). It seems that different ports in Greece are interpreting this law differently, as always, but if this is EU-legal, then they have discovered a new way of milking the goose that lays the golden egg, but which is more likely to go sit on another fence. Beat that for a mixed metaphor.)

There is no point in going minutely into documentation country by country because the detailed rules are constantly changing. Please let us reassure readers who are planning their voyages: be sensible, but don't worry. The requirements are different in virtually every country, and often in different ports within the same country. Do not worry. I assume the boat is properly registered in your own name, because boats registered in the name of companies in Panama, Guernsey, Gibraltar, etc can get into difficulties, this being occasionally a signal of someone up to no good.

If the boat is in your name, the formalities pertaining to the craft will give no trouble. They may take a long time, but time is not of the essence. You can save time if you make out copies (several) of your crew list. These lists should not only have the names in full of everyone on board but also passport numbers, dates and places of birth, and maiden names (and once we were asked for names, dates and places of birth of our parents too). Do not worry; stay calm.

We know of a Frenchman who cruised his yacht with an old British SSR registration certificate of a yacht that had been scrapped. The administration of the Small Ship Register encourages this, but the RYA dismissed this glitch as unimportant (The RYA are no longer responsible for the SSR). He had renamed his boat to match. He never had any trouble. You, being honest and essentially law-abiding, are not going to have any either.

No one has, so far, *ever* checked the number carved on our main beam, to see if it matches the ship's papers.

I assume you have proper passports that are in date. I assume you have taken the precaution of getting a visa for those countries who are scared to let you in without one, or who wish to extract the maximum cash from your visit. I assume you have found out if any vaccinations or inoculations are required, both for yourselves and any pets, and that you have the appropriate certificates. It's all tedious on occasions, but really quite simple. Do not worry.

If planning to go to both Israel and Arab countries, or if you wish to go to Northern (Turkish-occupied) Cyprus and also want to go to Southern Cyprus or Greece afterwards, then you can get a second passport in advance if you tell the passport office what you want to do. Greece cannot refuse entry under EU law to an EU citizen but they can be difficult. Don't mix the passports up, keep one for the sheep and the other for the goats.

Be careful about giving passage to persons of countries that are regarded as 'difficult' in the country you are heading for. Even this is not as bad as it sounds.

• *Stories* •

While apartheid was at its worst, we arrived in Antigua with two South Africans on board in the days when the redoubtable Sergeant King was in charge of immigration there. Our friends wished to disembark and fly home. Within a short time, thanks to a friendly approach, our friends went ashore with Sergeant King himself, the scourge of the Caribbean, smiling happily and helping them with their baggage.

People, even officials, are fundamentally approachable if you are tactful.

Some friends of ours embarked the young Greek boyfriend of their daughter for a short cruise and headed for Turkey without thinking. Their guest, when he discovered which harbour they were entering, was petrified. He expected to be decapitated or worse. The Turkish immigration officer told the quaking youngster he was very naughty to have come without a visa, then threw his arms round the boy's neck, kissed him, and said 'Welcome to Turkey'. Well, he was a good-looking young lad.

Turkey now demands visas for Britons in retaliation for something they imagine Mrs Thatcher did to one of their diplomat's children. Visas can usually be obtained at the port of entry without any difficulty, and are more of an irritant than a penalty. Do not worry.

Some countries are beginning to demand evidence of third-party insurance cover. Not many. We advise getting a certificate in the local country's language from your insurers. Some marinas are now demanding it as a condition of entry, not to the country, but to their *marina*. (Suppose you set on fire the boat in the berth next to you! France and Greece are the only places which we know to be affected, but have heard of this applying in Spain too.)

In all our cruising (except for ex-Iron Curtain countries) we have never been asked for documents issued by the port we have left, nor for de-ratting certificates, though once we were asked to produce evidence of good health. Any evidence. We wrote out our own certificate and stamped it with the ship's own 'official' stamp, which we put over the top of some leftover British postage stamps. It did the trick. Do not worry.

Check:

- Passports in date: visas.
- Boat registration.
- Boat insurance if applicable.
- Vaccinations and inoculations (including those of pets)
- Someone has Yachtmaster or appropriate evidence of personal competence.
- If European, that you have VAT evidence.
- You have form E111, or E112, your health reciprocation document. (This will save you endless trouble in case of illness or accident.)

Remember that people do arrive in the most awkward countries improperly documented and still have a good time, provided they are not aggressive or tactless. *So do not worry.*

We have made certain exempting clauses with respect to ex-Iron Curtain countries. It is likely these will be visited more and more in the future, and as they have not yet adapted their systems to the notion of freedom of passage, especially in yachts, you may find some difficulties. These are often soluble by the gift of a bottle of wine, costing (in Romania, for example) 80p, or vodka (in the Ukraine) costing 30p, and well worth it.

One meets more and more yachties coming from these countries. One, Andreu, from Moldova, told us hair-raising stories of the problems he had had getting permission to sail away from Odessa in the Ukraine in the boat he had built himself from government surplus items he had salvaged from the scrap-heap of an armament factory. (You do meet some interesting people in this mode of life.)

We have described in another book our experience of a recent impromptu visit to the port of Ismaila in the Ukraine. They wouldn't let us enter the country, as we had no visas and could not go to Kiev to get them, but they were perfectly polite about it, and we could have obtained provisions and shelter if we had needed them. All we suffered was inconvenience. (The cats were allowed ashore without a visa, with much chortling.)

In Romania, on the other hand, the bureaucracy was labyrinthine and byzantine: crooked in both senses of the word. The moral is that if visiting a country whose border forces are subject to political paranoia, you will need to have both patience and papers in apple-pie order, and probably have to drop dollar notes into various palms as well. This last is more difficult. We cruise with a small wad of one-dollar bills for use in this sort of emergency. They are often of more use than a passport. DO NOT WORRY.

'It is to be supposed by this time the ship is victualled and manned, the voiage determined . . . and all things else ready to set sail'

INLAND PASSAGES

For passages through the French canals and rivers to the Mediterranean, there are so many books giving detailed advice, and written by people with great knowledge of these waterways, that much comment here is not appropriate.

It is not a quick passage: there are very many locks, and navigation at night is not permitted. In our view it should be a lingering cruise, not to be taken at the rush. The French canals are an experience in themselves. The quickest passage we know of was made via the Marne, mast down to mast up 19 days, but how they must have sweated, and what delights they must have missed.

The maximum length should not worry the type of cruising yacht that falls in our categories, but beam is limited to 5 metres, and draught officially to 1.8, though

A quiet mooring on the tranquil Somme at Abbeville, northern France.

over 1.6 may involve some ploughing. The lowest bridge obstruction is 3.4 metres, and there are facilities for striking masts at both ends of the system. It is worth thinking of entering at Gravelines, rather than Calais. The latter is busy and dangerous with ferries and the Canal de Calais is infested with pondweed which will block engine cooling. This is getting steadily worse as commercial traffic declines.

Some yachts have sailed into the Bay of Biscay and passed to the Mediterranean via Bordeaux and the Canal du Midi, emerging at Sète. Not all yachts who do this originally intended to, it being sometimes difficult to get out of the bay any other way. The Gironde estuary with its many banks can be dangerous for small craft in strong westerly winds. One catamaran with the spoonerish name of *Cupid Stunts*, bound for Gibraltar in Autumn, was carried to leeward by several days of bad weather and actually blown into the Gironde river willy-nilly. Her crew, who were mostly inexperienced, learned a lot, and enjoyed their passage through this marvellous canal. Bear in mind that the Canal du Midi might be closed in times of drought, as in 1989.

The Rhine-Main-Danube Canal, has opened, and vessels should be able to navigate across Germany, Austria and down to the Black Sea. We have done it (see our book *Back Door To Byzantium*), and it is by no means the relaxing journey that one would have via the French canals. From sea to sea it is 4000 kilometres (2162 nautical miles), and both the navigation and the old Iron Curtain countries present difficulties.

ELSEWHERE

The Panama Canal is a substantial undertaking for a yacht, and I have never done it. Some people have had uneventful passages; others have had events and damage. The Panama is not an expensive canal to pass through because the charge is tonnage based, but yachts without engines capable of 5 knots or more have to be towed. We are reliably informed that the formalities for yachts are much simpler now than they were, but that pilotage is still compulsory.

There is nowadays quite a bit of yacht traffic from Australia via Galle in Ceylon and on into the Red Sea. A good alternative is the route via Christmas Island, the Cocos Keelings, Mauritius and Cape Town. A practical problem is the Agulhas current off the south east coast of South Africa; here the seas in bad weather can cause difficulties even for big ships.

The main problem about the Suez Canal route to Europe (provided one is not daft enough to try to cross the Indian Ocean against the monsoon) is getting up the Red Sea. In spite of the political complexion of the government, yachtsmen are usually well received at Aden (though events in October 2000 call that into question), but a similar welcome cannot be relied on at any Red Sea ports. This is a pity, for with the virtual certainty of head winds most will want to make a stop or two. Even Port Sudan, once quite popular, has to be approached with caution nowadays, and Saudi Arabia, for all its wealth and its religious teaching, and in spite of the millions of pounds worth of yachts owned by their citizens, has not learned yet how to give a civilised welcome to travellers.

The Suez Canal necessitates having an agent, unless one has unusual persistence, patience and a very cool head. The big trouble is that Egypt is openly and unashamedly corrupt. The actual cost of the transit is modest, but the agency fee will probably exceed the canal dues. A pilot is compulsory (I was one once, for a short time), who will have little to do except watch the signal stations. You may be lucky and get a pleasant fellow for half the journey; you would be very lucky indeed if both pilots were congenial. The chances are that even the pilots will demand and expect 'gifts'.

The reverse voyage, down the Red Sea, presents few problems and is best done non-stop in the present world disorder.

I offer no advice on rounding Cape Horn. In my view it is a rotten part of the globe, and the only reason I can think of for going there is to prove something that one ought not to have to prove.

It remains to wish you all calm seas, pleasant breezes, and safe arrivals.

• *Epilogue* •

A night in harbour is a precious thing,
  No waves to rock the boat, a full night's sleep:
But we are wishful to be journeying,
  With islands yet unknown a tryst to keep.

They call and beckon, coax and draw us forth,
  A pull as strong as the relentless tide.
They draw us like a magnet, South and North,
  Their soft insistence cannot be defied.

We'll sail the ancient ways, the quiet ways
  By dolphin path, salty, and silver blue;
The saffron sun shall circumscribe our days
  Of hopeful travelling to Xanadu.

A night in harbour is a precious thing,
  But when we go to sea again we sing!

• Appendices •

TABLE OF DISTANCES

	Aden	Barbados	Bermuda	Brindisi	Chesapeake	Cork	Cristobal (Panama)	Dover	Fayal (Azores)	Genoa	Gibraltar	Istanbul	Madeira	Malta	Marseilles	NewYork	Las Palmas (Canaries)	Plymouth	Port Said
Aden																			
Barbados	6550																		
Bermuda	6230	1220																	
Brindisi	2320	4530	4210																
Chesapeake	6630	1680	640	4600															
Cork	4400	3400	2730	640	4210														
Cristobal (Panama)	7630	1220	1640	5620	2380	3000													
Dover	4600	3710	3080	2580	3390	1750	4310												
Fayal (Azores)	4430	2250	1800	2400	2220	1180	450	4660											
Genoa	2810	4100	3770	750	4170	1950	5180	3260	1480										
Gibraltar	3300	3250	2930	1280	3330	1100	4340	1230	3260	850									
Istanbul	2190	5050	4730	790	5140	2900	6150	3030	1310	850	1810								
Madeira	3900	2630	2520	1900	2880	1250	3740	1400	670	600	1450	2420							
Malta	2330	4230	3910	360	4320	2080	5330	2220	2110	580	990	850	1590						
Marseilles	2900	3940	3620	840	4020	1790	5030	1920		200	700	1390	1290	650					
NewYork	6500	1830	700	4480	260	2820	1970	3250	2100	4050	3200	5010	2770	4190	3900				
Las Palmas (Canaries)	4000	2640	2560	1980	3060	1480	3800	1610	900	1550	710	2500	290	1680	1390	2930			
Plymouth	4400	3501	2870	2380	3430	233	4450	225	1275	1950	1038	2840	1205	2020	1730	3051	1421		
Port Said	1400	5150	4830	930	5240	3000	6240	3140	3040	1430	1900	790	2500	940	1500	5100	2610	2945	
Ushant	4230	3420	2810	2200	3120	230	4380	310	1170	1770	920	2720	1090	1910	1610	2990	1310	110	2830

APPENDIX A

• *Shopping basket in certain countries* •

	UK £	FR FFr	EU	Singapore $	Australia $	US $	W Indies $
12 eggs	1.35	15.00	2.28	3.12	1.19	1.99	6.95
250g butter	0 72	8.30	1.27	2.00	0.38	1.41	8.67
4 litres UHT milk	1 56	23.8	3.64	10.60	1.97	3.24	18.68
1kg sugar	0.45	6.95	1.06	0.95	0.45	2.18	2.13
1kg flour	0.75	5.85	0.89	1.95	0.50	0.75	4.62
200g Edam	0.78	10.48	1.59	2.98	1.16	3.80	4.62
100g Nescaé	1.75	22.30	3.40	10.75	1.69	2.56	9.79
3kg potatoes	2.26	12.00	1.80	0.78	1.38	1.73	2.40
1kg onions	0.52	1.99	0.30	4.90	0.67	1.73	5.17
2 lettuces	1.20	10.00	1.52	2.80	1.12	1.98	16.00
1kg tomatoes	0.99	16.95	2.90	0.40	1.22	5.47	13.20
2kg apples	2.58	9.95	1.52	0.40 ea	2.70	1.73	16.00 ea
4 pork chops (500g)	2.66	25.00	3.81	6.45	1.87	3.89	8.74
2 sirloin steaks (500g)	5.90	83.90	12.79	9.30	2.43	9.62	20.85
1kg mince	5.49	49.07	7.48	13.90	2.24	6.05	21.78
1 chicken (1.5kg)	3.79	47.90	7.30	3.99	2.36	4.97	11.12
1kg oranges	1.56	7.95	1.21	0.85 ea	1.10	2.17	
250g tea	1.29	31.4	4.78	2.25	0.96	2.69	
500g dried pasta	0.76	8.50	0.30	2.75	0.54	2.17	
500g rice	1.09	8.95	1.38	1.84	0.63	2.17	
24 x 25cl beer (Eurofizz)		39.45	6.01				
Simple meal for two with wine or beer	35.00	200.00	30.49		24.00	30.00	70 00

In order to compare prices, we give below currency rates at the time of compiling the table

Pound sterling	xxx	10.08	1.64	2.50	2.68	1.43	3.86
French francs	0.09	xxx	0.15	0.22	0.24	0.13	0.35
Euros	0.61	6.59	xxx	1.533	1.63	0.87	2.35
Singapore dollar	0.40	4.30	0.78	xxx	1.07	0.57	1.54
Australian dollar	0.37	4.00	0.61	0.92	xxx	0.53	1 43
US dollar	0.70	8.20	1.15	1.75	1.88	xxx	2.70
E Carib dollar	0.26	2.86	0.43	0.65	0.70	1.27	xxx

£ sterling	FFr		Sing $	Aus $	US $	E Carib $

APPENDIX B

• *Books and book websites* •

Seamanship, maintenance and repair

Rigging Handbook, Brion Toss, Adlard Coles Nautical

Metal Corrosion in Boats, Nigel Warren, Adlard Coles Nautical

Heavy Weather Sailing, Peter Bruce, Adlard Coles Nautical

Navigation for Yachtsmen, Mary Blewitt, Adlard Coles Nautical

Celestial Navigation for Yachtsmen, Mary Blewitt, Adlard Coles Nautical

VHF Radiotelephony for Yachtsmen, (GMDSS edition), RYA

VHF Radio Operator Examinations, (GMDSS edition),RYA

Cruising the French Waterways, Hugh McKnight, Adlard Coles Nautical

The Yachtsman's 10-language Dictionary, B Webb, Adlard Coles Nautical)

Health and victualling

The Ship Captain's Medical Guide, (HMSO)

Where there is No Doctor and *Where there is No Dentist*, TALC (Teaching Aids at Low Cost) PO Box 49, St Albans, Herts AL1 4AX Tel 01727 853869

North Atlantic Seafood, Alan Davidson, Penguin Books

Mediterranean Seafood, Alan Davidson, Penguin Books

Charcuterie and French Pork Cookery, Jane Grigson, Penguin Books

Diet for a Small Planet, Francis Moore Lappe, Ballantyne Books

Recipes for a Small Planet, Ellen Buchman Ewald, Ballantyne Books

Websites

www.amazon.co.uk (Web Bookshop)
www.adlardcoles.co.uk (Nautical publishers)
www.bookfinder.com (Worldwide secondhand hard-to-find books)
www.bookharbour.com (Kelvin Hughes, books and charts.)
www.nauticalbooks.co.uk (New and second-hand nautical books)

APPENDIX C

• *Useful websites and addresses* •

General

GJW Direct, Silk House Court, Tithe Barn St, Liverpool L2 Z11
e-mail: insure@gjwltd.co.uk (yacht insurance)
www.ybw.com (IPC magazines: Yachting and Boating World Forums)
The Foreign Office Tel 020 7238 4503/4504 (Information about political risks abroad)
www.cruisermart.co.uk Tel:01489 77 44 44 (Chandlery by mail order)

Health

www.dentanurse.com Tel 01981 500135 (Dental repair and first aid kit)
www.cigua.com (Ciguatera poisoning)
www.healthatoz.com (health A to Z, USA)
www.fitfortravel.scot.nhs.uk (NHS Scotland)
www.doh.gov.uk/traveladvice (Department of Health, UK) Tel 020 7210 4850
www.surgerydoor.co.uk/tril (Clinic by Internet)
www.masta.org (Medical Advice Service for Travellers Abroad) Tel 0891 224100
www.sentex.net/~iamat (International Assoc-iation of Medical Assistance for travellers)
TALC Teaching Aids at Low Cost) PO Box 49, St Albans Herts ALl 4AX Tel 01727 853869 (Spoon for babies)

Weather
www.met-office.gov.uk/datafiles/offshore.html (British Met Office)
www.meteo.fr (Meteo France)
www.nws.noaa.gov/om/marine (USA Weather Service)
www.nhc.noaa.gov (National Hurricane Centre)
www.wetterzentrale.de (German source giving a nine-day forecast)

Pet passports
www.maff.gov.uk/animalh/quarantine (Ministry of Agriculture, Fisheries and Food) Tel 0870 11710

Navigation
www.nms.ukho.gov.uk (Notices to Mariners for UK charts)
www.imo org/imo/library/piracy623rev1.pdf (Information on piracy.)
www.rin org.uk (Royal Institute of Navigation)
www.pcmaritime.co.uk (Nav and met programs)
minories@kelvinhughes.co.uk (charts)

Communications
www.bbc co.uk/worldservice (BBC World Service)
www.shiptoshore.co.uk (Organises mail forwarding etc)
www.ipass.com (How to access your ISP when abroad via a local number)
www.stargate3.co.uk (Pocketmail)
www.marinecomputing.com (Installation and advice on Inmarsat Mini-M and C)
www.inmarsat.org (Inmarsat organisation)
www.kvh.com (Makers of Tracphone for Mini-M)
www.tt.dk (Thrane and Thrane phone-makers for Mini-M and C)
www.rme.com (Inmarsat C compression software)
www.pinoak.com (Pinoak)
www.globewireless.com (Globe Wireless)

www.sailmail.com (Sailmail)
www.pentacomstat.com.au (Seamail)
www.xaxero.com (Software for Seamail)
www.airmail2000.com (Info on e-mail by ham radio)
www.win-net.org (Radio ham e-mail shore-stations)
www.shortwave.co.uk (Shortwave shop for HF radio gear)
www.gmdss.com.au (For comprehensive info on GMDSS and DSC)
www.icselectronics.co.uk (Ditto but this is a slow downloader)
www.radio.gov.uk (Radio authority for British Government)

Domestic
Hozelock Ltd Haddenham Aylesbury Bucks HP17 8JD (Plastic clothes pegs)
www.aqua-marine.co.uk (Domestic gear including refrigerators)
www.tek-tanks.com (Makers of fridge cabinets and tanks in plastics)
www.penguineng.com (Refrigerators, etc)
www.spectrawatermakers.com (Watermakers)
www.lakelandlimited.com (Stainless kitchen tools, Bamix, Stayfresh bags, Tefal cheese-keeper)
www.yachtpeople.com (Scootguard non-slip sheeting)

Education
Calvert School 105 Tuscany Rd Baltimore MD USA. e-mail: inquiry@calvertschool.org
www.bbc.co.uk/education
www.atschool.co.uk (to Keystage 2)

Yachting clubs and organizations
www.rya.org.uk (Royal Yachting Association)
www.cruising.org.uk (The Cruising Association, London)
www.ssca.org (Seven Seas Cruising Association, Fort Lauderdale, US) e-mail: office@ssca.org (Seven Seas Cruising Association)
www.oceancruisingclub.org (Ocean Cruising Club)

• Index •

soil 113
taxation 35-7, 38, 40
tenders 87-9
theft 225-8
thrush 310
ticks 151-2, 294
tides 249
tinned foods 196-200
tins 191
tools 164-8
    list 167-8
transferring funds 41
transom, sloping 69
Travelift 158
travellers' cheques 42
Turkey 61, 113
twin screws 70
types of anchor 92
types of boat 55-8

Ulysses Quotient 13
USA, east coast 324-6

vaccination, pet 146
value, yacht 72-3
varnish 157
VAT 35, 37
vegetables 197, 208-10
Vendee Globe round the
    World Race 63-4
ventilation 101, 110-11, 173
Visa/Barclaycard 43

warp 79
washing 113, 220
wasps 151
watchkeeping 129
water 218-22
    contamination 310
    systems 108
water-makers 108
weather 342
weather forecasting 137-9
weather on the internet 139
websites 341

weevils 152, 193
West Indies 316-19
    sailing conditions 64
West System 71
wet-bikes 153
wheelhouse 76
winches 83
Windboats 71
windlasses 76
windows 111
windvanes 175
wintering 331
wishbone rig 81
wood stoves 181
wooden hulls 71
worms 311

yacht clubs 278-9, 342
Yachtmaster's Certificate 124